THE SECOND ADMIRAL

ADMIRAL DAVID DIXON PORTER
(From an oil portrait by Carl Becker)

THE SECOND ADMIRAL

A Life of
David Dixon Porter
1813-1891

By RICHARD S. WEST, Jr.

ILLUSTRATED

NEW YORK

COWARD-McCANN, INC.

1937

PRINTED IN THE UNITED STATES OF AMERICA

AT THE VAN REES PRESS

TO
MARIE McELREATH WEST

A well built keel beneath him
Successful guns on his gun decks
And a gala, four-starred flag awaving
at the mainmast head...

CONTENTS

LIST OF ILLUSTRATIONS

LIST OF MAPS

INTRODUCTION

I T IS a curious fact that both the Union Navy and the most spectacular officer produced by that unusual organization require an introduction to the modern reader. The name of the "Lord High Admiral of the U. S. Navy," as General William Tecumseh Sherman affectionately called this great American fighter, has been virtually forgotten. But David Dixon Porter's penchant for bright discipline and smart appearance, his readiness to apply inventions to naval uses, his fondness for vast new undertakings, however complicated they might be by politics and economics, his buoyant, dare-devil, fighting spirit—these live on in the United States Navy today.

General U. S. Grant recorded in his *Memoirs* that "Among naval officers I have always placed Porter in the highest rank. I believe Porter to be as great an admiral as Lord Nelson." During the same decade a journalist named F. Colburn Adams wrote that "The future historian of the late war will have two very difficult tasks to perform—one in sifting truth from falsehood as it appears in official records; the other in giving Admiral D. D. Porter his proper place among the heroes of the conflict. We say this without any disparagement to Admiral Porter as a brave officer. He will, however, find in the Admiral a character very unevenly balanced and one of the most difficult to analyze correctly. He has at times reminded us of one of those strange characters we read of in Italian history, who live entirely within themselves and for themselves, who are never so happy as when they are making mischief."

Historians have neither echoed the friendly judgment of General Grant nor separated the chaff from the grain as the hostile journalist demanded. With the exception of a brief biography by Professor J. R. Soley undertaken in fulfillment of Porter's desire, historians have almost completely ignored Admiral Porter.

There are two reasons why Admiral Porter is not well known today, and in a perspective of seventy years both appear inadequate. The first reason is that the effective but surreptitious and indirect censorship exercised by the Federal Navy Department during the Civil War curtailed naval publicity and in turn influenced later historians and biographers. The second is that for twenty-six years after the war Porter was embroiled in controversies with the political general, Benjamin F. Butler, who succeeded in dragging the Admiral along with himself into eclipse.

The naval censorship was unobtrusive but effective. Porter and the six other active rear admirals created during the war were regular naval officers. They had no political ambitions. Newspaper reporters when permitted to accompany naval expeditions did so as guests, and their stories were subjected to censorship. Of the Army's 104 major generals more than ninety were volunteer political generals with political ambitions to satisfy. Save for a few notable exceptions like Tecumseh Sherman, the generals catered to the reporters, who wrote their dispatches from Army headquarters in the field and who were not dependent upon the good will of commanding generals for their means of locomotion and subsistence. The admirals, on the other hand, discouraged reporters and evolved a system for withholding information which might aid or comfort the enemy. Knowing that the Secretary of the Navy was expected to make official reports public, they deliberately made these as sketchy and innocuous as possible, and supplemented them with confidential dispatches to the Secretary and private letters to the Assistant Secretary. In this way the amount of contemporary publicity received by the Navy was limited to a mere fraction of that received by the Army. Unaware of the naval censorship, and impressed by the greater bulk of military source material, historians of the Civil War have scarcely as yet appraised the work of the Federal Navy.

It is true that the Federal industrial resources and reserves in man power were overwhelmingly superior to the Confederate. But the ingenuity and resourcefulness of the Confederate forces which opposed the Federal Navy have been underestimated. The Confederates drew upon the shipyards of England and Scotland. They fought the Union Navy with new devices—ironclad ships, rams, torpedoes, submarines. They fought with coast defense guns in casemated forts, with batteries of mobile artillery, with roving bands of bushwhackers and guerrillas. Nature fought on the side of the Confederates with snags, sandbars, shifting channels in the rivers and harbors, with northers in the Gulf of Mexico, with storms in the open sea off Cape Hatteras, Cape Fear, and Charleston. The naval war was by no means a one-sided conflict.

David Dixon Porter was born during the war of 1812, with

parents and grandparents powerful in naval and political circles. As a boy on his father's flagship he watched the suppression of pirates in the West Indies. At fifteen he became a midshipman in the Mexican Navy, fought in the war for Mexican independence, was captured and imprisoned in Havana. Becoming a midshipman in the U. S. Navy in 1829, he was irked by the peace-time regime. For many years he was attached to the Coast Survey. He won a wide reputation for his survey of the Hellgate and the Buttermilk Channels in New York Harbor. In 1846 he undertook for the State Department a secret exploring mission to Santo Domingo. Gallantry in action during the Mexican War won him the command of the steamer *Spitfire*.

His interest in steam engines carried him into the mail steamer service. During the gold rush he took the mail steamer *Panama* around Cape Horn to San Francisco. As captain of the *Crescent City* he became involved in the *Crescent City* incident in 1852, when he almost provoked a war with Spain and won for himself a national reputation. In the *Georgia* he broke all speed records between the cities along the Atlantic Coast, and in 1853 won a world reputation when his vessel the *Golden Age* broke in succession the records for the Atlantic crossing to Liverpool and from Liverpool to Australia. Commanding the U. S. storeship *Supply* in 1855, he transported camels from the Near East to Texas for Jefferson Davis' experiment in using these animals as cavalry mounts.

Preferring the role of lone wolf, when the Civil War broke out in 1861, he obtained orders direct from the President and behind the back of the Secretary of the Navy sailed the *Powhatan* to Fort Pickens off Pensacola Harbor and saved that outpost from the fate which overtook Fort Sumter. By ignoring the Department he incurred the hostility of the Secretary of the Navy. Nevertheless, on returning to Washington after a dashing cruise in pursuit of the Confederate raider *Sumter,* he induced the Navy Department to undertake the capture of New Orleans. With his foster brother Farragut he pushed that campaign to a successful issue. After New Orleans came his assignment to command the Mississippi Squadron for the great campaign against Vicksburg and the vital opening of the Mississippi River. In the unfortunate campaign up the Red River, he incurred the hostility of political generals, Federal cotton traders, Confederate guerrillas. Then followed the last great naval operation of the war, the capture of

Fort Fisher, which sealed the last Confederate port to blockade runners.

In spite of the antagonism of the Secretary of the Navy Porter rose in rank during the war from lieutenant to rear admiral. His spectacular victories alternated with spectacular reverses. He obtained more difficult assignments, commanded more ships and men, won a greater number of victories, and was more often awarded the Congressional vote of thanks than any other officer who ever served in the United States Navy.

After the war, when the grade of Admiral was created for Farragut, the grade of Vice Admiral was created for Porter. As Superintendent of the U. S. Naval Academy, he transformed the Annapolis institution into a flourishing professional school of national importance on a parity with West Point. During the war scares of President Grant's administration, Porter attempted to transform overnight the run-down Navy into an efficient fighting machine. He ignored laws, recklessly attempted to scuttle the system of political patronage that had fastened itself upon the Navy Department. His brusque methods antagonized powerful elements in politics and throughout the naval service.

After Farragut's death in 1870 Porter's enemies, led by General Butler, tried to deflate his prestige by elevating the memory of Admiral Farragut. Nevertheless Porter managed to secure the rank of "Admiral of the Navy." During the last twenty years of his life Admiral Porter turned modern inventions to naval uses. He invented torpedoes and torpedo boats, installed electrical equipment on warships, turned his hand to propaganda, and laid the foundations for the victory over Spain which came seven years after his death. He established a tone for the United States Navy which dominates at the present day.

Seventy years after the Civil War we need not be blinded by post-war controversies. It is not necessary, perhaps, to accept General Grant's sweeping judgment that Porter was "as great an Admiral as Lord Nelson." The present writer has preferred not to speculate upon the proper height for Admiral Porter's pedestal or to make invidious comparisons of the second "Admiral of the Navy" with Farragut or Dewey, the only other Americans who have received that rank.

ACKNOWLEDGMENTS

To the following relatives of Admiral Porter the author is grateful for access to manuscripts, extracts from family papers, and general information:

Mrs. Carroll Van Ness, Owings Mills P. O., Md.
Mrs. Carlos Cusachs, Annapolis, Md.
Brigadier General David D. Porter, U. S. Marine Corps, Washington, D. C.
Mrs. Albert Gleaves, Haverford, Pa.
Mrs. Robert W. Adams, Jamestown, R. I.
Mrs. David Porter Heap, Philadelphia, Pa.

Assistance has been cheerfully given by the staffs of the following libraries:

U. S. Naval Academy Library, Annapolis, Md.
Naval Records and Library, Navy Department, Washington, D. C.
Library of Congress, Washington, D. C.
Naval History Section of the New York Historical Society, N. Y.
Hall of Records, New York, N. Y.
Chicago Historical Society, Chicago, Ill.
Henry E. Huntington Library and Art Gallery, San Marino, Calif.
Delaware Historical Society, Chester, Pa.

To the many who have assisted him in research the author expresses his sincerest thanks. He feels a special debt to Associate Professor R. J. Duval, Librarian, and Mr. Louis H. Bolander, of the U. S. Naval Academy Library; to Captain Dudley W. Knox, U. S. Navy (retired), Librarian, and Miss Elizabeth Craven, of the Naval Records and Library; and to Mr. Richard C. McKay, of New York City.

The following have read the manuscript in various stages of preparation and offered invaluable criticism:

Mr. Victor F. White, Ridgewood, N. J.
Dr. Louis C. Hunter, St. John's College, Annapolis, Md.
Lieutenant Ernest M. Eller, U. S. Navy.
Dr. Allan F. Westcott, U. S. Naval Academy, Annapolis, Md.

The author gratefully acknowledges the permission of the following publishers to use material or quotations from the books listed:

D. Appleton-Century Company. *Battles and Leaders of the Civil War.* R. J. Johnson and C. C. Buel, Editors. 4 vols. 1884; *Incidents and Anecdotes of the Civil War.* By D. D. Porter. 1891; *Admiral Porter.* By J. R. Soley. 1903; *Adventures of Harry Marline.* By D. D. Porter. 1885.

Bobbs-Merrill Company. *Surgeon of the Seas.* By C. S. Foltz. 1931.

Christopher Publishing House. *The Chequered Career of Ferdinand Rudolph Hassler.* By Florian Cajori. 1929.

Arthur H. Clark Company. *Commodore John Rodgers.* By C. O. Paullin. Cleveland. 1910.

Houghton Mifflin Company. *The Diary of Gideon Welles.* (With an Introduction by John T. Morse, Jr.) 3 vols. 1911.

Macmillan Company. *A History of the National Capital.* By W. B. Bryan. 2 vols. 1914.

Naval History Society. *Confidential Correspondence of Gustavus Vasa Fox.* Edited by R. M. Thompson and R. Wainwright. 2 vols. 1918, 1919.

Oxford University Press. *The Growth of the American Republic.* By S. E. Morison and H. S. Commager. 1930.

G. P. Putnam's Sons. *Memoirs of Thomas O. Selfridge, Jr.* Rear Admiral, U.S.N. With an Introduction by Captain Dudley W. Knox, U.S.N. 1924; *The United States Naval Academy.* By Park Benjamin. 1900.

Charles Scribner's Sons. *The Sherman Letters.* 1894; *The Home Letters of General Sherman.* (Edited by M. A. DeW. Howe.) 1909.

Frederick A. Stokes Company. *From Reefer to Rear Admiral.* By B. F. Sands. 1899.

The following libraries have granted permission to use quotations from manuscripts:

Library of Congress, Manuscript Division. Washington, D. C.

New York Historical Society, and Naval History Section of the New York Historical Society. New York City.

PART ONE
THE KEEL

A well-built keel beneath him...

MERIDIAN HILL

Dᴀᴠɪᴅ Dɪxᴏɴ Pᴏʀᴛᴇʀ, the second son of Captain David Porter and Evalina Anderson Porter, was born in the borough of Chester, Pennsylvania, on June 8, 1813. He was born in the old colonial house known as Green Bank, which stood on a green hill between the town of Chester and the wide and peaceful Delaware River. The massive old house, built of rusty gray stone, with kitchen and carriage-house wings, parthenon façade and decorative cupola rising from the roof midway between the massive end chimneys, had been Major William Anderson's bridal present to his daughter Evalina Porter.

As she lay in the low-ceilinged, upstairs bedroom at Green Bank with the infant at her side, the twenty-two-year-old mother could look out the many-paned windows over tulip trees and see the masts of British ships of war on blockade duty in the Delaware River.

She was safe here in her own house, for the town of Chester was not likely to be molested by the blockaders. The citizens of Chester were chiefly landsmen who were off with General Gates's army fighting the British on the Canadian frontier. The oystermen at Chester had not turned privateers against British trading craft—as had the deep-sea fishermen of Maine—and would not provoke the blockade ships to fire their broadsides into Green Bank and the town which lay behind it.

Evalina Porter was thankful that the black-and-yellow-striped ships of the British had not arrived seven months earlier. Had they arrived then, they would have found Captain David Porter with his little 32-gun frigate *Essex* anchored in the river not two hundred yards from Green Bank; and there would have been instantaneous battle. Vividly she could recall the scene of her husband's departure on October 28, 1812. Out on the veranda beneath her window David Porter had kissed her good-by and patted the tousled head of three-year-old William. She could still see

David Porter's short legs jumping down the slope and scrambling out through the reeds to where the seamen had his gig ready for him. She could still see her husband's round red face very small in the distance as he waved farewell to her, and she remembered the swish of the long oars carrying him out to the *Essex*.

Where Captain Porter had gone in the *Essex* she did not know. No one knew. One by one the sister ships of the *Essex* had been heard from. One captured, another bottled up in New York Harbor by numerous blockaders. But for the last seven months Evalina Porter had heard nothing which might even suggest her husband's whereabouts.

She named her new baby David Dixon, after his father and after her witty sister-in-law, who was a Dixon of Norfolk.

Fifteen other months passed without any word from the *Essex*. Then the news of Captain Porter's arrival in New York came down by post to Chester. The *Essex* on March 28, 1814, had been battered to pieces by two British men-of-war in Valparaiso Harbor.[1] Captain Porter had been sent to New York a prisoner on board a cartel ship, but had made his escape off Sandy Hook. The citizens of New York had taken the horses from his carriage and themselves drawn David Porter through the city. Her David Porter! He was safe, he was free, he was being honored by the people.

Broadside ballads appeared on lamps and hitching posts everywhere to tell the wonderful story. The hero of the *Essex* had annihilated the entire British whaling industry in the southern Pacific.

When the hero of the *Essex* reached Green Bank in September 1814, Evalina Porter could make his home-coming doubly joyful by introducing to him his second son. David Dixon Porter was now an active little black-haired youngster of fifteen months. His large snapping brown eyes were his father's. The soft little nose had now lost its infant flatness and become aquiline like his father's. Captain Porter lifted the child high in the air and swore with deep content.

After resting three days at Green Bank, Captain Porter left his family and went by post to Washington.[2] During the next month Evalina Porter heard from her father, Major William Anderson, who was a Congressman, how British warships had sailed up the Potomac and a regiment of Redcoats had burned the Capitol, the Government buildings, and the navy yard. A letter from Captain Porter told how he had set up a land battery at a bend in the Potomac a few miles below Washington and raked the British vessels as they passed down the river.

After the close of the war David Porter received his commission as commodore, and an assignment to duty in Washington on the Board of Navy Commissioners, along with Commodores John Rodgers and Stephen Decatur. His duties requiring him to live in Washington, he purchased a 110-acre tract on the brow of a hill about a mile north of the White House and built a large mansion.[3] Meridian Hill, as he called his estate, because of its position on the map of Washington, was ready for occupancy early in 1819; and he sent for his family to come down from Chester.

Mrs. Porter brought the children to Washington by stage coach, the last leg of the journey being accomplished over the new Baltimore-Washington turnpike which had just been opened. There were five children in 1819: William, Elizabeth, David Dixon, Thomas, and Theodoric, the last an infant in arms.

On clear days David Dixon, now an inquisitive boy of six, could see through his father's long spy glass the stone masons at work rebuilding the Capitol. He could see the White House and the grove of trees at the right of it which screened the Navy Department from view. Washington was a low stretch of forest not unlike the flats of New Jersey opposite Green Bank, except that here there were occasional knolls and villages rising above the general level of tidewater swamp. Meridian Hill was higher than any other spot in Washington. There were days when David Dixon could not see the city at all for the fog. On clear days he could see far over the city to the Potomac. He could make out sailboats and occasionally a midget steam ferry like the ferries that came down to Chester Landing from Philadelphia.

Meridian Hill was largely isolated from Washington by bad roads, but it was not so desolate as any of the farmsteads his grandfather Anderson owned in the hill country back of Chester. Meridian Hill was a village in itself. There were many servants about the house, nursemaids, kitchenmaids, dairymaids, boys to cut wood, stable boys to groom the horses and keep the mud washed off the carriage. There was Nathan who drove the carriage for the family whenever they went to see Grandfather Anderson or to pay a visit at the Navy Yard. And there was Nathan's boy, no bigger than David Dixon, whose job it was to clean the house for Commodore Porter's prized Barbary pigeons. There was the English gardener who did nothing but cultivate the five-acre kitchen garden and take care of the fancy cattle his father imported at $1200 a head. There were families who worked in the grain fields.

In addition to its large domestic establishment Meridian Hill was always alive with visitors. Both Commodore and Mrs. Porter were fond of entertainment. When the roads were passable, people came by horseback and carriage from miles around to attend Mrs. Porter's levees. The Marine Band, the best in the country at that time, played for the levees and the stately quadrilles in the ball room.

There were always guests in the house. Naval officers who came to see Commodore Porter on business accepted the hospitality of Mrs. Porter during their stay in Washington. Lieutenant and Mrs. David Glasgow Farragut spent several weeks of their honeymoon at Meridian Hill. Commodore Porter had a fatherly affection for the serious, rock-faced, young naval officer, now in his early twenties whom he had adopted as a child and taken with him on the cruise of the *Essex*. David Dixon admired Dave Farragut and little dreamed that one day he himself would fight side by side with Farragut in two of the most important naval campaigns of the Civil War.

On March 1, 1819, when the Porter family had been but a few months at Meridian Hill, the Commodore took them all over to the Navy Yard to see the launching of the new ship-of-the-line *Columbus*.[4] Commodore Porter wore his full regimentals. Mrs. Porter in a new muslin dress set off by a dark spencer wore a bonnet tied under her chin and carried a large muff. David Dixon wore his long tight trousers and blue jacket with shining buttons.

As they started down the hill toward the city, it began to rain, but David Dixon did not mind the rain so long as the horses could pull the carriage through the muddy places in the slashes.

Navy Yard Hill was crowded with people. At the iron foundries and rope-walks, which surrounded the Navy's forty-acre reservation on the East Branch of the Potomac, the workmen were idle today. Everyone was out to witness the ceremonies. As Commodore Porter's carriage wheeled through the gate of the Navy Yard, the sentries stiffened and saluted.

The Marine Band marched across the yard playing the "Star Spangled Banner." Bluejackets ran down the long file of guns with their little torches. Flames and loud reports and smoke burst from the guns. The Navy vessels anchored off shore also fired salutes.

Commodore Porter now joined the official party which included President Monroe and Secretary of the Navy Thompson. Ten-year-old William D. Porter had permission from Commodore

William Bainbridge, whose namesake he was, to go aboard the ship for the launching. David Dixon danced with excitement. He too must go. Commodore Bainbridge nodded. David Dixon followed William up through the tall wet scaffolding to the glistening deck of the *Columbus*.

David Dixon scarcely noticed the crowd of four thousand that lined the shore until he felt the broad deck quiver a little, and saw the people on shore moving back, back away from him. A memorable thrill went through his small wiry body. In later years he told newspaper men how he had felt that he was himself being launched into the United States Navy!

The Washington Navy Yard fascinated David Dixon. On pleasant summer days when Nathan the coachman drove Mrs. Porter and the children to the navy yard, the sentries always saluted. While his mother called at Commodore Tingey's house, David Dixon was allowed the run of the yard. He climbed into the sentry boxes, queer little medieval turret affairs atop the walls, to talk with the sentries. Some of these men were old experienced sailors with funny beards under their chins who had served under Commodore Porter in the early wars with the Barbary corsairs and had been imprisoned in Tripoli when Commodore Porter and Commodore Bainbridge had both been prisoners there. David Dixon liked their droll stories.

Far better he liked the sea stories his father told around the great fireplace on winter evenings. His father could make his stories seem more real than could the old seamen at the navy yard. And he could illustrate them with the store of trophies hung on the walls of the living room: cutlasses, duelling pistols, harpoons, oriental scarves, and implements used by the savages of Nukahiva.

Many naval heroes of 1812 came to Meridian Hill to see Commodore Porter on business. But often they came merely to smoke and drink whiskey from wide decanters and recall their wartime experiences. On the latter occasions, when the conversation was not on matters current and confidential, David Dixon was permitted to come into his father's study and learn naval history from the lips of Stephen Decatur, William Bainbridge, John Rodgers, and Oliver Hazard Perry—the men who had made that history. This was brilliant, fascinating history. Sometimes his father and Decatur would quarrel, and dignified old Commodore Rodgers would have to separate them as if they were mere boys.

During his first three years at Meridian Hill David Dixon grew rapidly. Though frail in appearance he was wiry and his muscles were strong. He tried them often in fights with William, in which he was always worsted. But he never admitted defeat and was always ready on the instant to come back for more.

On a memorable day in July 1822 David Dixon decided to try out his father's double-barreled Joe Manton. He wanted to perfect his marksmanship. And he decided that his father's pet Barbary pigeons would make excellent targets.

Nathan had brought the stallion around to the house, and the Commodore had cantered away to the office. His sharp-eyed mother and Jane, the English maid, were in the nursery attending to Hambleton, the new baby, and did not see David Dixon unhook the weapon from above the fireplace and slip out with it.

As he ran out from the hall into the sunlight, disturbing memories of his father's malacca faded away. There was a chance that his father might not bother to count the pigeons afterwards. He would take that chance.

He raised the long shiny twin barrels until they looked up over the roof of the pigeon house. Unmolested for generations the pet pigeons had multiplied to fill their numerous compartments. They now crowded every door and window and jostled one another as they basked in the hot sunshine.

Sighting along the v-shaped depression between the barrels of the gun, David Dixon's eye found a target of soft, iridescent feathers. He held the hand-carved gunstock tightly against his shoulder and fired. Then through the black center of the powder cloud he discharged the second barrel.

The nine-year-old boy saw pigeons drop by the dozen while the cloud of wings spread out quickly over the house, over the roads, over the cornfields, and over the orchard garden.

Nathan's boy who witnessed the destruction from the cool shade of the stable came tearing up the driveway to find David Dixon admiring the gun. To him David Dixon belittled the kick of the gun against his shoulder. The little balls of smoke that puffed from the gun when he tapped the gunstock on the ground fascinated David Dixon, as did the acrid fumes. For a moment he forgot the pigeons.

But a sudden sound of hoofs ascending the hill reminded him sharply when it was too late to pick up his kill. He and the other boy ran to the orchard garden, where they propped the Joe Manton against the gate and sought refuge in a cherry tree.

David Dixon pitted several cherries against his teeth. Sour cherries.

33. Former site of the Porter (Lloyd) House, called "Green Bank" on the River, east of Welsh Street. Built by Chief Justice David D. Lloyd 1721; bought by Major William Anderson 1806. Residence of Com. David Porter, the son-in-law of Maj. Anderson and father of Admiral Porter, who was born in this house in 1813. The building was used in later years for the manufacture of fireworks and was destroyed by an explosion 2, 17, 1882, when eighteen persons lost their lives and fifty-seven were wounded.

BIRTHPLACE OF DAVID DIXON PORTER AT CHESTER, PENNSYLVANIA.

EVALINA ANDERSON PORTER AND HER DAUGHTER, EVELINA CORA, AFTERWARDS WIFE OF GWYNN HARRIS HEAP. MOTHER AND SISTER OF ADMIRAL PORTER.

The garden gate squeaked, and there at the foot of the tree stood his father, riding whip in hand, eyes snapping up at him, and grim little mouth crisply barking for him to come down at once.

David Dixon climbed down from the cherry tree. The riding whip cracked around his thinly-clad buttocks. He broke and ran, round and round the garden with the Commodore in pursuit. At length his father, wearying of the chase, returned to the tree to thrash Nathan's boy.

A few days later Commodore Porter called David Dixon into his study and gave him a half interest in the pigeons. If discipline at Meridian Hill was sometimes naval in character, the laws that were laid down were wise laws that would enforce themselves.

But the gay, extravagant life at Meridian Hill was not to continue indefinitely. James K. Paulding, the witty young Secretary to the Board of Navy Commissioners, who knew Commodore Porter both on and off the record because he boarded at Meridian Hill, playfully satirized Commodore Porter's system of farming in his book *John Bull in America*. According to Paulding the dairy-maid at Meridian Hill ran off and married a prosperous farmer, and the English gardener, having been told that whiskey would ward off intermittent fever (which was epidemic in Washington in 1822), concluded that he could not get too much of a good thing and remained in a stupor from morning to night. Meridian Hill was highly satisfactory to the casual observer, but yielded absolutely no financial return.[5]

By the winter of 1822 Commodore Porter had spent his wartime prize money and his salary of $3,500 was not sufficient for his needs. He began to look for a midshipman's appointment for William, and put in at the Navy Department a request for sea duty for himself.

On December 31, 1822, Porter resigned from the Board of Navy Commissioners. The next day William's appointment as midshipman arrived. Enviously David Dixon watched his proud brother set out for New York to join the frigate *Brandywine*. But the shifting conditions at Meridian Hill were soon to bring to David Dixon his first experience of life at sea.[6]

2.

THE COMMODORE'S DISGRACE

In January 1823 Commodore David Porter hung up his cane and reached for his sword. The mortgages against Meridian Hill had given him cause to doubt his ability as a business man.

He was nearing his middle forties. His sons were growing up untrained to life at sea. David Dixon was now a quick, wiry, impetuous youth of ten who needed the stern regimen of life at sea.

The enterprise that whetted Commodore Porter's passion for adventure was the suppression of piracy in the West Indies. The fledgeling republics of Venezuela, Santo Domingo, and Mexico had broken their bonds with Spain during the Napoleonic convulsions; but Spain had refused to recognize their independence and had sent a naval force to blockade their ports and paralyze their coastwise trade. In answer to Spain's blockade the republics were sending out privateers against their mother country's commerce. These raiders did not stand on ceremony. Few took the trouble to provide themselves with letters of marque.

Bold ruthless adventurers from every nation flocked to Spain's West Indian islands to capture merchantmen, massacre crews, ransack and burn vessels. Some even boarded their prizes in the harbor of Havana, beneath the battlements of Morro Castle. The buccaneers defied the Spanish officials of the islands or corrupted them with bribes. And their victims were not always Spanish caravels, but frequently American traders out of Boston, New York, Philadelphia, and Baltimore.

While Commodore Porter's orders called for decisive suppression of piracy, they repeatedly emphasized the necessity for caution. The West Indies was Europe's back yard, and the United States in sending her officers into it wanted to make clear that her motive was neighborly and humanitarian; that if she insisted on protecting her merchantmen from pirates, she wanted only to cooperate with the established authorities of the islands. The wordiness of Secretary of the Navy Thompson's orders to Porter reveal an uneasy distrust of his man. It was a ticklish mission and the Secretary did not want the impetuous commander of the West Indian Squadron to provoke hostilities with Spain.[1]

Commodore Porter's campaign in the spring of 1823 was so successful that the Secretary of the Navy gave Porter carte blanche in the outfitting of vessels for 1824 and approved his request that he be permitted to take his family with him.

When the Porter family came aboard the *John Adams* on December 10, 1823, David Dixon found much that was new and exciting.[2] The seamen ran cheerily around the capstan to the noise of the drum and fife. The anchor was soon atrip, the cable coiled around the capstan. The boatswain's mate shouted to the men aloft. The foresail was set and at ten o'clock the vessel was under way. At noon a salute of seventeen guns was fired as they passed Mount Vernon.

At sunrise on the fifteenth the *John Adams* anchored off Norfolk. Here were many tiny schooners of the Mosquito Fleet fitting out for the cruise, but David Dixon found the midget steam galliot *Sea Gull* more interesting than any vessel he had yet seen. The *Sea Gull* was a converted ferry boat with high sides to keep the waves from washing over her deck and quenching her fires. Her side wheels, located amidships, were of a dimension equal to a third of her length. She had a stump of a mast forward and two tall funnels. As her cumbersome machinery and her coal took up practically the whole of her buoyancy, she had little space for bunking her crew. Invaluable for chasing pirates when sail-driven schooners were becalmed, she had the distinction of being the first steam vessel of war actually to engage in warfare on the open sea.

In January 1824 the fleet was ready to sail. But the Secretary of the Navy now ordered Commodore Porter to stand by in Norfolk to testify before a court-martial. This meant six weeks of delay. David Dixon was compelled to watch the *Grampus,* the *Spark,* and the *Weazle* put to sea while the *John Adams* swung idly at anchor.

During these weeks David Dixon explored the *John Adams* from hull to topmast. Whenever it was not sleeting or raining he was over the vessel's black-painted sides, swinging in the main and mizzen chains, or scurrying up her ratlines to dangle his legs from the high crosstrees, and pinch little gobs of tar from the lace lines that secured the sails to the long horizontal spars. He learned the names of a thousand details of the rigging.

David Dixon helped the seamen clear the tiers and stow a new 18-inch cable. He helped break out the spirit room and replace the sixteen casks of condemned whiskey with an equal number that were guaranteed "first proof and clear of still burn."[3] The spirit room on the *John Adams* was the medicine chest for the fleet. The good whiskey would save many a man from dying of yellow fever, "His Saffron Majesty," as the seamen called the terrible black vomit plague of the tropics. When Captain Dallas, the captain of the *John Adams,* condemned all the old rat-eaten jackets and sent the seamen ashore for new ones, David Dixon went with them. He watched the carpenters install new cabinet work in the after cabins to make life easier for Mrs. Porter, the children, and the maids who had been brought from Meridian Hill.

On February 18, Commodore Porter, having completed his testimony before the court-martial, came aboard; and the *John Adams* followed by the *Sea Gull* sailed out past the Virginia Capes into the open sea.

David Dixon Porter's first voyage was over a cross and squally sea. At 9:30 A.M. on March 4, while the *John Adams* was standing down for St. Bartholomew, a marine fell overboard and drowned before a boat could be lowered.

The *John Adams* and the *Sea Gull* touched at St. Bartholomew, St. Christopher, St. Thomas. On the south coast of Porto Rico they nosed into the Dead Man's Chest and Ponce, which had been notorious rendezvous for pirates. They touched at Mona, Santo Domingo, Beata, and Kingston. But no pirates were to be found anywhere.

On April 10 Commodore Porter arrived at Thompson's Island, or Key West, where he set his men to work on the navy yard he had laid out the year before. Carpenters were sent ashore to build a dwelling for his family. Squads of men were detailed to chop underbrush and fill in mosquito swamps. The between-decks of the *John Adams* was washed with lime and regularly fumigated against yellow fever.

The first week in May Porter moved his family ashore and transferred his flag to the *Sea Gull.* He planned to search for pirates along the southern shore of Cuba. But he contracted yellow fever. A few days later the only doctor at Key West also came down with fever.

Mrs. Porter proved her resourcefulness and endurance by nursing her husband past the crisis and in spite of the stagnant heat of early summer warding off the sickness from her children. As soon as Commodore Porter could sit up in bed, she moved him on board the *Sea Gull,* crowded David Dixon, the four younger children, and the maids in after her, and directed Captain Vorhees to return to Washington.

The futility of the search for pirates and the early return grievously disappointed David Dixon. But the voyage on the little steam galliot was an experience he could always remember with pride. After stopping at Matanzas to take on an enormous load of coal and to allow the Commodore to leave dispatches for the officers of his squadron, the *Sea Gull* on June 15 chugged out to sea. David Dixon watched eagerly every movement of the *Sea Gull's* engineers. The flares from the furnace fascinated him. The steam that leaked from the steam chest when the enormous piston came down, penetrated his nostrils and thrilled him as had the fumes from the Joe Manton. The vibrations which thumped through the boat when the great paddle wheels kicked the water awoke in him the desire to command some day a warship driven by steam.

In the fall of 1824 David Dixon was put to school at Columbia College, in Washington D. C., the campus of which joined Meridian Hill on the east. It was a little three-building Baptist school with an enrollment in 1825 of ninety-three students. Here for the next two years he applied himself chiefly to the study of mathematics, the fundamental requisite for all who would navigate a ship.

The two years from 1824 to 1826 were crucial years for Commodore Porter and were destined to have a peculiar influence on both the character and the career of David Dixon.

In the fall of 1824 several piracies occurred in the West Indies, and the newspapers reporting them cast aspersions on the Navy Department. Commodore Porter was particularly blamed for directing the activities of the West Indian Squadron from his home on Meridian Hill instead of from the scene of action itself.

In October, therefore, after attending President Monroe's banquet to the venerable Marquis de Lafayette, Commodore Porter posted to Chester where the *John Adams* was awaiting him and returned to the West Indies.

Cruising over the usual route, he came on November 12 to St. Thomas, where he met Lieutenant Platt of the *Beagle.*[4] Platt came aboard the flagship in great distress to report as follows:

On the night of October 25, the warehouse of an American

firm in St. Thomas had been robbed of $5,000 worth of merchandise. Pirates at Fajardo, on the east coast of Porto Rico, were at once suspected, as other stolen property had recently been located there; and the American consul at St. Thomas had requested Lieutenant Platt to go to Fajardo and conduct a search. Platt had done so. At Fajardo he had gone ashore in civilian clothes and revealed his mission to the alcade, or mayor, who agreed to have the local police make a search. Platt now strolled toward an eating house for dinner when suddenly two native policemen summoned him to return to the alcalde. The Spanish official now demanded his register. As the *Beagle* was a ship of war she carried none. The alcalde feigned considerable wrath and Platt left him to return to his ship. But he was overtaken by village officers who took him dogwise by the collar and brought him back. Another agonizing hour passed before the alcalde would allow him to send to the ship for his commission and uniform. When these came he put on his officer's clothes and unfolded his commission. The mayor studied the commission and pronounced it a forgery, Platt a damned pirate, and marched Platt off to a filthy guard-house. Further protests and foolish arguments ensued, and finally after a considerable lapse of time the American officer was turned loose, to be hooted and hissed out of the village.

When Commodore Porter heard the Lieutenant's story he set off at once to demand an apology. On the way he encountered a tropical calm which delayed him twenty-four hours. Finally on the morning of November 14, he cast anchor off Fajardo and landed two hundred seamen armed with muskets, boarding pikes, cutlasses, and pistols. It was 85 degrees in the shade.

Commodore Porter sent Lieutenant Stribling ahead with a flag of truce and a demand that the alcalde apologize to Lieutenant Platt. A company of Spanish soldiers had mounted two 9-pounder cannon along the road to the village. Commodore Porter, seeing them aim at his boats, dispatched Lieutenant Crabb with a file of seamen to spike the Spanish guns. The Spanish soldiery fell back in desultory order to Fajardo. Commodore Porter followed with the remainder of his men. In fifteen or twenty minutes the sailors arrived at the fringe of the town.

Stribling returned with the alcalde and requested Crabb to hold his men back two hundred yards. Crabb halted his column and rested them on their arms. When Commodore Porter arrived, four or five hundred gesticulating Spanish soldiers had gathered at the edge of the town to gaze at the Americans. Commodore Porter ordered his seamen to come to attention and face around toward the enemy.

The alcalde was brought through the American line to confer with the Commodore. The Spanish official professed that he had not known Mr. Platt was an American officer, but the Commodore brought him face to face with Platt and informed him that he had but eight minutes in which to make the required apology. The alcalde assented. Lieutenant Platt was asked whether the apology was suitable. He said that it was.

The alcalde now invited the Americans into the town, but Commodore Porter refused to accept the hospitality of Fajardo and hurried his men back to the beach. Nor did he wait to take on board the herd of sheep and hogs that were shortly driven down as a peace offering.

Commodore Porter's report of the incident created a flurry in Washington. Less than a twelvemonth after President Monroe had forbidden European aggression in the Western Hemisphere an American officer had landed on Spanish soil and browbeaten a Spanish official into making a dictated apology. Secretary of the Navy Southard, fearing a war with Spain, recalled Commodore Porter to Washington to justify himself before a court of inquiry.

Porter arrived in Washington on March 1, 1825, and reported his return. The next day the press printed letters from two Congressmen that were derogatory to Porter. Porter chafed with indignation. He waited two weeks for his court of inquiry. But Spain entered no protest, and the court was delayed. Commodore James Barron, on whose court-martial Porter had sat in 1807, was now one of the ranking men in the Navy. Porter suspected a malign influence from that quarter.

Porter wrote Secretary Southard a letter demanding action. Southard, "surprised" at his phraseology, felt constrained to remind him "of the relation that exists between you and the Department."

The court of inquiry met at the Washington Navy Yard on May 2. When asked whether he objected to any members of the court, Porter read a lengthy criticism of the Secretary of the Navy, to which the Secretary sent a written reply which was read before the court. Given an opportunity to question a witness Porter launched into a second tirade against the Secretary.

The Court cleared the room and decided that his remarks were so "highly objectionable" that hereafter whenever he wished to communicate with the court he should have to do so in writing through the Judge Advocate. Again he was asked whether he desired to question the witness. The Commodore politely declined, and observing that he would now take leave of the court, he picked up his cocked hat and his cane and nonchalantly left the room. The court was compelled to proceed without him.

Commodore Porter now set out to justify himself with his pen. His *An Exposition of the Facts* flamed with the robust wrath of an Andrew Jackson. Unfortunately he dedicated his pamphlet to the new President, John Quincy Adams—the man whose pen had had a large share in the composition of the Monroe Doctrine. President Adams was piqued; and the Secretary, thoroughly angry now, ordered a court-martial to try the irascible Commodore.

The court-martial was essentially a repetition of the court of inquiry, but Porter's continued onslaughts against the Secretary had greater justification since two of the judges the Secretary had appointed—James Barron and Jesse D. Elliott—were notoriously inimical to Porter. So too was Judge Advocate Coxe who had been kept over from the court of inquiry. Coxe had anonymously published defamations of Porter in the newspapers. To the original charge of hostile action against His Catholic Majesty King Ferdinand was now added the charge of insubordination toward the Secretary of the Navy.

The surprising feature of the court-martial was the leniency of the verdict. Although Commodore Porter was suspended for six months, his action at Fajardo was attributed by the court "to an anxious disposition, on his part, to maintain the honor and advance the interest of the nation and of the service!" If Barron and Elliott had, as Porter suspected, exerted a malign influence against him, his friends on the court-martial, James Biddle and John Downes, had so modified the verdict as to render it self-contradictory, if not flattering.

But Commodore Porter considered himself disgraced. He resisted all his friends' efforts to console him and sought an audience with President Adams to get the verdict set aside but was denied a hearing.

David Dixon witnessed his father's troubles from the close perspective of Meridian Hill. Since the early dawn of his consciousness, he had looked upon his father as his one great hero. His hero had now been publicly stricken from the pedestal. But the faith of the worshiper was not disturbed.

David Dixon Porter resolved solemnly to wipe out his father's disgrace by retrieving the lost laurels for the name of Porter. The early maturing of his one ambition gave a direction to his life from which he would never swerve. He had inherited many of the characteristics of his father—his audacity, his perseverance, his passion for the sea—and these were to carry him far in the achievement of his ideal.

David Dixon's first axiom was that the Commodore could do no wrong. His father's enemies became his enemies. Commodore Porter never made peace with any of his old friends who had sat on his court-martial. The son was destined to serve under four of these judges, and with his particular set of preconceived notions it is not strange that he was to be caught in many a squall and many a difficult seaway.

His father's disgrace inspired him with a general contempt for Secretaries of the Navy—no mean handicap for a man who would seek to rise in the Navy.

Another prejudice fastened upon him from the beginning was a fear and consequent respect for the importance of politicians. During the Civil War his dashing victories alone were to save him from the machinations of the political generals, but in the post-war imbroglios his reputation was not to escape unsinged. In a dozen ways his career was destined to parallel that of the old Commodore whom he idolized.

Meanwhile his father's disgrace was to have an immediate effect on David Dixon's career. After the six months of suspension, Commodore Porter resigned from the U. S. Navy and accepted the position of General of Marine of the Republic of Mexico. When he left home he was to take with him two of his sons: David Dixon, twelve, and Thomas, ten. David Dixon Porter was to begin his career as a midshipman in the Mexican Navy.[5]

3.
THE MEXICAN VENTURE

THE Mexican brig-of-war *Guerrero* in April 1826, swung jauntily at her moorings with the garbage-freckled water of New York Harbor smacking her sides and making a sucking sound. She was a trim black vessel with fine lines built for speed. As yet her identifying flag had not been run up, so that fresh from the East River shipyard of Henry Eckford, premier shipbuilder of the United States, she looked like any one of a dozen or more American brigs that from time to time swung from the nearby docks of the Brooklyn Navy Yard. Her twenty-two guns had been cast in the same foundries and bored by the same workmen who made cannon for the U. S. Navy. Her seventy-odd seamen, Americans, Englishmen, Irishmen, Swedes, not a full crew, but enough to take her to Vera Cruz, had been signed on in New York by David Porter, the new Mexican General of Marine.[1]

On the General's staff were his good friends, Dr. Boardman, signed on as surgeon, and Mr. Law, as secretary. In immediate command of the *Guerrero* was General Porter's nephew, D. Henry Porter, son of his sister Anne, who had married her own cousin Alexander Porter. D. Henry Porter was a reckless, venturesome youth who had served more than half of his twenty-one years in the U. S. Navy under some of its sternest martinets. The *Guerrero's* watch officers, Midshipmen Thompson and Hawkins, were also Americans, Thompson having been a passed midshipman in the Navy. Other American naval officers would have joined the *Guerrero* had not the General of Marine refused to permit them to leave their secure positions for a venture which he regarded as highly speculative.

The General of Marine was leaving behind his oldest son William, now a midshipman in the Navy. At Meridian Hill he had left Mrs. Porter with Elizabeth, fourteen, Theodoric, Hambleton, and the infant twins Henry Ogden and Evelina Cora. He had assured his wife,—who knew his susceptibility to yellow fever and deplored his Mexican plans as an angry aftermath of the Fajardo court-martial—that he was going for a lark, and would soon return with prize money to pay off the mortgage on Meridian Hill. He was taking with him his sons David Dixon and Thomas to become midshipmen in the Mexican Navy.

In the latter part of April the *Guerrero* cast off her moorings, hoisted her flag and tacked out of New York Harbor, dipping her colors by way of farewell. By the end of May she had crossed the Gulf of Mexico. The day before arriving at Vera Cruz she made out the Spanish man-of-war *Hercules* standing for her under full canvas. With but six men to a gun the *Guerrero* crowded on top-gallant sails, and reached the protecting fortress of Vera Cruz, San Juan de Ulloa, without an encounter.

Leaving the *Guerrero* secured to the brass rings imbedded in the landward face of San Juan de Ulloa, David Porter went ashore with his entourage. The party received a noisy welcome from the newly-fledged republican citizens of Vera Cruz; but since the fever season was approaching, they set out immediately for Mexico City.

David Dixon found the first day's horseback ride over the hot sands of the *tierra caliente* tedious and fatiguing. The crude huts where they halted for griddlecakes, stewed beans, and a drink of pulque could hardly be called inns. There were no beds in the shack where they stopped for the first night, but David Dixon slept soundly in one of the hammocks his father had brought along from the *Guerrero*.

At Jalapa, the first of the upland towns, they rested three days. The air here was fresh and invigorating. David Dixon enjoyed the official courtesies rendered his father as though they had been arranged for himself.

On June 5, the party halted to gaze on Beautiful Lake Tezcoco and the landscape of Mexico City in the distance. Riding around the lake and over two miles of causeway, they entered the capital city at five in the afternoon, just when fashionable folk were out for their usual airing in the Alameda. Mexican ladies in native costumes paraded in gaily painted Spanish coaches. Men on horseback wore gaudily embroidered jackets and glittering spurs; their saddles and bridles flashed with studs of brass and silver.[2]

In Mexico City the General of Marine leased a two-story stone house, built in Andalusian style around a courtyard. Outside stairways led up to bedrooms with ceilings eighteen feet high, and the paved roof overhead served as a veranda from which David Dixon could survey a wide area of the city.

Joel R. Poinsett, the American Minister to Mexico, who had been a personal friend of David Porter's since the days of the *Essex,* introduced Porter to the aged President Victoria and his cabinet. Porter found the Mexicans to be shifty politicians; but, nevertheless, he managed to secure control of the navy and the Castle of San Juan de Ulloa, to adjust the matter of salary and perquisites, and to obtain commissions as midshipmen for David Dixon and Thomas.

Since they would not return to Vera Cruz until after the hot season, David Dixon and Thomas were placed in school, where they were taught to read and write Spanish, to repeat prayers, and to cross themselves. Poinsett wrote that the boys might be heard a square away bawling out their lessons all together like a school of Arabs. Although David Dixon acquired little formal education in the seven months he was here, the hidalgos took him under their protection and taught him to play monte and to sing Spanish love songs in a piping tenor voice, strumming his own accompaniment on the guitar. He was glad when in November his father announced that it was time to go down to Vera Cruz to fit out the squadron.

The Castle of San Juan de Ulloa held a fascination for the thirteen-year-old boy. He explored every passageway and casemate. He flung himself astride of every gun. He drew caricatures of seamen on its walls of soft coral rock. He could imagine himself with a few doughty companions stationed at the head of the narrow stone stairways slashing out with cutlasses to defend the fort against the Spaniards.

He watched his father whip the old hulks tied up alongside the *Guerrero* into something approaching seaworthiness. There were the frigate *Libertad* and three brigs, the *Victoria,* the *Bravo,* the *Herman;* and the old Spanish ship-of-the-line, *Asia,* which a mutinous Spanish crew had turned over to the Mexicans. Having found the *Asia* worthless as a warship, Porter dismasted her for use as a prison hulk.

Most knotty of all Porter's problems was that of personnel. There being no merchant marine, few Mexicans were good seamen. To fill out his crews the government sent him a company of mutinous soldiers, as if sending them to sea were a kind of condemnation to the galleys. Porter found the native officers little better than the seamen; but lethargic and dissolute as some were, they came from politically influential families, and it was not expedient to replace them immediately.

General Porter with a tradition of stern discipline in his blood had the U. S. Navy Regulations translated into Spanish and imposed as the law of his new command. He curtailed shore leave and ordered daily drills with small arms and exercises at the great guns. He court-martialed offenders and let it be known that he would not tolerate officers who slept on watch, played monte on the quarter-deck, or smoked their long cigars anywhere in the ship, except forward of the chicken-coops where sparks could not endanger the magazines. He applied the cat liberally to the backs of his seamen, and finally brought them to a semblance of obedience.

In May 1827 he took the Mexican squadron to Key West to draw the Spanish blockade ships away from the Mexican shore and to threaten Spain's trade with Cuba. Though the U. S. Navy had abandoned its station at Key West in favor of a new one at Pensacola, the Mexican squadron was not welcome. President Adams, impelled by the Spanish Minister's protests, sent an American squadron to Key West to observe.

A Spanish fleet under Commodore Laborde attempted a blockade. But the Mexican commander in chief, familiar with all the obscure, uncharted entrances to the harbor, sent out his ships and brought in prizes almost at will.

During the summer and early fall of 1827 David Dixon was broken in as a midshipman on the flagship *Libertad*. In many ways his surroundings illustrated what naval etiquette and discipline ought not to be. But his father so forcefully pointed out the shortcomings that the fourteen-year-old boy never forgot. His father treated him like any ordinary midshipman, and David Dixon loved him for it. For the first time in his life he began to have a realistic appreciation of his father's character—no longer the vague romantic hero who could tell glorious stories of the past, no longer the impractical gentleman farmer whose pet pigeons a nine-year-old son would not hesitate to shoot, but the stern militarist who could transform a company of scrawny, ill-fed Mexican soldiers with balls and chains on their legs into hard, husky, moderately dependable seamen.

By the fall of 1827 David Dixon was prepared for more active duty than that offered on the *Libertad*, whose primary job had been simply to lie in harbor and keep the Spanish squadron occupied blockading her. In October he was transferred to the *Esmer-alda* for a raid on the shipping lanes of Cuba.

The *Esmeralda* was a captured merchantman with high poop raised still higher by a pile of mahogany logs and machinery which had once been destined for sugar plantations. David Dixon was rated as a midshipman under his cousin Captain D. Henry Porter, commanding. The crew consisted of an English carpenter named Barret, an old Swedish quartermaster, Sims, an English cabin boy, Vizatelly, two Americans, and twenty-three Mexicans.

The *Esmeralda* needed no disguise to enable her to run through Laborde's blockade except an extemporized flag of cotton cloth freshly striped with red paint. Rounding Cape San Antonio on the western lizard's-tail of Cuba the raider coasted eastward. At midnight off Broa Bay Captain Henry Porter lowered his four-teen-oared launch and look a landing party ashore, leaving Midshipman David Dixon Porter in charge of the *Esmeralda*.[3]

The boat party surprised and captured several small schooners in the harbor, landed at the village of Batabanoa and captured a mule train with coffee and sugar, which they loaded on the schooners and brought off to the *Esmeralda*. By daylight the plunder had been shifted aboard the high-pooped raider and the schooners sunk. On the following night four vessels were seized in Seguanca Bay on the Isle of Pines. One was a beautiful craft, as large as the *Esmeralda* herself, and would have brought a fair price if she could have been taken to Key West, but the orders were to burn, sink, and destroy. Only cordage, sails, and naval stores were saved for the use of the Mexican squadron.

At Cienfuegos the Mexicans in the landing party threw off all discipline and indulged in private looting. Captain Henry Porter sent back this plunder and whipped the thieves at the mast.

Though flogging was perfectly good theory, it appeared in this instance to be poor practice. David Dixon noticed that the Mexicans dragged at their work and that Barret, the English carpenter, who had been punished many times for drunkenness, was shut-tling from one group of Mexicans to another talking in excited undertones. Barret had been drinking again.

After the landing party's weapons had been returned to the cabin, David Dixon, who had them in charge, counted them. Some were missing. He counted again. Two muskets, several cut-lasses, all of the fourteen bayonets were missing. He called Viza-telly, the wide-eyed cabin boy, who quoted one of the Mexicans as saying that the *Esmeralda* would have a new captain within twenty-four hours.

Remaining in the cabin to guard the weapons, David Dixon sent Vizatelly after Captain Porter, to whom he reported his discovery.

Directing his young cousin to stand in the cabin door with cutlasses and pistols ready and stationing old Sims the Swedish quartermaster by his side, Captain Porter called the men to muster.

Barret appeared on the forward deck with the Mexicans around him.

"Barret," Captain Porter called out, "come aft here, you drunken scoundrel!"

"I'm no more a drunken scoundrel than you are!" retorted the mutineer. Shouting for his companions to follow him he rushed upon the captain brandishing a weapon.

David Dixon handed his cousin a pistol and Sims a cutlass. Sims cut down Barret, and Captain Porter put a shot through the head of the leading Mexican. The other Mexicans retreated, while the stout, blood-spattered Swede, flinging aside his cutlass, ran into the mob and knocked down a number of Mexicans with his fists.

Captain Porter stood over them with cocked pistols while David Dixon and the quartermaster clamped the mutineers in irons and pulled the missing bayonets from under their greasy jackets.

With his effective crew now reduced to Sims, the cabin boy, and the two American seamen, Captain Porter ran the *Esmeralda* into a mangrove shelter in the Mangles Islands. If he marooned the Mexicans here they would starve. He devised a better plan.

Heaving overboard the mahogany logs that were piled on the poop, he sawed twenty-two pairs of holes through the deck straddling the carling over the cabin. The mutineers' feet were run through and chained below. In this way no one could touch the irons without the knowledge of the Captain. A simple but effective expedient.

David Dixon and his cousin, with the skeleton crew, sailed the *Esmeralda* back to her base, where the General of Marine flogged the malefactors through the fleet and sent them home to hard labor on San Juan de Ulloa.

Not long after the *Esmeralda's* voyage, uncertain political conditions in Mexico induced the General of Marine to return his squadron to Vera Cruz. The party in power from whom he held his command was seriously menaced by bands of roving guer-

rillas led by the party out of power. There was a formidable
Masonic agitation against the Catholic priests, who, like the old
Tories in America, retained their loyalty to the mother country.
The finances of the Republic were poorly managed, and the idea
of the navy's prizes being disposed of in Key West, where the
politicians could not hope to finger the rewards of victory, dis-
pleased the party in power.

Early in 1828 the General of Marine fitted out his best vessel
the *Guerrero* for a cruise similar to the *Esmeralda's*. Captain
Henry Porter was appointed to command her, with an English
officer, Williams, as her first lieutenant, Vanstavern, an American,
as second lieutenant, David Dixon Porter and several other American boys as midshipmen, and a picked crew—one third Mexicans
and two-thirds Americans and Englishmen—of 186 seamen.

Weighing anchor at Vera Cruz on February 7, the *Guerrero*
embarked with fair winds for Cuba. On the ninth, as she swung
across the route from Havana to the Guiana coast, she overhauled
and captured two Spanish Guianaman brigs, which she manned
and sent home to Vera Cruz. On this same day she also spoke an
American vessel two days out of Havana and obtained the inac-
curate information that there were in Havana two dismantled
Spanish frigates and but a single brig, the *Hercules,* which was
ready to put to sea.

On Sunday morning, February 10, the jagged sky line of Cuba
arose out of the sun-streaked sea. The *Guerrero's* sails, heavy
with night-fog, dripped peacefully as they dried in the mild air.
Suddenly the man in the foretop shouted "Sail Ho!"

Close to the shore were about fifty midget schooners heading
toward Havana with produce for ocean-going bottoms. Midshipman David Dixon Porter's heart thumped happily.

As the *Guerrero* bore down upon them, the fleet of sailing
boats came about and fled into the port of Mariel thirty miles
to the west of Havana. Through his cousin's glass David Dixon
discovered that the merchantmen were being convoyed by the
Spanish brigs *Marte* and *Amalia* and that upon the spit of land
behind which the fleet and the brigs took shelter stood a Martello
tower, a huge cylindrical pile of masonry built up to give elevation to two long guns.

The *Guerrero* stood in close for a hammering, battering fight.
Two of her guns were assigned to take care of the cannon on the
tower, whose missiles, hurled by bad powder, fell harmlessly into
the water. The gunners on the Spanish ships overestimating the

range sent their cannon balls whistling high into the *Guerrero's* rigging, puncturing sails and snapping stays but doing no serious injury. The *Guerrero's* American and English gunners silenced many cannon on the Spanish vessels before a lucky Spanish shot severed the *Guerrero's* cable and caused her to drift out of action.

The Mexican backed on to a submerged rock, but managed to get off without damage and after repairing rigging, tacked again to her former position and dropped her port anchor. The battle now continued as before. The *Guerrero* presented a smaller target than her enemies and got off her broadsides quicker. Her missiles that flew wide of the mark pounded into the tightly-packed merchantmen, sinking several of them. The merchant crews took shelter ashore, where the crew of the *Amalia* shortly joined them.

Midshipman David Dixon Porter sprinted along the smoky length of the ship from quarter-deck to forecastle to shriek Captain Henry Porter's orders to Lieutenants Williams and Vanstavern. Dodging flying splinters, leaping over corpses and wounded men and pools of blood that dotted the deck, swerving clear of the recoil of guns, he shuttled back again to his station beside the captain to receive other messages. He darted down the gangway under the rumbling deck to the magazines with a word for the quartermaster and the sweating Mexicans who heaved the rounds of ammunition to the gunners. He ran to the foremast to have the boatswain's mate card the shredded rope's ends and splice the rigging. He was hit once by a spent ball and bruised, but he was too excited to feel anything but exultation in his first battle.

The *Guerrero* was badly crippled aloft, sails torn, spars shot away, ropes cut. Both topgallant masts, sniped off by Spanish missiles, hung by broken spider webs of shrouds to foul the foresail and mainsail. But Captain Henry Porter was elated by the punishment his gunners were giving the enemy. He told David Dixon that in a few minutes the Spanish would surrender. As he spoke the *Guerrero's* port cable was shot away.

Again the Mexican drifted out of gunshot, and her men scurried aloft to repair. They wanted to get back and force the surrender before nightfall. But from their vantage point they beheld in the distance a new and formidable foe—the three tall masts of a Spanish frigate.

The guns at Mariel had been heard in Havana, and the 64-gun Spanish frigate *Lealtad* (whose presence had not been reported by the American merchantman the day before) had commandeered all the rowboats in Havana to tow her out to sea. When the *Lealtad* got within ten miles of Mariel, a fresh breeze bellied her broad courses, studding sails, and topgallant sails, and she bore down upon the *Guerrero* under full canvas.

The little *Guerrero's* twenty-two guns were no match for the frigate, and Captain Porter made all haste to get away. Maneuvering across the *Lealtad's* bows he discharged his guns at long range. The frigate's wide spread of studding sails prevented her from turning away and the cannon balls raked her fore and aft along the length of her deck.

In spite of her crippled rigging the *Guerrero* hauled away to the north and by nightfall had left her powerful antagonist hull down.

Captain Porter now forgot how narrowly he had escaped destruction. He remembered only the panic-stricken, prize-packed harbor of Mariel and the feeble response the brigs had made to his parting blows. If he ran on into Key West he would doubtless be blockaded there by the *Lealtad*. If he dodged his cumbersome pursuer and dashed back to Mariel he might under cover of darkness rush in with his boats and cut out the brigs and with these additions successfully encounter the *Lealtad*.

He put his helm up and tacked south. He did not get far. Abruptly the blackness was illumined with many patches of flame and the *Lealtad's* broadside crashed into the *Guerrero*. Captain Porter worked feverishly with his crippled masts and spars, and the black night once more sheltered him. But at daybreak the frigate was disclosed within striking distance.

With her long guns the *Lealtad* was able to stand off at a distance and pound the *Guerrero* to pieces. Captain Henry Porter strove to keep his short carronades within effective range, but the wind failed him. He delivered several good blows which brought the Spaniard's topsails down by the run, but his own decks were shortly reduced to a shamble. Twice the *Guerrero's* colors were shot away, and twice they were again run up the mast. At length Captain Porter called a conference of officers. It was decided to surrender. The colors were hauled down.

In the smoke of battle the *Lealtad's* commander did not notice the surrender but thought he had again shot the *Guerrero's* colors down. He kept on pounding broadsides into the *Guerrero*.

Midshipman David Dixon Porter now saw the *Lealtad* close upon the Guerrero and pour in grape at short range. He saw dozens of the crew crumple to the deck in agony. He saw his cousin double and fall. David Dixon caught him under the armpits. But the gored body was lifeless.

David Dixon raged helplessly on the deck. He never ceased to regard this action of the Spanish commander as the grossest and most loathsome cowardice. For four hours the *Lealtad* stood off to repair before sending a boat party to board the stricken *Guerrero*. As the boarders were hustling David Dixon and the other officers over the side to be taken to the *Lealtad*, David Dixon thought he saw his cousin's body thrown into the sea. He was filled with a violent hatred.

Hours later the *Lealtad* towed the dismantled hulk of the *Guerrero* in triumph to Havana. David Dixon Porter spurned the parole the Spaniards offered him, preferring to remain with his fellow prisoners on the filthy guard ship in Havana Harbor.[4]

Several months later his father effected his exchange and sent the fifteen-year-old boy home via New Orleans. The journey by river sailboat from New Orleans to Pittsburgh and by overland stage to Chester, David Dixon made alone. His brother Thomas had died in Vera Cruz of yellow fever.

The first day out of New Orleans he fell in with a group of card sharks who stripped him of his stage fare. The gamblers left the boat at Vicksburg. Years later, when David Dixon Porter was bombarding the town of Vicksburg with 13-inch mortar shells, he would recall the pleasant gallantry of these gamblers and wonder if they were still in the town.

A kindly old gentlemen he met on the journey paid for his ride on top of the stage from Pittsburgh to Chester. His mother welcomed him home to Green Bank, and put him to school in Chester. There were new lines about the corners of her straight small mouth, but her blue eyes were as sharp as ever, and her profuse, curly brown hair was as lovely. The prize money which David Dixon had helped his father to win in the navy of Mexico had been wholly absorbed by the navy itself. Meridian Hill had been sold under the auctioneer's hammer for a third of its value.

Through his grandfather, Congressman William Anderson, David Dixon on February 2, 1829, obtained an appointment as midshipman in the U. S. Navy. The sixteen-year-old youth had already had more experience in actual battle than many a full-fledged American lieutenant. This experience had begotten in him a certain cockiness surprisingly like that of his father. Too much, in fact, for any midshipman in the peace-time U. S. Navy of that day.

4·
THE DIFFICULT CAREER

Davɪᴅ Dɪxon's appointment as midshipman came in February
1829; yet his orders to duty did not arrive for months. During these months of waiting the short, wiry, sixteen-year-old
veteran of the battle between the *Guerrero* and the *Lealtad* won
a reputation around Chester for madcap pranks. The neighborhood credited him with setting fire to a carpenter's barn, which
severely exercised the bucket brigade of the village. His mother's
family in Chester lamented that he would probably turn out
exactly like his father, whom, indeed, he resembled.

It was June before David Dixon finally received orders to
report to Captain Alexander C. Wadsworth on board the U. S.
frigate *Constellation* at Norfolk. Since his father had not yet
returned from Mexico, David Dixon was accompanied as far as
Washington by his soft-spoken grandfather Anderson, now retired
as a Congressman, and his grandparent introduced the boy to
Mr. Branch, the Secretary of the Navy. Incidentally while in
Washington he visited in the home of Commodore Daniel Tod
Patterson, his father's old friend and successor on the Board of
Navy Commissioners, and met Commodore Patterson's youngest
daughter George Ann.

David Dixon Porter met his future messmates in a large, cot-
filled room on the top floor of a Norfolk hotel. He thought that
preparatory to going on board the frigate these boys from two
to four years younger than himself needed to have their trouser-
legs tied into sailor's knots and their boots filled with water, and
these it appears from his semi-autobiographical *Adventures of
Harry Marline* were his first pranks after his entrance into the
Navy. After they had all completed their business with the Norfolk tailors and crowded into the steerage mess of the frigate,
David Dixon at once became their leader.[1]

The *Constellation,* as flagship of the Mediterranean Squadron
under Commodore James Biddle, had the most dignified assign-

ment now open to any American ship. Her duties were entirely pacific. Yet to David Dixon she was the ship on which his father had served as a midshipman thirty years ago when she had captured the French frigate *L'Insurgente*. Both Commodore Biddle and Captain Wadsworth were distinguished officers; but inasmuch as both men had sat as judges on his father's court-martial, David Dixon regarded them as personal enemies.

After his experiences in the Mexican Navy, David Dixon found life on the Mediterranean station too tame to satisfy his taste for adventure. And he found Captain Wadsworth's discipline strict. The rigid Captain, contrary to the custom of officers on this assignment, had left his wife at home, declaring emphatically that he wanted no domestic obligations to interfere with his official duties.

David Dixon played midshipman pranks on the negro slaves whose owners in Norfolk had hired them to the ship as messboys. When the midshipmen were forbidden to bring liquor on board, David Dixon contrived to obtain it through the portholes from the bumboats. Instead of the dry history lessons the schoolmaster assigned, David Dixon devoured *Childe Harold* and *Don Juan,* and wrote Byronic rhymes satirizing his elders. Once he presumed to tell Lieutenant Paulding how things had been done aboard his father's flagship the *Libertad,* and the Lieutenant reported him for impudence; whereupon the midshipman sketched cartoons of the Lieutenant which kept the steerage mess in uproar. His most ingenious deviltry, as he afterwards recalled, was reserved for the fumbling Irish schoolmaster. Many times he was summoned to the Captain's cabin, and seldom were his explanations satisfactory.

In the fall of 1830 Captain Wadsworth refused to approve young Porter's warrant as midshipman. The blow carried an added force because David Dixon's father was visiting him at the time. In his extremity David Dixon appealed to Commodore Biddle, and the latter perhaps as a friendly gesture to Commodore Porter leaned over backward to temper Captain Wadsworth's stern justice. Behind his youthful peccadilloes was a fierce ambition. He meant to vindicate his father. He submitted to the hard discipline of Captain Wadsworth.

When the *Constellation* returned to New York in December 1831, after two years in the Mediterranean, David Dixon requested three months' leave of absence. He returned at once to Chester and reëntered school. In February 1832 he obtained an additional three months "to devote a little time to the scientific part of my profession." Learning that Commodore Patterson was to be the new commander of the Mediterranean Squadron, he wrote the Secretary of the Navy on April 30 requesting duty afloat to finish his sea service for the probationary grade and requesting if practicable that he be assigned to the command of Commodore Patterson on the frigate *United States*. Fortunately Commodore Patterson had had nothing to do with the wretched court-martial. The Secretary did not resent the youth's forwardness but acceded to his request.

Commodore Daniel Tod Patterson was an able commander with a distinguished career behind him. In 1815 while in charge of the naval station at New Orleans he had helped General Andrew Jackson win the first great battle of New Orleans, and Congress had awarded him a vote of thanks. While on the Board of Navy Commissioners from 1828 to 1832 he had taken a brilliant part in the social life of Washington. In 1832 he had but to ask for the command of the Mediterranean Squadron to get it. Unlike the stern Wadsworth, Commodore Patterson was taking his family with him.

Cholera was raging in Manhattan when David Dixon arrived there in June to join his ship. Ignoring the plague, he purchased a year's supply of bear's oil to make his hair shine and had a tailor measure him for more clothes than the first lieutenant. On the frigate *United States* in the Brooklyn Navy Yard he found the ship's carpenters preparing the after cabins for Commodore Patterson's family. A fine piano had been hoisted aboard. Georgy Patterson was going on the cruise.

On June 30, 1832, Commodore Patterson's red pennant was run up to the mainmast head. The seamen manned the yards. Thirteen guns were fired as the Commodore with his family came aboard. Georgy was now almost as tall as her elder sister Elizabeth. She had a graceful athletic figure and quick brown eyes. Her skin was tanned a rich ruddy brown, only a shade lighter than her luxurious hair. Her luggage was as bulky as that of her marriageable elder sister.

Although discipline prevailed on this crack ship of the Navy, it was made easy for David Dixon by the friendliness of the Commodore and the presence of Georgy Patterson on board. David Dixon developed a pride in the efficient performance of his duty. That his conduct should become the subject of a letter of commendation from the Commodore to the Secretary of the Navy is partly attributable to the happy hours he spent between watches in the Commodore's salon paying court to Georgy.

Though David Dixon was half a head taller than Georgy, he carried himself erectly to take full advantage of his scant five feet six inches of height. He dressed immaculately in a handsome blue coat with diamonds of gold lace two inches square on either side of his standing collar. He wore a closely fitted white vest, tight buff trousers, brilliantly burnished half-boots, and a smart cut-and-thrust sword with yellow mountings. Beneath his mat of black hair, heavily pomaded with bear's oil, his features were striking if not handsome. He had piercing brown eyes. His nose, though high, was gracefully arched. His small frank mouth, quick and sometimes stinging at repartee, was hidden behind a curly, well-groomed beard. The stories he told in a voice half an octave higher than anyone else's sparkled with droll exaggeration. Georgy found him magnetic, irrepressibly buoyant of spirit, prone to say anything that popped into his head about anyone—except herself.

During 1832 and 1833 the *United States* visited every important port in the Mediterranean.[2] Genial and affable Commodore Patterson made a practice of taking his lady folk and junior officers ashore to visit places of historic and scenic interest. David Dixon escorted Georgy when the party visited Rome, Jerusalem, Constantinople. Commodore Porter, now *chargé d'affaires* at Constantinople, introduced them to the aged Sultan Mahmud II and obtained a permit for them to visit the Seraglio.

As a representative of Jacksonian Democracy abroad, Commodore Patterson opened his ship to visitors of all classes. At Naples a crowd of vermin-infested lazzaroni swarmed on board. Cameo and lava sellers were permitted to expose their wares on the gun carriages, surrounded by the Commodore's daughters and the midshipmen. Fruit-venders hailed the sailors through the ports. Boatmen held up chickens and pigs with a recommendation in broken English. Cantadini in their best dresses walked up and down on the spar deck smiling on the officers. Punch played his tricks under the gun deck ports. Bands of wandering musicians rowed round and round the ship singing and playing and holding their hats for coins. Commodore Patterson hired twenty of the best of these Italian musicians and kept them on board the frigate for festive occasions.

There was a pomp and circumstance about the flagship that fascinated David Dixon. The warlike appointment and impressive order of which he was a part, the readily-manned boat, the stirring music of the band, and the honor and attention with which the *United States* was received in every port awoke in him a kind of chivalrous elation.

Everywhere the American vessel was received with the most attentive diplomatic gestures. Dinners of state and balls were given for the Commodore and his family and officers, to be returned by Commodore Patterson with like entertainments aboard ship.

At Trieste on August 7, 1833, David Dixon and Georgy helped to decorate the spar deck for a grand ball in honor of Austrian nobility. To clear the deck the guns were run through the ports. The main and mizzen masts were wound with red and white bunting; the capstan was railed with arms, and the wheel tied with nosegays. A stuffed American eagle was placed against the mainmast under a star of yellow-hilted midshipmen's swords. The Commodore's skylight was covered with cushions, and around the chalk-marked square for the dance, seats were laid between the gun carriages. Chandeliers were made of bayonets and battle lanterns.

That evening Midshipman Porter and George Ann Patterson danced the quadrille and the minuet, and in the promenades followed Midshipman George M. Bache and Elizabeth Patterson. Midshipman Bache and George Ann's older sister had already announced their engagement. Along with the gala company David Dixon and Georgy went below to the gun deck for refreshments. The dancing continued until daybreak, when a gun was fired and the guests were rowed ashore.[3]

Midshipman Porter and George Ann spent so much of their time together that Commodore Patterson thought it necessary to admonish Georgy that both she and David Dixon were too young to become engaged. Midshipman Porter's pay at this time was but $33.33 a month. The Commodore also directed the orderly at the door of his cabin not to admit Midshipman Porter except on formal occasions. To give young Porter and his fellow midshipmen something practical to occupy their leisure the Commodore instructed Chaplain Jones to establish a school for them aboard ship. Henceforth from ten every morning until noon all midshipmen not on watch were taught mathematics and navigation; from one to three in the afternoon they were taught foreign languages by a French schoolmaster. The Commodore, however, did not permit the lessons to deprive the young gentlemen of their trips ashore, and he expressly stipulated that their study should be rendered as attractive as possible.

Georgy was too favorably impressed by the fiery young man not to flout her father's orders. On moonlit evenings when the Commodore was enjoying his after-dinner nap, David Dixon climbed over the vessel's side along the mizzen chains and entered the afterlounge by the port gallery window. Georgy was there to meet him. Despite the Commodore's warning they became engaged.

One evening while the vessel was coasting under easy sail off Corfu the Commodore arose early from his nap and discovered young Porter with his daughter behind one of the windows of the stern ports.

"Young man," thundered the Commodore, "how did you enter this cabin contrary to my orders, sir, to the sentry?"

"The orderly is not to blame, sir. I came over the mizzen chains and through the quarter gallery window."

"Mr. Porter, when you again visit my family you must come in by the cabin door like a gentleman." [4]

Midshipman Porter set out to win favor with Georgy's family and by February 1834 had succeeded so well that, when Commodore Patterson in this month shifted his flag and his family to the ship-of-the-line *Delaware,* Midshipman Porter was also transferred. In October, when he was sent home to take his examinations for passed midshipman, he took with him the Commodore's as well as Georgy's best wishes. Commodore Patterson wrote the Secretary of the Navy that he regretted losing Midshipman Porter but thought that he would pass his examination with credit. [5]

After a brief furlough at Chester, David Dixon appeared before the examining board in the Barnum Hotel in Baltimore and passed his examination, standing number ten in a class of twenty. With his classmates he sallied into the hotel bar and in the time-honored tradition of the navy "spliced the main brace" with a glass of champagne.

Passed Midshipman Porter, now twenty-two years of age, bent his energies toward a career in the most difficult of all fields—the U. S. Navy in time of peace. For six months he was given duty at the Philadelphia Navy Yard under his father's ancient enemy Commodore James Barron. Here he was assigned to clerical work on the station ship *Sea Gull,* the same little steam galliot on which as a boy he had made the homeward voyage from

Key West. The *Sea Gull's* engines which he had once so proudly watched were now rusting away.

In December, after a siege of bilious fever, he returned on furlough to Chester. His mother, head of the house since Commodore Porter's removal to Constantinople, continued to live in the mansion that had been her wedding present. Already the industrial section of the town was crowding in around Green Bank; the old house was running down at the heel; and his father's remaining real estate was being poorly managed by a weary succession of agents employed by his mother. In March 1836, when Commodore Patterson returned home from the Mediterranean to become commandant of the Washington Navy Yard, David Dixon went to Washington to see Georgy.

His pay now as a passed midshipman on waiting orders was $50.00 a month. If he could get sea service it would be $62.50. He and Georgy could manage with $62.50, for his brother William had married on that pay. But William was supporting his wife under conditions little removed from poverty. Georgy was young and willing to wait. David Dixon must have something better to offer her.

At the Navy Department he learned that naval officers of his rating were being assigned to the Coast Survey, now newly reorganized by Professor Hassler. In this service they were allowed sea pay, traveling expenses, and an additional thirty dollars a month. Save for the extra pay the Coast Survey work was dull and unattractive. It meant from six to nine months a year of nomadic life along the mosquito-plagued coast of New Jersey, alternating with brief periods aboard a crowded survey schooner where endless soundings were taken and countless angles were measured between the markers set up by surveying parties ashore. In winter the Coast Surveyors worked in Washington in the two connected houses leased by Professor Hassler. Here they performed calculations, collated geographic data, and inked in their rough pencil maps and redrew them to scale. Tedious, unhealthy, eye-straining labor. But from three to six months of the year would be spent in the city of Washington—near the Navy Yard where Georgy Patterson lived. David Dixon applied for duty in the Coast Survey and on April 28, one month after Georgy Patterson returned from the Mediterranean, received his assignment to the Coast Survey schooner *Jersey*.

For six years Porter remained on the Coast Survey, despite his preference for more active employment. The duty was better suited to his needs than anything else in the Navy at this time, and his friends Midshipmen Carlisle Patterson, George M. Bache, and B. F. Sands were in this service. Young Porter sought relief from the routine in scribbling bombastic, satirical rhymes which he enclosed in his letters for Georgy to burn as soon as read. But also he developed a buoyant optimism, a pride in his work, and a genius for getting things done, with whatever makeshift means there were at hand.

Professor Hassler, Superintendent of the Coast Survey, was an eccentric Swiss political refugee who was continually getting into altercations with the innkeepers of the New Jersey countryside. He carried his own imported wines and cheeses into the inns with him and went to the law courts whenever he was charged prices which he thought exorbitant. He needed spectacles, but scoffed at the notion, preferring to stimulate his vision with the tobacco snuff he carried in the pockets of his vest. When he examined the sketch maps made by the midshipmen, he returned them corrected but smudged with snuff, and created much amusement in their ranks. He held the young naval officers to a high degree of accuracy, and if he could not imbue them with a scrupulous regard for scientific truth he ejected them without ado.[6]

Under Professor Hassler, Midshipman Porter quickly perfected his mathematics and learned the fundamentals of intellectual honesty. He became proficient in charting channels and developed an almost intuitive ability to pilot a vessel over tortuous shallows— an ability which would later be of inestimable value to him. Of more immediate consequence, however, his work on the Coast Survey enabled him by the spring of 1839 to save enough money to marry Georgy.

Commodore Porter returned home early in 1839 to persuade the State Department to establish a more important diplomatic mission in Constantinople, and to be himself elevated on March 3 from *chargé d'affaires* to Minister to Turkey. As it happened his visit home enabled him to attend two weddings. William D. Porter, whose first wife had died, was married on February 28 to Elizabeth Beale, of Norfolk. And on March 10, 1839, precisely on the thirty-first anniversary of the marriage of Commodore Porter and Evalina Anderson, David Dixon Porter and George Ann Patterson were married.

On the afternoon of March 10, 1839, the home of Commodore Patterson at the Washington Navy Yard was gaily decorated. The groom's parents attended with many of their friends and the friends of the Pattersons. David Dixon's younger sisters Evelina and Imogen were present. Theodoric Porter, whom David Dixon loved more than any of his brothers, now a junior officer in the Army post at Baton Rouge, Louisiana, was so prostrated by the severe intermittent fevers of the river country that he could not attend the wedding; but he sent Georgy his compliments and a pair of beaded Indian moccasins.

At three o'clock a group of singers from St. John's Episcopal Church began the wedding march. Two lines of naval officers, smartly clad in full regimentals, crossed their swords over the aisle to the altar. The rector of St. John's read the service and pronounced them man and wife.

The first joyful years of his life with George Ann were limned against a cloud of trouble. In August while Porter was attached to the survey schooner *Washington* off the coasts of Long Island and New Jersey, Commodore Patterson died; and George Ann and her mother moved from the navy yard to a small rented house in Washington. A few weeks after the wedding Commodore Porter returned to Constantinople without having placed his finances in order, and in September Evalina Porter was compelled to apply to her aged uncle Joseph Anderson for a loan of $500 on her silver plate.

One after another of David Dixon's brothers came to grief. Young Henry Ogden Porter contracted the liquor habit and came near to losing his position as junior midshipman in the Navy. Hambleton, also a midshipman, died of yellow fever and was buried at sea. Porter's elder brother William, a firebrand who for years had claimed the right to administer the affairs of the family while Commodore Porter was abroad, brought scandal into the family by fathering the child of a servant girl. The Commodore in Constantinople, vowing that he would never give William half a chance to repent, disinherited him. Thus to David Dixon fell the right of priority over William which he had always desired. In the violent correspondence with William which the new situation evoked, David Dixon developed a flair for controversy which rivaled even the Commodore at the Fajardo court-martial.[7]

In the winter of 1840 while David Dixon Porter was attached to the headquarters of the Survey in Washington George Ann bore her first child, a daughter whom they named Georgianne.

Porter was elated over the chubby little brown-haired infant.

He played with her at breakfast and got up to look after her at nights.

During the winter after his first child came, Porter's own health began to suffer. While surveying the mosquito flats of New Jersey he had been inoculated with malaria. At the office the fine detail work of inking in maps strained his eyes. He developed liver trouble and headaches. He was turning twenty-eight—with twelve years of service to his credit—but his promotion to lieutenant, expected at the time of his marriage, had not yet come. He groaned at the prospect of supporting his family indefinitely on the pay of a passed midshipman!

At the office one wintry day Midshipman Porter was seated on the edge of a work table dangling his legs. A colleague, Lieutenant Stephen C. Rowan, was at the same table inking a map. Lieutenant Rowan was a brusque, red-haired Irishman, who stood many numbers above Midshipman Porter, for he had entered the navy about the time Porter had gone to Mexico. Like Porter, Rowan was newly married, his wife was expecting a baby, and he was irked by the lax discipline which permitted midshipmen in the Survey to call him by his first name. When Porter began prodding the soft wood of the table with a pair of dividers, Rowan demanded irritably that he put the instrument down. Jab, jab, jab went the points of the dividers.

In an instant the two men sprang upon each other with oaths and blows. They clinched. But their friends separated them.

By Midshipman Benjamin Sands, Porter sent Rowan a challenge to a duel on any terms he pleased. Sands carried the challenge and found that Rowan had already appointed his second. The seconds, being friends of both principals, met in the room of a neutral party, where for two days they wrote and exchanged a series of notes so delicately worded as to effect a peaceful settlement without compromising the honor of either of the principals. The Code which had stricken Decatur and many another famous romanticist was on the wane, and the Navy Department was shortly to issue its most drastic prohibition of dueling.[8]

In March 1841 Midshipman and Mrs. David D. Porter attended the inaugural ball of President William Henry Harrison, and a few days later David Dixon Porter received his long-awaited commission as lieutenant. His increased rank gave him a jaunty air of independence. When the new Secretary of the Navy, Mr. Badger, undertook to regulate the style of whiskers worn in the

Navy and decreed that naval officers should only be permitted sideburns extending to the lobe of the ear, Lieutenant Porter stropped his razor and shaved away the whole of his luxurious beard.

In April 1842, Lieutenant Porter was detached from the Coast Survey and ordered to the *Congress* on the Mediterranean Station. Late in the summer he paid what was to be his last visit to his father at Constantinople. The aged Commodore, now suffering from angina pectoris, invested David Dixon with full control of his affairs in America, including his claims against Mexico, the papers for which he had lost. In a short time Commodore Porter was dead.

Upon his return home Lieutenant Porter found that his second child Nina had been born. Georgy had had an illness. At the Washington Navy Yard, his brother William had invented a shell which had exploded in the hands of the workmen, killing and wounding several; and William had defended himself so vociferously in the newspapers that he was now standing court-marial for insubordination. David Dixon had no sympathy for William. "He must lie in the bed he has made for himself," David Dixon wrote his mother. "He goes about telling the most ridiculous stories about his being able to leave the service having been offered $160,000 for his shot." Evalina Porter was now in desperate straits financially, and William in spite of his own difficulties was still pressing his claim to the management of her estate. Since the Commodore's death, William whose middle name was David, had begun signing himself "David Porter"; whereupon the post office in Washington became confused and delivered part of William's mail to David Dixon. "Somehow his plans all come to our knowledge," David Dixon joyfully wrote his mother ". . . It would astonish him to know how much of his correspondence I have on file!" [9]

Obtaining three months' leave, David Dixon set about righting the chaos of his mother's finances. He took over the management of her rental properties in Washington. He applied for a pension for her on the basis of Commodore Porter's services in the Navy. But the Navy Department demurred over the technicality that the Commodore had resigned to go to Mexico.

Commodore Porter had destroyed over a half million dollars worth of British shipping in the War of 1812. He had stopped the piracies against American shipping in the West Indies. David Dixon Porter felt that his mother's pension was morally justified, and he determined that if he could not get it one way he would try another.

At Chester it happened that the office of customs inspector was vacant and that his uncle Thomas Anderson wanted this job, but had not the necessary political influence to get it. His mother, Evalina Porter, had influence through the friends of the late Commodore. To his mother, therefore, David Dixon unfolded his plan: "Show the enclosed to Uncle Tom. If Mr. Anderson gets the job it's because of Commodore Porter, and you might as well get $500 a year out of it. Burn this letter." [10] Mr. Anderson obtained the job, and his mother in all probability, her $500 a year—though the written records, if any, were not preserved.

In the settlement of his father's estate an old note came to light. Years ago Commodore Porter had borrowed a large sum from his friend Commodore John Downes to settle his accounts with the Navy Department. Evalina Porter claimed that the naval debt was merely a technical claim against her husband and that the Commodore had paid it in a fit of anger. But here was the note to Downes with Commodore Porter's signature. Whether or not the debt was just made little difference to David Dixon Porter.

On October 16, 1845, when everyone in the house was ill with fever—Georgy; her sister, Elizabeth Patterson Bache; her mother, Mrs. Patterson; the children, Georgianne and Nina—when he himself was busy being "chief cook and bottle washer," David Dixon wrote his mother that he considered his father's note to Downes "a debt of honor" that he would have to pay.[11]

How? He did not know. He hoped soon that there would be a war. There were thunderheads looming over Mexico. In another note he told his mother, "I waited on the President last night with a deputation from the Navy headed by our Secretary, and I think he is going to give us something to do . . ." [12]

5.
THE WAR WITH MEXICO

A<small>FTER</small> two months of furlough to disentangle his mother's finances, Lieutenant David D. Porter was assigned on May 21, 1845, to the Hydrographic Office in Washington, where for nine months he worked with Lieutenant Matthew Fontaine Maury to produce the first wind and current charts of the ocean. These were the first efforts to systematize man's knowledge of the complicated phenomena affecting navigation. The "Mariner's Bible" as these charts came to be called, was one of the most important milestones in science since the work of Galileo. But it was a tedious statistical job involving the examination of countless log-books and the collation of information sent in from all parts of the world. Porter wanted action. Action was now looming in the direction of Mexico.

With the banner of Manifest Destiny flying in the political breeze, James K. Polk from Tennessee had won the Presidency on a platform calling for annexation of Texas. Mexico let it be known that the annexation of Texas meant war. Amid the ecstatic jubilations of the Randolphs, the Clays, and the Calhouns, Texas was annexed in July 1845. Mexico bided her time, but President Polk ordered a concentration of troops in the Far West. In July Lieutenant Theodoric Porter's detachment under General Zachary Taylor was moved to a position on the Nueces River on the southwestern border of Texas in anticipation of attack by Mexico.

In Washington Lieutenant David D. Porter with a naval delegation headed by the Secretary of the Navy visited the President and requested something for the Navy to do. The Secretary sent secret orders to Commodore Sloat of the Pacific Squadron to seize San Francisco the moment Mexico declared war.

In spite of James Russell Lowell's denunciation of Manifest Destiny as half ignorance and half rum, its advocates preferred to think of it in terms of gold and glory and revels "in the halls of the Montezumas." Not only Mexico and California were embraced in Manifest Destiny but also the backward islands of the Caribbean.

The first week in March 1846 Lieutenant D. D. Porter was called in by Mr. James Buchanan, Secretary of State. In the West Indies the little one-quarter white Republic of Santo Domingo, which in 1844 had broken away from the still smaller and 100 per cent black Republic of Haiti, was negotiating for American loans and recognition. It was necessary to investigate Santo Domingo's political and social stability, economic resources, and the suitability of the Bay of Samana for possible use by the U. S. Navy. Mr. Buchanan offered Porter the opportunity to make this semi-secret investigation.

Porter gladly accepted; as the Mexican issue had not yet ripened, he could probably get back from Santo Domingo before the war with Mexico broke out. The Secretary of the Navy detailed Porter for temporary duty under the State Department; and on March 15 Porter left Georgy and the two children (a third was now expected) in Washington and set out for Pensacola, via Pittsburgh and New Orleans.

He carried papers to Commodore Gregory at Pensacola which would give him command of a schooner in which to execute his mission, unencumbered, he thought, by the assistance of any officer senior to him.

Before Porter could reach Pensacola, however, the vessel which the Secretary had assigned to him had been sent on other duty; and it was twenty days before the senior officer present was able to detail the brig *Porpoise* under Lieutenant William E. Hunt to participate in Porter's mission and inspect the coast and harbors while Porter traveled through the interior of Santo Domingo.

In the ancient city of Santo Domingo on the southern side of the island, the mulatto president, Santana, was ill when the *Porpoise* arrived, and Porter lost twelve days entertaining officials of the port and waiting for an audience. Santana welcomed the investigation.

At four A.M. on May 19, 1846, Porter set out upon his trip across the island toward Puerto Plata with two horses, a guide, and letters to the commandants of the villages in the interior. The journey carried him over three difficult ranges of mountains, through forests of gigantic mahogany trees, across numerous uncharted rivers almost dry one day and raging torrents the next, over the pleasant savannah of La Vega, through tropical valleys where he had to cut his way with machetes. He swung his hammock at night in the huts of the natives and rose early to push on for fourteen hours the next day.

Ascending the mountain passes, he had to drive his horses ahead of him and carry his revolver at all times ready to shoot them in case they turned and stampeded back down the narrow trails. He had great difficulty getting sufficient food for his horses. From weariness they stumbled frequently, and only the scraggly trees that grew along the path saved them from toppling over the precipices. He had to mount and spur his animals to get them down steep declivities.

In the gorges the trails shuttled back and forth across the rivers. One day when he was pushing to make the next town ahead of a storm, he forded a single river fifty-one times. Usually he waded across, but often both he and his horses had to swim for their lives against strong currents. In swimming the rivers Porter ruined his watch, $92 in paper currency, and a number of kits of food. He lost three horses on the trip, one being pushed over a waterfall by a guide whom Porter had threatened for striking a horse over the head. Porter beat the guide and dismissed him.

The people, who everywhere received him kindly, were by nature indolent. "For a hoe or a plough," he wrote, "they have an aversion not to be described." Food was a major problem. At one place he was fortunate to buy an egg and a tough chicken for $5. Though he refused to eat at the table with his negro guide he was compelled to swing his hammock in the same hovel with him. At nights he was pestered by the mosquitoes and fleas.

In the villages old women with nothing above the waistline sat in their doorways sweating and smoking home-made cigars. Porter conversed with them in Mexican Spanish. Often he found women with their dresses open behind; yet, since they showed no mawkish embarrassment and simply turned their backs to the wall, he soon forgot that there was anything out of the way. Marriage among this semi-tropical people was the exception rather than the rule, and Porter's Victorian ideas of morality were exercised. Black women as well as mulattoes seemed to consider it a disgrace to have a child not whiter than themselves. In one hut where he put up for the night he was assured by his host, a white man, that he might change his clothes in safety; however at the most embarrassing stage of this process two enormous negresses entered the room and refused to leave until the toilet was completed.

When he reached Puerto Plata on June 19, 1846, he was covered from head to foot with insect bites. His left eye was com-

pletely closed from the sting of a hornet. His feet were so badly
bruised from wading rivers that he could scarcely walk. His legs
were swollen to twice their normal size.[1]

When he boarded the *Porpoise* at Puerto Plata, he found everyone on the ship excited. *War had actually broken out between
the United States and Mexico!* General Taylor's army had already
won several initial skirmishes. At once forgetting the discomforts
of his journey, Porter wrote a most chipper and enthusiastic report to the Department in Washington. He hurried home hoping
to be assigned to active duty in the war.

When he reached Washington in July, he found joy and grief
awaiting him. Georgy had borne him a son, whom he proudly
named David Essex Porter, after the late Commodore and the
famed naval vessel of 1812. He had gained a son but lost his
favorite brother. The War Department delivered to him the remains of Theodoric Porter, of the Fourth U. S. Infantry, killed
in action a few miles north of Matamoras. He conveyed the remains to his mother's home in Chester, Pennsylvania, for burial.[2]
Returning post-haste to Washington, he applied for duty in the
Home Squadron off the Gulf coast of Mexico, urging that his
experience in the Mexican Navy had especially fitted him for that
service. But Mexico had no navy and the Home Squadron was
crowded with officers.

He was disappointed when the Navy Department assigned him
to the Naval Observatory in Washington. On chilly September
evenings as he sat with Georgy in the little upstairs back room in
his Washington house, warming his toes before the open grate
after putting the three children to bed, he recalled his early experiences in San Juan de Ulloa. The ancient fortress, he believed,
might easily be reduced by newly invented contrivances for exploding powder charges under water.

On the night of September 19, Porter wrote a letter to the
Secretary of the Navy recommending that several 100-pound
drums of powder be imbedded in the soft coral foundations of
San Juan, and exploded from a distance by means of wires from
galvanic batteries; also he drew a sketch of the fortress to show
where he proposed to place the powder: "The effect of these cases
of gunpowder will be to throw down the bastions and burst in
the door; and the middle section, if it will not be thrown *down*,
will be so rent and shaken that it will paralyze those within, and
create a panic. Fifty well trained men will be able to gain the
top of the castle and hold it while any number of boats are

pulling to support them . . ." Finally, he volunteered to assist a submarine engineer in carrying out the exploit. His bold offer was placed on file.[3] For another eight weeks Porter was held in bondage at the Observatory.

Had it not been for the children—chubby little four-year-old Georgianne; two-year-old Nina, slender and fair; and robust baby Essex, nicknamed "the Mogul,"—he would have broken his bondage and gone to Mexico as a privateer. But he needed money, all he could scrape together, to pay on his father's debt of honor to Commodore Downes and to clothe Georgy, who having always lived well was inclined to be extravagant.

He was impatient. His work at the Observatory entailed duty several nights a week, and his eyes ached from strain.

The war dragged on into November 1846. The blockade off the hot, unhealthy coast of Mexico so depleted the Home Squadron that new men had to be secured. On the last day of November Porter was ordered to New Orleans to open a naval recruiting station. He was glad that he would at least be nearer to the scene of action. Packing his trunk, he kissed Georgy and the children and was off post-haste to New Orleans.

At New Orleans he rented an office and advertised for seamen. Enlistments, however, were few, since his competitors, the merchants of New Orleans, prospering from the war, offered better wages than the Government. Men asked Porter how much bounty the Navy would pay them. The Navy had not authorized a bounty. Porter could hint about the prize money they might earn by capturing shipping and raiding Mexican villages along the coast, but most of the unimaginative prospects he buttonholed walked away shaking their heads. Porter began to chafe at his enforced detention in New Orleans while the squadron was operating against the enemy upon his old familiar fighting ground.

In January 1847, he had rounded up barely three hundred seamen when he received welcome orders to close the recruiting station and report with his men to Commodore Conner at Vera Cruz. In a chartered steamer he embarked with his recruits for Vera Cruz, where Commodore Conner assigned Porter as first lieutenant on the tiny, side-wheel steamer *Spitfire* under smart, turtle-jawed Commander Josiah Tattnall.

The war had now been in progress for nearly a year. General Taylor's army in the north had won the battles of Palo Alto and Resaca de la Palma, and bonfires had been lighted back home in celebration of these victories. The flotilla in the Pacific under

Commodore Stockton had captured the Spanish missions along the California coast and claimed the country for the United States. In the Gulf, on the other hand, the Navy had failed to give a proper account of itself. Instead of illuminations and ovations the Home Squadron had won only witticisms from the newspapers. Commodore Conner was generally rated a good seaman who could take a ship in safety through the wildest norther and make an impressive parade along the coast in his flagship. He also had the reputation of being the best dressed officer in the Navy. But because he refused to take his indifferent fleet into the harbor of Vera Cruz and breach the walls of San Juan de Ulloa—as the French Admiral Baudin had done in 1838—the newspapers condemned him. In March the Department dispatched Commodore M. C. Perry to relieve him.

It is true that Commodore Conner had added little lustre to the American cause. He had fought no naval battles, for Mexico had no navy to oppose him. He had, however, made one important contribution which the newspapers overlooked. By becoming a scapegoat he had indirectly influenced Washington to strike the enemy in a vital part. The new strategy brought General Scott with a large army to Vera Cruz about the time Perry took command of the squadron.

The city of Vera Cruz lay like a giant crab on the sands of the *tierra caliente,* with its straight edge toward the water. It was surrounded by walls and battlements of the same soft coral rock as was in the Castle of San Juan. At the north corner of the sea face stood Fortress Conception, at the south, Fortress Santiago. The curtain between these castles bristled with cannon of all descriptions. For fragile, wooden-walled steamers to enter the narrow harbor, about eight hundred yards in width, under the cross-fire of San Juan and the defences of Vera Cruz, was considered impossible. Coral reefs at both northern and southern entrances to the harbor created additional hazards. The obstacles in the way of a purely naval attack influenced General Scott to invest the city by land.

On March 10 General Scott's army of 10,000 men was landed on the beach a few miles south of the town. General Scott could not have selected a balmier day, and Commodore Conner's preparations were carried out with the perfection of a well organized parade. The *Spitfire* and the *Vixen* with five sail-driven schooners of the Mosquito Fleet stood in to the beach and anchored in line abreast to cover the landing. Lieutenant Porter on the bow of the

Spitfire trained his pivot gun upon the bush-clad hillocks. He was eager for the enemy to dispute the landing, for with many other young men in the fleet he felt "that the Navy had a big butcher's bill to pay." [4]

From the transports off shore the soldiers climbed down into sixty-seven boats manned by sailors. General Winfield Scott in dress uniform stood in a man-of-war's boat ahead of the semi-circle of troop boats, and reviewed them as they passed. When the keels touched, the soldiers leaped into the surf and dashed up the sand hills to meet the enemy. They shouted and combed through the stunted growth of thorny mimosa and prickly pear. But there were no Mexicans to welcome them. The soldiers planted American flags on the sand hills, and throughout the fleet arose a great cheer.

While the troops were dragging field pieces over the dunes, cutting through chaparral, and fording the sloughs to invest the town, a terrific norther set in, which for two days cut off communication with the ships. On the 13th the windstorm abated. A few horses were landed and supplies were rushed to the farthest end of the line. Heavy mortar guns were landed to throw bombs into the besieged city. Since the guns of the Army were of too small a caliber to breach the walls in preparation for an assault, six pieces of heavy naval ordnance were also landed with their crews of seamen. It required several hundred men to drag each of these guns into position.

On March 21, the day before the investment was completed, Commodore Perry relieved the unfortunate Commodore Conner as commander in chief of the squadron.

On March 22, Perry sent the Mosquito Fleet to bombard Fortress Santiago and the batteries along the southern wall. The fleet anchored in line about a mile from the city, beyond range of San Juan, and poured in a steady, well-directed fire. Porter got off round after round from the *Spitfire's* bow gun. He enjoyed the work, the thundering of guns and crashing shells, the grotesque clouds of flame and smoke.

At night when the Mosquito Fleet returned, Porter volunteered to sound the southern channel into the harbor in order to secure a better position for the *Spitfire* on the morrow. While the burning fuses of the mortar shells described great arcs across the sky from the land batteries into the beleaguered city, Porter rowed far into the inner harbor and made a practical chart of the channel.

The next morning to the Commodore's amazement the *Spitfire* and the *Vixen*, each with two sail-driven schooners in tow, did not stop at the entrance to the harbor according to his plan but steamed on inside. From this vantage point the Mosquito Fleet quickly routed the gunners along the southern flank. When the *Spitfire* came abreast the main gate of Vera Cruz, the guns of San Juan de Ulloa opened upon her. The shot falling around her sent up columns of water that splashed her decks. Commodore Perry, whose flagship was anchored at a distance, signaled the *Spitfire* to retire from action. But Porter did not look toward the flagship. Commander Tattnall, the *Spitfire's* skipper, did not look, and had previously instructed his quartermaster not to look. An order delivered by special messenger finally brought the *Spitfire* out of action.

The *Spitfire* was applauded by the troops on shore and by the sailors of the neutral ships anchored in the opposite end of the harbor. Luckily for Porter and Commander Tattnall, the commodore suspected nothing out of the way in their failure to read his signal. Commodore Perry was a brave fighter who expected bold deeds from his subordinates but who also expected them to follow the letter of the plan he laid down for them.

Commodore Perry did not permit the *Spitfire* to repeat her hazardous exploit but kept her thereafter with the rest of the fleet well out of range of San Juan de Ulloa. At nights he brought his vessels to anchor in the lee of Sacrificios Island, a short distance out from the landing beach. New vessels—transports loaded with men, horses, and supplies—were daily added to the host already under his surveillance. The bombardment continued steadily.

On the 26th another norther swept the coast and for two days severed communications between the army and the squadron. The sand dunes were literally blown from under some of the besieging batteries, and many townspeople sought refuge in the consulates, which had escaped bombardment. Some twenty craft at the northern end of the harbor were pounded into wreckage under the walls of Vera Cruz.

The tempest marked the surrender of the Mexican garrison. When the winds abated, General Scott was able to inform Commodore Perry that commissioners from the opposing armies were already arranging terms; whereupon the Commodore sent delegates to represent the Navy at the conferences.

The 29th, the day of the surrender, was fair and warm with a light southeast breeze. A meadow south of the town was the site chosen for the ceremony. Commodore Perry sent a number of officers, including Lieutenant Porter, to represent the squadron. At ten o'clock the Mexican batteries saluted their flag for the last time. The Stars and Stripes was run up over the city and over the Castle of San Juan de Ulloa. Cannon on shore and throughout the fleet thundered salutes. The garrison, about five thousand strong, now sallied from the Merced Gate between files of Americans; and as each corps of Mexicans reached the designated spot they laid down their muskets.

With Vera Cruz taken, Scott's army moved on toward Mexico City, and the Home Squadron set out to capture the Mexican strongholds along the coasts and rivers.

In April Commodore Perry took the sailing vessels in tow of the flagship *Mississippi* and steamed up the coast 100 miles northwest of Vera Cruz to capture the fortified town of Tuspan. Seamen for a landing party had been chosen by lot from the vessels left at Vera Cruz so that all might share the dangers and successes.

At the mouth of the Tuspan River the masts were taken out of the *Spitfire* and the *Vixen* to lighten and enable them to cross the bar. On the 18th Commodore Perry boarded the *Spitfire* and steamed up the river with sailing schooners in tow. When they came under fire from the batteries, the schooners were cast off; and Porter sent shells from the *Spitfire's* pivot gun into the cliff batteries, La Peña and La Palma Sola. The landing party pulled ashore and scaled the forts while the Mexicans dropped rammers and sponges and fled in every direction. Sailors carousing that night in the town of Tuspan broke into the house of the fugitive Mexican General Cos and drank to the general's health in his own champagne. On the day the squadron captured Tuspan, the army, too, won a victory, at Cerro Gordo.

In June Commodore Perry led an expedition into the interior of southern Mexico to capture the town of Tabasco. At the mouth of the Tabasco River the port of Frontera, which the Navy already controlled, was continually being threatened by bands of guerrillas. The task now ahead of Porter and the other officers of the Mosquito Fleet was to clear the entire seventy miles of river to the head of navigation at Tabasco. This was the most ambitious purely naval accomplishment of the Home Squadron during the war. Sixteen miles below the city of Tabasco the *Spitfire,* the

Scourge, and the *Vixen,* with several bomb vessels were stopped by obstructions in the river bed. Here to Porter's dismay Commodore Perry landed with a detachment of 1,064 seamen and marines to make his way by land through the chaparral to Tabasco.

Porter and the men who remained on the vessels determined to have a share in the coming battle. Under the direction of Captain Taylor, the submarine engineer, they attached drums of gunpowder under water at the base of the piles. By means of long wires which he hooked to a galvanic battery, Captain Taylor exploded these drums and blew a mound of mud and water into the air. Porter hurriedly bent the *Spitfire's* hawsers to the loosened logs and cleared a passage the width of his vessel.

With everyone working and cheering, the *Spitfire* and the *Vixen* squeezed through the passage to race the Commodore's landing party to Tabasco. The steamers won.

Covered by a bombardment from the steamers, Porter leaped ashore with an extemporized force of sixty-eight seamen, coal-passers, and engineers, and captured the fort! Commodore Perry and his men scrambled exhausted through the chaparral two hours later.

For his distinguished services Porter was made skipper of the *Spitfire*—his first naval command. By an irony of fate, however, there was nothing further to be done in the way of naval fighting. After a few months of chasing guerrillas and supervising the revenue of the occupied ports, the war was over. Porter was detached from his first command and ordered home.[5]

The War with Mexico added to the United States a territory 100,000 square miles vaster than the Louisiana Purchase. For Porter it had meant a few hours of exhilarating experience in battle, remotely reminiscent of his experiences as a midshipman in the navy of Mexico. He could remember with satisfaction a few minutes in the harbor of Vera Cruz, a few at Tuspan, a few at Tabasco. But the nature of the war in the Gulf had worked against him. However greatly he had coveted fame and fortune, they had thus far eluded him.

Returning to Washington, he learned that Georgy had taken the children for the summer to Warrenton, Virginia, and that Nina, his second daughter, was ill with intermittent fever and not expected to live.

Porter caught the first stage for Warrenton. Little Nina was a mere skeleton, but alive. Porter wrote to his mother in Chester that the little four-year-old invalid smiled like an angel when she saw her father.[6] Georgy, too, had a light case of fever; but Georgi-anne was a bright growing youngster, a trifle too plump; and he had never seen a more delightful tyke than the Mogul, Essex.

Somehow he managed to load them all on a stage coach and get them home.

6.

PLAIN CAPTAIN DAVID

W HEN the curtain fell on the war with Mexico, it arose immediately to reveal a fantastic scene in California. Two weeks after
Lieutenant Porter, on January 10, 1848, had been ordered back
to the Coast Survey a workman in Sutter's mill race in the Sacramento valley discovered gold.

For civilians the return of peace and the gold rush brought
activity many times greater than that during the late war. For
Porter the spectacular peace brought only depression. The war
had netted him no prize money, and he was now mortgaging his
pay checks three months in advance. The children needed clothes.
Georgy was indulging in the extravagance of sending eight-year-
old Georgianne to dancing school.

In the Navy, now reducing its personnel to peace-time needs,
his future looked gloomier still. He was thirty-five years of age.
Having enjoyed a brief period in command of the steamer *Spitfire,* he wanted responsible duty afloat in a modern steamer.
But the Navy was selling its steamers and reverting to the old types
of sail-driven craft, which were less expensive to operate. The
summer, however, brought a responsible assignment which was to
lead directly in the next few years into peace-time services that
would win him an international reputation.

In August 1848, he set out as commander of the Coast Survey
schooner *Petrel* to survey the Hell Gate and Buttermilk Channels
in New York Harbor. For New England shippers the nearest route
into New York was through Long Island Sound and Hell Gate.
Hell Gate was also a practicable exit for south-bound sailing ships
when adverse winds closed to them the main outlet via Sandy
Hook. Of the hundreds of vessels that passed through Hell Gate
every week, dozens were holed by unseen shelves of rock and
were badly bilged if not sunk.

During six weeks of August and September while Porter was
surveying Hell Gate Channel, no less than fifty vessels were

snagged. While he was taking soundings over Bald-Headed Billy fifteen yards from Hatter's Dock, three vessels grounded on this ledge. One of them freed herself without damage; and, as Porter was pulling the second vessel out of his way, the third wrenched herself loose but lost her bowsprit, anchor, and chains. Two vessels striking Ravensworth Reef were bilged and nearly ruined, and a full-rigged brig sank at Pot Rock with a valuable cargo.

The New York Chamber of Commerce was so anxious to get the results of the survey and begin blasting out the channel that, as soon as Porter had made a third of the necessary soundings, he sent a special preliminary report to the Department to make the data available.

The survey of the Buttermilk Channel between Governors Island and Brooklyn, which Porter next undertook, was important to the Navy because this channel gave access to the Atlantic Dock, whose facilities would be valuable to the Navy. Because of its hazards this channel had never been used by ocean-going ships, but Porter charted it and discovered a usable passage.

The Secretary of the Treasury, interested in the project because of its bearing on revenue but skeptical of the accuracy of Porter's chart, invited Porter to accompany him on a trial trip through these channels aboard a large ocean steamer.

On September 22 Lieutenant Porter with Secretary of the Treasury Walker, a number of shipowners from the New York Chamber of Commerce, and a delegation of New York pilots boarded the revenue steamer *Jefferson* at the Battery. The *Jefferson* was unwieldy and, because she responded awkwardly to her helm, needed plenty of room to turn around.

She made the passage through Hell Gate and back over the line indicated on Porter's chart. Soundings were taken, and the shipowners were well pleased. Then came the run through the highly doubtful Buttermilk Channel to the Atlantic Dock. This too was accomplished, notwithstanding a stiff northwest wind, an unfavorable tide, and a lumber sloop with planks projecting on either side lying at anchor in the middle of the passage.[1]

While Porter was being applauded in New York for his success as a channel surveyor, the demand for transportation to the California gold fields increased out of all proportion to the existing facilities. Mr. John L. Aspinwall of the banking firm of Howland and Aspinwall, offered Porter the job of taking the U. S. mail steamship *Panama* around Cape Horn to San Francisco.[2] This chance of a lifetime to command a large ocean steamship came simultaneously with the news from Washington that Georgy had borne him a second son.

Porter returned to Washington to see Georgy and the new baby and to request of the Secretary of the Navy a leave of absence. The survey had now reached the stage where it could be carried on by assistants and Porter urged that as skipper of the *Panama* he would gain experience in handling a steam vessel which would be invaluable to him if the Navy ever increased its small number of steamers. The Secretary, Mr. John Y. Mason, gave his permission. After having attended to the repair and rental of his mother's property in Washington, borrowed money for Georgy, and christened the new infant Carlisle Patterson after the brother-in-law who endorsed his note, Porter returned to New York the first week in February, to take command of the *Panama*.

On February 15, 1849, Porter got the *Panama* to sea. Among his cabin passengers were the financier, Henry Livingston, a distant relative of Georgy, and two young Army officers, Joe Hooker and William H. Emory, who were later to become major-generals in the Union Army. Every inch of the steerage was packed and jammed with gold-rush farmers, laborers, preachers, clerks, gamblers and horse thieves.

After a few days at sea the *Panama's* engines became partially disabled, and Porter was compelled to turn back to New York, where he repaired quickly, took on a considerable cargo of tools and extra parts for his engines, and once more put to sea, this time for a successful nonstop voyage.

The *Panama*, pounding vigorously in the race southward, over-hauled dozens of similarly crowded windjammers, and on each occasion her cabin passengers lined her rails and cheered the ship. From the steerage came groans of the seasick, and hoarse but hopeful voices chanting:

> Oh, California,
> That's the land for me;
> I'm off for Sacramento
> With my washbowl on my knee.

There were deaths and burials at sea. At the worst season of the year Porter safely navigated the Straits of Magellan, and steamed up the Pacific, over the cruising ground of his father's famous *Essex* in 1812. On June 4, 1849, he docked the *Panama* at the bustling little village of San Francisco with the applause of his passengers ringing in his ears.

After delivering the *Panama* to the officials of the Pacific Mail Steamship Company, he returned in her as a passenger to the Isthmus. In midsummer he crossed this fever death trap, where workmen were already chopping a right of way for a railroad, and at the mouth of the Chagres River Porter boarded a mail steamer for New York.

Law, Roberts and Company now offered him the command of the mail steamer *Georgia,* which was being built in New York for the run to the Isthmus via Havana. If only he could induce the Secretary to grant him the assignment immediately he could superintend the installation of the *Georgia's* double engines. He rushed to Washington.

This time he was asking too much; at least so thought Mr. William B. Preston, the new Secretary of the Navy, who had been in office only the few months since the inauguration of President Taylor. As a mail steamer to be subsidized by the Government, the *Georgia* had to be completed and approved by Government inspectors before officers could be assigned to her. Since this experience in a technical branch of his profession was not to be had by any officer of his rank in the naval service, Porter requested that red tape be set aside. But the Secretary chose to follow the letter of the law and told him to apply after the *Georgia* had been accepted. Chafing bitterly, Porter went home. He came down with Chagres fever and lay in bed for weeks. In odd moments he found an outlet for his emotions in scribbling lampoons against the Secretary. During his convalescence he enjoyed being with his family. He wrote his mother about this time that the children were all healthy and a trifle too fat. Georgianne was improving rapidly in school. Nina had lost her beauty, the Mogul, Essex, was a great rascal, and baby Carlisle Patterson, "Ki," was "a perfect cherub." On December 14, 1849, another son was born, whom he named Theodoric after the brother who had been killed in action in the Mexican War.

The *Georgia* having been completed and approved by the Government, Porter on the twenty-sixth of January 1850, was given the job as her skipper.

As captain of a privately-owned vessel Porter's duties were of a civilian character. On his way to Havana he landed passengers and mails at Charleston and Savannah and took on other travelers and mail bags. He set a good table for his passengers and pushed the *Georgia* through calm and storm at her utmost speed. He worked to make new records from point to point and was

Lieutenant David Dixon Porter (*right*), with Captain S. F. Du Pont (*center*), and Commander S. S. Lee (*left*). About 1850.

continually making comparisons of the *Georgia's* speed with that
of the crack Collins Line steamship *Atlantic,* which was smash-
ing all former records for the voyage from New York to Liverpool. He found that he lost much time stopping at both Charleston
and Savannah and wrote emphatic letters opposing stops at
points so close together. When he discovered that the Post Office
Department was not interested in the *Georgia's* sailing record, he
took matters into his own hands. Outside the bars of one harbor
or the other he would stop fishing craft or any boat whatever in
hailing distance, transfer his passengers with their luggage and
the mail, and then push on, leaving outgoing passengers and mail
to catch the next steamer. Sometimes passengers grew angry with
Captain Porter, and he supplied them with hydrographical reasons, though their feelings were not always pacified by his logic.

One disaffected passenger, a journalist by the name of Colburn
Adams, ridiculed Porter for imposing a naval regimen on board
a civilian vessel. In a boisterous satire called "High Old Salts" he
recorded that "Plain Captain David was nearly always in a state
of rebellion, now with the company, now with the Government,
then with the passengers... Now there would not be enough
water, then the seas would be running too high. He had a mild-
mannered, but very wicked way of dumping passengers and mails
into fishing smacks... outside the bar, leaving them to make their
way in as best they could..." [8]

Porter was, indeed, different from the ordinary civilian captains,
and the distinction went deeper than the shining lace on his collar
and cuffs. He was first of all a lieutenant in the Navy. The civilian
character of the *Georgia* did not prevent him from writing reports
to the Secretary of the Navy relative to the condition of his vessel, the performance of her engine, the discipline of her civilian
crew. He tried to make everything on the *Georgia* conform to
Navy regulations.

When he ordered the *Georgia's* engineer to keep a minute log
of the engine's performance and on the first trip found him neg-
lecting orders and leisurely writing up the required data from
memory, Porter clapped him in irons. Three others in the engine
room struck out of sympathy. Porter called it mutiny, and thrust
these men also into the brig.

When he got back to New York, each of the men threatened
lawsuits against their late commander; and Porter wrote the Secretary at length to explain that on the mail steamers the crews
ought to be subject to naval discipline, since it was obvious that

on lieutenant's pay no man could afford to fight lawsuits, however petty. The company neither approved nor disapproved of Porter's disciplinary measures, but the successors of the "mutineers" entered their data in good form. Porter spent much time in the engine room, and reported that his engineers were all excellent fellows.

In May Porter yielded to his wife's importunings and took her and the children on his fourth trip to the Isthmus.[4] But this was the first and last time. In spite of the comforts of the staterooms opening on the gaily appointed Ladies' Saloon, Porter felt that the *Georgia* was no pleasure boat, and Aspinwall, the terminal town on the Atlantic side of the Isthmus, certainly was neither scenically beautiful nor healthy. The oldest daughter, Georgianne, fell ill with Chagres fever on the return voyage and never completely recovered.

Porter and his officers were half-sick much of the time with chills and fever. After five months' service Midshipman Shufeldt had to be detached. Midshipman James D. Bulloch was very anxious for the job, and Porter urged the Secretary to give it to him. Midshipman F. A. Roe, also ordered to the *Georgia* at Porter's request, though for eight months afflicted by fever, kept himself on duty and begged Porter not to trouble the Secretary. Roe and Shufeldt later won high rank in the Union Navy, and Bulloch was to distinguish himself abroad as a special naval agent for the Confederacy.

In the fall of 1852 occurred a flare-up of Manifest Destiny—with Captain David D. Porter as the central figure—which just missed provoking war between the United States and Spain. In August when the *Georgia* was laid up in New York for repairs, Porter had been transferred temporarily to the command of the mail steamer *Crescent City* for the run from New York to New Orleans via Havana.

A Mr. Smith, purser on "an American vessel recently at Havana," according to a New York correspondent of the Havana *Diario*, had circulated a rumor that in the city of Havana one thousand political prisoners were incarcerated.

When the *Crescent City* enroute from New Orleans to New York, put into Havana on September 15, 1852, the governor of the port sent a guard of Spanish soldiers on board Porter's vessel to charge that the purser on the *Crescent City* was the Mr. Smith who had spread the obnoxious rumor and to prevent Mr. Smith from going ashore.[5] Porter called the purser, an old man kept on the company's books for length of service. The purser denied the charge. Porter then ordered the soldiers off his ship and wrote a letter to the governor denying that the *Crescent City's* officer was the Mr. Smith in question. He then landed passengers and mail and proceeded to New York.

On October 3 when the *Crescent City* returned to Havana with Purser Smith on board, the port authorities demanded that Smith himself write a denial of the charge. In view of his own previous statement Porter refused to allow this. He contended that the offense was merely alleged, not proved, and that even if it had been committed the indiscretion had occurred on American soil outside the jurisdiction of Cuba.

The *Crescent City* was not permitted to land either passengers or mail and was ordered out of the harbor. Should she return again with Mr. Smith on board, Porter was warned, she would again be refused entry. A Spanish gunboat would cruise off the harbor to enforce the governor's edict.

A few hours after the *Crescent City* had docked in New Orleans, the report of what had happened in Havana was in everybody's possession. The flag of the United States had been insulted! An officer of the United States Navy had upheld the honor of his nation. The authorities of Havana should be taught a lesson. Cuba ought to be taken and annexed to the United States. Mobs demanded that Manifest Destiny be fulfilled. Two engineers, who had set out to work in the cane grinding mills and had had to pay their way back to Cuba in another boat, were convinced that Porter had been unnecessarily contentious with the authorities. But the people of New Orleans acclaimed Porter in a voice vibrant with the excitement of war.

On the night of October 11 there were several big demonstrations. People were massed at Lafayette Square, in front of the City Hall, on the steps of the Presbyterian Church, in St. Francis Street, and alongside the American Theater. Bands of musicians rallied the people in every quarter of the city. Merchants displayed patriotic banners. Portraits of George Washington glued to shopwindows were illuminated from the rear by innumerable candles. There were speeches by prominent politicians and ardent, chauvinistic resolutions dictated by the crowds.

Most interesting was the gathering at Lafayette Square. At an early hour the community grandstand was packed and every street leading into the square jammed. At seven o'clock a salute was fired; and a Mr. N. R. Jennings, who had been a passenger on the *Crescent City*, gave an account of the outrage and read Captain Porter's spirited letter of protest to the American consul in Havana. The reading of the letter was interrupted by frequent applause. Judge Larue spoke as follows: "It is said that we have been endeavoring to raise an issue with Spain in order that we might take possession of Cuba. Well, suppose we had? Cuba naturally belongs to us!" An ovation greeted the Judge's remarks. A young politician, Mr. Judah P. Benjamin, arose—the same whose mental agility and obsequiousness would bring him many portfolios in the Confederate Government. Mr. Benjamin professed himself "appalled by the depth and intensity of emotion of the great ocean of humanity around me...In a time of profound peace an American vessel, commanded by an officer of the United States Navy—all honor to his name, for it is an honor to the Navy—entered the port of Havana, and was driven out of it with contumely and insult." He asked, "What will the people determine under such circumstances?" The people cried, "Fight! FIGHT!" [6] The cheers for Mr. Benjamin resounded for many minutes.

Captain Porter took no part in the public meetings, but his plans for his next move were spectacular—and he kept them to himself.

On the return trip the *Crescent City* arrived off Havana Harbor before daylight on October 14, hours ahead of time. Porter did not wait for a native pilot to come out to meet him but piloted his vessel himself through the difficult channel in defiance of the rules of the port, of the Spanish man-of-war detailed to intercept him, and of the guns of Morro Castle. At sunrise when the captain of the port came on duty, he found the *Crescent City* swinging peacefully at her usual anchorage.

The captain of the port came alongside and asked whether Mr. Smith was still on board. Porter told him that he was. The official then informed Captain Porter that as his ship was already in she would not be molested and might lie there as long as she pleased. But she could not land passengers and mail. Such were the governor's orders. Porter asked if he might communicate with the American consul. The Spanish official said that he would have to consult the governor, and after surrounding the *Crescent City* on all sides with guard boats went ashore.

The Spanish soldiers on guard duty did not relish their job. They had no awnings to protect them from the sun; and, when the gong sounded for breakfast on the *Crescent City*, they looked so miserable that Porter invited them to come on board for refreshment, which they declined. After breakfast Porter ordered out the paint pots and set his men to painting the outside of the ship. Observing this, the officer commanding the guards withdrew all but two of his boats.

At nine o'clock the captain of the port returned and informed Porter that he would not be permitted to lay his protest before the consul. After several hours an official of the steamship line and the acting consul were permitted to come alongside; and Porter delivered to them a second protest for the governor, after which he hoisted anchor and steamed out of the harbor, firing a salute to his flag as he passed Morro Castle.

At New York he was received by a committee of excited citizens who wanted to present him with a handsome sword as a token of their esteem. Porter declined the sword, saying that he deemed it inappropriate for an officer of the Navy to receive gifts for doing his duty.

The State Department, alarmed over the *Crescent City* incident, dispatched the U. S. S. *Cyane* and the U. S. S. *Powhatan* to Havana to prevent a repetition of the insult and make an investigation. Porter was ordered to Washington to report in person. Mr. Smith was induced to make a written denial of the charge against him, and his deposition was handed to the Spanish minister. On his return to New York Porter was transferred back to the *Georgia,* whose repairs had now been completed; and the threatening war with Spain was indefinitely postponed.

The excitement of the incident had weakened Porter physically, so that almost immediately he contracted Chagres fever. He nevertheless continued in command of the *Georgia* for seven months. In May 1853, he finally requested and obtained a year's leave of absence to recuperate. While he was recovering from his illness, however, the Australian Steamship Company offered him command of the *Golden Age;* and, before the year was out, he bade farewell to his family, now including a new baby, Elizabeth, and was off once more on the high seas, determined to surpass all speed records and if possible to make his fortune in the fabulous new country of Australia.

Fashioned like a river boat the *Golden Age* had no graceful, tapering prow to cut the waves. Her cabins towering high above the water reminded New England folk of their meeting houses. Westerners said that her walking-beam would make an excellent implement for sawing wood. With her paddle wheels billowing out on either side, she possessed neither grace nor beauty. Nevertheless, she made the run to Liverpool in faster time than any steamer had ever made the crossing before.

The postmaster in Liverpool seeing a chance to profit by her fame arranged for Porter to carry the next mail to Australia, and put up posters in the exchange to apprise the public of the fact. Enough mail was collected to take up the room of fifty tons of ordinary freight, and Captain Porter was criticised by rival shipping interests for taking this mail. It was charged that he was under no regular contract and that his hatches were not battened down and sealed with the government seal, but Porter did not mind so long as the postmaster was satisfied.

The voyage around Africa and across the Indian Ocean was accomplished in fifty-six days actual sailing—another record, for no ship had ever made it in less than eighty-six. The Americans in Melbourne celebrated the achievement of their fellow countryman by giving him "the handsomest banquet ever got up in Australia," which cost $2,500. Porter was flattered, but since his recent illness his stomach had not been good, and he wished that he had been given the money instead. Moreover, the long voyage had worn him out. His first officer had got drunk, and Porter had put him off duty and his second officer had been bedridden during the entire trip, with the result that Porter had been forced to do the work of three men.

At every street corner Americans buttonholed him and overwhelmed him with hospitality, but he found Melbourne a "horrid hole." It was difficult to get into the town from the *Golden Age,* three miles out in the harbor. He had either to take a rickety, smoky steamboat up a tortuous creek, or else ride four miles in a cart over the dustiest of roads. Secondly, a gale blew all the time. Whenever it blew from inland across the desert regions, Melbourne became as hot as an oven. The dust rose and hid even the carriages in the streets. All business had to be suspended, doors and windows boarded up, and as Porter witnesses, people lay panting ready to die until the breeze chopped around from seaward, and then it blew cold and damp and gave everyone rheumatism. A turkey cost $10, a chicken $5, and other commodities in proportion. Finally, he got terribly homesick. "What would I not give to peep in upon you just now, and see what you and the children are doing?" he wrote Georgy. "I can see you all in my mind's eye in the upper back room sitting around a coal fire warming your toes, while here I am almost suffocated. I should be glad to get on a fast horse and ride off home ... What would I not give to hear my dear little Lizzy's voice and see her running about; dear little thing, how interesting she must be ... It seems such a long pile of ocean between us ... I long to hear how my darling Georgy is.... I think of her poor little thin face night and day ... God bless you again and a sweet kiss for yourself." [7]

In spite of his homesickness Captain Porter stayed in Australia for six months carrying passengers and freight between Melbourne and Sydney. There were now ten vessels engaged in this traffic, and Porter's, having the ocean record to its credit, soon became the most popular of them all. The joy of competition seized Captain Porter, and he cut down the steaming time between the two cities from four days to two. The popularity of the *Golden Age* won trade from the rival boats, and one by one these began to drop out. Captain Porter came to be familiarly referred to as Yankee Doodle. Bets were placed in Sydney and Melbourne on the number of hours that Yankee Doodle on his next trip would cut from his own record.

Beaten on the water the owners of the rival boats now started a newspaper campaign against their dangerous competitor. There were dark hints about the illegality of his carrying the mail from Liverpool. It was alleged that the *Golden Age* was dangerously top heavy, and it was predicted that one day the "old meeting house" would topple into the sea. Porter now brought into the open the talent for rhyming which he had cultivated in secret lampoons against Secretaries of the Navy. He answered his critics in a lengthy burlesque poem entitled "Yankee Doodle in Australia." Its meter was not always regular; but, inasmuch as most of the piece was a characterization of himself, he turned it off with éclat. The following are sample stanzas:

Oh, Yankee Doodle, all around he is a clap of thunder,
He jumps up higher, comes down drier, and never will knock under,
He'll whip his weight in catamounts, and grin a bear to bits, Sir,
And as to electricity, he'll knock it into fits, Sir.

    Corn cobs twist your hair, cart wheels around you,
    Printer's devils, damn your eyes, and leaden types confound you.

He'll slide a rainbow any day with a planet on his back, Sir,
When his steam's up, take my advice, at once to clear the track, Sir,
For when his dander's up, you can't tell when his hand will fall, Sir,
He'll swallow up an Editor, his printing press and all, Sir.

    Corn cobs, etc. [8]

Porter caused this effusion to be printed on placards eight feet square and posted around Sydney and Melbourne. The result was more applications for passage than the *Golden Age* could handle. On his last trip, before leaving Australia for America, he carried 1,200 passengers.

He came home via Tahiti and Panama. With the profits of his trip to Australia he bought a modest house on East 33rd Street, New York, and moved his family there from Washington, hoping that the more healthful climate would benefit his oldest daughter Georgianne. The child, however, failed to improve and died within a year. But her place in the family was filled on May 23, 1854, by a new baby, Richard Bache. Porter himself came down with fever and exhaustion and was ill for more than a year.

At the end of his adventures as a "plain captain," Porter was so harassed by fever and chills that he forgot to report to the Secretary his return from leave. On July 21, 1854, when he finally attended to this matter he excused himself on the score that he had been too ill even to dictate it.

7.
CRUISING INTO CHAOS

WHEN Lieutenant David D. Porter returned to regular duty in the line of the Navy after his trip to Australia he had acquired fame and prestige. Hitherto the Navy Department with a penchant for cataloging had conceded him a sort of composite character which applied generally to all the Porters. His service at Vera Cruz and Tabasco had justified a flattering fitness report from Commodore Perry and a reputation for fearlessness and audacity which marked him as a true son of the late Commodore Porter. The *Crescent City* incident disclosed a high sense of personal honor—tinged with stubbornness, which was also a characteristic of all the Porters.

The *Georgia's* records for speed between the coastal cities, which to Porter were more important than anything else, did not impress the Department or the public so much as the expedients Porter employed in disciplining his civilian crews to make those records. The public, moreover, jaded by the speed rivalries of the Cunard and Collins liners in the Atlantic crossing, took little note of Porter until the record-breaking voyages of the *Golden Age* became the news of the day.

Then the trim, piercing-eyed Lieutenant David D. Porter ceased to be merely the son of the audacious, irascible Commodore of 1812, or the younger brother of the controversial Commander William D. Porter. Lieutenant David D. Porter became a personage in his own right. The Department recognized his impetuous energy, his zest for responsibility, and his ability to take over the direction of unusual enterprises.

Though the naval doctors had kept him in bed more than six months after his return from Australia, he wrote from his sick room on March 15, 1855, volunteering to command an expedition into the Arctic in search for the lost explorer, Dr. Kane, for whose safety the country was much concerned. His request was not granted, but the naval service recognized that even a series of exasperating illnesses could not impair his will to succeed.

There was, however, another unusual task to which a convalescent naval officer might be assigned.

Since 1848 Colonel Jefferson Davis had pondered the transportation problem facing the U. S. Army in the arid Southwest territories lately won from Mexico, and in particular had studied the British Army's use of camels as pack animals and cavalry mounts in the conquest of India. In the spring of 1855, when the wholesale employment of camels in the Crimean War evoked comment in the newspapers, Jefferson Davis, now Secretary of War under President Pierce, managed to secure an appropriation of $30,000 to finance an experiment of introducing camels into Texas.[1]

On April 12, Porter was assigned to command the U. S. storeship *Supply* on a joint mission with Major Henry C. Wayne of the Army to the Near East to procure camels for Davis' experiment.

Porter read all the material he could find about camels and at the Brooklyn Navy Yard designed and constructed on board the *Supply* a special stable to accommodate the camels. This consisted of a trunk 60 feet long, 12 feet wide, and 7½ feet high, extending from abaft the foremast to the quarter-deck. Amidships he provided a large hatch through which the camels might be lowered and cut other hatches in the forward and after ends to put wind sails down for ventilation. The twenty portholes on each side of the trunk he fitted inside with glass frames to be let down in cold weather and outside with wooden shutters to keep out the sea during storms. The main hatch he built up so high above the deck that it could be kept open in all weathers. The camels were not to be hoisted on board like horses, with straps run under their bellies, but conveyed in a special camel car which could be ferried to and from the beach on a shallow scow and lifted bodily into the ship.

Porter sailed the *Supply* past Sandy Hook on June 4, and arrived in Spezia, Italy, on July 12, a few days ahead of Major Wayne, his partner in the enterprise, who was traveling via London and Paris to acquire information about the nature and habits of camels. While the *Supply* waited in Spezia for Major Wayne, Porter made a trip to Florence and Pisa to examine the herd of camels on the estate of the Grand Duke. Since cholera was scourging the country at this time, most of the officials had fled, and Porter could learn nothing from the peasants.

Wayne had arrived by the time Porter returned to Spezia, and the *Supply* sailed to Tunis. Here Porter and Wayne bought a camel whose habits they might study while negotiating for the remainder of the cargo. They had no sooner embarked their experimental animal than the Bey of Tunis made them a present of two other specimens—one young, plump, and healthy, the other afflicted with itch.

On the way to Smyrna Porter scrubbed and curried the ailing camel, fed him sulphur in his oats, oiled his callosities and touched up his sores with sulphur ointment. At Smyrna camels were scarce and prices high. Mr. Offley, the consul, informed Porter and Wayne that the British had recently contracted for hiring 8,000 of the animals for service in the Crimea. At Salonica finding no camels of any description, they pushed on to Constantinople, where the only animals to be found were unfit for military use. The Sultan, who received them kindly, promised them "four of the best specimens in Asia"; whereupon they sold their two worst camels to a butcher.

While the *Supply* was in Constantinople, Porter and Wayne accepted the hospitality of British officers and made an observation trip to the Crimea aboard the British steamer *Imperador*.

They arrived in the Crimea in November, a short while after the famous charge of the Light Brigade. Porter, inspecting the captured fortifications of the Malakoff, was more impressed by the size and strength of the great fort than by anything he had ever seen. In the course of the naval bombardment the French had used a floating battery sheathed with armor plating. The backwardness of the U. S. Navy never struck him with greater force. He was also interested in the new style of equipment used by the British and French sappers and miners. When he returned on board the *Supply* he constructed models of this equipment, fired musket balls at them to test their strength, and sent them with a report to the authorities in Washington.

Concerning the military use of camels Porter and Wayne obtained expert information from an officer who had taken part in General Napier's expedition against Sind. The large, one-humped dromedary camel made an excellent mount for two men, who sat back to back and were both armed with rifles and sabres. The man facing the head was the animal's groom and driver. Upon arriving at the scene of operations the dromedaries were made to kneel in a square, under the charge of their drivers, forming a base of operations from which the other men operated as infantry. In case of extremity the square offered a cover, and the drivers a reserve. With their forelegs hobbled, the dromedaries afforded a living breastwork that would stop a bullet.

Unfortunately when Porter and Wayne returned to Constantinople the Sultan's "four best camels in Asia" were still at large and the *Supply* moved on to Alexandria without them. The winter gales were now commencing, and Porter had to stay by his ship while Wayne and Gwynn Harris Heap, Porter's brother-in-law, now a consul in Alexandria, ascended the Nile to Cairo to purchase camels.

Wayne wished to purchase twenty of the best animals in Egypt, but he encountered legal technicalities. So much livestock had recently been drained from the country by the war in the Crimea that the Egyptian viceroy had issued a general prohibition against any further exportation. Wayne informed the authorities that these camels were wanted for scientific purposes, to introduce them into a new country. The authorities finally authorized him to take out four animals, two males and two females. Wayne bought five camels and drove them back to Alexandria. To smooth the way for smuggling the fifth one on board he sent the viceroy's confidential secretary a present of two Minié rifles complete with bullet mould and swage. The gratuity at once dissolved the official scruples, and Wayne was told that he might take out ten animals. But it was now too late for him to make another journey into the interior to acquire them, and the camels in Alexandria were scrofulous and ill-suited to his purpose.

Although the governor of Alexandria wanted to make America a present of six choice camels from his own private herd, Porter found these specimens so poor that he refused to jeopardize his country's experiment by accepting them.

Leaving Alexandria, Porter reached Smyrna on January 30, 1856, where his brother-in-law, Consul Heap, whom he had sent ahead, had twenty-one reasonably healthy animals ready for loading when the *Supply* arrived. Porter engaged three Arabs and a Turk as native experts to assist on the voyage to Texas; and, as the animals were being loaded, the native craftsmen were fashioning harness to leash them in stormy weather.

Porter composed and posted a sheet of regulations to govern the routine on the camel deck. The attendants were to swing their hammocks alongside the animals at night and never leave the deck unless relieved. No open lights were to be used, and tubs of water were to be kept handy in case of fire. Feedings of hay and grain were to be carefully measured and the amounts consumed recorded. Dung was never to be left lying around on the deck. The camels' feet were to be washed with soap twice a week. Callosities were to be regularly oiled.

Since the object of the expedition was to introduce into the United States as many head of camels as possible, most of the females selected were with foal and the others were bred as soon as they were got on board.

Leaving Smyrna on February 15 for her homeward voyage, the *Supply* almost immediately encountered a storm. In the midst of the ship's lurchings a male calf was born. The storm continued with force until the vessel was well out into the Atlantic. On the 19th a female calf was born. Both calves died on the 25th for want of nourishment, their dams refusing to rise and suckle them. In vain the attendants beat the poor brutes to get them on their feet. The Turk suggested setting fire to their humps, but perplexed as he was, Porter would not consent to this.

The log of the camel deck is unique in the annals of seafaring.

Six calves were born in the course of the voyage. One was laid on and crushed by its mother through neglect of the Arabian attendant. Another sickened and died, it was thought from teething. Another was born dead, and the mother suffered such agonies that Porter had her killed. Deciding that his native experts were too anxious to hurry nature, Porter himself took charge in the next emergency; and by simply leaving the mother alone for a sufficient length of time the delivery was successfully accomplished. Porter caught up the calf, breathed into its nostrils, swaddled it in warm wrappings, and was pleased with his skill as a veterinarian.

Four of the calves were lost, but two healthy specimens survived, thanks—Porter believed—to numerous dosings with paregoric, mineral oil, dough balls, and other baby foods prepared from the captain's larder. In clear weather the two calves pranced up and down the camel deck on their perfect sea legs, taking their nourishment indiscriminately wherever they found a fresh cow that was standing up. One of them, named Uncle Sam for having been born under the flag, was taught wrestling tricks and soon became so proficient that whenever he leaped on the attendants unawares he toppled them to the deck.

After another season of storms in the Gulf Porter got his

camels ashore at Indianola, Texas, in good order. On being landed, and feeling once more the solid earth beneath them, they screamed, reared, bit and kicked one another, broke halters, and tore up pickets before Major Wayne's soldiers could bring them under control.

The authorities in Washington were so pleased with the venture that they sent Porter for a second boatload of camels—this time without Major Wayne, who remained behind to care for the first lot. By the time Porter returned with the second cargo, President Pierce and Secretary Davis had gone out of office. The Buchanan administration discontinued the experiment, and the immigrants were turned loose on the plains, where they survived for several generations to the terror of all horses they encountered. Three of their descendants were caught in 1862 by General Curtis' pickets and shipped up the Mississippi to the General's home in Keokuk.

In 1857 after squaring his accounts with the Treasury, sitting on courts-martial, and seeing his mother's pension through Congress, Porter was ordered to duty as one of the two junior officers at the Portsmouth, N. H., Navy Yard. In May of 1857 he moved Georgy and the six children into a rented house on the outskirts of the Portsmouth yard to begin three of the most uninteresting years of his life.

The climate agreed with him. His health improved. But the petty detail work to which he was assigned in the little, out-of-the-way navy yard exasperated him. A single ship was overhauled and fitted for sea during the three years he was there. Unable to be idle for long he read widely in naval ordnance, strained his eyes. He invented and patented a contrivance for controlling the elevation of a gun for firing at unseen targets or during the night time.[2]

He also landscaped the navy yard and tutored his children in Latin. His oldest son Essex, once called the Mogul, was now a handsome boy almost as tall as his father. Carlisle and Theodoric, Ki and Tod, respectively marking one and two stairsteps below Essex in height, were also growing slender and tall. His boys were fond of Portsmouth, and threatened to "mutiny" whenever their father spoke of leaving the place. Essex and Ki enjoyed nothing so much as rowing their father across the harbor in their gig. After much hammering, eight-year-old Tod constructed a bird house and then planted a chestnut bur to grow a special tree in which to hang it.

Mrs. Porter, however, shared her husband's dislike for Portsmouth and longed for the society of her genial Southern friends, the Barrons, the Baches, and her own family, who lived in Washington. Mrs. Porter's health was poor after the birth of her eighth child Elena in 1856. She was an invalid during the greater part of the years spent in Portsmouth, repeatedly undergoing operations from which she recovered slowly. The second daughter Nina died during the first year at Portsmouth.

On April 14, 1858, when Porter received from the vice-president of the Pacific Mail Steamship Company an offer of a permanent position as commander of a large steamer being built to operate in the Pacific, he was tempted to accept it. "I see no reason why I should decline the honor (i.e. money) if it is thrown at my head," he wrote his brother-in-law Heap. "Before I embark in the business, however, I must know if it will pay (mercenary dog you will say)...I don't care about lifting my anchor from these diggins until I am sure of having a fair wind into a better roadstead...I suppose if I was to be appointed I should be cursed to death by every other fellow in the Navy (I should like that), and doubtless by the time the ship was constructed I should be denounced everywhere as a damned vallain... *que importe,* as long as I get what I want? I don't think it suits me sitting down so quietly here." [3] To his mother—whom he had to console because the rest of the family were nagging her for having sold a Washington property and because the youngest son Henry was drinking again—Porter confided that he himself sometimes felt as if he would like to jump overboard, "and should likely as not if I had not so many kedge anchors [Essex, Carlisle, Theodoric, Elizabeth, Richard Bache, and Elena] holding me back."[4]

Since the steamship company's offer could not go into effect until after the proposed vessel had been designed and built, Porter had about eighteen months in which to accept or decline.

Meanwhile the spring of 1859 brought his restless spirit a few months of relief from his trivial duties in Portsmouth. He was assigned as junior member of a board to make a general inspection of the navy yards at Portsmouth, Boston, New York, Philadelphia, Washington and Norfolk. Porter was now forty-six years old. His commission as a commander was three years overdue. His rank was, and for the last eighteen years had been, that of lieutenant.

The president of the board was elderly Captain George S. Blake, Superintendent of the Naval Academy at Annapolis, an affable gentleman with whom Porter had been associated twenty-four years ago when he had first gone to the Coast Survey. Another member of the board was Commander Andrew Hull Foote, one of the most highly respected officers of his time.

The survey of the navy yards revealed everywhere a general inertia. Only a few vessels in the lighter categories were being constructed. None of them were ironclad, such as had already appeared in the British and the French Navies. Along the Atlantic Coast there were but two yards having dry docks, and these needed extensive repair. Only the small yard at Washington had any facilities for reconditioning steam engines. Because the Naval Appropriations Bill of 1859 prescribed the most rigid economy, few ships that required expenditures in excess of $1,000 were being repaired. Ships manifestly unfit for sea duty were being dispatched to foreign stations. Others were being laid up in ordinary or decommissioned. Here and there a few hundreds of dollars were being expended annually on buildings and sea walls. Different systems of organization prevailed in the various yards. Porter found that the station at Portsmouth was paying better wages than the yard in New York, where the cost of living was much higher.

Porter loved the Navy in which he had now spent thirty years of his life, and deplored the conditions that existed.

In the Navy afloat Porter knew that conditions were as bad as in the Navy ashore. As the number of ships steadily diminished from want of extensive repair and almost total lack of new construction, jobs afloat for officers became fewer and fewer. The officer personnel of the Navy languished. No one was ever retired. Congress had not yet provided for the retirement of older officers. Promotion, dependent upon seniority, had been brought to a standstill. Lieutenant Porter had been more fortunate than most officers of his subordinate grade. Generally officers in the lower ranks grew gray-headed never having had the experience of commanding a vessel, and with little chance of getting it. Many promising young men—Gustavus Fox for instance—solved their problems by resigning and entering private business.

The ships' crews were probably no worse than they ever were, but the War with Mexico, which should have raised the standards of discipline, failed to accomplish that result. Lieutenant Rowan, who shared Porter's ideas about discipline, had testified a few years before that crews were "all made up of persons who are disqualified by their vices from employment on shore—thieves, gamblers, drunkards, play actors, circus riders. Many of them escaped civil punishment by enlisting." [5] Only three of the representative group of officers whom the Department asked to submit opinions on the subject advised doing away with flogging, but the Department in spite of this overwhelming verdict had recommended it; and on September 28, 1850, Congress had formally abolished flogging in the Navy. Even many old seamen grumbled over this. Bravery to endure lashes from the cat had for generations been the criterion for distinction among seamen. [6]

In an age of invention the Navy Department had shut its doors to inventors. John Ericsson was not encouraged, but abused as an eccentric fool by Navy officials. The memory of a single disaster—the explosion of an experimental 12-inch gun on the U. S. S. *Princeton* in 1844, which had killed Secretary of State Abel P. Upshur, Secretary of the Navy Thomas W. Gilmer, Captain Beverly Kennon of the Navy, and Colonel Gardiner of the Army—survived even the War with Mexico.

In some ways the Navy of the 1850's shone. Lieutenant John A. Dahlgren in the Bureau of Ordnance had been able to apply his principle of the "curve of pressures" to the manufacture of muzzle-loading guns. In the Depot of Charts in Washington Lieutenant Maury produced his Mariner's Bible, the wind and current charts. The work of the Coast Survey, now extending into the distant Pacific, was a significant achievement. Naval ships had penetrated into the Arctic. Commodore Perry's expedition to Japan had resulted in a treaty of amity and commerce which opened that medieval oriental empire to occidental influence.

In the summer of 1860 Porter was at last detached from what he considered a dreary exile in Portsmouth. On the return to Washington he transported his family down as far as Annapolis on the honored relic of 1812, the U. S. S. *Constitution*. What he coveted for the Navy was not a squadron of ancient ships dependent upon wind for motive power, but a fleet of modern steam vessels like the mail steamers whose engines he had himself tested.

In the fall of 1860 preparatory to accepting the job with the Pacific Mail Steamship Company, Porter secured an assignment to duty on the Pacific Coast as commander of the Coast Survey schooner *Active*. Luckily for him events preliminary to the Civil War delayed his departure.

After the election of President Lincoln in the fall of 1860, Porter went often to the galleries of the Capitol to listen to the speeches of ill-tempered Congressmen.

On the rainy evening in December, 1860, when news arrived that South Carolina had seceded from the Union, Porter tramped through mud and drizzle to call on Senator Jefferson Davis, whose friendship he had made at the time of the camel voyages. Davis of Mississippi was a calm, intellectual gentleman, and Porter delighted in his company. He felt that Davis would view the situation in the most philosophic light possible. A considerable crowd had already gathered when Porter arrived. He entered the house, just as the genial and witty Varina Davis in bonnet and shawl was descending the stairs.

"Ah, Captain," she called to Porter, "I am so glad to see you! I want you to escort me to the White House to congratulate the President."

Porter hailed a carriage and accompanied Mrs. Davis to the White House. On the way he asked why she should feel so highly elated.

"Because," she said, "we will now have a monarchy South, and gentlemen to fill official positions."

On his return to Davis' house Porter found the crowd of men pulling on their coats to follow Mrs. Davis. They all spoke of the mild-mannered President Buchanan as being in sympathy with them.

Porter called at the Davis house several times during the months that followed. He heard much talk about naval officers being offered high commands in the new government. Varina Davis laughingly offered Porter a job as admiral if he would come over to the Southern side. Porter was noncommittal. But both Varina Davis and her husband believed Porter to be "a sort of secessioner."[7] In Porter's presence one day Senator Jefferson Davis spoke disparagingly of the Federal Navy, saying that he himself would not have voted for the last appropriation for small naval vessels had not Representative Stephen Mallory included in the bill a provision for the vessels authorized to draw too much water to enter Southern harbors!

In the last weeks of the Buchanan administration many of Porter's friends resigned their positions and went south. Commander Tattnall—a native of Georgia, under whom Porter had served during the bombardment of Vera Cruz—was among the number who resigned. In February, Porter's sister-in-law, Mrs. William D. Porter, packed her trunks while her husband was on duty in the Pacific and moved from Washington to Richmond taking her three children with her.[8]

At the Navy Department no one knew whom to trust.

As the demoralized Navy cruised into the chaos of war it was inevitable that in order to preserve secrecy certain important movements had to be conducted in the manner of conspiracies, behind the backs even of the Secretaries of War and of the Navy. Lieutenant David D. Porter was to have a share in secret missions as well as in the open warfare.

PART TWO
THE GUNS

Successful guns on his gun decks . . .

8.

THE DIVERSION OF THE *POWHATAN*

Dust swirled to the eaves of the sun-scorched houses along Pennsylvania Avenue. A queue of sight-seers in black frock coats trailed Lincoln's carriage to Capitol Hill, where two companies of soldiers stood ready if necessary to pull the lanyards of their cannon. When the frock coats collected with orderliness in the square east of the great half-completed dome of the Capitol, gray-haired General Winfield Scott heaved a sigh and leaned against one of his cannon to ease the throbbing in his gouty leg. On a back row of the speaker's platform sat Mr. Gideon Welles, the incoming Secretary of the Navy, a crusty old gentleman with a Longfellow coiffure who quietly stroked his beard and listened. Lincoln delivered his inaugural address.

The first three weeks of Lincoln's administration resembled the last three months of Buchanan's. Emissaries from the seceded States came to Washington to negotiate for peaceful recognition and peaceful surrender of Fort Pickens and Fort Sumter to the Confederate States of America. Already the forts on the mainland at Pensacola and Charleston had been seized by State troops. The policy of the new administration had not yet been decided. Lincoln remained in the background while Secretary of State William H. Seward treated unofficially with the emissaries.

At the Navy Department was recrimination and confusion. The retiring Secretary, Mr. Toucey, a Democrat with Southern sympathies, was being openly accused of having used his position to cripple the Navy in case of war with the South. The new Secretary, Mr. Gideon Welles, a small town politician from Mr. Toucey's own state Connecticut, was unknown. He was an ex-Democrat, appointed, according to rumor, not because his trenchant editorials in the Hartford *Evening Press* had swung Connecticut for Lincoln but because Lincoln hoped that his appointment might somehow conciliate the defeated Democrats. Few remembered that twenty years ago old Mr. Welles had headed the Navy Department's Bureau of Provisions and Clothing, for no politician before him had ever used that bureau as a stepping-stone to higher office. Lieutenant David D. Porter and his friends regarded the new chief as just another civilian Secretary, and nicknamed him "Grandfather Welles."

Every day brought fresh resignations from Southern officers. Convinced that his native Maryland would secede, Captain Franklin Buchanan, commandant of the Washington Navy Yard, resigned; subsequently when Maryland did not secede, he sought to withdraw his resignation, failed, and went off perplexed to Richmond, to emerge later as an admiral in the Confederate States Navy and commander of the great C. S. ironclad *Merrimac*.

Throughout these exciting first weeks of the new administration, Porter continued his preparations to leave for the West Coast. The ship on which he had engaged passage was sailing from New York on April 2. In drawing rooms and in lobbies of hotels he drank farewell toasts with his friends and discussed the impending crisis. Many of his friends rebuked him for leaving now. How, they asked, could the command of a Survey ship off the rocks of California compare to the opportunities here in the East? Secession! South Carolina had left the Union as long ago as December 20, 1860! By the first of February the six other States of the Deep South had followed South Carolina out of the Union! Secession inevitably meant war!

"Perhaps!" rejoined Porter. "But what has Lincoln done? Nothing! These Southern gentry who come so politely to ask for Fort Pickens and Fort Sumter! Are they arrested? No! Neither will there be a war!"

Among his brother officers Porter was outspoken against what seemed to him a repetition of the Buchanan regime. To him it seemed unthinkable that the Government should remain idle while the Southern States seized the Federal arsenals. Already Florida Secessionists had compelled the United States officers to evacuate the important navy yard at Pensacola, where the Confederate General Braxton Bragg was even now getting the captured guns into position for firing at Fort Pickens and Santa Rosa Island immediately across Pensacola Bay. It was time to act. If the Government did not immediately relieve its little garrison, Fort Pickens, too, would soon fall into Secessionist hands.

To his neighbor Captain Montgomery C. Meigs of the Army Porter remarked that he would like nothing better than a chance to carry an expedition into Pensacola Harbor to relieve Fort

Pickens and recapture the navy yard. Meigs agreed with Porter that the thing could be done and said that he too would like to participate in such a mission. The two believed it could be accomplished if managed in secret. But the number of Southerners still left in the War and the Navy Departments closed all regular channels to such a project, and Porter, having scant hope that decisive action would be taken, went ahead with his West Coast plans.

At noon on the first of April while he was eating the farewell meal with his family, he received a note from Mr. Seward, Secretary of State, requesting Porter to call and see him without delay. Hastily Porter whisked the crumbs from his beard and returned with the messenger to Mr. Seward's office.

Porter found the thin-legged Secretary of State reclining on a sofa, knees up, inspecting a document. Without changing his comfortable position Seward asked Porter if he knew a way to save Fort Pickens. Porter sketched briefly the plan he had outlined to Meigs; and, when Meigs himself presently appeared, Mr. Seward asked the two of them to accompany him to see the President.

Lincoln was in the doldrums, pacing back and forth with lanky strides between his desk and the window. His hope that he might win the Secessionists through mildness was growing fainter as the Southern separatists waxed more violent. The situations at Pensacola, Charleston, and Norfolk were rapidly becoming desperate. He had to do something, but his slightest move might strike the match of rebellion. A "secret" expedition (about which everyone knew) was even now being prepared to carry relief to Fort Sumter; and Gustavus V. Fox, an ex-naval officer soon to become Gideon Welles's prompter in the Navy Department, was fitting out the vessels and begging the President to give his approval before it should be too late. Lincoln dreaded to give the word, knowing that as soon as he did it would at once be relayed south by sympathizers in the Navy Department.

Porter and Meigs talked so confidently that the President was favorably impressed by their scheme. Porter asked for a sizable steamer, carrying a large number of guns and plenty of ammunition. He stated that at the navy yard in New York lay such a vessel, the *Powhatan,* which the Navy Department had recently ordered to be decommissioned. Porter thought that she could with slight repairing be made fit for the purpose. If the President had ever been informed that the *Powhatan* was designed for another mission, he did not remember it. Lincoln sat down and thumbed through a pile of papers on his desk, but the *Powhatan's* name was not on the memorandum listing ships for Fort Sumter. So far as he knew, Porter might have the *Powhatan*. Porter urged that the entire matter should be kept secret even from the Navy Department itself, where many officers and clerks were disloyal.

It was not difficult to get the President committed to the secrecy part of the Fort Pickens expedition, nor did it seem unusual to him that the Secretary of State was meddling in the affairs of the Navy Department, for Mr. Seward, a sort of self-appointed major-domo to the President, had already dabbled in the routine business of departments other than his own. Only once did the presumption of Porter and Meigs seem to strike Lincoln. He uncrossed his long legs and with a twinkle asked, "But what will Uncle Gideon say?" [1]

In passing it might be observed that Mr. Gideon Welles was tempted later to discipline Porter, but that the President's connivance in the Fort Pickens matter so effectually restrained the Secretary that he could do no more than confide his interesting thoughts to his diary.

Having jestingly begged the question, the President consented in his capacity as commander in chief of the Army and Navy to give Porter and Meigs direct orders, without consulting the Secretaries of War and of the Navy. But he himself could not write the necessary orders, knowing so little as he did of naval and military argot.

For this duty Porter and Meigs volunteered. The major issue settled, Porter took occasion to mention that his friend Captain Samuel Barron would be a good person to install in the Bureau of Detail in the Navy Department. To this Lincoln also assented. Porter and Meigs retired to an anteroom where Porter composed four letters for the President's signature. To require a veteran captain to turn over his ship to a junior or to risk his command by coöperating in what was at least a gross departure from naval procedure if not a Secession subterfuge, Porter would have to show an unequivocal set of orders.

So far as is known Meigs composed only one brief paper. If he showed this to Porter, Porter was too wrapped up in his own plans to read it carefully; but the probability is that Porter never saw Meigs's paper until his arrival seventeen days later in Pensacola Harbor. Meigs knew all of Porter's plans, for he copied the orders as they came wet from Porter's pen.

Porter's documents read as follows: [2]

a)   Executive Mansion, April 1, 1861.

Sir: You will proceed to New York, and with the least possible delay assume command of any naval steamer available. Proceed to Pensacola Harbor, and at any cost or risk prevent any expedition from the Mainland reaching Fort Pickens or Santa Rosa.

You will exhibit this order to any naval officer at Pensacola if you deem it necessary after you have established yourself within the harbor, and will request coöperation by the entrance of at least one other vessel.

This order, its object, and your destination will be communicated to no person whatever until you reach the harbor of Pensacola.

                                            ABRAHAM LINCOLN.
Lieutenant D. D. Porter, U. S. Navy.
Recommended: Wm. H. Seward.

b)   Washington City, April 1, 1861.

Sir: Circumstances render it necessary to place in command of your ship, and for a special purpose, an officer who is duly informed and instructed in relation to the wishes of the Government, and you will therefore consider yourself detached; but in taking this step the Government does not intend in the least to reflect upon your efficiency or patriotism; on the contrary, have the fullest confidence in your ability to perform any duty required of you.

Hoping soon to be able to give you a better command than the one you now enjoy, and trusting that you will have full confidence in the disposition of the Government toward you, I remain,

                                            ABRAHAM LINCOLN.
Captain Samuel Mercer, U. S. Navy.

c)   Executive Mansion, April 1, 1861.

Sir: You will fit out the *Powhatan* without delay. Lieutenant Porter will relieve Captain Mercer in command of her. She is bound on secret service, and you will under no circumstances, communicate to the Navy Department the fact that she is fitting out.

                                            ABRAHAM LINCOLN.
Commandant Navy Yard, New York.

d)   Executive Mansion, April 1, 1861.

Lieutenant D. D. Porter will take command of the steamer *Powhatan*, or any other United States steamer ready for sea which he may deem most fit for the service to which he has been assigned by confidential instructions of this date.

All officers are commanded to afford him all such facilities as he may deem necessary for getting to sea as soon as possible. He will select the officers who are to accompany him.

                                            ABRAHAM LINCOLN.
Recommended:
Wm. H. Seward.

Porter also wrote a memorandum to the Secretary of the Navy directing him to place Barron in the Bureau of Detail. Meigs copied it, and put it among the other papers for Lincoln to sign. Lincoln affixed his signatures without reading the papers, his only comment being, "Seward, see that I don't burn my fingers."

Porter and Meigs now returned with Seward to the latter's office where Seward gave them a draft for $20,000 to pay the expenses of the expedition. Also to avoid any direct dealing with the Navy Department, Secretary Seward requested the services of Porter's brother-in-law, Gwynn Harris Heap—who had given up his consulate in Alexandria to become a clerk in the Navy Department—and Secretary Welles without the slightest suspicion dispatched Heap, ostensibly on a State Department mission to New York, actually to become Porter's paymaster on the *Powhatan*.

Porter and Meigs next hastened to General Scott's office to obtain the necessary troops for their expedition. In the anteroom Porter was informed that the General was not at home to Navy men, but would admit Captain Meigs. The aged General's gout was troubling him, he was sitting with his feet in a tub of ice, and did not wish to be seen by anyone outside his military household.

Leaving Meigs closeted with the general in chief, Porter returned home. To Georgy he whispered that she should let their friends think that he was going to the West Coast as he had planned, but that he was really undertaking a secret naval mission on orders from the President. He had planned to take his seventeen-year-old son Essex with him to the West Coast, and now he decided that Essex should go on the *Powhatan* as captain's clerk. Porter bade farewell to his thirteen-year-old son Carlisle, who was soon to enter the Naval Academy in Annapolis. Essex and Ki hustled his bags out to the carriage. Porter kissed Georgy and the younger children, climbed into the carriage with Essex, and was off. On the train to New York that night he fell into conversation with some officers who thought he was going to California. He did not undeceive them.

Meanwhile Mr. Nicolay, private secretary to the President, delivered to Secretary Welles the instruction Porter had composed to ensconce Captain Barron in the Bureau of Detail. Without a moment's delay Mr. Welles left his table at Willard's and hurried to the White House to see Lincoln. At times even this restrained old gentleman, who prided himself on his calmness while under stress and whose delightful *Diary* is full of testimonials to prove it, could display excitement.

Without revealing the primary object of Seward, Meigs, and Porter, Lincoln managed to placate Mr. Welles; but the President in turn was made to realize in this interview that he had been unwise in sanctioning Porter's expedition without consulting the Secretary of the Navy. The next day, in completing the negotiations with astute old General Scott, the President virtually revoked Lieutenant Porter's special commission by assigning the general command of the military and naval force at Fort Pickens to a cautious Army officer, Colonel Harvey Brown. Attached to the document of revocation which carried the President's endorsement, signed April 2, was the paper Meigs had written the day before: [3]

Executive Mansion, April 1, 1861.

All officers of the Army and Navy to whom this order may be exhibited, will aid by every means in their power the expedition under Colonel Harvey Brown, supplying him with men and materials and coöperating with him as he may desire.

ABRAHAM LINCOLN.

The *Powhatan*, a large steam sloop-of-war with a full rigging of sails, and paddle wheels on the sides, had arrived in New York harbor about the middle of March, and was at first scheduled by the Department to be decommissioned. A few days before Porter was given his special mission, elderly Captain Mercer and the rest of the *Powhatan's* officers had been granted leave. However, Gustavus Fox, while preparing the expedition for Fort Sumter, discovered the *Powhatan* and considering that she might be useful in his expedition persuaded Mr. Welles to reverse his orders. Thus the *Powhatan's* officers had been recalled by the Department on the very day of Porter's interview with Lincoln and peremptory orders had been issued to the commandant of the yard to rush her repairs.

When Porter arrived at the Brooklyn Navy Yard on April 2, less than twenty-four hours after getting his orders, workmen were already busy on the *Powhatan*. He entered the office of the commandant, where he found his friend and recent colleague on the inspection board, Captain Andrew Hull Foote, acting as senior officer.

Porter briefly stated his mission, and handed over his orders for Captain Foote to read. Foote read and reread them and examined the Executive Mansion stamp.[4]

"These are ticklish times, Porter," said Captain Foote. "How do I know that you are not going to run off with this ship?"

Porter explained the circumstances more fully.

Foote called for the chief clerk to bring him a telegraph blank; but Porter detained him, pointing out the specific injunction not under any circumstances to inform the Secretary of the Navy or anyone else of the expedition.

Meigs arrived, and confirmed Porter's story. Captain Mercer was taken into their confidence, and seemed only too glad to be relieved of his job as he felt that the *Powhatan* was really unfit for sea.

Foote doubled the crew at work on the *Powhatan,* saying nothing to Porter about the Navy Department's order to fit out the ship for Fort Sumter. Foote was placed in a ticklish situation. To a certain extent the orders of the President and of the Secretary coincided. Both commanded him to fit out the *Powhatan* without delay; and he resolved to carry out this provision, letting the future decide who should have the vessel.

Meanwhile, determined to keep a close watch on Porter, Foote sent to the Irving House for Porter's belongings, and ensconced him as a guest in his own house. This arrangement pleased Porter, who also wanted to watch Captain Foote, and if possible prevent his writing to the Department. Porter sat up late at night relating the gossipy news of Washington and plaguing his host with tales of desertions among their common friends.

For four days the double crew of workmen labored on the *Powhatan.* On April 4 in disobedience to the spirit of the President's injunction, Foote wrote Welles:

Captain Meigs has called on me with a letter, showing his authority from the Government to have certain preparations made and things placed on board of vessels soon to go to sea, about which you are familiar; but as the orders do not come direct, I make this report; but as no time is to be lost, I am preparing what is called for and report my action.[5]

And on the following day he hinted still more broadly to the Secretary:

I am executing orders received from the Government through the Navy officer as through the Army officer. Will write fully, if possible today, certainly tomorrow.

I hope the *Powhatan* will sail this evening.[6]

These enigmatic notices caused Gideon Welles to hurry to the White House on the morning of April 6, when the *Powhatan* was all ready to sail from New York; and this time the President was compelled to call in Mr. Seward and make a clean breast of the affair to allay the Navy Secretary's wrath.

The departure of the *Powhatan* on April 6 was as peculiar as the events that led up to it. Captain Foote was anxious to have her get under way, so as to be free to communicate fully with Secretary Welles. Consequently, he left the question of the command to be settled by Porter and Mercer, each of whom had orders—though emanating from different sources. Porter had some of Meigs's guns aboard, and since Meigs was embarking his troops on the fast Collins liner *Atlantic,* Porter was anxious to get the slower *Powhatan* to sea as quickly as possible. In spite of his haste, however, he arranged with Captain Mercer a mode of procedure designed to clear Mercer in a technical way. Captain Mercer was to assume temporary command and remain on board until they reached Staten Island, when he was to be put ashore. Then the *Powhatan* was to proceed down the bay in charge of the first lieutenant. When the ship had crossed the bar and the pilot had left, Porter was to take command.

The *Powhatan* cast off at 2:30 P.M., her side wheels revolving slowly as she had not yet a full head of steam. The extraordinary procedure cost an hour's delay at Staten Island for the boat to take Captain Mercer ashore and return. Then she proceeded down the bay according to plans. Before she had cleared the bar, however, she was overtaken by a fast steamer bringing the following message for Porter: [7]

Give up the *Powhatan* to Captain Mercer.

Seward.

Porter faced a dilemma that demanded immediate decision. To return to New York would be to annul all of Meigs's preparations as well as his own. To face Secretary Welles with nothing in the way of success to justify his connivance with Seward might well mean the extinction of Porter's professional career. Should he disregard Seward's command? Since Seward had assumed all responsibility in the first place, his telegram revoked the original order. Technically, however, Porter would be justified in disobeying, for not Seward but Lincoln had signed his sailing orders. So far as Porter knew, Seward's countermand signified nothing more than an effort to pacify Mr. Welles. In his necessarily hurried deliberation Porter might have been moved by patriotism, by recklessness, by his own egregious self-confidence, or a mixture of motives impossible to unravel or explain. The fact is that as rapidly as possible he penned the following answer: [8]

Hon. William H. Seward: I received my orders from the President and shall proceed and execute them.

D. D. Porter.

Porter wrote Foote a hurried letter of explanation, and proceeded on his mission, fully confident that once inside of Pensacola Harbor he would be able to save Fort Pickens, but beyond that he hoped to tempt the Confederates into taking the offensive, when he and Meigs would lead the assembled United States forces to a victory which would not only save Pickens but recover the lost navy yard as well.

9.
THE RELIEF OF FORT PICKENS

Fort Pickens, toward which the *Powhatan* was laboriously steaming, lay on the western extremity of Santa Rosa Island—a ribbon of sand forty miles long which undulates with the mainland and serves as a breakwater for Pensacola Harbor. Fort Pickens was a small and ill-conditioned affair but it commanded the entrance to the harbor. West of it on the mainland lay the more powerful Fort McRee, and to the north Fort Barrancas, built originally by the Spaniards, but now reconditioned and added to. The three forts formed a triangle, the legs of which varied from one and a half to two miles in length. A few miles east of Fort Barrancas were the village of Warrington and the Pensacola Navy Yard. The city of Pensacola was seven miles farther up the bay.

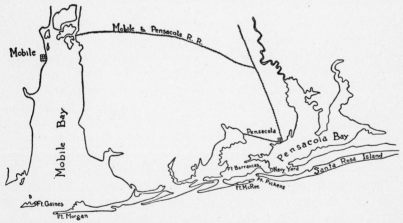

PENSACOLA AND MOBILE BAYS, SHOWING FORT PICKENS AND FORT MORGAN WHERE PORTER HELPED TO ESTABLISH THE BLOCKADE.

On the eve of Florida's Secession Fort Pickens was an unoccupied pile of brick and mortar with a few old guns on decayed platforms, rippled with drift sand. After the seizure on January

6, of the U. S. arsenal at Apalachicola, excited rumors reached Lieutenant Adam J. Slemmer at Fort Barrancas and the septuagenarian Commodore James Armstrong at the navy yard. Influenced by Confederate sympathizers on his staff, the latter made no preparation to secure the navy yard against an assault, but Slemmer with his garrison of forty men furtively began shifting ammunition from the outside magazine into the fort. While this work was in progress, Florida on January 10 passed the ordinance of Secession; and Slemmer, foreseeing the futility of resistance, floated his small garrison across the placid sky-blue harbor to Fort Pickens, avoiding the clash two days later when the navy yard and mainland forts were stormed and captured by State troops. When the victorious Floridians demanded that he surrender Fort Pickens, Slemmer refused and called on Washington for reënforcements. In response to his plea the War Department sent down eighty men under Captain Israel Vodges, but when these reënforcements arrived on the U. S. S. *Brooklyn*, Captain Adams, the senior naval officer present, would not allow them to disembark, his reason being that he had entered into an armistice with the Confederate General Braxton Bragg, who commanded the troops on the mainland. For months the relieving force under Vodges lounged on the rails of the *Brooklyn* and watched the Confederates line the opposite shore with guns captured from the navy yard. With no help from outside Slemmer could do little to strengthen his fort, and the situation remained unchanged until Porter and Meigs organized their secret expedition. However, on the very day of the *Powhatan's* sailing Secretary Welles dispatched Lieutenant John L. Worden—later captain of the *Monitor* in her classic duel with the *Merrimac*—overland to Pensacola with an order to Captain Adams commanding him to allow Vodges' men to be landed.[1]

On her way south the *Powhatan* encountered gales that reduced her speed. But Porter found time to exercise his gun crews. Porter paced restlessly from gun to gun. Finding the men slow and inefficient, he at length procured a stick of chalk and scrawled "Snail," "Turtle," "Slow Coach" on the breeches of the guns. Irked by Lieutenant Porter's sarcasms, the gunners improved in their work and Porter solemnly erased his chalk scrawls. One clear day Porter suspended his seamen over the side to paint out the gunport shutters so that the *Powhatan* might resemble a mail steamer. With this disguise Porter counted strongly on being able to run past the forts and batteries at the entrance to Pensacola

Harbor before the Confederates discovered his identity. Once inside and beyond Fort Barrancas, he had nothing to fear from the enemy and would be able to prevent any attempt on their part to land a force on Santa Rosa Island. Confederate General Bragg would then be compelled to assume the offensive and in all likelihood would wear himself out fighting Fort Pickens at long range, with the *Powhatan* and other U. S. warships countermarching inside the harbor to unsettle his range.

During the *Powhatan's* eleven-day voyage, Fort Sumter was bombarded, surrendered, and evacuated. Lieutenant Worden, traveling overland, arrived at Fort Pickens and delivered his message to Captain Adams. Vodges debarked his troops upon Santa Rosa Island on April 12. On April 16 Meigs and Brown arrived with the chartered steamer *Atlantic* and twenty-four hours later Porter came in with the *Powhatan*.

Through his glasses Porter saw the *Atlantic* some five miles below Fort Pickens on the Gulf side of the island. Meigs and Brown were unloading her, and the beach was crowded with disembarked troops. With his own decks cleared for action and his men at battle stations Porter steered directly for the gun-swept entrance of the harbor.

Meigs divined Porter's purpose and knew from their early conversation that Porter wanted a fight. He knew also that the Confederates were on edge because the armistice between Captain Adams and General Bragg had been flouted and troops landed. On the previous night while Meigs was debarking his troops, the Confederates lighted bonfires in the ditches around Fort Barrancas to celebrate the fall of Fort Sumter. Meigs, however, interpreted the Confederates' display as preparation for opening on Fort Pickens. With the Federal cannon not yet unloaded from the *Atlantic* and the *Powhatan*, Fort Pickens was not ready to withstand attack. Meigs obtained a note from Colonel Brown and steamed out in the tug *Wyandotte* to intercept Porter.

Porter disregarded Meigs's signals and veering off course several times to avoid hitting the *Wyandotte* continued to make for the channel. Finally Meigs succeeded in placing himself directly in the path of the *Powhatan*. Porter halted.

Meigs came aboard the *Powhatan* and handed Porter Colonel Brown's letter:

From the wretched condition of the defense of this place [Pickens] and the very elaborate range of batteries put up on the opposite side it is desirable that we put off the day of collision as long as possible. If Porter runs the gauntlet now a collision is inevitable, and we shall suffer the most. I, too, doubt the possibility of his escaping. I am told that Fort McRee alone mounts one hundred guns. Would it not, then, be best to stop him? I think so.[2]

Porter, still unconvinced as to the seriousness of entering the harbor, compelled Meigs to endorse Brown's views in an official letter to himself. Meigs insisted that Brown's decision had almost the authority of a verbal order from the President.

Porter hoisted the U. S. flag in the hope that the enemy would open fire, but the enemy guns remained silent. Reluctantly Porter turned the *Powhatan's* head toward the steamer *Atlantic* and anchored within twenty fathoms of the beach with hawsers to keep her guns bearing on the navy yard across the narrow Santa Rosa Island and the bay. The work of unloading the *Atlantic* went on in safety under the guns of the *Powhatan,* and Meigs's 600 soldiers were lodged in the fort with provisions sufficient to withstand siege.

The second day after the arrival of the *Powhatan,* a Confederate flotilla of about twenty-five tugs, schooners and launches filled with men steamed down the crystal blue bay and headed toward a landing on the island immediately opposite the *Powhatan's* anchorage. When it approached within range Porter cast loose an 11-inch gun on board the *Powhatan* and fired a shell. Porter's missile exploded directly over the flotilla, and the Confederates turned back to Pensacola.

Porter wanted to run the *Powhatan* into the harbor and give chase, but Brown forbade this since his guns had not yet been mounted in Fort Pickens. Chafing at the delay, Porter that night wrote a note to Brown in which he went as far as he dared in an attempt to prod the reluctant army officer into action: [3]

If you think that in two days' time you will be ready for me to make the attempt please notify me, for after that time I shall have to run the gauntlet by moonlight... I can not do much in cutting off [Confederate] boats where I now am. Will you please make any suggestion[s] as your good sense may dictate, and I will endeavor to follow them as near as I can.

He made no promise to follow Brown's conservative policy. Two days later when he saw Meigs's 600 soldiers haul the last cannon into Fort Pickens, Porter went to Captain H. A. Adams, the senior naval officer on the station, and asked permission to blockade the harbor. Porter wanted to capture the many coastwise vessels that were running in supplies for General Bragg. Captain Adams objected to establishing a blockade in advance of orders from the Department. Porter offered to assume the responsibility, but still Adams refused. He did, however, allow Porter to police the entrance and turn back all save foreign vessels; but he would not consent to his seizing them as prizes of war.

On April 28 a Confederate spy came off to Santa Rosa Island. After he had examined the Federal batteries being erected opposite the navy yard, he was accosted and taken before Colonel Brown. He claimed to be a Union man, and professed a desire not to be returned to the mainland. Brown sent him to the *Powhatan* where all his movements were watched. When he discarded some bits of paper in the spit-box, Porter had them collected and pasted together. They read: [4]

J. C. Morris, Esq.

Dear Sir: I wrote you from Atlanta. Was my note received and attended to? Please telegraph my friends that I spent a couple of days at Pensacola previous to my departure for Texas. I want to see a besieged fortress once in a lifetime. Everything goes on finely here. Hope to hear of surrender of Fort Sumter today; next Pickens, and then Washington.

Very truly, Joe.

Porter sent the note to Colonel Brown. Two days later a constable from Pensacola came over under a white flag, and presented a warrant for the spy's arrest for theft. Brown let him go!

The behavior of his two senior officers irked Porter into a sardonic humor. "I have no great opinion of flag officers generally," growled Porter in a letter to his friend Gustavus Fox, "especially after they have arrived at the age of one hundred years. It is time then for the government to take care of them and [not to] let them go abroad where they eat Uncle Sam's rations without any adequate return . . . and I tell you that if the U. S. is going to employ worn out men without brains, merely because they hold a certain position, why then they will get rich of it . . . !" [5]

Today the record of Captain Adams's fumbling evokes sympathy. He was an elderly man lacking the stamina and energy necessary to handle the complicated situation that had now developed around him. For three months the Confederates had deprived him of his usual supply of fresh beef and vegetables from the mainland. In Mobile the mob had hanged a man he had sent to purchase foodstuffs, though he had the written permission of the Confederate Governor and the military commandant to do so. The crews of his own vessel and the others that had now drifted into the sphere of his direction were rapidly coming down with scurvy. The chaotic situation in Washington had made it impossible for him to secure help from that quarter. At one time his ship's funds had run out, and he had had to use his own money to pay the Government's bills. The enlistments of seventy of the *Sabine's* crew had expired, and the senior captain did not know what to do, being short of men already. When he heard of the secession of Virginia and the loss of the Gosport Navy Yard at Norfolk, with the defection of so many of his one-time friends, he wrote his old shipmate, Captain Samuel F. Du Pont, "We are fallen upon fearful times, and I have had my share of troubles and perplexity." 6 He wished himself in his grave.

The Confederates having now shut off the overland mails, orders for the squadron came slowly around the long distance by sea. It was not until May 12, twenty-five days after Lincoln proclaimed the blockade, that the order to blockade Pensacola arrived.

On this day Captain Adams wrote General Bragg to inform him officially of the blockade of Pensacola Harbor; whereupon with mock seriousness Bragg replied that he considered the blockade an act of aggressive war and that Captain Adams would please consider the harbor closed against all boats and vessels of the United States! More seriously General Bragg also interpreted Lincoln's blockade proclamation as a virtual acknowledgment of the national existence and independence of the Confederate States.

Nor were the Southerners alone in this view of the matter. Foreign nations who wished to continue their trade accepted it, and textile workers in England and France held demonstrations and attempted to secure national recognition for the Cotton States. For months Mr. Charles Francis Adams, the U. S. ambassador in London, found himself in a very uncomfortable and disagreeable position. Instead of proclaiming a formal blockade which conceded belligerent rights to the South, Lincoln should merely have closed the Southern ports to trade. Such procedure would have given the Confederates the technical status of insurrectionists. But so loud and persistent were the cries of "rebels," "traitors" in the North that what the rest of the world might say seems to have been overlooked.

So far as the war was concerned, however,—and this was the angle which alone interested Porter—the establishment of the blockade was a step in the right direction. At last the period of uncertainty was at an end. Shots had been fired, the war had begun, one knew exactly where one stood. Of course, the prolonged period of chaos in Washington had resulted in the serious losses of Fort Sumter and the navy yards at Norfolk, Charleston, and Pensacola. These losses would have to be charged to experience and recovered as soon as possible now that the decks had been cleared for action.

About the middle of May, while Porter was blockading off the harbor, he received a signal from Colonel Brown to come to Fort Pickens for a conference. Landing on the island, Porter noticed that the Confederates had pulled the dry dock out of the basin at the navy yard and maneuvered it into position athwart the harbor channel near Fort Pickens. There were a number of men on the huge structure and four heavy anchors were hanging from its ends. When Porter reached the fort, he found that Captain Adams and Colonel Brown had written to ask General Bragg's intentions and he had been told that the dock had "unaccountably" got adrift and that Bragg would soon return it to its place. Four hours later the dry dock sank inconveniently in the middle of the channel.

Early on the morning of May 25, Captain William W. McKean arrived off Fort Pickens in the *Niagara* to supersede Captain Adams. Captain McKean, a younger and more energetic man, taking in the situation at a glance, decided that Colonel Brown did not need all the ships in the Gulf to protect Fort Pickens, and at once dispatched the *Brooklyn* and the *Powhatan* to the mouths of the Mississippi to establish the blockade. He, in the *Niagara*, was to station himself off Mobile. Colonel Brown sought to prevent McKean from removing the fleet by once more producing the Meigs-composed letter from the President; but McKean's orders were of a later date and the wrinkled epistle failed to alter McKean's decision.

Porter was off in the *Powhatan*, relieved to get away. He wrote later, "There is a fascination about Pensacola Bar that kept the commanding officers there day after day gazing at the harbor, and fancying, perhaps, that they were acquiring experience in the art of war... Months passed away. Bragg built his fortifications and never molested Fort Pickens. Colonel Brown piled up sand bags and never troubled Bragg. Neither of them committed an 'overt act.' A more innocent war was never carried on."[7]

THE BLOCKADE BEGINS

Stung by the loss of Fort Sumter, President Lincoln plunged the Federal Navy into its most ambitious undertaking of the entire war—the blockade of the seceded states from South Carolina through Texas. By isolating the rebellious states, stopping their coastwise traffic, and severing communication with the world outside, the Federal President hoped not only to check the militant spirit of the Deep South but to prevent Virginia, North Carolina, and inland border States from leaving the Union. Within a week, however, South Carolina's victory at Fort Sumter had won not only a feeble island fortress but the Old Dominion and North Carolina as well. Whereupon Lincoln issued a supplementary proclamation to include Virginia and North Carolina in the blockade.

But the Federal Navy at this time was far too insignificant to maintain an effective blockade along the 3,549 miles of Confederate coast line which included 189 harbors and river mouths. At best the blockade could now be effective at only a few points. Months and years would be required to purchase and convert merchant vessels, yachts, tugs, ferryboats and to build wooden gunboats, experimental ironclad monitors, torpedo boats, and armor-belted battleships in sufficient numbers to accomplish the giant mission. Many Confederate forts, including a number not yet in existence, would have to be taken. Only Great Britain in the wars against Napoleon had ever undertaken so mighty a task as this blockade which Lincoln assigned to the diminutive Yankee Navy.

When Porter on his way to the delta paused off Mobile to notify the Confederate garrisons of the blockade, Fort Morgan answered by hoisting the Stars and Stripes union down, while about it they ran up a Confederate States flag of large dimensions. Porter resisted the impulse to reply to this insult with his broadsides and went about his business of turning away inbound merchantmen who had not yet learned that war was on. When Captain McKean appeared in the *Niagara*, Porter steamed on toward his own station off the Mississippi delta.[1]

Overhauling the schooner *Mary Clinton* of New Orleans, Porter sent two of his lieutenants on board to warn her of the blockade; and, when the latter discovered from the endorsement on her register that she had been previously warned, Porter seized her as prize and took her in tow. Porter and his officers drank a toast to their good luck and crowded on all possible steam. In a few hours they passed the *Brooklyn* at Pass à l'Outre. Porter saw the masts of many vessels stranded on the bar beyond the *Brooklyn*.

The next morning Porter sent his prize to New York, anchored the *Powhatan* athwart the South West Pass with broadside bearing upstream and notified Confederate authorities at Pilot Town of the blockade and the fifteen-day period of grace during which vessels of foreign register might pass through on their way home.

The Confederates inquired whether Porter would permit their tugs to draw outbound neutrals over the bar, as Captain Poor was doing at Pass à l'Outre. Porter agreed not to molest the tugs provided they would also give assistance to Federal ships. Some of the tug boats, Porter learned, after hauling northern vessels across the bar, had then captured and tugged them back to New Orleans as prizes!

Tow vessels were at such a premium and so mad was the scramble to get to sea before the expiration of the time limit that many neutrals attempted to navigate the lower bar without assistance and invariably went aground. Other ships trying to pass around them also stuck. Within 300 yards of the *Powhatan* there grew up a forest of vessels with keels fast in the mud and rigging entangled.

A multitude of human problems arose. Vessels arrived with immigrants, too short of provisions to get them to the nearest neutral port. Out of their own short stores of provisions the *Powhatan* and the *Brooklyn* had to supply them with bread and beef, taking in exchange any miscellaneous stores the distressed vessels might have. On May 31, an English vessel out of New Orleans failed to heave to for inspection and a shell was fired across her bow. A Northern woman fleeing from the Southern metropolis was on board and the shock brought on premature travail. Could the vessel be permitted to put in at Mobile against the regulations of the blockade? There were many such contingencies for which the Department had not as yet issued instructions.

Peculiarly irksome was the case of vessels owned in New Orleans with American captains and American crews who carried provisional English registers obtained from the English consul in New Orleans. Porter searched them carefully to see that none were equipped as commerce raiders, even after the consul assured him the English Government would be responsible for his act. He wrote Secretary Welles: "If we allow vessels with provisional registers to depart in one instance, we must in all, though I should take the responsibility of sending north any vessel of a suspicious character... no matter what kind of papers she might have. It would no doubt be a relief to all commanding officers to be instructed on this point." [2]

From the river pilots, many of whom remembered Porter as the captain of the *Crescent City,* Porter learned that five Confederate naval vessels were fitting out at New Orleans and were nearly ready for sea. The most formidable was the steamer *Sumter,* formerly the fast packet *Habana,* with one 68-pounder and two 32-pounder guns. The *Sumter's* skipper was Commander Raphael Semmes, late of the U. S. Navy, whom Porter had known as the first lieutenant of the *Porpoise* in the mission to Santo Domingo and who had been a member of Commodore Perry's staff at Vera Cruz. "The vessels cannot get out of this pass," Porter wrote Welles, "but they can get out of two other passes where there is no vessel blockading." [3]

The *Powhatan* and *Brooklyn* inconvenienced many Confederate and foreign merchantmen but they alone could not seal the port of New Orleans. The river divides before emptying into the Gulf and resembles a huge chicken foot with four toes: Pass à l'Outre, North East Pass, South Pass, and South West Pass. Only the first and last of these were blockaded and the distance separating them by sea is thirty-five miles. The unguarded intermediate passes, though shallow, were practicable for light-draft vessels. The chicken foot was completed above the Head of the Passes by a sort of spur known as the Jump, which, too, was open to small craft. In addition to the river outlets, New Orleans had lateral waterways through Lake Ponchartrain on the east and Barataria Bay on the west, which were not so convenient as the passes of the Mississippi River, but still practicable for shallow vessels.

The *Powhatan* and the *Brooklyn* in these early weeks of the blockade had no supporting force of light drafts. One of Porter's most trying temptations was to leave his muddy anchorage to chase vessels from the secondary channels. Porter could not even consider running up the river after any of the numerous prizes that ventured down almost within his reach, for the heavy, deep-draft *Powhatan* could not cross the bar. The Confederates on the other hand could and did dash out through shallow passages and make captures of Union-owned merchantmen, many of whom re-

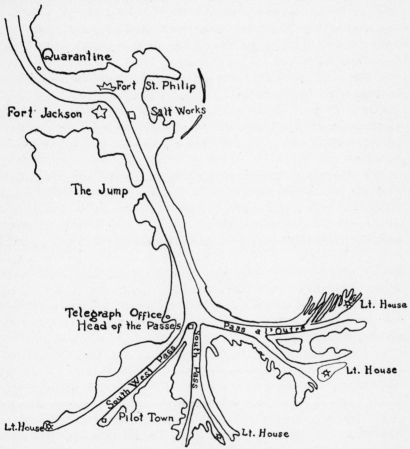

THE MISSISSIPPI DELTA, SHOWING THE PASSES AND FORTS JACKSON AND ST. PHILIP, WHICH PROTECTED NEW ORLEANS

turning from Europe were unaware of danger. Secretary Welles was daily exhorted by shipowners and presidents of insurance companies to make the blockade effective, stop commerce raiders, or at least to warn uninformed captains against running in to New Orleans.

After the fortnight during which neutrals were permitted to leave, activity at the South West pass abruptly ceased. The *Powhatan* could seldom leave her anchorage on the mud bar for fear of vessels slipping out or in. Occasionally Porter was able to speak a Union merchantman and learn of depredations by Confederate raiders from Apalachicola, Florida, or from the countless shelters of the Texas coast. In the direction of Barataria Bay, about thirty miles west of him, he could see smoke, which indicated an active commerce between New Orleans and Texas. There was nothing he could do about it, however, since peremptory orders held the *Powhatan* fast at her anchorage and lack of coal compelled obedience to these orders.

A coal ship finally arrived to break the dullness, and Porter learned that conditions on other blockading stations were much the same. When a new flag officer, Captain Mervine, assumed the direction of the Gulf Squadron, Porter wrote him about the *Powhatan's* boilers and requested him to send to Havana for certain necessary castings.

The last days of June brought mosquitoes and wet, uncomfortable weather. Across the wide, flat delta on late afternoons the air was black with insects hanging in thick layers like mist. Every day dreary entries found their way into the *Powhatan's* log: sultry weather, atmosphere charged with moisture, occasional squalls of rain, thunderstorms, heavy rain. Fogs were often so dense that Porter could not see the length of the ship, but usually they were so low that from the crow's nest he could look over the fog blankets and see across the deltas the smoke of busy blockade runners. Fog condensed in the rigging and dripped to the deck, soaking everything.

The dull monotony at South West Pass increased Porter's desire for excitement. He knew that there was unusual activity up the river at the Head of the Passes. Every day he saw the tiny Rebel gunboat *Ivy* nose downstream as far as the Confederate telegraph station at Pilot Town, peek down the pass at the *Powhatan,* and then run back upstream. Once he saw the *Sumter* come down as if to test his watchfulness.

On the night of June 27, Porter sent Lieutenant Watson Smith with thirty-five picked men up the river into Secession territory. They paddled quietly, keeping close to the dark alluvial bank. Abreast of the enemy's telegraph station at Pilot Town they landed quickly, seized the enemy operator, and cut the wires. They then hid themselves, according to Porter's instructions, and lay in wait for the *Ivy*. But the *Ivy* did not come down the next day as usual. Nor the following day. The crafty Raphael Semmes, who was awaiting an opportunity to run the *Sumter* through the blockaders' guard, had noted the telegraph's failure and become more cautious. When after three days a mail steamer came down and tied up on the opposite side of the river, Smith stowed sixteen men in the bottom of an old boat and proceeded under sail across the river. He got almost near enough to board when the Confederate vessel departed up the river under full steam. Porter's intention had been to seize the *Ivy,* put 200 men in her at once, carry the *Sumter* by boarding, proceed to New Orleans under the Secession flag, and burn the remaining Confederate vessels. "The only thing that prevented this," Porter moaned, "was the want of one more minute in time..." [4]

Sunday, June 30, marked a triumph for the Confederates. While Lieutenant Smith and his companions were returning down South West Pass, Raphael Semmes in the C. S. S. *Sumter* steamed out through Pass à l'Outre to the open sea.

Captain Poor in the *Brooklyn* had left his station to run down a sail making for a secondary pass. At 11 o'clock he sighted the *Sumter* coming out of Pass à l'Outre and gave chase, but the little black bark-rigged raider had an eight-mile start over the more cumbersome *Brooklyn*. In three and a half hours the *Brooklyn* failed to gain on the Confederate; and Captain Poor, being out of sight of his station and seeing another sail standing in that direction, gave up the pursuit.

The escape of the commerce raider *Sumter* revealed the weakness of the blockade more forcefully than letters from the commanding officers. Porter had already written that light vessels were needed to block the secondary passes. Instead of one heavy ship at each of the two major passes there should have been two vessels, one to remain on the station and another to give chase. The Department, however, did not have vessels enough to meet the needs. Instead of sending ships, Mr. Welles was compelled to send only suggestions. Why not sink prize vessels in the less frequented channels? Flag Officer Mervine now had to release some of his vessels from their blockade stations and send them in chase of the *Sumter;* and while they were away, it was obvious that other raiders—or pirates, as they were called by the Northern press— might escape.

A few ships from the Atlantic Blockading Squadron were detailed to catch the *Sumter,* and Captain McKean in the *Niagara* made a futile dash around Cuba. But the intelligent commander of the *Sumter,* like all successful commerce destroyers of the past, darted from one intersection of trade routes to another, remaining in no locality for very long.

Soon after the *Sumter's* escape a lookout from the *Powhatan's* masthead reported unusual activity at the Head of the Passes. A hulk and tents had been placed there, with men at work. Porter climbed into the tops to see for himself and wrote to Mervine advocating that the Federals themselves, unable to blockade all mouths of the Mississippi from the outside, ought to ascend the river, set up batteries, and seal the entire river at one point above the passes:

There is a field here for something to do. The steamers they have up the river could be captured by a proper combination of force, and we could very easily be in possession of the lower part of the river and cut them off from important supplies. When the hurricane months come on we will have to enter the river or go to sea, and the sooner we get in with our forces and prevent them from putting up forts at any of the Passes the sooner this war will be brought to a close. I am an old cruiser in this river, and know every inch of the ground. I assure you that an expedition up the river is an easy thing for vessels not drawing over 16 feet...I know most of the pilots, light-house keepers, etc., and this is their feeling.[5]

The more he thought about this plan, the more enthusiastic he became.

Porter wanted a proper combination of force, naval and military, to attack New Orleans. He became much exasperated because the Department in Washington delayed sending vessels of proper draft to enter the river. He told his officers that if he had six good vessels he would undertake to run by Forts Jackson and St. Philip and capture New Orleans. The Government, however, already had too many irons in the fire. A board of ranking officers meeting in Washington at this time to consider the Navy's objective declared an immediate conquest of New Orleans incompatible with the other nearer and more urgent operations.

The flurry occasioned by the *Sumter's* escape subsided for the moment, and Porter continued to mark time in nervous pacings of the *Powhatan's* quarter-deck. On July 4, Porter again reported to Flag Officer Mervine the *Powhatan's* condition:

We cannot raise a tack, scarcely a nail to repair any damages with. We have not an ounce of paint on board, nor whitewash. The ship is actually going to ruin for want of her wood being covered. It is now over a year since she had any paint put on her. We could not repair a boat for want of a plank, and our machinery having broken down, brought to my notice that there was no rope in the ship to make sheets, bowlines, halyards, etc... but feel it my duty to say that she is very rotten...I doubt if we could save her in a heavy blow, the spirketing (to the middle of which the rigging screws set up) is almost entirely decayed.[6]

Porter's list of the *Powhatan's* defects is perhaps a more accurate description of his own feelings at the time. It was written in mid-summer in a semi-tropical climate, with humid, swampy surroundings exhaling fog, with millions of flies, midges, mosquitoes, and nothing for the ship to do but wait at her anchorage and hope for some guileless merchantman to drift down within range of her broadside guns.

While in the midst of his troubles on this particularly unhappy Fourth of July, a boat flung on to the *Powhatan's* deck a sack of mail with a chipper letter from Gustavus Fox, now Assistant Secretary of the Navy. Fox was offering a prize of an advance in rank to the first naval officer who should take a fort.

Porter devoted the whole of the next day to writing Fox a 3,000-word letter. For five years Lieutenant Porter had been waiting for his overdue promotion to commander. "A man don't associate down here with alligators, sand-flies, mosquitoes and rattlesnakes for nothing, he soon gets his eye teeth, and gets wide awake—take a fort indeed! I don't think it likely that any body will take anything down here unless it is the fever or the Scurvy ...whoever sends us Ice and lemon juice shall have a Fort sent to him...Engine is broken down for a time and I can't chase or be chased—I shall be all right in a week, barring 25 holes in the boilers, a split in the steam chimney all round, caving in of the smoke stack, bursting up of condensers and a general state of decayitiveness...this blockade is the greatest farce on earth...I will let you know when I take a fort. I have my eye on one now, but I must have my Commander's Commission first, and then I will look out for the next peg...take this home and read it Sunday night when you have nothing to do..."[7]

Within the past week the Confederates had darkened the lighthouse at Pilot Town. While Porter was writing to Fox, a party of his sailors pulling upstream to get the lanterns failed to find them for the very good reason that Semmes had removed them and placed them in storage.

Reliable information had now ceased to reach Washington from New Orleans. Among the tips and rumors was a story that the Confederates were converting the propeller steamer *Enoch Train* into a sort of naval monstrosity. Above the water she would resemble the shell of a turtle, her only tophamper being her funnel. She would have but one gun, located in the bow, the porthole for this providing the only entrance from the outside. A heavy eyelid of iron would cover this port whenever the gun was not firing. Unseen beneath the waterline she would carry a metal-sheathed ram. This vessel—shortly to be rechristened the *Manassas* in honor of Stonewall Jackson's victory of July 21—was preparing to run down and stave in the Union blockaders. Mr. Welles passed on this scarcely credited intelligence to the blockaders. Before receiving this information, however, Porter had sent one of his rowboats twenty-five miles up the coast toward Barataria Bay and captured a party of Southerners who had left New Orleans to avoid being drafted into the Confederate Army. Professing to be tired of the war, they talked freely. The blockade, they said, had put a stop for the present to fitting out privateers. Porter wrote the Department, "There is no danger to be apprehended from the boat with the iron horn. She will likely never be finished..."[8] The subsequent career of this naval monstrosity, however, was to invalidate the testimony of Porter's Confederate draft-evaders.

On August 6 Porter again implored Mervine to hurry the castings for his patched and repatched boilers. Happily the materials arrived from Havana during the following week and repairs were made.

Early on the 13th Porter's lookouts described a sail standing toward Barataria Bay. Porter gave chase and captured the Confederate prize schooner *Abby Bradford* of New York. The C. S. S. *Sumter* had captured her on July 25. Commander Semmes of the *Sumter* had attempted to take his prize into Puerto Cabello, but the governor of that place had denied his plea, and on the 27th Semmes had placed a prize crew aboard her with orders to proceed to New Orleans. Her prize master had been intrusted with Semmes's first dispatch to the Confederate Secretary of the Navy since his escape from the Mississippi, as well as other correspondence giving a detailed account of the *Sumter's* movements.[9]

Porter hastily examined these revealing documents. On the morning of July 3, Semmes had doubled Cape San Antonio, the western extremity of Cuba, and on the same day had captured off

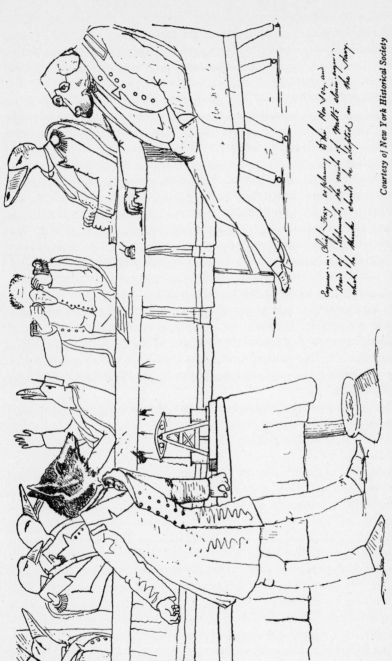

Courtesy of New York Historical Society

THIS BURLESQUE SKETCH, TYPICAL OF THE CARTOONS WHICH PORTER SENT TO INTIMATE FRIENDS, REVEALS PORTER'S ATTITUDE EARLY IN THE WAR TOWARD HIS SUPERIOR OFFICERS.

the Isle of Pines the *Golden Rocket* of Bangor, Maine. He burned her. The next day he captured the sugar-laden brigantines *Cuba* and *Machias,* also of Maine, and sent them to Cienfuegos. On July 5 he captured the brigs *Ben Dunning* and *Albert Adams,* owned in New York and Massachusetts. The next day the barks *West Wind* and *Louisa Kilham* and the brig *Naiad* of New York, Rhode Island, and Massachusetts, respectively. These, also laden with sugar, were sent to Cienfuegos for adjudication. Semmes himself ran into Cienfuegos on the 6th, appointed an agent, took on coal, and was off. On the 17th at Curaçao he coaled again. On the morning of the 25th he captured the *Abby Bradford* off La Guayra and dispatched her two days later from Puerto Cabello.

Porter induced one of the men in the *Abby Bradford's* crew to turn state's evidence and gathered from the man's story that the *Sumter* was now lying outside the harbor of Puerto Cabello, in a disorganized state, short of coal and money and without credit.

In his excitement three pictures flashed before his imagination. First: an old bulging, paintless, side-wheeler, with her bilges half stuck in the mud, and her broadside guns pointing up a brown, drift-littered river. The second picture: a trim black vessel, bark-rigged, propeller-driven, newly outfitted and freshly painted, lying at anchor off a picturesque West Indian harbor. The third picture: the bulging side-wheeler overhauling and capturing the slender black vessel.

Porter did not return the *Powhatan* to her anchorage. He raised a heavy smoke and steered east northeast.

11.

STALKING RAPHAEL SEMMES

STEAMING eastward to the flagship off Pensacola, Porter laid his plans before the elderly Flag Officer Mervine, who despite the weakening of his blockading force sent Porter off at once on the even more urgent mission to capture the commerce raider *Sumter*.

The *Powhatan*, encountering stormy weather, arrived off Cape San Antonio on the 17th. Many sails dotted this busy traffic intersection at the western tip of Cuba. Porter spoke five vessels and learned that another prize, the *Joseph Maxwell* of New York, had been sent to Cienfuegos to join the seven already there but that the authorities would not allow her to remain; that Semmes's crew had put to sea in her and returned the next day in an open boat, reporting her foundered.[1]

Finally at Cienfuegos Porter learned from the U. S. consul a truer and sadder version of the *Maxwell's* story. The ship had merely been abandoned by Semmes's prize crew and a passing merchantman had towed her back into port and released her to the consul, who by now had obtained possession of Semmes's other prizes. The Spanish authorities, however, alleging that an old Spanish law required abandoned vessels to be held by their government, had peremptorily demanded that the *Joseph Maxwell* be turned over to them, and the American consul had yielded! [2]

Enraged at the actions of the Spanish officials, but restrained by a vivid memory of what had happened to his father at Fajardo, Porter took a disgruntled leave of Cienfuegos and again pointed the *Powhatan's* prow to the southward.

At Kingston, Jamaica, where he put in on August 21 to get coal, he was made to feel like an unwelcome guest. The British authorities were indisposed to sell him coal, and private merchants increased their already exorbitant prices. Captain John Pope of the U. S. S. *Richmond* was coaling in the harbor when Porter arrived, and the presence of two Federal men-of-war using their docks at the same time was indeed disconcerting to the Jamaican officials. Months earlier England had announced a policy of neutrality, but her need for raw cotton inclined her to be more friendly toward the Confederacy than she was toward the Northern States.

Porter procured coal from his indifferent host, but gained little useful information about the *Sumter*. An old newspaper from Trinidad stated that the *Sumter* had entered that port on July 30, taken coal, and departed on August 5. This intelligence, however, was sixteen days old. According to Porter's interpretation of the news story, the "Rebel pirate" had been welcomed by Her Britannic Majesty's officials, and supplied with the necessary coal to continue his maraudings against loyal citizens of the United States.

Again Porter put to sea on a southerly course, hoping against hope that the *Sumter* might be zig-zagging back from Trinidad towards Cienfuegos to collect money for the prizes sent into the latter port. He sailed four days, saw nothing, heard nothing.

On August 29, Porter ran the *Powhatan* into the little Dutch harbor of Curaçao, landlocked by jagged mountain peaks overhung by fleecy clouds. Bumboats with hucksters of all nationalities swarmed around as the *Powhatan* dropped anchor.

Porter hurried ashore to the American consulate, where he learned that the governor of Curaçao had at first refused entry to the *Sumter,* but that Semmes had got in by pretending that his ship was in distress. The *Sumter's* foretopmast had been slightly sprung. Once inside, the cunning raider had ingratiated himself with the governor, procured coal and provisions, repaired his boilers, fitted a new topmast, and painted his ship. A deserter from the *Sumter* had spread vivid tales of Semmes's depredations, which irked the American consul at Curaçao.

Porter called on his Excellency, Governor J. D. Crol, who professed a neutral attitude, and justified his kindness to Semmes on the score that the *Sumter* was a man-of-war in distress.

Porter explained that the *Sumter* was a pirate, that there was no "Confederate States of America" and that if the governor allowed another such vessel to coal it would be an unfriendly act toward the United States.

Porter set his mechanics to work patching the *Powhatan's* boilers, sent divers down to inspect her hull, and while this work was in progress wrote letters of protest to the governor. The divers reported that most of the *Powhatan's* false keel had carried away, that some 500 of her copper plates were missing, others loose, and that there were barnacles everywhere below the waterline, and opening seams above.

Important news was now discovered in a recent number of the *Price Current* of Trinidad. The *Sumter,* reported as sailing westward, had been sighted off the tiny island of Margarita on August 5. Semmes evidently was doubling back toward Cienfuegos. At least he was still in the Caribbean. This news was three weeks old!

Porter made a quick dash to St. Thomas in the Virgin Islands, hoping in this busy little Danish outpost on the intersection of Caribbean traffic lanes to pick up fresher clues.

Three days earlier, he was told, the *Sumter* had been sighted in the Surinam River (Dutch Guiana) apparently short of coal, since a freighter that Semmes had sent for fuel had been seized by the British authorities.

Once more the *Powhatan* dashed ahead, this time but three days behind her prey. To Porter's ears the heavy sobbing of her engines and the pounding of her side wheels were as exhilarating as the baying of a hound.

On the way to the Guianas Porter showed his colors off Frederiksted and looked into Martinique. At noon on the 10th he entered the harbor of Bridgetown, Isle of Barbados, saluted the British flag, but kept steam up and did not anchor. The U. S. consul, Mr. Trowbridge, came aboard to tell Porter that the *Sumter* had left Surinam on August 21, with her funnel lowered, and was last seen standing under sail toward the west. Mr. Trowbridge had this information direct from the consul at Surinam.

To make certain that the *Sumter* had actually sailed westward, Porter veered slightly to the west and spoke the lightship off Demerara. As he suspected, Semmes's movement had been only a ruse. The *Sumter* had not been sighted off British Guiana. After proceeding westward until he had lost sight of land, Semmes had doubled back toward the Atlantic. Porter ran eastward to Surinam.

The U. S. consul at the "little codfish and cheese village" of Surinam was a Mr. Sawyer of Connecticut. Mr. Sawyer's mulatto wife owned slaves, but this in no way affected his allegiance to the Union. Sawyer had not only protested to the governor against allowing the *Sumter* to coal, he had openly bribed the lighters. But Semmes had overmatched the consul's arguments, found other boats, and taken on enough coal to run all the way to Rio. Further verification was obtained from pilots at Surinam who described how the *Sumter* had lowered her smokestack and sailed in a westerly direction. In the town Semmes had spread rumors that he was going to Jamaica and would return in three weeks. He had not sailed as far west as Demerara. Porter rightly guessed that his quarry had gone east toward Cape St. Roque and perhaps down the coast of Brazil.

On then to Maranham, Brazil. From the fragments of information in hand Porter calculated that the *Powhatan,* falling to pieces as she was, could make fifty more miles per day than the *Sumter.* All night the *Powhatan's* broad paddle wheels dipped and swished in endless rhythm. On September 14, the day after he left Surinam, the equatorial sea was as smooth as glass. Steady vibrations eddied through the ship, as the *Powhatan* gained mileage upon her prey. Suddenly there arose a tremendous hissing noise, and the side wheels dragged to a slower rhythm. White clouds burst through the hatches from the bowels of the ship. Porter hurried below. One of the boilers that he had patched and re-patched had broken. He examined the rupture hurriedly. Nothing could be done about it now. Though her steam was cut to five pounds pressure, she could still make eight knots on the smooth sea. Porter gave orders to hold her on her course.

But for the mishap to his boiler Porter would probably have caught the *Sumter* off the harbor of Maranham. Semmes had gone out just five days earlier. He had hovered around for two of these days hoping to capture the New York brig *Maria,* whose arrival was daily expected.

The American consul in Maranham, the first Brazilian port under the equator, could attribute his failure to have Semmes excluded to the fact that the sympathies of Brazil, the largest slave-owning country outside of the Confederacy, swung naturally toward the South. For nine days Semmes had outmaneuvered him. A lively pro-Secessionist party in Maranham had entertained Commander Semmes, C. S. Navy, and allowed him to make Secessionist speeches.

Porter gave orders for adjusting more patches upon the *Powhatan's* boilers, and in place of the usual courtesy call sent the governor of Maranham a protest of some 2,000 words. In this interesting document he painted a full length portrait of Raphael Semmes as the Federals saw him. The "pirate" had captured and wantonly destroyed vessels and goods owned partly by neutral foreigners. He would burn property of Brazilian ownership if he got the chance. He had compelled neutrals against their will to furnish him stores and coal. Inhuman toward his captives, he held them for the express purpose of stringing them up to the yardarm in case the United States should so treat captured pirates. In bold contrast to the picture of Mr. Semmes the document quite unnecessarily praised the governors of Cienfuegos, Curaçao, and Surinam.[3]

After a week of repairing and coaling Porter again sailed after the *Sumter*. One item of information gave him hope. On entering Maranham, Semmes had been unable to get a pilot and had grounded upon a hidden ridge of sand, knocked off the false keel and sprung a leak. Porter hoped that the concussion might have jarred Semmes's engines out of line. At least this injury would cut down his speed under sail. From the Maranham pilot who had guided the *Sumter* out to sea, Porter learned that she had taken a northeasterly course.

Plowing due north Porter saw nothing of his prey. When he reached the much frequented traffic lanes in the latitude of St. Thomas, he shuttled the *Powhatan* back and forth for a week in a final effort to catch the *Sumter*. His thoughts ran more and more on conditions at home. His impatience increased daily. Not since he had left Jamaica had he spoken an American warship. At last he abandoned his fruitless marching and countermarching and stood westward for St. Thomas.

In St. Thomas on October 10, Porter learned that the merchantman *Spartan* had been boarded on the 5th by the *Sumter* in latitude 9° north, longitude 47° 25″ west. Excitedly Porter leafed back through the *Powhatan's* log. On October 5 the *Powhatan* had been countermarching but seventy-five miles distant from the object of her chase!

Captain Charles Wilkes and Commander James S. Palmer, who were also at St. Thomas with the U. S. S. *San Jacinto* and the U. S. S. *Iroquois*, had both made flying pursuits of the *Sumter*. From these officers Porter learned that the elderly Captain Mervine had been ordered north and that Captain McKean was now flag officer of the Gulf Blockading Squadron. He heard rumors, too, that there had been a little light fighting at Fort Pickens!

Porter rushed on to Pensacola hungry for news after his protracted and futile chase. When he arrived, the officers on the station greeted him as commander. Flag Officer McKean had received Porter's new commission several weeks ago, but McKean was now off the Mississippi delta.

In his excitement Porter could hardly refrain from blowing the

Powhatan's rusty whistle. The breezy letter he had written to Fox had brought him his long deferred promotion to commander.

There was other news more exciting. In addition to the recent fighting at Fort Pickens there had been an engagement up the Mississippi at the Head of the Passes. A Confederate ironclad ram had damaged the U. S. S. *Richmond.* The U. S. S. *Vincennes* had thrown her guns overboard. The officers off Pensacola were full of animated conjectures but knew nothing aside from the important general fact that fighting had started at the mouth of the Mississippi.

The world Porter had dropped back into was in many ways the same as when he had left it, and yet it was not the same. Federal war vessels had ascended to the Head of the Passes—and had been forced to retreat by a Confederate ironclad ram! Was this the "turtle-backed monstrosity" of which Porter had heard while off South West Pass? It was possible.

Porter sat down to his desk and shut himself off from the Fort Pickens world of uncertainty. He wrote McKean a comprehensive statement of the *Powhatan's* condition and requested to be sent north to repair. Since August 14, when he had left the delta, the *Powhatan* had run more than 10,000 miles. She was rotten throughout. Only the barnacles frozen to her bottom kept the oakum from washing out. Her planks would not bear caulking. One could run a knife through her seams. The *Powhatan* could not, in his judgment, ride out the forthcoming winter storms in her present condition. Greatly pleased with the *Powhatan's* accomplishment, however, Porter concluded, "but for her condition ... there would be no more efficient ship afloat." [4]

This report was written and signed at Pensacola. But Porter determined to deliver it to the flag officer in person.

McKean gave Porter his commission and cordially gripped his hand. He admired Porter's energy, and had written this to the Secretary with a request that Porter and the *Powhatan* be returned to his squadron. But when he saw the *Powhatan* and heard Porter describe her, he agreed that for the safety of those on board she should be sent to New York at once.

Before setting out Porter gathered the following facts about the occurrence at the Head of the Passes. Several efforts had been made to erect land batteries and thus blockade the river at one point on the inside rather than at many entrances on the outside. The Confederate gunboat *Ivy*—the same that Lieutenant Watson Smith had attempted to ensnare—had each time come down the river and prevented the Federals from landing guns. Before daybreak on October 12 the Confederate ram *Manassas,* with several gunboats, had rushed down upon the Federal vessels, the *Richmond,* the *Vincennes,* the *Preble,* and completely surprised them. The *Richmond,* loading coal at the time, was dealt a glancing blow that ripped off several planks. The Federals retreated down South West Pass firing as they fled. In their haste the *Richmond* and the *Vincennes* had grounded on the bar.

The signal "retire from action" was flying from the *Richmond* and Commander Handy of the *Vincennes* had misinterpreted it to mean "abandon ship." This last he proceeded to do. He heaved all but four of his guns over the side, sent his men off in boats, and himself lighted a fuse to the magazine. The Confederates now retired up the river having captured one of the Federal supply vessels, and Commander Handy and his crew fidgeted on the decks of the *Richmond* and the *Preble* waiting for the *Vincennes* to be blown to atoms. But the *Vincennes* did not explode. An old quartermaster — believing that the commander might shortly change his mind—had snipped off the burning end of the fuse as he followed his superior over the side.

From the Head of the Passes came a note of derision. "Perhaps the most brilliant and remarkable exploit on record!" proclaimed the *Daily True Delta* of New Orleans.[5]

When Porter arrived in New York on November 9, he had forgotten Raphael Semmes and the *Sumter.* His thoughts were absorbed in the more significant problem of New Orleans. After the occurrence at the Head of the Passes perhaps he could induce the authorities to undertake an expedition against New Orleans.

When he tied the *Powhatan* to the dock at the Brooklyn Navy Yard, Porter definitely ended the lone wolf period of his Civil War career. In April he had obtained a gambler's stake and played the role of an adventurer. His dream of recapturing Pensacola Harbor and its important navy yard had failed to materialize for the simple reason that a timid and over-cautious old man had possessed the authority to direct his moves. On the blockade of the delta, he had gathered a few prizes, small ones. Lack of resources had handicapped him, and under the conditions his opponents had known most of the moves ahead of the game. The frustrated attempt of his boarding party to capture the *Ivy,* which in turn was to have carried the *Sumter* and rushed New Orleans—that too had been a romantic pipe dream, possible perhaps in such a struggle as the War with Mexico, but not feasible against such opponents as the Confederates. The idea of rushing New Orleans, however, was a good one, if attempted in a modern and scientific manner with a sufficient naval force. In the chase of the *Sumter* Porter had almost won. Here the margin of failure had been tantalizingly small. He had enjoyed the chase as it could remind him of the exploits of his famous father Commodore David Porter of 1812. But steam had come in since his father's day, and the glamorous tactics of the past, which depended so largely on individual courage, were not so fruitful in a mechanized age.

In tackling the problem of New Orleans Porter was firmly determined not to rely too heavily on fortune. As a lone wolf off the delta he had envisioned the coördinated effort of a large naval force in attacking New Orleans. The pursuit of the *Sumter* had given him time to orient himself and make plans. The recent ridiculous episode at the Head of the Passes clearly demonstrated the necessity for the campaign he hoped to wage.

NEW ORLEANS MUST BE TAKEN!

Porter's train chugged into Washington on November 12 just two hours after the arrival of the first great naval news of the war. Working through the crowd, he bought a paper, and as he rode to his home on Gay Street in Georgetown he read headlines about the victory of Flag Officer Du Pont's squadron over the Secession forts guarding Port Royal, S. C. Located between Charleston and Savannah, Port Royal would afford the Atlantic Blockading Squadron an excellent base for operations. More than that, by giving the Navy Department a taste of victory it would, Porter hoped, prepare the way for the acceptance of his New Orleans plans.[1]

Porter stopped an hour at his home to greet his wife and four of his children whom he had not seen for seven months. Carlisle was away at the Naval Academy, which upon the threatened secession of Maryland had now been removed to Newport, Rhode Island. Tod was an inch taller than he had been seven months ago. Mrs. Porter was in good health. He had difficulty convincing his wife that he had not had time to write her more than a single letter during his entire absence. Essex, who returned with his father, found a captain's commission in the Army of Virginia awaiting him.

Porter hastened across town to the Navy Department. The tulip poplar trees surrounding the unpretentious, three-story brick building to the west of the White House grounds were shedding their yellow leaves as he stepped briskly up the walk way.

As he entered the Navy Department building for the first time since the outbreak of the war, Porter no doubt experienced a twinge of conscience for having diverted the *Powhatan* without the knowledge of Secretary Welles. It is true that his friend Gustavus Fox, the Assistant Secretary, had obtained for him his commission as commander; but how Mr. Welles might receive him and how the Secretary might respond to the proposal for attacking New Orleans were matters about which Porter could only conjecture.

In his *Incidents and Anecdotes* of the Civil War Porter depicts his own feelings at this crucial moment:

Assistant Secretary Fox was not communicative; Faxon eyed me askance; Wise was jocose, but knew nothing; old Commodore Joe Smith said, 'Well, you didn't run away after all!' etc.; and I wandered about like a cat in a strange garret . . .[2]

In the anteroom to the Secretary's office he fell into conversation with two Republican Senators of the Naval Affairs Committee, Mr. Hale of New Hampshire and Mr. Grimes of Iowa. Porter told them his plans for the capture of New Orleans, and they insisted on accompanying him and reënforcing his appeal to the Secretary.

Mr. Welles, his gray eyes lighted by an excitement he could not conceal, received the Senators' congratulations over the Navy's victory at Port Royal. When Senator Grimes introduced the short, hard-muscled, black-bearded naval officer, the Secretary greeted him genially and to Porter's relief seemed to have forgotten the matter of the *Powhatan*. Mr. Welles's chief foible—the one which retarded his actions as executive of a war machine—was his habit of sifting and eliminating from his thoughts as a public official all the prejudices he had as a man. And this peculiarity was now a point in Porter's favor. Porter related in detail the situation at the mouth of the Mississippi. So numerous were the delta passes and the secondary entrances through Barataria Bay and Lake Pontchartrain that it was virtually impossible for the Federals to blockade New Orleans from the outside. The simplest and best way to blockade New Orleans was to capture and occupy it. Porter offered a plan which included one of his original ideas. He believed that wooden ships could rush by the enemy's casemated forts and capture the city if they were preceded by a smothering forty-eight-hour bombardment of 13-inch mortar shells. Mortar fire had long been the Army's chief weapon for bombardment. Porter's proposal was to mount mortars on dismantled schooners and thus eliminate the necessity for military operations ashore. After the city had been captured the isolated forts would be compelled to surrender. A few thousand soldiers to garrison the forts and occupy the city would be all that the Navy would have to ask of the War Department to carry out its mission. Mr. Welles was favorably impressed. He said the Department had for a long time been considering an attack on New Orleans. After the Senators departed, the Secretary called in Mr. Fox and suggested that the three of them go to the White House and talk the matter over with the President.

Six months earlier Porter had entered the White House in the company of the Secretary of State. He now entered Lincoln's study with the Secretary of the Navy. The thoughts of Welles and Porter were no doubt interesting and tinged with irony.

Lincoln was calm and thoughtful, and he was pacing the floor. He listened with keen interest to Porter's résumé of the situation at the mouth of the Mississippi and his proposal for capturing New Orleans. The gaunt President from the backwoods of Illinois, who had once made the journey by flatboat down the river to New Orleans, was also favorably impressed. Porter told the ludicrous story of the fight at the Head of the Passes, and Lincoln reciprocated with a rustic anecdote that augured well for Porter's plan. At length the President arranged for a conference that evening with General McClellan, who had recently superseded the aged General Scott.

Welles had Porter and Fox come to his house about an hour before the meeting at McClellan's for further discussions, after which the three proceeded to the General's residence at the corner of 14th and H Streets. They arrived just as the President drove up in his low-swung carriage.

McClellan, cautious after the reverses suffered by the armies in Virginia, believed that wooden ships would never get past Forts Jackson and St. Philip. They could run by Fort St. Philip, perhaps, as Du Pont had run by the simple parapet and earthwork fortifications at Port Royal. But they could not pass Fort Jackson which, with its tier of heavy coast-defense guns in casemate, was one of the strongest military defenses in the country. Any number of ships attempting to pass it, McClellan believed, would be smashed like so many eggshells. These forts would first have to be besieged and captured by the Army and such an operation would require at least 50,000 troops, too large a number to be spared from the Virginia front.

But the enthusiasm of the naval men over Porter's novel idea of bombardment by mortar fire from schooners finally convinced McClellan that even if the forts were not reduced their gun crews would be demoralized and driven to shelter long enough for the fleet to run by. Since Welles assured him that 10,000 men in addition to the 2,500 which General Butler was now raising in Massachusetts to be sent into the Gulf Department would be sufficient, McClellan agreed that they ought to try the plan.

Lincoln approved the plan, and because there were still many Southern spies in the Federal capital it was decided to keep the object of the campaign a close secret. Mobile, Pensacola, or some port in Texas might be talked of as the destination. Even Charleston and Savannah might be mentioned. New Orleans must not be mentioned.[3]

The decision to launch a naval attack against New Orleans was one of the great strategic decisions of the war, but it was curiously shortsighted. No adequate plan was devised for following up a possible victory. In the case of Port Royal—where the harbor itself was the ultimate prize—no special provision for subsequent operations was necessary. Not so New Orleans. The great Southern metropolis was at once the gateway to the Mississippi and the keystone to the arch of Confederate ports around the Gulf. In the event of success the Federal armed forces should have been equipped with a well prepared, well coördinated plan for further operations to be undertaken immediately before the enemy recovered from his shock at the loss of New Orleans. The Federal high command at this time, however, had available neither ships of suitable draft nor sufficient numbers of soldiers to enable it to plan anything beyond New Orleans. For their shortness of vision they would pay dearly. The pity is that the historian must deplore their mistake even while praising their courage.

Meanwhile for Porter the decision to attack New Orleans brought great personal satisfaction. Instead of being disciplined by the Department, he had seen his plans adopted. A few days later Fox informed him unofficially of the Department's decision to place him in command of a flotilla of mortar boats to effect the bombardment while a fleet of fourteen or fifteen of the best steam vessels in the Navy was to attempt the passage of the forts.

Porter set to work at once to create the Mortar Flotilla. The mortars had to be built by foundries in Pittsburgh. Schooners had to be purchased and carriages for the mortars built and installed. A fleet of half a dozen light draft steamers for towing the mortar schooners up the river had to be assembled. The task would require months of preparation.

While men in the street rejoiced over Du Pont's victory at Port Royal, Secretary Welles closeted himself with Assistant Secretary Fox to select the commander for the fleet which was to run by the forts after Porter's preparatory bombardment. The merits of each possible candidate were carefully weighed, for a mistake in selecting a flag officer might doom the entire venture.

To Mr. Welles, an experienced politician, the storm of applause that greeted Du Pont's victory at Port Royal clearly indicated that the Federal Government could not afford a failure in the New Orleans venture. The enlistments of the ninety-day volunteers had run out. Large new levies of men had been made. In the East General McClellan had committed himself to the tactics of a protracted war. In the West General Frémont had made a political blunder and had been superseded by the scholarly General Halleck. Already the inability of the Federals to match the early military victories of the Confederates had created dissension at home, even within Lincoln's own party. Failure of the deep-draft steamers and slow sail-driven craft to make the blockade effective was multiplying diplomatic troubles abroad. British and French sympathies were so frankly pro-Secessionist that a war with either France or England was not unlikely.

The Secretary's most cherished diversion was judging men. He would have enjoyed personally interviewing each of the older captains in the Navy. But the records revealed a dearth of candidates. Compelled finally to rely on the judgment of others, he instructed Fox to ask Porter's opinion.

Fox mentioned several names to Porter; and Porter urged the appointment of Captain David Glasgow Farragut, his own foster brother. Farragut at sixty years of age stood number thirty-seven on the active list of captains. In Porter's judgment the majority of the captains above Farragut were like the older officers at Fort Pickens and South West Pass. They had forgotten that their primary job was to fight.

With his characteristic enthusiasm Porter stated that, while he did not think Farragut a Nelson or a Collingwood, he did consider him the most competent officer of his rank.[4] Although brought up in the old school Farragut had seen more fighting than most of the older officers. He was still vigorous. He was not lacking in professional energy. Since his mind was still open to suggestion, he would not be too greatly handicapped by tradition; where many of the older officers might hesitate to accept the New Orleans task because they had not been consulted about the plan of campaign, Farragut would not cavil over such trivialities. As to his loyalty there could be no question. He was a Southerner by birth (if East Tennessee could be considered Southern), and until Virginia seceded he had lived in Norfolk; but on the very day that Virginia seceded, Farragut had crowded his family aboard a dingy coastal steamer and gone to live in New York.

Mr. Welles, in order not to commit his Department to anything that he might regret, had the Assistant Secretary direct Porter while in New York on the business of the Mortar Flotilla to pay Farragut a visit and sound him out. This Porter did without delay. A month later Welles ordered Farragut to report to the Department, where he took the further precaution of detailing Fox to invite Farragut to dinner. Finally the Secretary interviewed him, and the selection of Farragut as flag officer of the newly organized West Gulf Blockading Squadron and leader of the forthcoming New Orleans expedition was settled.

During the months of preparation Porter divided his time between the Navy Department and New York City, where he pushed the work of purchasing suitable schooners and getting them outfitted. Most of the twenty schooners were located by Commander Henry H. Bell, acting as naval purchasing agent, but Porter had the Secretary's permission to approve or reject as he saw fit. In emergencies, to expedite the work, Porter consulted in New York with Mr. George D. Morgan, who as Mr. Welles's lifelong friend had been empowered to act as the Secretary's proxy.[5]

To foundries in Pittsburgh Porter telegraphed orders for twenty giant, keg-like mortars and 30,000 13-inch shells. The iron manufacturers of Pittsburgh were now far behind in their orders, and Porter had to keep continually pushing them. His chief competitor as purchaser from the Pittsburgh concerns was his former colleague Captain Foote, lately detached from the Brooklyn Navy Yard and loaned by the Navy to the Army. Foote was rushing the construction of the ironclad gunboats needed by General Grant in his forthcoming attacks on Forts Henry and Donelson. Spurred by Porter's letters and telegrams, the Pittsburgh foundries turned out Porter's work first. Some of Foote's gunboats scheduled for completion months earlier were not completed until January 1862. By this time Porter's mortars had begun to arrive in New York. Gun carriages were already installed aboard the schooners, and Porter mounted the mortars immediately as they arrived.

In the Navy Department during January and February Porter attended to a variety of essential details: ammunition stores, food supplies, medical supplies, the transfer of seven shallow-draft steamers and converted ferryboats to the Mortar Flotilla, the transfer of officers and crews, the clerical work of assigning stations to his men. As Porter hurried from one naval bureau to

another, Secretary Welles noted his restless energy and called it
a Porter characteristic.

Fox and Porter thought alike on many subjects, especially on
the subject of mortar fire. They were both intensely interested
in giving the new project of a wholesale, smothering bombardment with mortar shells a good tryout. At Porter's house they
drank whiskey punch and criticised their superiors. But for the
technicality of rank, Gustavus Fox would have preferred Porter
to Farragut as the head of the New Orleans expedition.[6] Fox had
once been in the Navy, and irked by the slow advancement had
resigned five years before the war to enter business. He could
appreciate Porter's feelings toward such senior officers as Porter
had had at Fort Pickens.

Through Fox, Porter was detailed to examine and report on the
naval vessels under construction at Philadelphia, New York, and
Mystic, Connecticut. Porter was thus enabled to meet the blunt,
broad-chested, Swedish inventor John Ericsson, and to inspect
John Ericsson's iron-turreted *Monitor,* the famous "cheese box
on a raft" which was soon to outclass all wooden vessels and reverse the unfriendly attitudes of France and England toward the
United States.

By February 3, the last of the mortar schooners and five of
the steamers had been fitted out and dispatched to Key West.
Another delay now threatened. The *Octorara,* last and best of his
seven steamers, which Porter had picked for his flagship, broke
down and had to undergo major repairs to her boilers in New
York. Several days later when he learned that the *Octorara's*
repairs would require three weeks, Porter decided to leave without her.

On February 11 he bade his family farewell and boarded the
Harriet Lane at the Washington Navy Yard to set out for the
rendezvous of his flotilla at Key West.

The *Harriet Lane,* under Lieutenant Wainwright, was an ex-
revenue cutter taken over by the Navy from the Treasury Department. Though her side wheels gave her an air of spaciousness,
they belied the fact. Her quarters were narrow and stuffy, but
she had the redeeming virtue of speed. When Porter came aboard,
Wainwright met him at the gangway with a smile.

"I don't see how we shall be able to stow that trunk in the
cabin, Commander."

"Put it in the maintop," said Porter, "and get under way at
once." [7]

With the great unfinished dome of the National Capitol settling into the tidewater terrain behind him, Porter was at last on his way. He was one week behind Farragut.

So close were the Confederate lines drawn around Washington at this time that the *Harriet Lane* was compelled to run the gauntlet of Confederate batteries recently set up along the Potomac River. She received a shot through one of her paddle wheels, which did small injury and was speedily repaired at Hampton Roads. Captains of the wooden frigates blockading in the James River told Porter that the Confederate ironclad *Virginia* (the name Southerners gave to the rebuilt *Merrimac*) was expected to be completed within a week; Porter relayed this cheerless news to Fox and pushed the *Harriet Lane* on toward the rendezvous of the Mortar Flotilla at Key West.

The *Harriet Lane* steamed rapidly and steadily down the coast. So smoothly did she sail that her heaviest rifled guns might have been cast loose with safety. Even through the gales off Cape Hatteras her mess attendants did not have to put racks on the table.

There was a brief delay at Port Royal to deliver dispatches to Flag Officer Du Pont and take on coal and another in the exciting capture of a blockade runner off St. Augustine, Florida.

On February 28 the *Harriet Lane* shut off her racing paddle wheels and drifted into an anchorage among the mortar schooners at Key West.[8]

Porter signaled for his officers to come aboard. All twenty of the schooner captains climbed over the *Harriet Lane's* side. Dividing them into three groups under Lieutenants Watson Smith, W. W. Queen, and K. R. Breese, Porter sent them out at once to maneuver in divisions and practice firing their mortars at barrel targets.

The success of Porter's plans depended entirely on speed and scientific accuracy in carrying them through. He had planned target practice for the mortars at Key West. As soon as his steamers appeared, Porter would join Farragut at Ship Island. From Ship Island the Flotilla would quickly enter the Mississippi and strip for action at Pilot Town. From the anchorage with Farragut's ships at the Head of the Passes the experts Porter had brought would survey the treacherous channel of the river up to the forts. Then the mortar schooners would be placed by divisions at ranges scientifically determined by the Coast Survey to bombard the forts. The barrier of hulks and chains which the Confederates had thrown across the river below the forts was to be broken at the last minute. While Farragut's ships ran by the forts, the mortar schooners would double and redouble their fire; the mortar steamers led by himself in the *Harriet Lane* would move in close abreast the water battery of Fort Jackson and draw the Confederates' fire away from the passing fleet. Porter had been meticulous in the preparation for the needs of the Mortar Flotilla, and the firing practice at Key West elated him as the first step toward the accomplishment of his aim.

Thus far only one of his seven steamers had arrived, the *Owasco* under Lieutenant John Guest. Guest reported that the *Owasco* was a perfect beast in a seaway, floundering like a porpoise, rolling the green seas over her waist nettings. While waiting for the other steamers, Porter took a run in the *Owasco*, verified Guest's opinions, and reported by letter to Fox.

The captains of the mortar schooners were not all regular naval officers but men Porter had recruited from the mail steamers and given temporary commissions as acting masters. Many of them were irked by naval discipline—as the crews on the mail steamer *Georgia* had been. At the first sign of grumbling Porter clapped them in irons and put other men in their places. In a week's time he noted an improvement in discipline.

During the week of waiting only the steamer *Miami* arrived. Porter still had heard nothing concerning his three other steamers. As these latter were converted Manhattan ferryboats of doubtful seaworthiness, Porter feared they might have foundered in the storms the *Miami* had encountered along the Atlantic Coast.

However, he could delay no longer. On March 6 he ordered the sailing schooners to proceed to Ship Island and pushed on ahead with the *Harriet Lane*, the *Miami*, and the *Owasco* to pick out anchorages for the schooners and report to Farragut.

FARRAGUT AND THE BOMBARDS

SHIP ISLAND lies across the sound about thirty miles south of the little resort town of Biloxi, Mississippi. Its stretch of flat, barren sand rising but slightly above the tides of the Gulf, resembles in shape the long hull of a ship. Its "bowsprit" points toward Lake Pontchartrain and New Orleans. Mobile lies E.N.E. off its starboard quarter, and Pensacola lies directly astern somewhat farther to the east. In the early days of the war, since the railroad from New Orleans to Pensacola had not at that time been completed, the Confederates had seized Ship Island, in defiance of Flag Officer Mervine, and erected a few small batteries to protect their coastal vessels. After the Confederates burned their camp and abandoned Ship Island in the fall of 1861, the Federal blockaders moved in and established on it their most important base west of the Florida Keys.

Farragut arrived here on February 20, 1862, to relieve Flag Officer McKean in the territory from St. Andrews Bay, Florida, to the Rio Grande.

Farragut now made a show of normal routine blockading. Since he did not wish to alarm the Confederates by premature gestures toward New Orleans, he remained at Ship Island instead of moving to Isle au Breton, which was much closer to the Mississippi and just as well suited for his avowed purpose of blockading. He wanted the Confederates to believe that he might attack Mobile or Galveston. Meanwhile he dispatched orders to the blockading stations and quietly drew in the steam gunboats to locations close by. He studied the plans of Forts Jackson and St. Philip, which the War Department had supplied from its files.[1]

The two forts guarding New Orleans were placed at an elbow in the Mississippi River some eighteen miles above the Head of the Passes. Fort St. Philip, which from the eastern bank at the peak of the elbow commanded a long raking view down the river, was a simple affair like Fort Barrancas or the fortifications at Port

Royal. On the river face it had a scarp of masonry and a wet ditch. Its guns peeped over the wall and were open to the sky. Originally built by the Spaniards, it had been reënforced after 1812 when U. S. Army engineers had bombproofed its magazine and dug a shelter for the garrison. But in spite of these improvements Fort St. Philip was still essentially the same as when the Spaniards had left it. On the point across the river, however, was a modern and far more formidable structure, Fort Jackson. It was a heavy pentagon with fronts of 110 yards and bastions at each of its corners. Its walls of solid masonry arose 22 feet from the bottom of the surrounding ditch. Like St. Philip it had a tier of parapet guns looking over the walls, but unlike St. Philip, and unlike any fortification the old wooden Navy of the Federals had yet encountered, Fort Jackson had a tier of guns in casemate. The casemate, protected from above by the vaulted roof that supported the parapets, was virtually bombproof, and no amount of bombarding with the ammunition of that day could drive out the men who served the casemate guns. Farragut would have to accept a pounding from these guns as he ran the gauntlet into the upper river.

"The Department and the country require of you success," Secretary Welles had stated specifically in Farragut's orders. Farragut was determined to give them success. He was prepared to sacrifice half of his vessels if necessary. "Success is the only thing listened to in this war," he wrote, "and I know that I must sink or swim by that rule." [2]

While waiting for his forces to assemble, Farragut on March 1 sent a boat expedition to raid the post office at Biloxi, and learned from Confederate newspapers that Captain Foote and General Grant had taken Forts Henry and Donelson on the Tennessee and Cumberland Rivers. Foote was moving on down the Mississippi toward Island No. 10. The Confederates were stampeded. The time had come to move against New Orleans. Farragut feared that if he delayed some Army officer might make a blunder and the Confederate morale might swerve to the opposite extreme as after Fort Sumter and Bull Run.

Accordingly on March 7, without waiting for Porter's Mortar Flotilla, or, indeed, for his own coal, ammunition, and hospital stores, Farragut moved on to Pass à l'Outre and began the work of tugging his ships across the bar into the river. Since the destination of his expedition was now revealed to the enemy, Farragut worked as rapidly as possible. However, the delta channels, having collected silt during a twelvemonth without traffic, proved a considerable obstacle to seagoing vessels.

While Farragut was shoving his ships through the mud, the Confederate terror, *Merrimac*, slid into Hampton Roads, rammed and sank the U. S. S. *Minnesota*, burned and sank the U. S. S. *Congress*, terrified all Washington and threw it into stampede. Only the timely arrival of Ericsson's *Monitor* eight hours later stopped the *Merrimac's* maraudings and saved the day for the Union. Welles immediately sent Farragut all the information he could gather about the ironclads now building at New Orleans. Farragut would have to move up the river before these monsters were completed. Fox wrote confidentially to Porter asking whether Farragut was equal to the task ahead of him.[3]

On March 11, when Porter arrived at Ship Island with three of his steamers, the *Harriet Lane*, the *Miami*, and the *Owasco*, he received word that two of his converted ferryboats had collided in a fog and that one had sunk. Porter greatly feared that he would not have enough steamers to tow his sail-driven mortar schooners into the river. Since Farragut was now laboring to get his heavy ships across the bar, Porter did not want to have to ask him for help. While waiting anxiously for his mortar schooners which were proceeding under sail from Key West, Porter relieved his feelings by writing a burlesque description of a drunken paymaster and sending this, along with a captured Confederate love letter, to his friend Fox.[4] As soon as the schooners had arrived, Porter hurried them on to Pass à l'Outre.

On the 18th while the *Harriet Lane* and the *Owasco* were towing mortar schooners up Pass à l'Outre, two of Porter's delayed steamers arrived. Though the *Clifton* and the *Westfield* had weathered a tempestuous voyage, Porter set them immediately to work towing schooners into the river.

The Mortar Flotilla now went down South West Pass to dismantle at the abandoned and flooded village of Pilot Town. Pilot Town's dozen shanties which were built on piles proved invaluable as a storeplace for sails, spars, and other naval gear. Porter's men worked swiftly, and their eagerness to get away from Pilot Town was increased by the mosquitoes. In the early morning and late evening the men found it impossible to breathe without inhaling midges, and their faces were covered with blotches.

The correspondent for the New York *Times* found Porter's officers at Pilot Town as impatient as Porter himself. He wrote: "The mortar captains, a jolly set of fellows, may become ill...if something is not done soon. They begin to fret at the lack of opportunity for ridding themselves of the large amount of super-fluous energy with which they are imbued." [5]

While the schooners were stripping for action, Porter took his steamers on down South West Pass to the *Powhatan's* old blockade station to help tug Farragut's larger vessels across the bar. [6]

It was imperative now to get by Forts Jackson and St. Philip as soon as possible. The Confederates had been warned and must not be given too much time to prepare. Fortunately Jefferson Davis and others in high command in the Confederate camp be-lieved New Orleans to be more seriously threatened by Foote's iron gunboats from the upper river than by the wooden vessels at its mouth. Troops continued to be withdrawn from New Orleans and sent north to strengthen General Beauregard. Time, man power, and materials were used to erect batteries looking upstream above New Orleans. And many of the "old salts" in Farragut's fleet shared with the Confederates the belief that Forts Jackson and St. Philip would prove impassable to wooden ships.

The task of towing in Farragut's fleet was not an easy one. The side-wheeler *Mississippi* could not be careened and dragged through on her side as the screw steamers *Richmond* and *Pensa-cola* could. Four of Porter's steamers ran cables to her and dragged her a foot or two at a time through the mud. The *Mississippi* slashed madly with her side wheels, but the soft mud created a vacuum along her bottom retarding her progress. At last on April 4, after eleven days of labor, they dragged her through to deep water.

Although the *Pensacola* started with the *Mississippi*, she did not get through until the 7th. This was due in part to the whims of her commander. When the *Pensacola* had been towed across the worst place, her captain, Morris, waved Porter's vessels aside, although Porter insisted that the tow was necessary. Belching black smoke and with a full head of steam, the *Pensacola* barged ahead and rammed squarely into the mud and onto a sunken hulk a hundred yards from the main channel, nosing over so far that her screws were lifted clear of the water. Porter had not been so exasperated since the early days at Fort Pickens. He vowed that he would have nothing more to do with the *Pensacola*. Cap-tain Morris asked Farragut to order Porter to his assistance, but this Farragut would not do. Captain Morris was finally compelled to request Porter's aid; whereupon a stream cable was passed to a heavy vessel outside the bar; and the stranded *Pensacola* was hauled out of her uncomfortable berth, to be careened and finally towed by Porter's steamers into the river.

Meanwhile Farragut made a reconnaissance as far as the chain of hulks below Fort Jackson. This was the second barrier the Confederates had thrown across the river at this point. The earlier one had been made of 3- and 4-foot logs about thirty feet in length joined by underslung chains. Part of this log barrier had been carried away in the spring current, and eight schooners had now been anchored athwart the channel, and chained together across their bows and amidships. Masts had been removed from all but one of the hulks. Riggings, ratlines, and cables had been left to trail astern to foul the enemy's propellers. Before the fleet could run by Forts Jackson and St. Philip, Farragut would have to break the chain barrier.

Farragut's ships, now anchored at the Head of the Passes, were of every size and description; and they varied in speed, draft and maneuverability. Some were weak in guns; some like the *Hartford* had nearly twice as many guns as they rated. They were anchored with little regard to formation, more or less in the order of their arrival in the river.

On the day Porter finished dragging the *Pensacola* over the bar the first of Farragut's coal ships at last arrived. Farragut was overjoyed. He sent Porter a message that he was ready and waiting for him.

"Waiting for me, indeed!"

Early the next morning Porter brought the Mortar Flotilla up from Pilot Town, trim and clean, with a brisk jauntiness. Farragut's miscellany of ships had never seen such a dress parade. "They looked very pretty," wrote a seaman on the *Hartford,* "as they ranged along the shore in line of battle, with their flagship, the *Harriet Lane,* at their head." [7]

From his experience navigating mail steamers to New Orleans Porter had known beforehand that the narrow and continually shifting channel from the Head of the Passes up to the forts would have to be mapped and anchorages marked before the twenty-six vessels of the Mortar Flotilla and the fifteen larger ships of Farragut's fleet could push ahead. Consequently, while preparing for the expedition, Porter had secured the services of the steamer *Sachem* and Mr. F. H. Gerdes of the Coast Survey to do this work.

As soon as the mortar boats had come to anchor opposite Farragut's fleet in the wide basin at the Head of the Passes, Porter directed Mr. Gerdes to commence triangulating the river up to the forts. Farragut detailed a gunboat to escort the *Sachem*.

Confederate sharpshooters were posted along both sides of the swollen river. Some had hidden in the crotches of cypress trees. Others were crouched behind willows and cottonwoods along the fringes where the river spilled over into the swamps. Many of them, waist deep, stood up like cypress knees from the drift-littered backwater. These men watched the small boats put out from the *Sachem* and prowl along the shores, they saw them drive small stakes with white markers into the levees. They watched them pull down the overhanging willow branches and affix little flags to them. They saw them land under cover of the gunboat and mount little weather-vane affairs on the roofs of deserted houses. Whenever opportunity offered the hawk-sighted watchers would blaze away with their indifferent shotguns and duck to cover, for the gunboats would always retaliate with a shower of shells.

On April 10 and 11, a windstorm swept down the river and greatly handicapped the Confederate defense measures. The waters rose in the swamps. So many sharpshooters were sick from exposure that two companies of them had to be returned to New Orleans. The regiment guarding the rear of Fort St. Philip against a possible landing of Union General Butler's army from Ship Island had to be transferred to the higher ground on the west bank of the river above Fort Jackson. Driftwood came down in huge floats. Two of the fire rafts the Confederates had prepared broke from their moorings above the forts and swept against the barrier with such impact as to break the chains and scatter the hulks. Despite the raging current the Confederates so quickly rechained their barrier that no one in the Federal fleet was aware that it had been broken.

After the storm Porter spent much of his time with the surveying party and completed the map by the 14th. But Confederate scouts removed the markers during the night, and they had to be replaced under cover of a continuous fire from the gunboats.

Farragut's ammunition had not all arrived, and he lacked fuses of the size used on the gunboats. But these he improvised by whittling down the larger ones made for the mortar shells. Others of his vessels which had taken on coal now moved up and dropped anchor in the order of their arrival. Porter brought up the Mortar Flotilla past Farragut's ships and anchored near the west bank under the trees. In preparing to receive the Federals, the Confederates had felled the trees only as far as the lower limit of Fort Jackson's casemate fire. Thus they had left below this line a perfect natural screen for Porter's mortar schooners.

On Wednesday the 16th Porter towed three schooners up to the 3,000-yard marker and let fly a few shells to get the range. Farragut's gunboats in midstream diverted the enemy's fire. The current was too swift, and the rifled guns from both forts made navigation too difficult for the latter to risk themselves long at a time. A fire raft sent down by the Confederates caused such confusion that several of Farragut's ships fouled each other in working clear of the blaze. The fire raft consisted of an enormous pile of pine knots smeared with resin and tar. Its flames, according to Midshipman Bartlett of the *Brooklyn*, attained the height of 100 feet.

Thursday April 17. Once more the surveyors paddled in their boats along both banks of the river. They set markers for each of the twenty-one mortar schooners. Much of the time the surveyors were under fire from walking-beam Confederate river steamers that ventured downstream between the forts. Along the west bank the Mortar Flotilla dressed its masts with cottonwood boughs. Some of the more energetic crews covered their entire broadside.

"The 'bummers' think this is a holiday!" was a comment by amused onlookers in Farragut's fleet. "The bloody bottoms of the 'bummers' will drop out at the tenth fire!" was another.

Friday the 18th—Good Friday. Before daylight a Coast Surveyor came aboard the *Harriet Lane* to assist Porter in locating the schooners. The *Clifton* and the *Westfield,* each towing two or three of Lieutenant Watson Smith's first division chugged upstream and cast off their charges under the lee of the wooded point. As soon as the schooners were anchored the mortars began firing. The bushes on shore quivered from the kick of the explosions and presently deepened in color as fine black débris settled on their leaves. As soon as Smith's division was placed, that of Lieutenant K. Randolph Breese was hauled into position just below the first. The first and third divisions were now splitting the air with explosions and the nerve-tickling whine of 13-inch shells. These shells had a trajectory of 2,850 yards, at the end of which lay squat and heavy Fort Jackson.

The second division of the Mortar Flotilla was now tugged across the open river. Lieutenant W. W. Queen's mortars were placed in the most dangerous position, open to the unobstructed view of both forts and 3,680 yards below Fort St. Philip, which was its target.

In midstream struggling against the current Lieutenant Guest in the gunboat *Owasco* attempted to attract the fire of the forts away from the mortar schooners. After Guest had dodged rifled shot for an hour and fifty minutes, Porter went on board Guest's vessel and ordered him to retire before the *Owasco* was blown to pieces. A relieving force detailed by Farragut took the place of the *Owasco*.

All day the firing continued. Each of the thick iron kegs discharged every ten minutes. Although the gunners were not aware of it, they were firing with great accuracy. Porter, rowing from one schooner to another, kept a watchful eye on the foundations of the mortars, but they did not drop out at the end of the tenth round. By midday the Confederate gunners had spotted Queen's division. A 120-pound Confederate shell hit Queen's leading schooner, the *T. A. Ward,* tore through the cabin, damaged the magazine, broke out a hole in the starboard side near the waterline. Other shots ripped her rigging. Porter went on board and ordered Queen to shift the *Ward* to a position 200 yards astern of the others. The next in line, the *George Mangham,* was also hulled and Porter shifted her down below the *Ward.* The spirited remonstrances of Lieutenant Queen and Acting Master Collins pleased Porter. He loved a good fight and kept himself in the thick of it all, but he was determined to take no unnecessary chances.

At 4:30 P.M. a solid 8-inch shot struck the face of a mortar in Lieutenant Smith's division, killing Seaman James Lebar and knocking the trucks off the mortar but not putting it out of action.

About five o'clock great flames appeared over Fort Jackson. Porter believed he had ignited some of the enemy's fire rafts. The mortars continued firing long after Fort Jackson's guns had ceased; at nightfall Porter silenced them. While his men rested, Porter pulled up the river in the darkness and discovered that the flames had been inside Fort Jackson itself. The ruins of the citadel and barracks were still aglow. Realizing now that he had made a mistake, he resolved henceforth to keep his mortars thundering night and day.

On Saturday April 19, General J. K. Duncan, the Confederate commander in Fort Jackson, noted: "Mortar Flotilla again opened at 6 A.M. and the fire was constantly kept up throughout the day ... The enemy's fire was excellent, a large proportion of his shells falling within Fort Jackson. The terre-plein, parade plain, parapets, and platforms were very much cut up as well as damage done to the casemates ... magazines were considerably threatened." [8] Five of the parapet guns and two rifled guns in the water battery were disabled.

Across the swamp and behind the point of woods the Mortar Flotilla was also suffering damages. Lieutenant Queen's division was not again towed across the river but stationed below the other divisions along the west bank. At 10 A.M. a shot struck the *Maria J. Carlton,* passed through her magazine floor and out her bottom. Porter rushed to the scene. The *Harriet Lane* wedged the stricken vessel against the bank until most of her movables were taken out before she filled and slid down the muddy incline weighted by her mortar and shells. When the bubbles ceased to rise her upper rail and her slanting bush-clad masts stuck up opposite the print of her hull on the levee.

The firing from Fort Jackson was still so vigorous that Porter began to despair of demolishing that fortification. It would not have been so bad if he had not claimed that he would reduce it in forty-eight hours of bombardment.

General Butler, leaving his soldiers encamped on the sand flats of Ship Island, came on board the *Hartford* for a conference with Farragut. Farragut told the General that he had no muslin in the fleet to dress wounds.

"The Chief of Bureau thought my requisition extravagant," said the Flag Officer. "I have been on the parish." [9]

Butler offered to share anything the Army had.

The fleet surgeon, unable to understand why the squadron should be short of ether and chloroform, thought Farragut brave and full of fight, but nevertheless a Quixote who "evidently does not know what he is going about." [10]

Night came on. Porter ordered the mortar fire to continue, each piece to fire once in thirty minutes instead of ten. As the sky darkened the seamen on Farragut's ships discovered a grim beauty as the burning fuses described the trajectories of the mortar shells. Because too many shells exploded in midflight, Porter cut the fuses longer. Here and there a man lay down on the thundering decks and tried to sleep.

Sunday, April 20—Easter Sunday. When morning came the bombards quickened their steady, monotonous explosions. The gunners were beginning to look like slaves, their hands and faces black with powder and grime. A light rain that fell during the morning streaked their blackened faces.

A mud-spattered deserter from Fort Jackson floundered across the swamps to the point of woods and surrendered to Porter's men. Identifying himself as a Pennsylvanian formerly attached to Dan Rice's Shows, he assured Porter that he had been coerced into joining the rebel garrison of Fort Jackson and stated that there were others among the six or seven hundred men in the fort who had been similarly coerced. He told Porter that the fort's parapets were torn up, casemates in places broken in and flooded. While the garrison was fighting the flames in the citadel, he said, he had made his escape through an embrasure the shells had made in the wall of the fort. Porter felt much encouraged and took the man to Farragut.

The Flag Officer was pleased with the deserter's account. He was pleased with the work of Porter's mortars, but since his supply of ammunition for his gunboats was running low, he was anxious to start up the river. He did not think Porter could destroy Fort Jackson's casemates, though Porter was now hopeful. Only the fierce winds driving down the channel necessitated delay.

That night at 8 o'clock Farragut sent Fleet Captain H. H. Bell up the river with three gunboats to break the chains that held the hulks together.

Monday, April 21. At 1 A.M. Captain Bell returned to the *Hartford* having broken the chain barrier. At 3 o'clock the Confederates released a fire raft which caused the *Sciota* and the *Kineo* to collide and together, with their rigging entangled, to foul the *Mississippi*. The *Sciota* lost her mainmast and the other ships suffered minor damages, but the raft was successfully fended from the fleet.

Tuesday, April 22, the fifth day of the bombardment. Fort Jackson's casemate guns were still firing, and the Mortar Flotilla's ammunition was dwindling. The gunners were grimy and exhausted, having slept only a few hours on the decks beside their thundering mortars. For five nights Porter had slept in his clothes. Farragut came on board the *Harriet Lane* and told Porter that a party of French and English naval officers he had permitted to pass up the river to communicate with their consuls in New Orleans had returned and expressed the opinion that Farragut's wooden ships would never survive the fire of the forts.

Porter offered to bet all his old clothes that Farragut would get through to New Orleans without losing more than one vessel.

"Ah, Porter," said Farragut, "I'd give a great many suits of new clothes to think and feel as you do!" [11]

Farragut returned to the *Hartford,* and signalled for his captains to come aboard. He told them they must pass up the river that night. Two of the older captains opposed the move, because their carpenters' crews were absent down the river. Farragut agreed to postpone the passage another twenty-four hours, but no more.

The strong wind down the river was still blowing steadily. On the 21st, Farragut had written Welles: "I shall await a change of wind and a consequent less violent current before I attack the forts as I find great difficulty in avoiding collisions among the vessels." [12] He now issued general orders to his fleet preparatory to the great thrust up to New Orleans.

THROUGH JACKSON AND ST. PHILIP

T HE Confederate Government in Richmond refused to believe that New Orleans was more seriously threatened from below than from above. General Mansfield Lovell, commanding the defenses of New Orleans, sent frantic telegrams to which President Jefferson Davis replied that Foote's ironclads descending the river were more to be feared than Farragut's wooden-walled vessels. The defenses above New Orleans consisted of antiquated smooth-bore cannon on clay banks and cottonclad river steamboats; whereas the approach from below was defended by two good modern forts. The troops withdrawn from New Orleans in March and sent north to help Beauregard at Corinth against Grant and Halleck were not returned. The Confederate ram *Manassas,* terror of the Federal blockaders, was withdrawn up the river. The fourteen converted river boats known as the Confederate River Defense Fleet were also ordered up the river. Guns shipped from the Pensacola Navy Yard continued to be placed behind fresh clay mounds looking upstream above New Orleans. If the C. S. S. *Mississippi* and the C. S. S. *Louisiana,* now being built at New Orleans with heavy iron casemates modeled after the *Merrimac,* had been nearer completion, they would also have been sent up the river to check Foote.

When the Mortar Flotilla began its long bombardment, General Lovell on his own authority telegraphed to Beauregard for the *Manassas.* Beauregard sent her down. Lovell then withheld half of the River Defense Fleet and sent it down to the forts. He persuaded Governor Moore of Louisiana to arm several of the walking-beam "Steamboat Bills" that were tied to the New Orleans levee and sent these down. Several rifled guns intended for the *Louisiana* he sent to Fort Jackson—though imperative orders from Richmond forced him to return one of these. Additional fire rafts were prepared.

Confederate General Johnson K. Duncan who commanded in

Fort Jackson had to remount his parapet guns under a constant rain of mortar shells. Thousands of sand bags, rushed down to him from the city, he packed in the embrasures and over the magazine. But in spite of its five-foot covering of sand bags the magazine was greatly endangered. Duncan's urgent calls for help brought the half-completed *Louisiana* down from New Orleans on the night of April 20. The *Louisiana's* sixteen guns were unmounted, and her curiously arranged screw propellers and paddle wheels, located one behind the other amidships, had never functioned. Several hundred mechanics and carpenters were carried down with her to continue their work on her just above Fort St. Philip.[1]

On the eve of the battle the Confederate forces on the lower river were divided into three commands. In addition to the *Louisiana,* of which he was captain, Commander J. K. Mitchell had the general direction of the regular Confederate States naval vessels including the ram *Manassas,* and a miscellany of small boats and tugs. Captain Stevenson with six converted river steamers of the River Defense Fleet refused to come under Mitchell's orders, and the same was true of the vessels outfitted by the State of Louisiana.

Between the triarchy of commands afloat and the garrisons in the forts there were no bonds except the loose unity of a common purpose. It was the theory of the commanders in the rear that each of the officers at the front would have enough to do to look out for himself alone. Events proved they were partially correct.

Porter's mortar shells wrought great havoc inside Fort Jackson. They tore open the levees, flooding six to eighteen inches of water into the casemates. When Porter cut his fuses longer, many of the shells buried themselves twenty feet in the slushy parade plain. One shell struck a man between the shoulders and carried him down out of sight and another falling in the same spot hurled his corpse high into the air. The explosions of buried shells shook the ground inside the fort like an earthquake. Duncan pleaded hysterically with Mitchell to take the *Louisiana* lower down and draw some of the fire from the forts. He was asking the impossible.

At midnight on April 23 the Mortar Flotilla ominously diminished its uproar.

The Confederates set torches to piles of cordwood along the river. The first hour of the new day was silent, but for the crackle and rustle of the bonfires.

In the darkness three miles below the broken barrier of hulks, lay Farragut's wooden warships. Farragut had prepared for battle in many ways. Sheet cables were hung over his vessels' sides abreast the boilers. Some ships were smeared with mud to make them less visible. Others had their decks whitewashed around the gun carriages so that not even dark lanterns would be needed to serve the guns. Berth decks over engine rooms had been packed with a miscellany of shock absorbing materials—hammocks, clothes bags, cordage, sacks of sand and ashes, cables and anchor chains. Even ships' biscuit were put to this use.

In the *Harriet Lane* Porter led his steamers up the west bank of the river. As he rounded the wooded point he could see three legs of the huge stone starfish of Fort Jackson dimly lighted by flares from the bonfires. Indistinguishable in the darkness was Fort Jackson's water battery, a series of low earthworks detached from the fort and extending toward the Point of Woods. It was this water battery which Porter with his steamers was to attack from close range during Farragut's attempted passage. Across the fire-flecked river Fort St. Philip loomed larger than it really was. Porter waited at the edge of the cleared field below Fort Jackson.

The lieutenant whose sledges had broken the chain three nights ago now passed Porter's mortar steamers, pulling his row boat up in midstream a little beyond one of the hulks. Dropping a sounding lead over the side and drifting downstream, he made a last-minute test of Farragut's channel. A flare from a raft discovered him to the enemy and drew their fire, but he was not hit. He rowed swiftly down with the current and made a signal to Farragut.

At 2 A.M. on April 24, two small red lanterns—the signal for the Federal fleet to weigh its anchors—were run up to the *Hartford's* masthead.

From below Porter's silent mortar schooners came the noise of capstans reeling in cables and chains. The complaint of cables grinding through many hawseholes made a roar that carried up the river beyond Porter to the Confederate listeners. The Confederates lighted fire rafts and prodded them into the current. Porter moved up to within 200 yards of Fort Jackson's water battery.

At 2:30 the black shapes of Captain Theodorus Bailey's Division of the Blue sped upstream past Porter's steamers toward the broken barrier. The fast little *Cayuga* and the large rough-and-tumble *Pensacola* burst suddenly into the glare of the Confederates' rafts and bonfires.

Simultaneous flashes came from the guns of Fort St. Philip, Fort Jackson, and the water battery.

Porter opened his guns on the water battery. From below the Point of Woods the mortars, resuming their bombardment, doubled and redoubled their rate of fire as if jealous of their prestige. The mortar shells shrieked across the sky, describing sharp arcs of flame. But one scarcely noticed them now. The *Cayuga* and the *Pensacola* dashed through the broken barrier, adding their broadsides to the pandemonium. The *Mississippi* churned through the gap. At this moment a shot from Fort Jackson struck the *Harriet Lane,* carried away a stanchion and a portion of the railing of the bridge between the wheelhouses. Whirring splinters killed one man, wounded another stationed near Porter at the 9-inch gun on the quarter-deck. Only the upper decks of Porter's steamers were vulnerable for Porter kept their hulls rubbing against the levees to protect them at the water line. Behind the *Mississippi* raced the stately *Oneida,* and the swift little *Varuna,* whose indistinguishable wood smoke gave her an air of graceful and effortless motion. The *Katahdin,* the *Kineo,* and the *Wissahickon* brought up the rear of Bailey's division.

Farragut's second column—the Division of the Red—followed immediately astern of the Blue. The flagship *Hartford* sped through the shell-splashed entrance. The *Brooklyn* close behind but too near the west bank ran afoul of a sunken hulk. The *Brooklyn's* nose swung round and bumped into the levee while the *Richmond* veered around her and took her place astern of the flagship.

The *Hartford* and the *Richmond* let go their broadsides into Fort Jackson. Howitzers in their tops spat down upon the open-air parapets, which were well illuminated by the mortar shells. The flagship on the other hand was a beautiful 225-foot target for the Confederates, and their firing converged on the *Hartford* from both sides of the river at once.

The current flowed swiftest along the west bank as it rounded the bend where Farragut was now. From above the forts the turtle-backed ram *Manassas* zigzagged downstream toward Farragut's division. Fire rafts came swirling down. Tugboats shoved the blazing fire rafts and guided them by means of iron claws fastened to long poles.

One of the rafts suddenly bore down on the *Hartford.* In maneuvering to avoid it Farragut ran across the river and grounded directly under Fort St. Philip. In this predicament the

Copyrighted by the Review of Reviews, from the Photographic History of the Civil War

DECK OF ONE OF PORTER'S MORTAR SCHOONERS.

FARRAGUT'S FLEET PASSING FORTS JACKSON AND ST. PHILIP, APRIL 24, 1862. ENGRAVED BY GEORGE E. PERINE FOR THE *Eclectic*, AFTER AN ORIGINAL DRAWING.

fire-fangs licked down upon the flagship. Flames enveloped her port side, funneling up the rigging. The diminutive Confederate tugboat *Mosher* was driven off, in a sinking condition. When her flames were subdued, the *Hartford* backed free of the bank and pushed ahead up the livid, flame-splotched river.

The *Brooklyn* was hit many times by Fort St. Philip before she slipped her port anchor which had caught in the wreckage, and sped up the river. The ram *Manassas* now butted into the *Brooklyn*, at the moment of impact firing its stubby carronade through its single forward port, but did little damage. The *Brooklyn* raced upstream where the ram's feeble engines would not allow pursuit.

The sky to the east of Fort St. Philip was tinged faintly with gray as the *Sciota* with Captain H. H. Bell's distinguishing pennant of red and blue appeared. But the brilliant fires on the river with the thick canopy of smoke overhead created an artificial night under cover of which the Indian namesakes, the *Sciota,* the *Iroquois* and the *Kennebec,* dashed by the forts. These swift gunboats came through with hardly a scratch on their paint. The three ships got past the forts in time to witness the destruction of the heterogeneous Confederate vessels. Many of these fragile death-traps had been run into the banks in the last stages of consumption by fire. Some had been sent to the bottom in midchannel, and only the tips of their smokeless funnels were to be seen above the tawny water.

Daylight prevented the *Pinola,* the *Itasca* and the *Winona* from getting through. One by one these last of Farragut's gunboats ran by the hulks into the concentrated fire of Forts Jackson and St. Philip. Unsupported by the larger vessels they were compelled to drop their crews flat on deck and drift downstream out of action.

Porter sent up two rockets as signal for the Mortar Flotilla to cease firing, and at the same time ordered his steamers to retire from their exposed position.

When the smoke cleared away at daybreak Porter could get an idea of the condition of the Confederate defenses. The forts had not been demolished. The ram *Manassas* drifted down about 7:30 A.M. but the boatmen Porter sent out under a flag of truce discovered that the "portholes," from which smoke was escaping, were punctures made by Farragut's fleet. An hour later the "pigmy monster" which earlier had so successfully frightened the Federals, feebly exploded and sank abreast the line of mortar schooners. Porter could see the ironclad *Louisiana* still tied to the bank above Fort St. Philip, and the *McRae* and the *Defiance,* as well as several of the River Defense Fleet, moving about the forts. Porter did not yet know how many of Farragut's ships had got through nor what damage they had suffered.

The Navy Department's dispatches had described the *Louisiana* as more formidable than the *Merrimac;* and Porter, without knowing that she was yet unfinished, had every reason to fear a second Hampton Roads disaster. Neither his flotilla nor Farragut's rear gunboats which had been forced back by the forts carried rifled cannon to pierce the *Louisiana's* armor.

General Butler came up from his troop ship at the Head of the Passes to confer with Porter, and in the conference with Butler Porter concealed his fears. He urged Butler to land troops on the seaward side in the rear of Fort St. Philip, and detailed the shallow, round-bottomed *Miami,* to take the general to Ship Island and assist in transporting the troops.

Porter then sent the *Owasco* under a flag of truce to demand the surrender of the forts. The Confederates replied that surrender was inadmissible.

Porter dispatched an appeal to Farragut and another to Flag Officer McKean at Pensacola. Meanwhile he sought to bluff the enemy by renewing the bombardment of Fort Jackson. From 8 A.M. to 12 noon, and from 2 to 5 P.M. the faithful mortars thundered reassuringly.

At 5 o'clock the endangered mortar schooners were all sent down to Pilot Town with the mortar steamer *J. P. Jackson* and Farragut's sailing sloop *Portsmouth* to protect them. The *Itasca,* badly mangled in her attempt to run the gauntlet, Porter also sent to Pilot Town to repair.

All the effective gunboats were held at the Point of Woods to watch the enemy. In the *Harriet Lane* Porter shuttled anxiously between the schooners and the gunboats.

At last Commander Boggs came around by land with news of Farragut's passage. Captain Bailey in Farragut's leading gunboat, the *Cayuga,* had made prisoners of the Chalmette regiment above Fort Jackson. Eleven of the enemy's river boats had been sunk or burned. Captain Beverly Kennon of the C.S.S. *Governor Moore* was reported to have set fire to his vessel and burned her wounded with her. Boggs's ship, the *Varuna,* rammed by half a dozen Confederates at once, had been sunk. Farragut's loss was a little over a hundred killed and wounded. Farragut had stopped at Quarantine just long enough to collect his vessels, sluice their decks, and bury his dead and was now pushing toward New Orleans. Farragut wanted some of the mortar vessels to appear in the bayous behind Fort Jackson. Porter gave orders for this to be done.

Meanwhile up the river everything was quiet at Fort Jackson and Fort St. Philip. On April 25 the sky was lighted by fire and smoke in the direction of New Orleans. The Confederate commanders in the river became alarmed. Commander Mitchell wanted to get the *Louisiana's* engines started on this day, but most of his volunteer seamen were drunk. Toward evening bits of burning wreckage floated down the river past the forts.

On Saturday Mitchell sent the *McRae* under a flag of truce to carry the wounded of the Confederate forts and fleets to New Orleans. At 4 P.M. the gigantic uncompleted Confederate ironclad *Mississippi* floated down from New Orleans a burning wreck. No shots were exchanged during the day.

At daylight on Sunday April 27 Butler's troops began landing at Quarantine behind and above Fort St. Philip. At noon Porter again demanded the surrender of the forts. Again it was refused. The Confederates had not yet been officially notified of the fall of New Orleans.

At midnight the troops of Fort Jackson suddenly mutinied en masse. They seized the guards and posterns, reversed the guns, and fired upon their officers who tried to check the disorder. So many of them filed out of the gates into the swamps to be picked up by General Butler's army that Butler promptly conceded the victory to himself and so reported to the War Department.

General Duncan sent a rowboat down the river to the *Owasco* with the word that the forts were ready to accept Porter's terms of surrender. The *Owasco's* crew broke into wild cheering as they raced downstream with the news, flying Confederate colors beneath the Stars and Stripes at the *Owasco's* masthead.

On Monday at 2 P.M. the *Harriet Lane,* the *Westfield,* and Farragut's gunboats, the *Kennebec* and the *Winona,* steamed up to Fort Jackson, holystoned and dressed for parade. They anchored athwart the channel about thirty yards apart. A boat from the *Harriet Lane* brought off General Duncan and Colonel Higgins to the flagship. Porter met the Confederates at the ladder and they went at once to the cabin.

The articles of capitulation had already been prepared. Porter signed. Renshaw of the *Westfield* signed. Wainwright of the *Harriet Lane* was about to affix his signature when he was called on deck. Wainwright returned at once with the report that the Confederate ironclad *Louisiana* was on fire and was drifting down the river upon them. The Federal vessels being broadside to the current, she would not have room to pass.

"This is sharp practice," Porter remarked to the Confederate officers, "but if *you* can stand the explosion when it comes we can. We will go on and finish the capitulation."

To Wainwright he said, "Pass the word to each of the other vessels to veer to the end of their chains and use steam if necessary in sheering clear of the wreck. They are not to leave their anchorages." [2]

There was enough danger in the *Louisiana's* fire-threatened magazine to add drama to the situation in the cabin of the *Harriet Lane.*

The two Confederate officers, General Duncan and Colonel Higgins, signed with a boldness that Porter never ceased to admire. One, two, three minutes passed. Then there was a stir on deck, a rumbling in the air. The *Harriet Lane* swayed gently. As the noise of the explosion was heard, everything in the cabin of the *Harriet Lane* was jostled from side to side, but not a man left his seat.

Porter and the officers with him now came out on deck.

The Confederate ironclad had exploded within a few hundred feet of her moorings, opposite Fort St. Philip and well above Porter's vessels.

The Confederate military officials aboard the *Harriet Lane* stoutly urged that they had no responsibility whatever for the doings of the forces afloat. They had just joined Porter in a cacophony of abuse of Commander Mitchell when Mitchell's lieutenant climbed up the *Harriet Lane's* ladder with the belated warning that the *Louisiana* was "about to explode."

"Say to Captain Mitchell I am much obliged," said Porter.[3] Then he ordered Wainwright to steam up the river and capture Mitchell. Mitchell and his associates were held in close confinement and denied the rights of ordinary prisoners of war.

The U. S. colors were now run up the flagstaffs of Fort Jackson and Fort St. Philip. Boats were dispatched to bring General Butler's troops to garrison the forts.

On April 29 Captain Bailey came down from New Orleans on his way to Washington as bearer of dispatches. Porter sent with him his report on the "surrender of Forts Jackson and St. Philip to the Mortar Flotilla."

New Orleans, the South's richest and most colorful city, had fallen to the Federals. As a demoralizing blow to the South's economic sinews of war its capture ranks with Sherman's march to the sea. The greater was the blow for having descended early in the war. For three long years the Confederacy would be deprived of two important forts and her largest port of entry for military and economic supplies from the outside world. For the Federals the bold stroke yielded immense advantages. The blockade was sealed at its most difficult point. Potentially powerful enemy iron-clads were destroyed while yet in their cradles. The most suitable of all bases was secured for the Western Gulf Blockading Squadron. But greatest of all was the possession of the southern gateway to the great Mississippi . . .

For Porter, as for Farragut, the capture of New Orleans was one of the crowning achievements of his career. As we have seen, Porter had been largely responsible for initiating the campaign and for selecting Farragut as chief. His novel conception of a smothering bombardment of 13-inch mortar shells had been his most original contribution. He had personally created the Mortar Flotilla, using the only vessels available at the time—ferryboats, miscellaneous shallow-draft steamers, sailing schooners. Under the most trying circumstances he had got these indifferent units into the river, helped several of Farragut's unwieldy ships over the bar, surveyed the river, directed the entire bombardment, and in the immortal passage of the forts he had "taken the enemy in flank." Throughout the entire operation he had unleashed a tremendous energy. In addition his sarcasm, his jokes, his buoyant spirits, his dogged courage had worked a sort of magic in upholding the morale of the fleet. And at the end he was thoroughly exhausted, thoroughly happy, but withal anxious to push on to the next step in the suppression of the great rebellion.

"New Orleans falling seems to have made a stampede in 'Secessia,'" Porter wrote to Fox; "You may put the rebellion down as 'spavined,' 'broken-backed,' and 'wind-galled' . . . you good people at home can go to work now cut down the Navy pay, and disrate us to your heart's content . . . It will take me ten years to rest and recover from the exhaustion caused by vexation of spirit, in the last year. My liver is completely turned upside down. My eyes are failing me and I want to go to roost—One more slap at the Rebels through Mobile and I will be satisfied." [4]

TELL THE LADIES . . .

On April 27, the third day after the Navy's thrust up the river, General Butler arrived in the rear of Fort St. Philip with a boat-load of troops. The clever Massachusetts politician who had for-feited a seat in Congress to assume a more glamorous role as major general of volunteers was chagrined to find that Farragut had gone on to New Orleans without the Army.

He deemed it a "wholly unmilitary proceeding" on Farragut's part to leave forts behind him unreduced, and he felt piqued that Porter, a naval commander, should have received the surrender of the military garrisons within the Confederate forts. To the Sec-retary of War he complained that all the steamers captured and in repair were claimed by the Navy so that he had had no means of transportation to get down the river to participate in the surrender.[1]

A few minutes after Porter's officers had raised the U. S. colors over the forts and paroled the garrisons, a transport loaded with Butler's troops arrived at the forts, having been towed up the river from the Head of the Passes by the mortar steamer *Clifton*. The Navy now turned the forts over to the Army and placed the steamers of the Mortar Flotilla at General Butler's disposal.

While the mortar schooners vied with blockaders and Army boats in sweeping up such crumbs of victory as Fort Livingston and minor Confederate batteries along the lateral approaches to New Orleans, Porter hurried into Fort Jackson to examine the work of his mortars. His mortars he found had executed their work with great zeal and accuracy. He noted that hundreds of shells had sunk deep in the soft mud; whereas if the ground had been solid the fort might have been pounded to atoms. From prisoners he learned that about three thousand shells had fallen inside—though only 1,100 holes could be counted. He ordered Coast Survey assistants Gerdes and Harris to make an accurate plan of all the works, noting every bomb that fell and the injury the fort sustained, every distance and position being accurately measured by tapeline and compass, and the comparative size of fractures noted. Mr. Harris affirmed that the casemates were cracked from end to end, one of the bastion casemates had the roof broken through in three places; another in one place; and its walls were so badly cracked "that daylight shines through very plainly, the crack being about 4 inches wide." [2] Mr. Gerdes noted that craters in the parade plain were from 3 to 8 feet deep and very close together; "The destruction goes beyond all description. The ground is torn by the shells as if a thousand antediluvian hogs had rooted it up . . ." [3]

Porter attached the surveyors' map to his report to the Department, and Fox immediately assured him that in the records soon to be published by the Senate "your speckled Fort shall come in for a good share of photograph." [4]

Butler in turn commanded General Weitzel to examine the damage wrought by the mortars. The Army official's report contained not even faint praise. It stated that although Fort Jackson to an inexperienced eye seemed badly cut up, "It is as strong today as when the first shell was fired at it." [5] The discussion thus started waxed warmer and warmer and continued for many years, with many individuals contributing their verbal or foolscap wrath to the support of one side or the other. Neither civilian surveyors nor Army engineers, however, were competent to render a final verdict. An inspection of the carpenters' reports of the damage to the passing fleet would have settled the question without ado. More than half of Farragut's injuries were inflicted by Fort St. Philip—which was rated but two-thirds as powerful as Fort Jackson. Porter's mortars, by concentrating on the stronger fort, had materially lessened Farragut's casualty list, and had, as the flag officer phrased it, "taken the enemy in flank."

At New Orleans Farragut commandeered all the river boats the Confederates had not destroyed or sent up the river with refugees and dispatched them down to help Porter bring up the troops. On the first of May, General Butler and the Army arrived to occupy the city. The troops were so thickly packed aboard the white painted river boats that they were compared by Mrs. Butler to bees swarming over their hives, and by a Confederate witness to "lumps of sugar covered with flies."

The paroled Confederate soldiers from the forts were greeted with sticks and stones by the people of New Orleans. Several of the late defenders of Fort Jackson were killed by the mob. In one section of the city a group of foreign-born citizens including women and children cheered for the old flag, and a squad of taut-nerved Louisiana militiamen fired their shotguns into the crowd.

When General Butler and his staff marched down the gang-plank to land at the foot of Canal Street, the Secessionists hissed and split their throats with cries of Jeff Davis and General Beaure-gard. Butler prudently landed his troops after nightfall and marched them through the solemn gas-lighted streets to the City Hall, where they were billeted. For headquarters he took possession of the St. Charles Hotel, placed a guard with howitzers at each of the street corners, and brought up Mrs. Butler from the transport. The cabman whose horse and carriage were impressed made it clear to the mob that he performed this distasteful duty only at the point of a pistol.

Four of Porter's steamers came up to New Orleans on this mo-mentous May Day. When the *Harriet Lane* arrived, the crew of the *Richmond* gave three cheers for Commander Porter. The greeting was returned by three cheers for Captain Alden—the only one of Farragut's officers, besides Lee and DeCamp, whose friend-ship for Porter was at all enthusiastic.

To celebrate the great victory of Farragut and Porter and the hasty retreat of the Confederate General Lovell from New Or-leans, a Union rhymster produced "The Ballad of Lord Lovell." [6]

> "Oh! Tarry, Lord Lovell!" Sir Farragut cried.
>   "Oh! Tarry, Lord Lovell!" said he;
> "I rather think not," Lord Lovell replied,
>   "For I'm in a great hurry."
>
> "I like the drinks at St. Charles Hotel,
>   But I never could bear strong Porter,
> Especially when it's served on the shell,
>   Or mixed in an iron mortar."
>
> "I reckon you're right," Sir Farragut said,
>   "I reckon you're right," said he,
> "For if my Porter should fly to your head,
>   A terrible smash there'd be."

Porter found Farragut sadly perplexed. Farragut had relatives in New Orleans, who might be subjected to mob fury if they had anything whatever to do with him. The multifarious duties of his command required the Flag Officer's attention in all directions at once. Should he stay a while in New Orleans and catch up with the general work of the blockade of the Western Gulf? Should he ascend the river to join Flag Officer Davis? * Should he go at once to attack Mobile? The Confederates were stampeded. He needed to carry out all three of these objectives at once to take advantage of the enemy's confusion.

The Navy Department's orders issued in January, and substantially reiterated in February, indicated but did not solve Farragut's dilemma: "If the [Army's] Mississippi expedition from Cairo shall not have descended the river, you will take advantage of the panic to push a strong force up the river to take all their defenses in the rear. You will also reduce the fortifications which defend Mobile Bay and turn them over to the army to hold."

At the beginning of the second year of the war Washington's strategy was still seriously shortsighted. It is true that they saw desirable objectives beyond New Orleans, but they had devised no workable plans and provided no adequate material for carrying them out. Clearly Farragut's orders failed to recognize what a purely naval force could and could not do against the inland river forts. The capture of river defenses above New Orleans called for military as well as naval force and only enough troops had been sent to accomplish the original mission.

Most of Farragut's lighter gunboats suitable for ascending the river had been so badly battered in the passage of the lower forts as to need extensive repair. His large sea-going ships were unsuited for navigation beyond Baton Rouge. If he penetrated far into the interior, as he should likely have to do since Flag Officer Davis' flotilla was still above Memphis, Farragut's supply vessels would need a convoy, and this would diminish his effective force at the far end of the line. Towns along the river would have to be occupied by troops; but General Butler had barely enough to control New Orleans—where he had not only a rebellious civil population, but a large body of paroled Confederate soldiers from the lower forts with nothing to do.

Under these circumstances Porter strongly urged Farragut to attack Mobile. Farragut's sea-going fleet could under cover of mortar bombardment easily thrust past Fort Morgan into Mobile Bay, and once inside they would be able to sever that Fort's communication with the city and compel its evacuation. The strategy

* Flag Officer C. H. Davis, now commanding in the upper river, had recently relieved Foote, whose broken health had caused the Department to transfer him to Washington.

so effective at New Orleans might easily be repeated at Mobile. The Confederates at that point had not anticipated an attack and owing to the present widespread panic would be poorly prepared to defend themselves.

Accordingly Farragut on May 1 decided to attack Mobile, as Porter desired. He ordered Porter on this day to take the Mortar Flotilla to Ship Island and await the coming of the main fleet before attacking Mobile.

Porter at once hurried his steamers out of the river, gathered his scattered mortar schooners, and on May 3 once more dropped anchor off Ship Island. Here he waited. The first week of May passed without any sign of Farragut's fleet. Porter suspected that some other older officer had persuaded Farragut to go up the river without the Mortar Flotilla. In his anxiety he wrote the Department that this action of Farragut's "may prevent my getting hold of some Fort. I think my discretion might be trusted." [7]

During the delay Porter found time to write for Georgy a burlesque description of the Battle of New Orleans illustrated with caricatures of several participants. A mild little duck and a crowing rooster represented Farragut before and after the battle. Porter depicted himself as a sort of gunswab rammed into the barrel of one of his mortars, hair down over his eyes, a scowl on his face, left hand and arm hanging limp and lifeless but his right smartly drawn up to thumb his nose at the enemy. [8]

He received a letter in Georgy's almost illegible handwriting telling him that all the women of Washington were praising the work of his "bummers." But Georgy also wrote that Carlisle had failed at the Naval Academy.

To Fox Porter wrote requesting him to do something for Carlisle. "If you can find time to...make any arrangement not conflicting with the rules of the school, I should appreciate it; he is a fine boy, and would make the right kind of an officer though he is not at present strong enough to go through the killing process which boys are subjected to at the Academy...I would ask nothing better after this war than to have command of the Naval Academy, and get the right set of officers into the Navy. A new era should be instituted. We don't want Miss Nancy's—we want fearless dashing men..." [9]

On May 7 Porter took his steamers and the survey boat *Sachem* to the main entrance to Mobile Bay to sound and place buoys along the channel, in order to have everything ready when Farragut's ships did arrive. The excitement of the Confederates in

Forts Gaines and Morgan was evident in the chasing to and fro of vessels inside the harbor. The Confederates appeared to be re-enforcing Fort Morgan at the expense of the smaller Fort Gaines, which lay across the shallows. The heavy buttresses of Fort Morgan arose almost from the channel itself.

The ferryboat *Clifton,* after throwing a few shells against Fort Morgan, ran aground within range of the fort. While the Confederates were making a target of the grounded *Clifton,* Porter sent in the survey boat, the only available vessel of sufficiently shallow draft, to assist the *Clifton,* but the latter managed to free herself without help.

The next two days being stormy, Porter returned all his vessels save his flagship to Ship Island and in the *Harriet Lane* rode out the storm. He was abundantly repaid for doing so.

At 2 A.M. on May 10 the *Harriet Lane's* lookout discovered a great light in the direction of Pensacola. Porter rushed eastward at full speed through the gale, bows under half the time.

For two months the Confederates under Colonel Jones had planned their evacuation of Pensacola. After the fall of Fort Donelson on the Tennessee-Kentucky line, the Confederate high command had decided not to attempt to hold all outposts along their frontier, but to withdraw their forces and concentrate them at the more strategically necessary points.

When the Confederate adjutant at Fort Morgan informed Colonel Jones that the Mortar Flotilla had reappeared, Colonel Jones hastily completed his evacuation, and simultaneously set fire to Forts McRee and Barrancas, their water batteries, the navy yard, the naval hospital, the barracks, wharves, ships, etc., and retired to Mobile.

The *Harriet Lane* steamed into Pensacola Harbor on the course Porter had formerly plotted for the *Powhatan.* Fort Pickens was shelling the retreating enemy. Unfortunately her commander, General Arnold, could do nothing else because he had no ships.

Porter turned the *Harriet Lane* into a ferry and by 3 o'clock had landed 400 men, 2 pieces of artillery, horses, and luggage carts on the Pensacola side of the harbor. Porter then steamed up to the town and warned the mayor not to permit activities hostile to the United States. The only loyalists to make a demonstration were negroes. If there were any loyal whites in the town, they suppressed their emotions. One could never tell when the Union troops might be withdrawn, and Secessionists knew how to be most unpleasant toward acknowledged Unionists in their midst.

The next day, after Porter had ferried to the mainland some 1,200 other soldiers with their camp equipment, his long-coveted flagship, the *Octorara,* arrived from Washington. The *Octorara* was one of the new double-enders called by Lincoln "a vessel with two sterns." Her arrival marked one of the most joyous moments of Porter's life. Although most of Porter's personal belongings were on board her, the *Octorara,* after her repairs were completed, had been further detained for the defense of Washington.

For nearly three months Porter had lived on the hospitality of his officers, borrowing their clerks to do his writing, and bunking here and there. "Every man should have a little privacy at times," he had written to Fox on April 8, "but I have not a place where I can retire to and shift my clothes when wet." He was so delighted by the *Octorara* that immediately he wrote Fox to strike out from his last report certain remarks about the Flag Officer that were not "exactly shipshape." "Though this is so," he wrote, "it won't do in a public dispatch to say so." [10]

Porter returned to Ship Island hoping to find Farragut there, but the latter was reported to be at that moment ascending the river with even his largest ships to Vicksburg. Porter wrote Fox begging to be allowed to attack Mobile. To Farragut he wrote, "Mobile is so ripe now, that it would fall to us like a mellow pear." [11]

In lieu of anything more important he made sail on his schooners and distributed them along the coast off Mobile to seal the blockade. In the open roadstead outside he placed several of the steamers to intercept anything that might outrun the mortar boats. In this way he captured three schooners and two sloops laden with sugar, cigars, tar, turpentine, and cotton. This work, however, was blockade duty; and Porter did not want the war to end before he got back into action.

The mails brought news of the evacuation of Norfolk. By a coincidence the Confederates had blown up the *Merrimac* and evacuated the Norfolk Navy Yard on the same day that they had set fire to everything in Pensacola. Porter promised that if Fox would send him the Ericsson *Monitor,* now that it was no longer needed to blockade the *Merrimac,* he would take the Mobile forts "or eat them." [12]

When he saw the New York *Herald's* account of the Battle of New Orleans, with its misplaced emphasis on the part played by General Butler, Porter unburdened his wrath to Fox: "*Butler* did it all!!! So I see it stated by that blackguard reporter of the

Herald..." Porter recommended a Departmental order "that no reporter should be allowed on board of our ships under any circumstances..." [13]

While Porter was engrossed with these meditations, he received a letter from General Butler proposing that he bring his mortars back into the river to attack Vicksburg. Farragut's guns could not reach the troublesome batteries on the heights behind Vicksburg, and Butler wanted Farragut to try again using the vertical fire of the mortars.

In the same dispatch vessel came Farragut's order for Porter to take the mortars to Vicksburg. The Department, explained Farragut, had sent him imperative orders to clear out the river.

To Porter it seemed clear that Butler had coerced the Department into giving the Navy an impossible assignment, for at this late season the water might fall at any time and leave the heavy ships landlocked many miles from the coast.

Though Farragut asked for six mortars, Porter returned with twenty. At the same time he sent a final appeal to Farragut to change his plan and make Mobile the first object of his attack.

"Tell the ladies," Porter wrote to Fox on June 2, "there are no jealousies out here that I know of, but kind brotherly feeling. ... There is glory enough for all ..." [14]

Not many hours later he received the following message from Fox: "Dear Porter: Somebody has made a most serious blunder, in persuading the Flag Officer to go at Mobile instead of obeying his instructions to go up the Mississippi River. We have sent out two steamers in all haste to require him to proceed at once, and cut off Beauregard who has but the line left viz. to Memphis. Davis has repulsed the iron rams of the enemy, but they are going at him again and if they should be successful, Halleck would have to fall back and we should lose St. Louis, Cairo and everything. It seems extraordinary how Farragut could have committed this terrible mistake... Mobile and the whole Gulf will fall at any time, but the Mississippi is a golden opportunity that I fear is fast slipping through our fingers ..." This letter was written on May 17. [15]

Porter rushed his vessels into the river. All his plans were now changed. Mobile was forgotten while Vicksburg became the immediate objective.

THE NAVAL ATTACK ON VICKSBURG

Washington's only means of communication with Farragut, by steamer from Hampton Roads to New Orleans, was a slow and tedious transit even during the more normal days of routine blockading. But when the victory at New Orleans imperiously demanded a follow-up campaign, the lack of speedy communication proved exasperating. Only by a farsighted strategy in the first place might Washington have avoided the confusion that now developed.

About the time Farragut's dispatch-bearer reached Washington there arrived also disquieting rumors from the western army. After General Grant had driven a deep salient into West Tennessee, he had been surprised and nearly defeated at Shiloh; whereupon General Halleck had come down in person to whip Confederate General Beauregard. The cautious Halleck had elbowed Grant into the position of second in command with nothing to do and placed a check on Sherman, who might otherwise be tempted to fight the enemy irregularly. The ensuing campaign against Corinth, Mississippi, had then dragged methodically throughout May, with Halleck's large army advancing a mile a day and devoting the remainder of the twenty-four hours to entrenching. Halleck's snail-footed invasion of Jefferson Davis' home state began quite naturally to tax the nerves of the leaders in Washington. Fourteen days won fourteen miles. By the time Corinth was evacuated on May 31, Washington had heard alarming rumors that Confederate troops were ferrying across the Mississippi River into Arkansas. New Orleans had inspired hope for an early termination of the war. But in case Beauregard should elude Halleck, and escape into Arkansas and Texas, Washington feared, he might continue the war indefinitely. In the upper river Flag Officer Davis had been checked by the Confederates at Memphis. In the emergency Washington's single hope was that Farragut would come up the river from New Orleans and cut Beauregard off from a westerly retreat.

In these difficult days when so much depended on immediate action and when facilities for rapid communication with Farragut did not exist, it was most unfortunate that Washington should be able to get quick news via Secessionist newspapers from Richmond. Washington recognized, of course, that such news was partisan; but until dispatches from their officers arrived—from two to three weeks later—they had no means of checking its accuracy or discovering to what extent it had been censored.

News of Porter's May 7 appearance off Mobile reached Washington via the Richmond press, along with Confederate conjectures that Farragut's fleet was coming from New Orleans to attack Mobile. The Navy Department recalled that Farragut's orders had mentioned Mobile and Secretary Welles began to worry.

At the end of May, just when it was most necessary to head off Beauregard, news came through Richmond that Farragut had ascended to Vicksburg, surveyed the formidable batteries on the bluffs and then retreated to New Orleans.

Lincoln conferred with Welles. Had Farragut disobeyed his orders? Mr. Welles sent the Flag Officer a dispatch in triplicate, via three fast steamers, one of which was chartered for this special mission. This dispatch demanded that Farragut go up the river at all hazards. It was this message, conveying the imperative command of the President, that caused Farragut to bring Porter into the river as fast as his boats could carry him. Washington, of course, knew little about the Confederate defenses along the cliff-bound east bank of the river, and nothing at all concerning the grounding of the *Hartford* and the *Brooklyn* even when the river was at flood stage. They did not know that Farragut had been ill the day his officers induced him to return with his large ships to New Orleans; and the Confederate censorship had withheld the information that Farragut had left a considerable force of gunboats to blockade Vicksburg from below.

When Porter arrived off Pass à l'Outre, the large congregation of merchant vessels reminded him of the scene a year ago, except that now they were pushing and crowding to get in, and noisily bidding against each other for the services of the few tugboats in the vicinity. Most of these tugs were engaged in towing supplies for Butler's army. Certain ones Porter recognized as prizes the Navy had turned over to the Army. He spoke several of these demanding that they draw some of the mortar schooners into the river. The tugboat captains informed him that he would have to consult the Army commander at Fort Jackson.

With several schooners in tow, Porter's new flagship, the *Octorara*, arrived at New Orleans on June 9. Porter requested General Butler to place two of the Army-controlled tugs at his disposal. Butler acceded to the request but informed Porter that the tugs were under the captain of the fort. Porter called on the latter, who also agreed to furnish the tugs, but in turn informed him that the tugs were under the immediate command of the quartermaster. Thus Porter was forced to unwind the red tape of officialdom.

Meanwhile Porter kept the Mortar Flotilla's steamers constantly busy. At last the Army tugboat *Fox* was reported at his service. Since the naval storeship was sorely needed, Porter ordered the *Fox* to tow this vessel to New Orleans, and then to take three mortar schooners up to Vicksburg. But the captain of the *Fox*, instead of returning to New Orleans with the supply vessel, brought up two merchantmen. So elated was he over his private prosperity that he presented himself drunk at the St. Charles Hotel in New Orleans, whereupon he was instantly dismissed by General Butler. Porter now applied for the *Empire Parish;* and this steamer was given him, upon the annoying condition that Porter supply her with provisions from the Navy and pay her crew.

To Farragut Porter wrote, "I don't hesitate to say that there has been a deliberate attempt made to deceive and trifle with me. ...We have traitors enough to fight against without finding them holding office under our Government... I wish we had retained for our own use the vessels we captured and turned over to the army, and I would earnestly suggest...that we obtain possession of them again and employ them for naval purposes." [1] Farragut sent this letter to Welles to give him "a slight idea of the difficulties with which we have to contend in our ascent of this river." Welles dispatched it to the War Department "to call attention to the abuses practiced." Thence it got back to General Butler, who called in witnesses, took affidavits, and wrote Porter a sarcastic letter, to which Porter replied that he "never supposed it was a high offense to inform a general that the public duty was neglected."

The situation at New Orleans was so complicated and exasperating that Butler can be held at least partially excused by it. For Butler, too, had his troubles. The Confederates had carried off much of the city's food supply and a large and impoverished population had to be fed. Trade had to be revived. The occupied region—once the entrepôt for millions of pounds of cotton—should have been able at least to feed itself; but Richmond had ordered its generals to burn all cotton throughout the occupied areas, that New Orleans might prove a barren victory.

By June 13 Porter had sixteen of his schooners started on their 400-mile journey against the current to Vicksburg. The remaining four left New Orleans within a few days, towed by Farragut's ships. The shortness of the food supply at New Orleans necessitated so much red tape that Porter rushed his flotilla ahead on half rations; and the heat, mosquitoes, and fetid atmosphere of New Orleans in this sweltering second week of June made all hands anxious to get away.

Between New Orleans and Vicksburg the great Father of Waters tortures through an almost unbroken succession of crescents and devil's elbows, flowing to the north and west almost as often as to the south and east. From New Orleans to Baton Rouge the water inside the levees was now higher than the surrounding bottom-lands, and one could look down upon the blackened clapboard roofs of the negro cabins and see the heads of horses and men passing along the roads. Now and again a bushwhacker would fire his shotgun at the passing flotilla.

At Baton Rouge the bluffs begin along the east bank of the river and continue up to Vicksburg. Baton Rouge stands thirty to forty feet above the high level of water. In 1862 it was a beautiful little town with green terraces, pleasant esplanades. The slate-roofed French and Spanish houses and the miniature Bastille, which was the arsenal, contrasted pleasantly with the neighboring specimens of Southern colonial architecture. Farragut's flagship, the *Hartford,* was tied to the wharf at Baton Rouge as the mortar steamers with schooners lashed alongside passed the town. Here and there groups of negroes shouted and made jubilant gesticulations toward the bombers. The white population kept sullenly indoors. A few days earlier a band of mounted guerrillas had fired upon a petty officer as he put in to shore to get his laundry, and two of Farragut's ships had emptied their guns into the town. Several regiments of Federal troops, which had been detached from Butler's command, occupied Baton Rouge.

To ward off scurvy from the flotilla, Porter sent boats to the plantations along the river to buy vegetables, fresh mutton, and beef. But even on the plantations food was almost as scarce as in New Orleans. The little he collected spoiled quickly in the summer heat. At night negroes escaped from the plantations and rowed out to the *Octorara,* to be signed on by Porter as coal passers.

Behind the hills at night the Confederates sent up rocket signals. Occasionally a vindictive artillery piece would fire upon the flotilla. The guns on Porter's steamers could not reply effectively, since the mortar schooners alongside masked their fire.

At the mouth of the Red River lay many suspicious looking flatboats. Porter could not stop now to investigate them. At Ellis Cliffs he was fired upon by batteries not hitherto reported. Porter pushed on by at his best speed.

Eighteen miles farther up at one of the bends in the river were two clusters of houses on different levels joined by an almost perpendicular red clay road. This was Natchez. The cliff here was ten or a dozen feet higher than at Baton Rouge. Natchez was also silent. Along the wharves of Natchez-Under-The-Hill, once notorious for rowdy boatmen, were piles of charred cotton that still exhaled a wretched smoke.

Twenty-five miles below Vicksburg the clay hills arose to a height of a hundred feet. Heavy cannon looked down across the burned village of Grand Gulf toward the river. These batteries were shelled by two of Farragut's gunboats as Porter passed.

Porter arrived below Vicksburg on June 20, after a seven-day trip from New Orleans. He cast off the schooners, tied them to the trees below the range of the Vicksburg batteries, and reported to Captain Craven—the senior officer left by Farragut in the vicinity of Vicksburg.

Many elements subversive to morale had fixed their tentacles upon Farragut's fleet. Food was short. Coal was running low. The river was beginning to fall, and several vessels were aground. The weather was so hot and the men so unacclimated that most of the heavy work was done at night, the men attempting to sleep in the heat of the day. The malaria mosquito caused the sick lists to increase daily. Worst of all, everyone in the fleet believed the forthcoming thrust past Vicksburg to be utterly useless.

Porter sent Captain Craven a memorandum warning that patrol vessels would have to be stationed at Ellis Cliffs. Craven sent a midshipman on board the *Octorara* directing Porter to send to the *Brooklyn* all negroes he had collected. Porter returned the midshipman with a request for a written order. Porter had already signed the negroes on as part of the flotilla. The reply nettled Craven. In a recent letter to his wife Craven had scoffed at the New York *Herald's* account of "Porter's mortar boats and Butler's expedition!" To Farragut, Craven reported that he did not wish to have any dealings with Porter.

On June 22, Porter wrote Fox, "I would be very much pleased if the Department would relieve me from this command or all connection with the Gulf Squadron. I have no reasons to assign, and am willing to serve anywhere else in a yawl boat."[2]

During the next few days while the rest of the mortars were arriving, Porter ran the *Octorara* up under the Vicksburg batteries and shelled them to get their range.

The Walnut Hills, on whose river slope the city of Vicksburg lies, mark the end of the three hundred miles of cliffs along the east bank of the river. The hills at this point rise to a height of 250 feet. As if to climax the advantage for the defenders the river at Vicksburg makes one of its most perfect horseshoe bends, giving the highest batteries a commanding diagonal sweep along both shanks of the horseshoe.

As soon as Farragut passed through Forts Jackson and St. Philip, the Confederate General Lovell had telegraphed for all available guns to be hurried to Vicksburg. Aided by two months of delay on the part of the Federals, the Confederates had now terraced the Vicksburg hills with every type of gun. Their batteries began near the water's edge and arose tier on tier to a final height of 264 feet for the rearmost on the crest of the hills about 1,500 yards from the river. Against the crest batteries Farragut's ships could do nothing, for the elevation was too great.

On the peninsula across the river from Vicksburg, Union General Thomas Williams projected a canal, to straighten the channel and isolate the Vicksburg batteries. To supplement his small number of soldiers General Williams robbed the surrounding plantations of a thousand blacks and on June 27 started them digging his canal. To his sorrow he found a very thick stratum of clay instead of the hoped-for sand. Nevertheless he mounted a few pieces of artillery to cover his operations, and continued digging. If he had had a sufficient number of troops to storm Vicksburg, as Butler had intended that he should, he might have been more useful, but he did not have the men.

Without the survey ship to make a careful triangulation of the river below Vicksburg, Porter resorted to trial-and-error methods for placing his mortar schooners and the imperfect fuses made the work exasperating. To avoid the midday heat he worked all night. On the right-hand side of the river (going up) he placed nine schooners under Lieutenant Watson Smith. This division was partly sheltered by overhanging trees, and was protected against boarding parties from the land by an almost impassable swamp. Along the edge of this swamp Porter dug trenches and stationed pickets. Since the primary task of the Mortar Flotilla now was to cover the passage of Farragut's fleet, and no such protracted night bombardment was planned as that below Fort Jackson, Porter had to fortify himself against surprise attacks. He swung a large bell at the water's edge with ropes leading to the pickets so that alarms could be sounded if the enemy approached. Howitzers were kept leveled at the swamps.

Against the Louisiana bank of the river he placed his other division of eight schooners under Lieutenant Queen. Since the schooners on that side were the more exposed, they were all dressed alow and aloft with bushes, as they had been two months earlier.

After these preliminaries, Farragut arrived with the *Hartford* and several gunboats and Porter began bombarding the enemy's batteries in and around the town. A troublesome Confederate battery erected just below the marine hospital was commanded by Captain Todd, the Secessionist brother-in-law of President Lincoln.

Farragut's plan for the thrust past Vicksburg resembled that used in passing Forts Jackson and St. Philip.[3] Porter's mortar schooners were to shell the batteries on the heights. Porter was to move his steamers up close to the city and attack the marine hospital battery while Farragut's larger ships, the *Hartford,* the *Richmond,* the *Brooklyn,* and seven smaller gunboats passed up above the city. Farragut's ten vessels were to form in two lines, the three large ships constituting the line nearest Vicksburg. The vessels in the two lines were to be so staggered that all of their broadsides could be simultaneously used against the enemy.

This was a good plan. But Farragut's general order was ambiguously worded, and although he explained it in conference and individually with his officers, his explanations were clumsily made. Captain Craven, next to Farragut in age and experience, rightly construed the written order to mean that the ships in the rear of the line should not pass above Vicksburg if any of the batteries remained unsilenced.

At 2 A.M. on Saturday June 28, red lanterns were run up to the *Hartford's* masthead as the signal to get under way. At three the fleet weighed anchor and proceded upstream toward the mortar schooners. At four the air was filled with flying mortar shells, and Porter, bucking the three-knot current with his steamers, commenced throwing a quick fire into the hospital battery.

The *Richmond* and four gunboats passed Porter's squadron. As the vessels passed they opened with broadsides of grape, canister, and shrapnel. Confederate shot splashed in the river. From the *Octorara* Porter could watch the explosions of his mortar shells. They smashed the clay mounds in the lower terraces but failed to silence the batteries on the crest, which in turn were raining shot dangerously close to the little mortar steamers. The *Hartford* at last came up. In the dusk her gunners took aim on the flashes from Confederate guns and wasted many a round of ammunition by shooting at exploding mortar shells.

No sooner had the *Hartford* passed by than the wheel ropes of the *Octorara* jammed, compelling her to fall back for emergency repairs. Porter hailed the *Miami* to push up and close the range to 600 yards. As he drifted down he came under the line of fire from the *Brooklyn* and a shell from the *Brooklyn* burst off the *Octorara's* port side. A few minutes later the *Brooklyn* fired a stand of grapeshot into the ex-ferryboat *Clifton*. Porter hailed the *Clifton,* the *Westfield,* and the *J. P. Jackson* and ordered them to go ahead while the *Octorara* was being repaired. Fortunately this required but a few minutes. The *Jackson,* now the foremost of Porter's steamers, received a shot through her wheelhouse which carried away the leg of her helmsman. Porter shouted for the *Clifton* to assist her. While passing a line to her stricken sister ship, the *Clifton* also was hit and her port boiler exploded. Six men in and about her magazine were scalded to death and several others seriously burned. A number plunged overboard; one drowned. The rôles were now reversed, and the *Jackson* became the helping ship. The *Westfield* was struck on her engine frame by a heavy, rifled shot, which fortunately landed butt end foremost and did little damage. The *Octorara* now managed to run a line to the *Clifton* and tow her out of action, while the others drifted down the river.

As daylight came the mortar shells could be seen distinctly against the sky. They grew smaller and smaller and barely skimmed over the ridge. From behind the cliffs the sun rose, and Porter ordered the mortar schooners to cease firing.

Across the peninsula the officers and crews of two heavy ships and six gunboats celebrated their passage by rolling out liquor kegs and splicing the main brace. Several of Colonel Ellet's ram vessels attached to Davis' squadron came down the river and welcomed Farragut. But Farragut was in no mood to celebrate. He had passed the Vicksburg batteries under the urgent orders of the President and the Department. He had demonstrated that it could be done, but many of his vessels had suffered as severely as in the Battle of New Orleans. The *Brooklyn* and the gunboats *Katahdin* and *Kennebec* had not come through—though Farragut at one time during the passage had deliberately slowed the *Hartford* to allow these rearmost vessels to close up. Farragut was worried. He sent a messenger across the peninsula to find out what had happened to them.

The messenger returned. The *Brooklyn*, the *Katahdin*, and the *Kennebec* were all safely anchored below the mortar boats. The messenger also reported that Porter had eight men killed and ten or twelve wounded and that two of his steamers had been badly injured. Captain Craven of the *Brooklyn* sent an informal letter: "Thank God there is nothing the matter with either of the three vessels below. After you left us, and Porter stopped throwing his shells, the rascals who had been thoroughly driven from their guns beforehand returned...it seemed as if a thousand new hands had come to demolish us... The *Kensington* arrived about noon with provisions, and the mortar boats have already besieged me with requisitions...I send requisitions to you... There is nothing new from New Orleans... Should you desire Porter to keep up a demonstration upon the hills, please write to him, for it is too evident that he does not like to receive instructions from myself..." [4]

Infuriated over what appeared to be disobedience of orders on the part of the *Brooklyn,* the *Katahdin,* and the *Kennebec,* Farragut directed Captain Craven of the *Brooklyn* to submit his official report. Craven now stated that by the time the *Brooklyn* arrived abreast the lower batteries the steamers of the Mortar Flotilla obstructed his passage in such a manner as to oblige him to stop his engines, and this delayed his progress. He had not passed up, however, because he had interpreted the Flag Officer's orders to mean that he must not do so *if any of the enemy's batteries remained unsilenced.*

Farragut was not easily moved to wrath. Craven was an old friend and a poor man with a large family. He was an officer who had distinguished himself in the Battle of New Orleans. Nevertheless Farragut could not allow his subordinates to depart from his general orders and take refuge behind a misconstrued phrase. Farragut's letter of censure brought Captain Craven's request to be detached, and no amount of mediation on the part of Bell or Davis could persuade Craven to withdraw his request. On July 1, Captain Bell came aboard the *Brooklyn* and took command, Captain Craven leaving the ship amid the cheering of the men who had served under him. The hardships to which the fleet had been subjected had strained everybody's temper, and Craven was a victim of the situation.

Porter's requisitions for provisions were ignored during this painful correspondence between Farragut and Craven. Neither Porter nor the men of the Mortar Flotilla on half rations could understand why they should not eat, now that the supply vessel had arrived, especially since their bombardment of Vicksburg was going steadily on. On June 30, Porter wrote Fox, "The weather is very hot here, and we of the mortar fleet are living on *half rations,* no flour served, no bread, no butter, no sugar, no molasses, and a store ship with all these articles lying alongside of us— But we are outsiders and not expected to eat— I have an infirmity of temper which never permits me to forget nor forgive, and the only pleasure I have is in knowing that a day of *Reckoning* will come." [5]

In his report to Secretary Welles Farragut praised Porter's perseverance in getting to Vicksburg and his steady work of demolition and annoyance to the enemy. "Porter's service has been hard upon his officers and crews, though they have performed it well, willingly and unflinchingly." [6] Porter in turn reported to Farragut: "I have to mention favorably the divisional officers and the acting masters commanding the mortar vessels. Anchored at all times in a position selected by myself, more with regard to the object to be accomplished than to anyone's comfort or safety, knowing that they will have to stay there without a chance of getting away until I think proper to remove them (no matter how thick and fast the shot and shell may fly) there has always existed a rivalry as to who shall have the post of honor (the leading vessel), almost certain to be struck, if not destroyed. They know no weariness, and they really seem to take a delight in mortar firing, which is painful to those even accustomed to it. It requires more than ordinary zeal to stand the ordeal. Though I may have at times been exacting and fault-finding with them for not conforming with the rules of the service (which [it] requires the education of a lifetime to learn), yet I cannot withhold my applause when I see these men working with such earnest and untiring devotion to their duties while under fire." [7]

Porter's men thrived upon hardships. Their work was hard, their food short, but Porter worked beside them, inspired them to compete with Farragut's squadron, outspokenly championed their rights upon such occasions as the tilt with Craven. Unlike Farragut, who fumbled reluctantly for words to praise his officers, Porter commended the men who served under him with a fulsomeness never known in the Navy before or since. He praised his men generously throughout his detailed report to Welles. Nor did he stop with a single report, but wrote again and again to impress his men's bravery upon the authorities. Mr. Welles, the Connecticut Puritan, frowned upon Porter's insistent praise and thought it developed sycophancy and clannishness in the Navy. But the men who worked with Porter appreciated his recognition, for this offset the bite of many a Porter sarcasm.

The steady bombardment of Vicksburg almost, but never quite, settled down into monotony. On June 30, and July 2, Confederate troops rushed through the swamps to board the mortar schooners. But Porter's pickets tolled the great bell, crouched down in their dugouts, and all the vessels opened howitzers on the bushes for a mile along. Mortar shells with half-pound charges were tossed into the thickets, and the attackers were routed. Porter's men leaped ashore and found the marsh strewn with knapsacks, cartridge boxes, boots and shoes. A pair of officer's boots with silver spurs was recovered from the mud. Three Confederates who had not been able to escape yelled their surrender to the approaching Federals.

From the prisoners Porter learned that whenever the mortars opened fire the men in the Confederate batteries always ran back 600 yards until the shells had exploded. Porter suggested to General Williams that he take his men up the hills under cover of the bombardment and capture the Vicksburg batteries. Ships alone could do little without the Army. "Ships can't crawl up those hills," he said. But General Williams declined the movement. He had but 3,500 men, and his scouts had reported 13,000 of the enemy within easy striking distance. For having promised 6,000 men and having sent only 3,500, Porter added another item to the score against General Butler at New Orleans.

On the first of July Flag Officer Davis brought his fleet leisurely down the river to join Farragut's across the peninsula. Davis was a mild-mannered man of scholarly temperament. In the Battle of Memphis (June 6) Davis' river ironclads had won their fight against the few remaining wooden vessels of the Confederate River Defense Fleet but had allowed the only important Confederate vessel, the ironclad ram *Arkansas,* to escape to a safe hiding place up the Yazoo River, whence she might at any time have surprised Farragut's unwieldy salt-water warships, near Vicksburg. For three weeks after allowing the Confederate ram to slip through his fingers Davis had delayed at Memphis before descending the river to join Farragut.

On the first day of July Davis sent down four mortar scows to echo Porter's fire from above the bend. The thundering of the iron kegs from two directions served to keep up the spirits of the fleet. Midsummer chills and fever, along with the dreaded dysentery, crowded the sick bays on every ship. The *Richmond* alone reported sixty-eight cases during the early days of July.

On the Fourth of July all the vessels of the fleet, excepting the *Richmond*, fired a national salute. Each division of the Mortar Flotilla supplemented its regular bombardment with a greeting of thirty-four holiday guns.

On the night of July 9, Farragut received telegraphic orders via Cairo to have Porter proceed immediately with twelve mortar boats and the *Octorara* to Hampton Roads.

Early the next morning Porter crossed the peninsula to take his formal leave of Farragut. For seven months Farragut had thought only of his own expedition. After the clean victory of New Orleans —the futile anticlimax of Vicksburg! Lives lost, vessels injured, lifelong friendships disrupted. By giving him a view of the larger problem the telegram from Washington had taken the Flag Officer out of his melancholy.

Porter arranged to take the twelve mortar schooners—leaving Commander Renshaw of the *Westfield* in charge of the remaining vessels of the flotilla—and at 3:30 in the afternoon Porter started down the river. At Warrenton and Ellis Cliffs a few Secessionist muskets volleyed farewell. The Confederates were glad to see the Mortar Flotilla depart. Far and wide they heralded the withdrawal of the twelve mortar boats as admission of defeat. Townspeople no longer sulked indoors but turned out en masse to witness the retreat. Lorgnettes and field glasses eagerly surveyed the vessels, "looking," Porter declared, "for mythical shot holes." But Porter had patched and painted over his damages. His crews in white, officers in full dress, he passed by the river towns in parade formation.

While anchored for the night at the mouth of the Red River, he noticed a steamer come out and another enter. He had the *Clifton* cast off her tow and rush into the river. The *Clifton* encountered and chased the Confederate ram *Webb* for ten miles up the Red River. While this was in progress Porter inspected Colonel Ackland's plantation on the east bank of the Mississippi and found a quantity of food which probably had been ferried across from Louisiana. From the mouth of the Red River down to Natchez Porter collected all the barges and ferries and carried them with him to New Orleans. Temporarily, at least, he would stop the eastern flow of Confederate supplies. River boats licensed by General Butler he allowed to continue their trade, although he found that some of these vessels abused their privileges by selling to the people contraband provisions easy to relay to the Confederate armies.

In New Orleans he noticed a great increase in Union shipping. Many foreign flags also gave a lively color to the scene. Porter found the people of New Orleans discontented with Butler's rule, and he thought that they had reason, but at the same time Porter considered them "great fools" for not approving of Butler's indirect supplying of salt, shoes, blankets, and flour to the Confederate armed forces.

The *Octorara* enjoyed an easy passage to Hampton Roads. Two days before her arrival she captured the *Tubal Cain,* a blockade runner with a cargo of munitions for the Confederacy labeled "hardware."

At Hampton Roads Porter learned that the Southern ram *Arkansas* had slipped through the combined fleets of Farragut and Davis and found shelter under Vicksburg! To Fox he wrote a letter hinting very pointedly that in the upper river a more energetic flag officer than the scholarly Davis was needed.

17.

THE NEWPORT INTERLUDE

THROUGHOUT the first twelve months of the war, newspaper wits cudgeled Mr. Welles for his sluggishness. A typical cartoon portrayed him sitting with his feet aloft and a spider web spun between his legs. After the capture of New Orleans the newspapers abandoned their witticisms for encomiums. "Mr. Welles has made the best and fullest report of any department...has furnished us a navy which both gratifies and surprises the nation," said one paper.

With a favorable press to back him Welles was now able to push through Congress the greatest naval bill in fifty years. The measure established two new grades in the Navy, commodore and rear admiral. Nine superannuated officers were retired as rear admirals to clear the way for four active rear admirals: Farragut, Goldsborough, Du Pont, and Foote. Eighteen senior captains were promoted to commodore; forty commanders, to captain. For the Navy Department the new bureaus of Ordnance and of Navigation were provided. Of more significance in view of the widespread rivalry between the military and the naval services was the formation of the Navy's new Mississippi Squadron.

These measures were enacted while Porter was on his way east with the Mortar Flotilla, and Mr. Welles in spite of a 100-degree heat wave was remaining in Washington to hear the pleas of disappointed elderly officers and their wives.

Unfortunately for Porter on the very day of his arrival in Washington Captain H. A. Adams, the one-time senior officer off Fort Pickens, was writing the Navy Department to know why he had been passed over. Captain Adams' letter recalled to Mr. Welles the curious episode of the *Powhatan*.

It was rumored in Washington that when Porter disregarded Seward's last-minute countermand of the order, Mr. Welles had wanted to court-martial him but was restrained by Lincoln, who alleged his own complicity in extenuation of Porter's misdemeanor. After this the conscientious Secretary of the Navy had smothered his wrath and tried hard to forget. But it was not in Mr. Seward's nature to allow Mr. Welles to forget that he, the Secretary of State, had saved Fort Pickens while the Navy Secretary's expedition to Fort Sumter had signally failed. The matter was frequently referred to in friendly badinage. At such times, when Mr. Welles declined to be amused, Lincoln would speak disparagingly of Porter.

While the Secretary undoubtedly desired to discipline Porter, it is clear that he did not consider it politic to do so at once.

When Porter returned at the end of the *Powhatan's* cruise, he had entered the Secretary's office flanked by two Senators of the Naval Affairs Committee whom Mr. Welles cordially despised. At one of the crucial moments of the war Porter had proposed the expedition to New Orleans, and with the support of Senators Grimes and Hale had seen his plans accepted and had himself been made Commander of the Mortar Flotilla.

Throughout the whole of the operations below New Orleans, Porter had sent his reports directly to the Secretary. For months Mr. Welles had never communicated with him in return but had sent instructions through Farragut—although Porter persistently urged Fox to dispense with red tape and save delay by sending his orders direct. Only once had Mr. Welles written directly to Porter: when it became his official duty to congratulate him on the victory of New Orleans.

When Porter arrived at Norfolk in the *Octorara* on July 26, 1862, he was ill with intermittent fever. Usually a victim of intermittent fever remained in bed about a week, was giddy and bilious, alternating between fever and chill. For weeks after the fever subsided he could expect fearful aches in his bones. If he remained quiet he might experience hours and even days of normal health, but the slightest exertion or eye-strain would send him back to bed.

On July 28 Porter left his bed prematurely, dispatched Lieutenant George Brown with the *Octorara* to Baltimore for repairs, left Lieutenant Watson Smith to take charge of the flotilla as it came in, and traveled by stage to Washington. Washington was sizzling in a heat wave.

Porter found that his home in Georgetown, No. 37 Gay Street, was vacant. Neighbors told him that his family had gone to Newport to get away from the heat. Not waiting to shift his clothes Porter went on to the Department to report to Mr. Welles.

The Secretary greeted him genially. Seeing that Porter was worn and haggard, Welles refused to allow him to exhaust himself by reporting on conditions in the Mississippi. Welles told Porter that when the mortars arrived they would probably be used along the James River to bombard Confederate batteries and protect the flank of the army under General McClellan. Meanwhile the mortar schooners would not arrive before August 10. Welles sent Porter home to bed. On August 1 when Porter again appeared at the Department the Secretary made out a two-weeks leave of absence for him and dispatched him to Newport to visit his family and rest.

Porter arrived in Newport with a high fever and so dizzy he could hardly stand. Georgy put him to bed at once and lectured him for not taking care of himself. By reading him the newspapers she managed to keep him in bed three days.

After eighteen months the fighting had reached a stalemate on every front. McClellan's large army in the peninsula below Richmond—where Porter's son Essex was stationed—was paralyzed. No one could understand why; yet everyone had his own conjecture. The army of 50,000 in northern Virginia had lost all trace of the opposing Confederates under Stonewall Jackson, and Washington was trembling with fear of an attack. Du Pont's fleet and the small coöperating army at Charleston were idling. After the passage of the Confederate ram *Arkansas* through their combined fleets both Davis and Farragut had left Vicksburg, one returning up the river to Helena, Arkansas, with his river ironclads and the other with his seagoing wooden ships to New Orleans. From Helena to Baton Rouge the Confederates held undisputed control of the Mississippi. At New Orleans were General Butler and an avaricious host of Northern cotton traders.

Defeatism stalked in every quarter of the North. The streets of villages were lined with men in uniform on leave of absence who ought to have been at their posts of duty. Secret societies opposed to the war, like the Knights of the Golden Circle, flourished in Ohio, Indiana, and Illinois. In New York and Connecticut the Lincoln administration was openly denounced by "doughface" anti-war Republicans and "copperhead" anti-administration Democrats. Everywhere the movement to oust General McClellan was angrily agitated.

On August 4 two clarifying executive orders came from Washington like lightning across a lowering sky. From the War Department came the cancellation of all leaves of absence. Henceforth no furloughs would be granted save by the Department itself. All able-bodied soldiers who did not report back to their posts of duty by August 11 would be classed as deserters. From the White House came not only a call for 300,000 volunteers but a threat to apply the draft in any State which failed to raise its quota by August 15. The immediate result was a storm of political speeches, torch-light parades, and anti-draft riots.

On August 5 Porter received a note from Fox: "Nearly all the Bummers have arrived with considerable sickness. The *Octorara* will not be ready under ten days so you have that length of time. I will telegraph you when she is ready." [1] Porter crawled out of bed and replied: "My dear Fox, I was much surprised getting *two weeks'* leave of absence. I did not expect more than ten days; two weeks is a great deal to lose in these times when a Rebel ought to be knocked in the head every five seconds and people ought not to stop to blow until the war is over. I am pretty sick, but not sick enough to lie idle, and I hope you won't let anything go on without me and the Mortar fleet being there, wherever it goes it has good luck; telegraph me at a moment's notice and I will be off—this is a lovely place and just where you ought to spend two weeks, it would set you up." [2]

On August 6 Porter felt well enough to go to the Newport Club for a game of billiards.

Inside the club a noisy argument was in progress over the latest dispatches. The Army of Northern Virginia was reported to have located the enemy and to be falling back upon Washington. Various members of the club denounced the Government for interfering too much with General McClellan's command. Bets were made that if McClellan were ousted the people would vote for McClellan as President in the next election. The crowd asked Porter's opinion of the situation.

"McClellan's troops," said Porter frankly, "have not been taught what discipline is. Is it not awful to get so incessantly worsted when we have such good material and such equipment! The troops have no discipline. They ought to shoot a thousand soldiers and hang a dozen or so of officers. After that they would have an army that could fight!" [3]

With the country divided into as many hostile camps as there were generals in the field, it was hazardous for so reckless and plain-spoken a man as Porter ever to have left the sanctuary of his quarter-deck. To speak so plainly in Newport—where every wall had eyes and ears that connected with the Navy Department—was doubly dangerous. But Porter was not the man to mince words. If he felt strongly on any subject he said what he thought and did not care a snap of his fingers who knew it. In some form Porter's criticism of General McClellan reached Washington.

The next day Porter received a telegram ordering him to proceed to Washington without delay and report to the Navy Department.

Porter arrived in Washington on August 8 at 6 P.M. and went straight to the Department. Mr. Welles had gone home, but the Assistant Secretary was still in. Chief Clerk Faxon lifted his eyebrows, said nothing. Porter entered Fox's office.

Fox greeted Porter formally and told him that his remarks in the Newport Club had greatly incensed Mr. Welles. Porter recounted what he had said. Fox agreed with him and hoped that on the morrow Porter would be able to explain things to the Secretary.

"Meanwhile," inquired Fox, "can you get your things out of the *Octorara?* Mr. Welles has given her to George Brown. He's to take her to Charleston."

"Tell Brown he can have all my things. What about the mortar vessels?"

"They are to be turned over to Wilkes. The organization is being broken up."

"So Wilkes is to get the James River Flotilla?"

"That's the order."

"Well, he's welcome to it. There's little reputation to be got in that quarter."

Porter then asked what his own duty would be, and Fox told him that his orders had not yet been made out.[4]

The next day when Porter returned to the Department, Fox informed him that Mr. Welles had decided to send him out to Cincinnati as aide to Commodore Hull, a superannuated officer recently placed on the retired list. Commodore Hull, inspecting the construction of gunboats, and having difficulties with the contractors, needed a younger man to work with him to get things done.

Porter then asked to see Mr. Welles, but the Secretary was engaged. Borrowing Fox's pen Porter wrote the Secretary a letter expressing his desire for active employment and requesting to be allowed to return to Newport. The permission was granted at once, and he left the building.

At last the disciplinary axe had fallen. Porter had fondly hoped that his part in the New Orleans expedition had cleared his record

in the Secretary's office, but it had not. When he had left Vicksburg, the men of the Mortar Flotilla had confidently predicted
that their commander would now be made admiral. Wainwright
of the *Harriet Lane* had even written the Assistant Secretary that
Porter should supplant Davis as flag officer of the Mississippi
Squadron. It is difficult to believe that Porter had no knowledge
of his devoted subaltern's machinations.

In his extremity there was but one thing he could do—go to
see Lincoln. This Porter did.

President Lincoln received Porter kindly.

"Well, what can I do for you, Captain?" asked the President.

Porter stated his case with considerable warmth. The understanding Lincoln praised Porter's work at New Orleans and proceeded to draw Porter out on present conditions in the river and
the details of the passage of the forts.

"I read all about it," Lincoln said at last, "how the ships went
up in line, firing their broadsides; how the mortars pitched into the
forts; how the forts pitched into the ships, and the ships into
the rams, and the rams into the gunboats, and the gunboats into
the fire rafts, and the fire rafts into the ships. Of course I couldn't
understand it all, but enough to know that it was a great victory.
It reminds me," he continued, "of a fight in a barroom at Natchez,
but I won't tell that now. It struck me that the fight at the forts
was something like the Natchez scrimmage, only a little more so." [5]

Porter's description of the fortifications at Vicksburg was a
revelation to Lincoln. Clearly the Confederates meant to hold this
great strategic point regardless of cost. So long as they held Vicksburg they could draw supplies of food from Arkansas, Louisiana,
and Texas. Through the Atchafalaya Bayou and the Red River,
as Porter had discovered on the trip down the river, Vicksburg
could even receive supplies directly from the Gulf.

In sanctioning the expedition to New Orleans Lincoln had recognized the Mississippi as the key to the general problem of crush-
ing the rebellion. The junction of Farragut with Davis was futile
so long as the magnificently fortified heights of Vicksburg remained in the hands of the enemy. If the Mississippi was the key
to the rebellion, Vicksburg was the key to the Mississippi.

The President then summoned a messenger and said, "Go tell
the Assistant Secretary of the Navy that I wish to see him at once."

Porter took leave on the plea that he had to catch his train to
Newport.

Porter's intermittent fever lingered for more than a month, but his hope for reinstatement through Lincoln kept up his spirits. When he heard that Watson Smith, one of his favorites of the Mortar Flotilla, had been detached from his respectable command and given the wretched Army transport *Stepping Stones* with one seaman and twelve negroes, one howitzer, one boat, one officer, and one engineer, Porter wrote to Fox in Smith's behalf. Smith was given a better command.

When Porter finally received an offer of the temporary command of the Potomac Flotilla, he declined it, stating that he preferred something more active. The idea of coöperating with McClellan did not entice Porter.

Porter anxiously followed the course of events through the newspapers. His elder brother, the stormy Commander William D. Porter, with whom he had broken off all relations fifteen years ago, was now coming into fame. In command of the ironclad *Essex* in Davis' fleet, William D. Porter dropped down below Vicksburg and defeated the Confederate ram *Arkansas*. His fame was widely heralded, though reporters attached to Butler's army disparaged the achievement by proclaiming that the *Arkansas* had been exploded by her own men. On August 30 the Confederates under Lee, Longstreet, and Jackson repulsed McClellan and Pope in the second Battle of Manassas.

On September 1 the Navy lost an ancient privilege—the daily ration of grog. Henceforth Porter, who enjoyed a toddy, could imbibe only medicinal liquors, labeled "vinegar bitters," "Mrs. Winslow's Soothing Syrup," etc.

On September 22 Mr. Welles telegraphed to Porter: "Sir: you will be assigned to duty West, and on your way report in person to this Department for further orders." [6]

When Porter appeared at the Department, Mr. Faxon smiled for the first time in months. Fox greeted him with something like the old time cheer.

When he was ushered into the Secretary's office, Mr. Welles quietly and deliberately explained that he had been thinking of sending Porter to relieve Davis as *flag officer* of the Mississippi Squadron. Although Porter was but a junior commander, he was to be entrusted with the temporary and local rank of acting rear admiral. The records dealing with the operations on the Western rivers were to be opened for his inspection so that he might familiarize himself with the task which the Department was contemplating for him.

Porter tried to accept his good fortune like a philosopher, with no visible show of his joy, but the stress was greater than he could bear. He said that if Mr. Welles ever ordered him to go over Niagara Falls in an iron pot he would do it!

At the end of seven days Mr. Welles again called Porter into his office and gravely handed him his orders to proceed to Cairo and relieve Davis. As commander in chief of the newly formed Mississippi Squadron Porter was to attempt to capture Vicksburg.

Welles, Fox, and Porter now hurried to the White House, where Porter, partly out of gratitude for the President's encouragement, agreed to coöperate with an army commanded by the Honorable John A. McClernand.

McClernand, a resident of Lincoln's home town and a politician of considerable influence in Illinois, had served with Grant at Forts Henry and Donelson and again at Shiloh. It had occurred to Lincoln that McClernand who seemed to understand the Western volunteers, might be a good man to send with Porter to capture Vicksburg.

Porter's willingness to coöperate with McClernand was also based in part upon his reading of the trials Commodore Foote had endured at the hands of the West Point generals, and he was glad enough not to be associated with one of them. His recollections of Colonel Harvey Brown at Fort Pickens and of General Williams digging his canal opposite Vicksburg instead of storming the heights had given him a distaste for the regular West Pointers. McClellan and Halleck, also West Pointers, he thought were little better.

On the night of October 1 Mr. Welles aired his emotions in the pages of his diary. He made a small list of Porter's virtues and a more comprehensive catalogue of the Porter infirmities. "It is a question, with his mixture of good and bad traits, how well he will succeed. His selection will be unsatisfactory to many, but his field of operations is peculiar, and a young and active officer is required for the duty to which he is assigned... If he does well I shall get no credit; if he fails I shall be blamed. No thanks in any event will be mine. Davis, whom he succeeds... is kind and affable but has not the vim, dash,—recklessness perhaps is the better word,—of Porter." [7]

Despite the fact that President Lincoln won in the obscure conflict with Secretary Welles, the latter protagonist never so much as confessed that there had been a battle. At the last minute before Porter left Washington Mr. Welles invited him to his house to tea, and between cups endeavored "to caution him on certain points and to encourage him in others."[8] Porter was aware of Welles's intentions and enjoyed the little causerie.

On the way to the train he posted a jubilant message to assure his anxious mother that he was taking the place of Admiral Davis, and not that of his own brother William. "How proud my old Father would be if he could see me an Admiral. Yet it gives me pain to be hoisted over the heads of those old veterans who have so long considered the Navy as belonging to them. It seems somewhat like the Justice of Providence who takes this method of mortifying them for their treatment of my Father."[9]

In his joke book years later Porter exulted, "I was now a flag officer, with the title of Acting Rear Admiral. Let those laugh who win. I won in spite of many obstacles, and enjoyed my victory immensely."[10]

THE FRESH-WATER NAVY

On October 1 while Secretary Welles was writing Porter's orders as commander in chief of the Mississippi Squadron, the War Department transferred its Western Flotilla to Flag Officer Davis at Cairo, and the Navy's new Mississippi Squadron came into existence. Even in the watery little village of Cairo it is probable that few citizens noticed the change. Not one of the large newspapers of the country mentioned it. The Union General Rosecrans was not aware of the new order of things until four months afterwards, when he peremptorily instructed the senior naval officer at Cairo to report to him and the transfer was called to his attention.

But the unheralded establishment of the Navy's Mississippi Squadron signified a new and clearer Federal strategy which was destined to split the Confederacy and hem in the Eastern theater of the war by a strict blockade. While Farragut's retreat to New Orleans and Davis' to Helena had damaged Federal prestige, and reduced the psychological advantage won by the capture of New Orleans, the Federals had learned important military lessons. The Navy Department had learned to its dismay that a naval force operating from the south single-handed without an adequate army could not take the Confederate river defenses, and the War Department had admitted that its Western armies invading from the north needed something more than a makeshift flotilla organization to coöperate on the rivers. As in other early errors in strategy, however, this failure sooner to launch a well-coördinated naval and military campaign along the line of the Mississippi can be excused by the lack of physical resources in the first years of the war. The Navy, wanting ships and adequate administrative facilities in the Department itself, had been compelled to devote its energies only to the most urgent naval objectives—the blockade, the capture of enemy cruisers, coöperation with the armies in the East wherever the military lines touched navigable water. Geographic isolation from contact with the Navy had given Western military operations a unique character and had led the War Department to improvise its own flotilla. In these early stages of the war the Navy Department had only been able to lend the Army a handful of naval constructors and officers of the line to superintend naval building, teach midwestern landsmen how to operate naval guns, and themselves command a few of these boats in battle. Henceforth the operations in the Western theater of the war would lose the romance of makeshift, pioneer experiments which had characterized the early single-handed efforts of both Army and Navy. Under General Grant and Admiral Porter the new Federal strategy of well-coördinated Army-Navy coöperation, with greatly augmented forces, would be executed in a professional, businesslike manner.

When Acting Rear Admiral Porter came west in October 1862, there was a general lull in military operations. Grant was at Grand Junction and Sherman at Memphis. Both were preparing to move on Vicksburg. In Kentucky all was quiet. By October Confederate General Bragg's offensive in that state had spent its force. In Missouri the war presented a panorama of two-penny skirmishes, and the same was true in Arkansas. For eight or ten weeks to come only rumors, bushwhackers, and guerrillas would ruffle the placidity of the Western theater of the war.

This quasi-peaceful interval gave Porter time to reconnoiter and reorganize according to the Navy pattern the miscellany of fresh-water boats which the War Department up to October first had euphemistically designated as its "Western Flotilla."

The Western Flotilla was a museum of naval freaks. Its units had been improvised and assembled piecemeal as military emergencies had dictated. It was marked with the pioneer's genius in makeshift.

For scouting and convoy duty three side-wheel river boats, the *Tyler,* the *Lexington,* and the *Conestoga* had been first pressed into service. After Commander John Rodgers had lowered their boilers, and erected breastworks of oak to protect their gun crews and machinery, these boats had shelled bushwhackers along the banks of the streams, and in an early skirmish near Columbus, Kentucky, had saved a large number of Grant's unwary volunteers from capture, when at the moment of victory the latter stopped fighting and began collecting loot. They formed a dignified nucleus for the fleet, but they could not stand up against forts.

To aid the Army against the river forts that barred the entrance into Tennessee, seven ugly but powerful ironclads had been built by Mr. James B. Eads in St. Louis. Designed by Naval Constructor S. H. Pook, their slanting casemates sheathed with railroad iron were mounted on flat-bottomed scows and driven by paddle

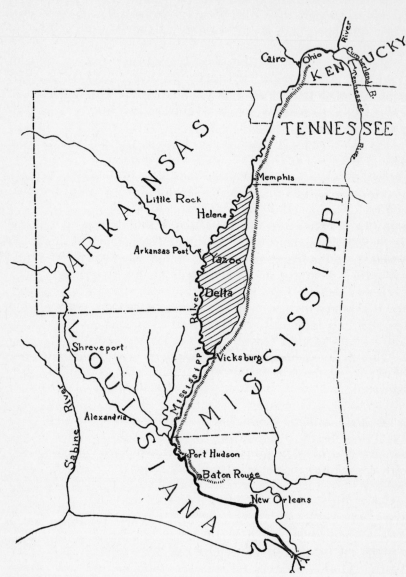

GENERAL MAP OF THE MISSISSIPPI RIVER, SHOWING PORTER'S BASE AT CAIRO, STRA-
TEGIC RIVER TOWNS, AND THE YAZOO DELTA.

wheels in the stern. Their novel design and want of speed caused them to be familiarly known as the "Pook Turtles," though on the Navy List they bore the names of river cities: *St. Louis, Cincinnati, Louisville, Mound City,* and *Pittsburgh.* Flag Officer Foote had used them to good effect against Forts Henry and Donelson, though they had been penetrated by plunging shot which tore open boilers and wounded many men, including the Flag Officer himself.

By the time the Federals had made their way down the Mississippi past the Tennessee-Kentucky line, the Confederates had organized their River Defense Fleet, consisting of steamers metal-plated across the bow for ramming. This Confederate measure had called into being the most romantic class of Federal fighting craft on the river—Colonel Ellet's rams. Provided with a special commission from the War Department, elderly Colonel Charles Ellet had bought a dozen boats of miscellaneous size and shape, strengthened them to withstand the shock of ramming with timbers braced lengthwise inside their hulls, and hurried them down the river to the front. They were mainly officered by members of his own family and manned by a set of dare-devil volunteers he had himself recruited. In the battles of Fort Pillow and Memphis his rams had woven their way through the slow Pook Turtles and dashed against the Rebel Defense Fleet with great success. The tall old Colonel, who bore a striking resemblance to the poet Wordsworth, directed his rams in a most unseamanlike way by waving his hat. Ellet's rams carried no guns heavier than pistols, and relied solely upon the audacity of their attack. Charging with magnificent gallantry, they broke up the enemy's formation in the manner of the modern destroyers.

The flotilla also included a host of miscellaneous units as varied in character as the individuals who remodeled them. The *Essex,*— a St. Louis ferryboat whose iron carapace weighted her deck dangerously close to the water line—was unique for that time in having every contrivance on board operated by steam. The *Benton,* which Foote and Davis had used as flagship, was a remarkable turtle about one and a half times the normal size of a river steamer; a catfish-view of her under side would have revealed two boats supporting a platform 200 by 75 feet with a huge paddle wheel churning aft between the twin hulls. To itemize and describe every unit in the Western Flotilla a rather fat volume would be necessary. There were tugboats, snag boats, supply boats, ammunition boats, and dispatch boats. There were barges for transporting coal and fodder, barges converted into machine shops and barges with negro shacks erected upon them as quarters for the contrabands who had escaped from the plantations.[1]

On his way out to Cairo Porter stopped at Pittsburgh, Cincinnati, and St. Louis. Pittsburgh with its forest of tall chimneys, its iron mills, its coal piles, its noisy freight yards and crowded water front was the source from which he must draw increasing quantities of engines and iron plating and fuel and guns for his Mississippi Squadron. He warned the Pittsburgh contractors of an immensely increased demand for their products and urged them to expand their facilities. Unfortunately the heavy river monitors projected by the Department could not be built at Pittsburgh because of shoals in the river. Much time was lost in floating the heavy materials down to Cincinnati and St. Louis.

At Cincinnati Porter inspected the ironclads *Indianola* and *Chillicothe,* which were nearing completion. He found that the *Indianola's* machinery combining both side wheels and screw propellers left no space for bunking her crew. Porter wanted apartments built on deck, but needed the sanction of the Department. This meant red tape and delay. Even worse were the structural blunders on the *Chillicothe,* whose turret gun ports had been cut out five inches too high, and then patched and whose steering wheel was jammed in between two of her forward guns so that pilot and gunners could not function at the same time. The general supervisor of boats under construction was a pleasant and refined old gentleman who reveled in red tape, and the thought that the outcome of a battle might depend on the aged officer's moving quickly exasperated Porter.

At St. Louis Porter was greatly pleased with the new tinclads. They had less than two feet of draft and could be used effectively to patrol many of the three thousand miles of rivers included in Porter's new command. The tinclads, Porter jocularly said, could float wherever the ground was a little damp. Porter also was pleased with the heavy turtles *Choctaw* and *Lafayette,* despite the fact that his brother William had drawn the designs for them.

On October 15 Porter arrived at the naval base of Cairo off the southernmost tip of Illinois, where Admiral Davis had collected most of the squadron. A salute was fired. Davis' distinguishing pennant was hauled down, and up to the masthead of the largest Pook Turtle of them all—the "old warhorse" *Benton*—was reeled the first white-starred, blue flag of Acting Rear Admiral David Dixon Porter.

The triangular river-bottom village of Cairo situated in the crotch where the Ohio joins the Mississippi hardly looked like the most important interior naval base in the country. There was no navy yard here, for the Government owned no land in the town. The station commandant's headquarters were in a rented building close to the long lines of wharves to which the host of heterogeneous vessels was tied up. The navy yard which lay a few miles up the Ohio at Mound City, was a ten-acre tract of muddy lowland containing several supply sheds and docks, but for the most part its stores, machine shops, blacksmith shops, and quarters were on barges.

When Porter went ashore at Cairo he was enthusiastically welcomed by Captain A. M. Pennock, commandant of the station, and by Captain Henry Walke of the *Carondelet*. Admiral Farragut's kinsman, Pennock, had an intelligent grasp of the complex situation and was honestly enthusiastic in his support of the new admiral. Porter considered Pennock a "trump." Walke was an active, impatient man whose ideas and fluency in expressing them were similar to the Admiral's. Porter at once sent him down the river to Helena, Arkansas, to take charge of operations between that advance base and Vicksburg.[2]

At Porter's request Lieutenant K. R. Breese, who had commanded a division of the Mortar Flotilla, was ordered to Cairo as his fleet captain.

The work of transferring the Western Flotilla from the War Department to the Navy had been under way for two weeks, but there were still many Army irregularities to be corrected before the Mississippi Squadron could be recognized as a naval organization.

The personnel of the squadron had been signed on by the Army as emergency had dictated and not according to Navy Regulations. Many of the recruits from the cornfields, swamps, and forests had been given higher ratings and higher pay than they deserved according to Navy standards. Easing them down to their proper ratings was a ticklish proposition since their morale had to be maintained. At the same time they had to be reduced in order to maintain the morale of the salt-water seamen who had joined the squadron. In the adjusting process many men had to be dropped and their places filled with contraband negroes.

About four hundred sick men had to be discharged at once. The river fevers had taken an alarming toll from the green and unacclimated recruits. Many of the leaky, makeshift, war vessels were unfit for human habitation, and yet a number of men had crowded their families in with themselves aboard ship.

There were no hospitals either afloat or ashore. Porter leased a hotel at Mound City for this purpose. Then the new Admiral sent out a general order that hereafter crews were to be inspected at morning and evening quarters to see if they were comfortably clad and had their under flannels on. In the ironclads, where the sun could not get to the decks, drying stoves were to be freely used. Fresh meat and vegetables were to be served three times a week. The men were not to be permitted to sleep in the open air where night dews could fall on them. Decks were to be kept clean but not wetted too often. "The comfort and health of the men must be the first thing to be looked after," Porter announced to his officers.[3]

During the first three weeks Porter worked at his desk from seven in the morning until ten at night and sometimes until twelve. To keep fit for this strenuous labor he treated himself to one hour each day on horseback. He loved horses as he loved a well-cut suit of clothes, private secretary, and other appurtenances of a gentleman. Later on when he went down the river he always carried along his horse on his ship, comfortably stalled behind timbers of heavy oak.

The construction of new vessels and repair of old was hampered by the maraudings of guerrillas. Bands of mounted soldiers would appear suddenly at a bend in the river and fire upon the coal and iron barges towing down from Pittsburgh. Guerrillas along the Mississippi also picked off the crews from private steamers surreptitiously engaged in the cotton trade. Many plantation owners smuggled their cotton to the Northern traders to keep it from being burned by their own government, and the traders in turn supplied Southerners with contraband salt, shoes, clothing, liquors, and coffee. These dealings filled the Rebels with disgust and hatred for the "Mammonish, nigger-loving Yankees" who aided them, and they endeavored to atone for their own disloyalty by encouraging their guerrillas.

Porter ordered his patrol vessels to retaliate fiercely upon the guerrilla-infested regions. There was no impropriety in wreaking vengeance against noncombatants who harbored these marauders. A taste of devastation, Porter thought, would bring them to their senses and teach them to inform the proper authorities whenever guerrillas appeared in the neighborhood. Contributions were levied upon offending towns, villages were burned, plantations were destroyed by shell fire.

In the first few weeks at Cairo Admiral Porter fitted heavier guns on the Pook Turtles, and replaced the old Army ammunition, which had no protection against dampness. The soft pine decks of several vessels had been deeply scored by the trucks of the guns and had to be replaced by oak planking. The *Eastport's* keel had buckled up under her engines and she had to go into dry dock. Porter purchased many steamers both big and little for his squadron. He bought many light-drafts which were to be used later by Farragut to seal the shallower inlets and bayous along the Gulf, but for the time being he was to use these craft in his squadron, and was especially instructed by Gideon Welles that their ultimate purpose was to be known only to himself.

For the benefit of untutored river captains recently taken into the squadron, Porter had to give endless directions of a most minute character. In a brief space of time he tried to whip his fleet into something like uniformity. He could not train naval officers and seamen overnight, but he did secure an immediate appearance of uniformity. All officers were strictly enjoined to follow the regulations in their dress. The uniforms to be worn by the crews were signalled daily from the newly purchased and spacious flagship *Black Hawk*. A white flag signified dress in white; a blue flag, dress in blue; white above blue meant white frocks and blue trousers; blue above the white, blue shirts and white trousers.

A hostile picture of Porter at this time depicts the "Terror of the Mississippi," as Porter came to be called by the Confederates, as a full-feathered admiral in all his glory and making things lively. "He was a terror to Rebels...his name and fame resounded over the valley where the great Mississippi rolls...He had the Treasury of the United States in his locker, and was under full sail." [4]

It was true that Porter was under full sail. His requisitions upon the Department were frequent and alarming in size. Scrupulous Mr. Welles, however, had not been so rash as to transfer the U. S. Treasury to Cairo. On the subject of money he had a New England conscience. He had given Porter secret orders to purchase vessels for Farragut, and he honored Porter's requisitions. But he caused Fox to suggest to Porter that the Navy must show an economical administration in comparison with the Army, and by this stratagem Porter was led to substitute contraband negro for white labor and to strain every muscle in the squadron to collect enough "C. S. A." cotton along the river banks to make the Navy as far as possible pay its own way.

At the outset Porter had difficulty in getting the Ellet Ram Fleet transferred to his squadron. The elder Ellet having died of a wound received at Memphis, the command had descended upon his brother Brigadier General Alfred Ellet; and, when on October 1, 1862, the gunboats of the Western Flotilla had been transferred to the Navy Department, Ellet had refused to surrender his rams on the technicality that they were not gunboats. Curiously enough Ellet was supported by General in Chief Halleck and by Secretary of War Stanton. A protracted correspondence accomplished nothing, but Porter was determined that there should not be two separate naval forces within the limits of his command. He tried argument, he tried praise, and finally he ordered the rams tied to the bank and instructed his officers to fire into them if they left their moorings. Porter wrote Secretary Welles an elaborate interpretation of the transfer law, pointing out that he could not permit the Army to have a separate naval force, and—not very consistently—Porter suggested that the ram fleet be converted into a sort of marine brigade which would place under his command a force capable of landing and routing guerrillas. The anomaly of allowing Porter a land force not under the military did not disturb the Secretary of the Navy.

On November 7 the difficulty between the two Departments was aired in a full executive session of the Cabinet, in which Stanton charged that the Navy was very unpopular in the West, boasted rashly that the Army would take Vicksburg by Christmas, and finally grew very angry. Gideon Welles, on the contrary, appeared very cool, with the knowledge of having right on his side, and won his case. Brigadier General Ellet was by Presidential decree placed under Porter's orders.

Because of the low stage of the water the ram fleet was at this time especially valuable. The deep-draft Pook Turtles, marooned between the various bars in the rivers, could not move until high water came. With the light and swift ram boats under his control Porter became anxious to get down to Vicksburg. For three weeks, however, he had heard nothing from General McClernand although McClernand's recruiting base at Springfield was within a short distance of Cairo.

Porter wrote to General Sherman at Memphis asking whether General Grant was going down and offering naval support. Sherman on the same day was writing Porter explaining the military situation in northern Mississippi.

Several weeks passed and still no word came from McClernand.

About the first of December Porter was entertained at a supper party by Captain McAllister, Army quartermaster at Cairo, aboard the latter's ramshackle river boat. During the meal Captain McAllister was called out of the room and on returning ushered in a short, bearded man in a citizen's brown coat with a velvet collar and gray trousers, covered with dust, seedy, and travel worn. Captain McAllister was a tall man, and the newcomer by his side was dwarfed. "Admiral Porter," said McAllister, "meet General Grant."

Grant shook Porter's hand heartily, as if he had been an old acquaintance. McAllister seated the two men apart from the rest of the company at a small table with roast duck and a bottle of champagne. "While I was looking earnestly at Grant, trying to make out how much of the man there was under the plain exterior," Porter wrote in his journal, "the General was regarding me to see what amount of work there was under all the gilt buttons and gold lace with which the Department had bedizened my coat." [5]

In a brief, matter-of-fact conversation Porter told Grant of his interview with McClernand before he left Washington, and of his desire to coöperate with Grant while waiting for McClernand to appear. Grant stated that he and Sherman were ready to move down over the high land east of the Yazoo through Holly Springs and Oxford toward Jackson and from there to approach Vicksburg from its landward side. If Porter could move down the river, embark General Steele at Helena, and make a demonstration on the river side, they might capture the great Confederate stronghold. This mode of procedure was agreed upon; and General Grant at once took leave of the party, stoically refusing to be tempted by any of the delicacies which Captain McAllister's stewards had set out for him. The conversation had taken barely an hour.

At once Porter ordered a general concentration of all available rams, tinclads, and Pook Turtles under Captain Walke at Helena. The turtles were warned to proceed slowly, sounding carefully over the bars and if necessary to wait for the expected rise in the river. Walke was ordered to move down to the Yazoo River, make a reconnaissance up that tributary and secure landings for the troops. Porter remained at Cairo to recruit men, push repairs, and work out the complicated arrangements for supplies to be sent down after he had left Cairo. In addition to the persistent annoyance of guerrillas, reports kept coming in that the coal barges at Memphis and Helena were continually being boarded by Federal soldiers who ignored the Navy's regulations and helped themselves. Porter ordered the coal barges to be guarded, Army pilferers to be arrested if necessary.

A few weeks before making his arrangement with Grant, Porter had heard from McClernand—not directly but by a message relayed through Halleck, Stanton, and Welles. In about three weeks, McClernand had reported, he would be ready to move down the river. This information was passed on by General Halleck on November 15. But the first week of December failed to bring McClernand.

On December 8 Grant and Sherman, who had now moved down to the little university town of Oxford, Mississippi, suddenly changed their plans. Through unofficial channels Sherman had learned that McClernand's commission entitled him to supersede himself. Grant and Sherman decided to attack at once and attempt to capture Vicksburg by the time the political general, McClernand, arrived on the scene. Sherman was to return to Memphis and take his armies down the river along with Porter, to join forces with Steele at Helena, and storm Vicksburg from the water front while Grant assailed the Confederates from the rear.

This intelligence was communicated to Porter, who wired Sherman his assent. Porter had now arranged that Captain Pennock should communicate directly with the Department so that important matters could be immediately attended to during his absence. On December 14 Porter left his desk, boarded the *Black Hawk,* and shoved off, taking every boat he could find men for. Some of his vessels were short as many as fifty men, but Porter took them even if they could fight but a single gun. Sherman had informed him that his thousands of new volunteers were so anxious to get at the enemy that it took hard handling to repress excesses, and Porter was not the man to hold back these energetic coal-pilferers from the front.

Halfway to Memphis Porter encountered the tiny light-draft *Marmora* steaming up river. She hailed the Admiral, lowered a boat, and the youthful Commander Selfridge, whom Porter had made captain of the ironclad *Cairo,* came aboard to report the first serious disaster to the squadron. The *Cairo*—one of the seven original Pook Turtles—had been sunk in the Yazoo by a torpedo.

This was the first news Porter had had of torpedoes in the Yazoo. Porter listened gravely to Selfridge's story. Then Selfridge asked whether a court of inquiry might be ordered.

"Court! I have no time to order courts!" Porter thundered. "I can't blame an officer who seeks to put his ship close to the enemy. Is there any other vessel you would like to have?" Then turning to the Fleet Captain. "Breese, make out Selfridge's orders to the *Conestoga*." [6] With that he turned the *Black Hawk's* nose downstream toward Memphis.

19.

DISASTER AT CHICKASAW BLUFFS

THE valley of the Mississippi was divided among three generals. General Rosecrans controlled most of Kentucky and middle Tennessee. General Grant with the XIII Army Corps held the eastern bank of the river from western Kentucky down into northern Mississippi. General Curtis commanded the Department of Missouri. When Grant detached Sherman to lead the west wing of his army from Memphis to Vicksburg in coöperation with Admiral Porter, he virtually created a separate command, for between Grant's line of operations along the high ridge of central Mississippi and the Mississippi River lay the Yazoo River and the impassable Yazoo Delta—a malarial region of lowlands and swamps veined north and south by the tributaries of the Yazoo and east and west by lateral water passes fed by overflows from the Mississippi. It was impossible for Grant and Sherman to communicate across the Yazoo delta. Messages had to be relayed through Memphis. If and when General McClernand appeared, a fourth separate command would doubtless be formed in name as well as fact. Porter had been specifically ordered to coöperate with McClernand, and with Grant, Sherman, Rosecrans and Curtis as far as it was physically possible to do so. There were so many generals acting independently of each other that, as Porter facetiously observed, the whole American Navy could not have complied with their demands.

On Thursday December 18 the *Black Hawk* docked at Memphis, and Porter sent a messenger ashore to tell Sherman that he would call on him at his headquarters. Some regiments were loading boats with guns and supplies. Thousands of green troops were toiling clumsily through the manual of arms. Many of General Sherman's sixty transports had not yet come down the river, and Navy men heard that Sherman was very impatient.

Thinking Sherman might be dressed "in full feather," Porter donned his own uniform coat, the splendor of which he said rivaled that of a drum major. Porter's letters, on the other hand, had led Sherman to believe that Porter scorned formality and the General wore his ordinary blue flannels. Each was surprised at the appearance of the other.

"Hello, Porter," greeted Sherman, "I'm glad to see you. Did you see anything of those transports of mine on your way down? Devilish cold, isn't it? Sit down here and warm up." As he stirred the coal in the grate, he flung out an assortment of orders to his aides. Then turning again to Porter, "Glad to see you, Porter. Do you suppose we can get all this crowd down to Vicksburg by Christmas? That's the plan." [1]

The two commanders examined a map of the swamps north of Vicksburg, and went over the general plan. Vicksburg according to reports was but feebly garrisoned. Confederate General Pemberton's army was in the neighborhood of Grenada, and Grant would either engage Pemberton there and keep him from reënforcing Vicksburg, or he would drive the Confederates into the town and besiege them from the east. Union General Nathaniel P. Banks, who had recently supplanted Butler at New Orleans, would move up the river, capture Port Hudson, and move on Vicksburg from the south. Porter and Sherman would make a quick descent from the north, bombard the batteries near the mouth of the Yazoo River, and attempt to take Vicksburg from the water front.

McClernand's name was mentioned, and Porter remarked to Sherman that McClernand's doings in Springfield sounded more like electioneering for Congress than recruiting an army.

Porter and Sherman parted like old friends, each surprised and pleased to find that the other was not "all feathers and fuss."

The remainder of Sherman's transports arrived during the next thirty-six hours and were immediately loaded with troops. Just before embarking, the troops were paid for the first time in several months; and as they piled aboard they sang "John Brown" and "Yankee Doodle." [2] They shouted, made lusty wagers that they would celebrate Christmas in Vicksburg, and invited one another to Christmas dinner in Vicksburg's fashionable Preston House. In the scramble they shoved their equipment aboard topsy-turvy. A newspaper reporter who was offended by the scent of corn whiskey and whose ribs were jostled by the uncouth soldiery wrote that the confusion was never paralleled, except by an army making a precipitate retreat. But the confusion was only apparent. Speed was the important factor.

After Porter took leave of Sherman, he dispatched Captain

William Gwin in the *Benton* down the river to get the gunboats which were waiting at Helena and move on to join Captain Walke at the Yazoo mouth. The gunboats were to clear the Yazoo of torpedoes and secure landings for Sherman's troops.

Porter then made a tour of inspection of the machine shops and buildings recently taken over by the Navy in Memphis. He moved about wearing his grandiose admiral's overcoat, partly because Memphis was shivering in the grip of its Christmas "cold snap" but mainly to advertise the Navy before the midwestern landsmen. That the fresh-water navy now had a soul of its own and was no longer under the Army, was a matter upon which the military had not instructed the public.

On Saturday December 20 the *Black Hawk* set off down the river at the head of a long file of transports, and on Sunday Porter arrived at the squat little cotton-ginning town of Helena just in time to catch a detail of soldiers from the Army transport *Key West No. 2* in the act of stealing coal from one of the Navy barges. Porter sent marines on board the *Key West* to browbeat her captain into respecting the Navy's order. Porter had but a few barges of coal, and he needed every bushel for his squadron.

Very little of Helena was visible from the water front because of the long line of Army tents stretched along the bank. As General Steele's division of Sherman's troops crowded into the already loaded transports, the tumult and general hilarity rivaled that at Memphis. A large mob of negro men, women, and children broke through the lines of soldiers, shouting and leaping and waving their arms.

They sang "Jubilo," a song that had recently become very popular with negroes along the Mississippi.

> Say, darkeys, hab you seen de massa,
> Wid di muffstash on he face,
> Go long de road some time dis mornin',
> Like he gwine leabe de place?
> He see de smoke way up de ribber
> Whar de Lincum gunboats lay;
> He took he hat an' leff berry sudden,
> And I spose he's runned away.
> De massa run, ha, ha!
> De darkey stay, ho, ho!
> It mus' be now de kingdum comin',
> An' de yar ob jubilo.[3]

VESSELS OF THE MISSISSIPPI SQUADRON AT ANCHOR OFF THE MOUND CITY NAVY YARD. THE LARGE BOAT AT THE LEFT IS A RIVER STEAMER CONVERTED INTO A "TINCLAD," THE ONE IN THE CENTER IS A RIVER IRONCLAD OF THE EADS TYPE.

Courtesy of Navy Department

THE U.S.S. *Black Hawk,* USED AS GENERAL HEADQUARTERS OF THE MISSISSIPPI SQUADRON.

THE U.S.S. *Benton*, PORTER'S FLAGSHIP DURING ENCOUNTERS WITH CONFEDERATE RIVER FORTS.

Two contrabands brought news of a large pile of wood the
Southerners had cached near the levee. Soldiers and negroes carried the fuel aboard the transports and stacked the decks high. At
Helena, according to General Sherman's strict orders, all women
who had come down from Memphis were put ashore amid colorful scenes of farewell—laundresses, nurses, sutlers, wives of the

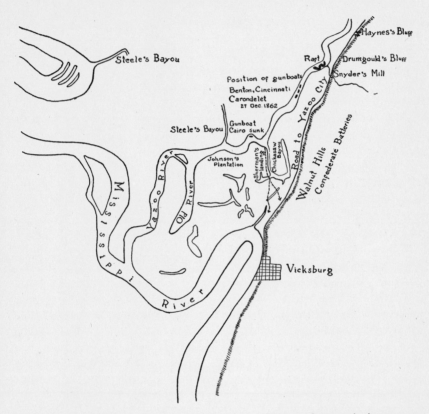

THE TERRAIN NORTH OF VICKSBURG, SHOWING THE LINE OF SHERMAN'S ASSAULT ON
CHICKASAW BLUFFS AND THE POSITION OF PORTER'S GUNBOATS ON DECEMBER 27, 1862.

steamboat captains, and women from the water-front dives. Their
places were taken by some hundreds of husky contrabands who
shouted and jabbered about emancipation. These joyous black
recruits had not yet caught sight of the thousands of picks and
shovels stowed in the holds, and they little dreamed how they
would spend their Christmas in the swamp muck near Vicksburg.

Porter pushed down the river and arrived at the mouth of the
Yazoo on December 24 a few hours ahead of the troops. The water

in the Yazoo had now risen sufficiently for the heavy Pook Turtles to ascend, and Captain Gwin had dragged out the torpedoes for about ten miles up the stream and secured landings for Sherman. For weeks the energetic Captain Walke had been on the sick list with severe intermittent fever.[4]

The Yazoo River enters the Mississippi opposite the little steamboat landing of Duckport, Louisiana, about eight miles above Vicksburg. Ascending the Yazoo the compass read north for three miles, then east for six, then northeast for six more before the river met the Chickasaw Bluffs, at John Snyder's mill. These bluffs, a continuation of the hills that veer away from the Mississippi at Vicksburg, overhung the Yazoo for three miles up to Haynes's Bluff, where the Confederates had driven a formidable barrier of logs and railroad iron into the river. Heavy rifled guns had been embedded all along these hills from Vicksburg to Haynes's Bluff.

The triangle framed by the Mississippi, the Yazoo, and the Chickasaw Bluffs was a dismal swamp across which Sherman's troops must make their way in order to storm the heights behind Vicksburg. Two spur-like waterways leave the Yazoo and penetrate the swamp in the direction of the hills: the first, a wide lagoon known as Old River, which had once been the bed of the Mississippi; and the second, a narrow inlet known as Chickasaw Bayou. Between these shallow waterways lay Johnson's plantation, a narrow strip of solid ground on which the troops were to land. From Johnson's plantation the Confederates had fired on the tinclads as they lifted torpedoes, and Captain Gwin had sent marines ashore from the *Benton* and burned the buildings. When Porter came up the Yazoo, the old brick mansion was a gaping, smoke-tongued ruin. The steam sugar refinery, the saw mill, the cotton gin, the machine shop, and the living quarters for three hundred negroes were still smouldering.

To accomplish the work of lifting torpedoes just above Chickasaw Bayou, Captain Gwin had the *Benton,* two light drafts, and two of the Ellet rams. The crews of the four light vessels were out in their rowboats dragging along either side and back and forth across the river. The *Benton* kept up a continuous fire into the bushes to protect the boatmen from sharpshooters. The Confederate torpedoes were home-made affairs, anchored in the channel with lines running to both banks. Most of them were set to be detonated by friction. Whenever the boatmen discovered a line they would lift it carefully and drag the entire mechanism up to the bank and secure it. Porter examined the hundreds of torpedoes and praised the men who were fishing them out. Some of the powder demijohns Porter ordered to be carried into the house of Benson Blake, an officer in the Confederate Army, and used to blow up this hiding place for sharpshooters.

Sherman's transports arrived above Duckport at Milliken's Bend on Christmas Eve, and the next morning Porter and Sherman set out from Johnson's plantation on horseback to reconnoiter. They did not ride far. Beyond the fields of blackened cotton stubble and cockleburs their horses sank to their bellies in the mire. The swamp was a natural cheval de frise, with magnolia trees, spear grass, underbrush, willows and briar vines all entangled. From the foot of the hills beyond the morass came the crackle of Confederate rifle fire. All day Sherman's scouts reconnoitered and after nightfall reported that Chickasaw Bayou might be forded at three or four places, but that these were apparently covered by cannon on the hills. Beyond the old bed of the river for miles along the defenders had felled the giant magnolias in such a way as to render that approach to Vicksburg impassable.

Christmas night was clear and frosty. Throughout the fleet there were no whistles blown, no bells rung, no lanterns lighted. Sheets of wet canvas were hung around furnaces to shut in the glare. The seamen were not allowed to light their holiday cigars.

Porter returned to the mouth of the Yazoo, divided his cumbersome squadron into two divisions under Walke and Gwin, berated a river captain for allowing the blacksmith boat *Sampson* to foul one of the coal barges, and answered a bag full of correspondence before he retired.

The next day was spent in convoying the sixty transports to their landings at Johnson's plantation.

By Saturday December 27 the torpedoes had been removed as far up as Snyder's Bluff, and Porter sent Captain Gwin with the *Benton* and six smaller boats up to this point to shell the enemy batteries. His object was to draw the Confederates away from Sherman's front and also to guard Sherman's left against a flanking movement by the enemy. The narrowness of the channel under the bluff compelled the vessels to ascend in single file. A stiff breeze and strong current swept down the river. Around a bend in the river Captain Gwin roped the *Benton* against the left bank, where he had a full view of the enemy, while the vessels below the *Benton* were sheltered by the forest.

The engagement lasted an hour and a half. By slacking and

tautening her lines the *Benton* was able to fire alternately her bow and starboard guns. The enemy soon ceased firing toward the vessels behind the trees and directed a concentric fire against the *Benton*, hitting her repeatedly. Many shots glanced from her sloping casemate, but others hit on her deck and penetrated with fearful effect. Three heavy rifled shot in quick succession entered one of her ports. Captain Gwin stood out on the open deck spotting the enemy batteries on the hills as they unmasked. "A captain's place is on the deck," he said, and refused to go inside.

Just then a cannon ball glanced from the *Benton's* armor and grazed Gwin. It gouged the muscles from his breast and right arm. He was quickly carried down the river, and Admiral Porter bedded him comfortably in his own cabin on the flagship *Black Hawk*.

A slight rain fell on this day, but not enough to check Sherman's deployment.

The next day Porter sent the turtle *Baron DeKalb* to take the *Benton's* place in shelling the Yazoo batteries. Into Old River, a drift-littered bayou extending from the Yazoo halfway through the swamps toward Vicksburg, Porter sent two tinclads, the *Marmora* and the *Signal,* to assist Sherman's right wing. Repairs were made on the *Benton* with as little fuss as possible, for the Confederates must not discover the vulnerability of Porter's strongest ironclad.

Sunday night was clear and cold. The armies bivouacking in the swamps listened intently for the sound of General Grant's guns. On the still air they heard the rumble of trains moving into Vicksburg. To the east of the town rocket signals were observed.

On Monday December 29, the day for the great assault on Chickasaw Bluffs, the sky threatened rain. All night Sherman's men had chopped down trees to fill the ditch under the bluffs, only to have the enemy destroy this labor at daybreak by a few well placed shells. Now there was but one practicable crossing, over a narrow corduroy road which sagged along the bottom of Chickasaw Bayou, but was nevertheless fordable. The wing divisions could keep up a distracting fire, but only a few brigades could participate in the assault. When these brigades sloshed through the ford they came under a terrific concentric fire from the cannon on the heights in front. One brigade dug in under a clay bank on top of which were large numbers of Confederates in rifle pits. Marooned here they could neither go forward nor retreat. The other brigade rushed up the heights in a gallant but futile charge. The few who reached the top, being unsupported, were forced down under a galling fire. The shrieks of 1,500 dying and wounded men arose above the impersonal din of rifle and cannon fire.

Throughout the assault Porter had his gunboats shelling enemy batteries at both ends of the line. He could do but little since the range was extreme. He sent a speedy vessel to Memphis to bring down mortar boats regardless of their condition. Sherman had too few tents to shelter his wounded, and Porter sent an emergency dispatch to Cairo for the hospital boat *Red Rover* to be rushed down the river.

A report from Captain Pennock informed Porter that the Confederates had broken General Grant's railroad south of Columbus, Kentucky, and had cut the telegraph wires between that base and Cairo. The Federal garrisons occupying Columbus and the near-by Island No. 10 were momentarily expecting attack and were beseeching Pennock to send gunboats for their protection. Pennock had nothing to send.

A few minutes after 4 P.M. a dispatch came from Sherman requesting Porter to send his fastest steamer to Memphis for a supply of ammunition. The ammunition boat *Blue Wing,* which had left Memphis in the wake of the transports, had failed to arrive. Within ten minutes the tinclad *Rattler* was speeding to Memphis on this urgent mission.

Late in the afternoon it began raining and by nightfall increased to a downpour. Firing ceased. Sherman withdrew the remnants of his advanced brigades and made his way out to the *Black Hawk* to see Porter. The General was drenched to the skin and covered with mud. He sat down in Porter's room and remained silent for several minutes.

Porter sent the steward to fetch the necessary ingredients and mixed a whiskey punch.

Captain Gwin lay in the cabin behind the thin partition, and the two men spoke in whispers. What should they do next? The loss of the ammunition boat *Blue Wing*—which had been last seen in the neighborhood of the Arkansas River—caused Sherman to suggest an expedition up that river to capture Arkansas Post. Their operations against Vicksburg would continue to suffer so long as the enemy held Arkansas Post, which being in the rear of the Federals could menace their communications. Moreover, a spectacular capture would give the reporters something to write about besides the disaster at Chickasaw Bluffs.

Porter agreed to coöperate with Sherman in the venture but suggested that they first try to secure a lodgment on the hills farther up the Yazoo at Haynes's Bluff, where the Confederates would least expect an attack. To this Sherman assented.

Further operations, however, were prevented by a fog so thick that the men could not see one another at ten paces. This fog proved both fortunate and timely since it prevented a repetition of the Chickasaw Bluffs disaster. General Grant, as Porter was shortly to learn, was not pressing Vicksburg from the rear as Porter and Sherman believed. On the very day when Porter and Sherman had set out from Memphis, the Confederate General Van Dorn had led a cavalry raid against Holly Springs and destroyed over a million dollars' worth of supplies upon which Grant had depended. Simultaneously the Confederate General Bedford Forrest had cut Grant's rail communications to Columbus. From the south Union General Banks had not even begun his attack upon Port Hudson. The neatly planned combinations of Grant, Sherman, and Porter had been broken up. By an irony of circumstance Vicksburg had received large reënforcements; and Sherman, lacking means of communication with Grant, had wasted his men in a futile assault.

On New Year's morning, as the fog lifted, a tug came alongside the *Black Hawk;* and a young colonel in a new uniform apprised Porter that General McClernand had arrived at Milliken's Bend near the mouth of the Yazoo.

Porter sent this cheerless news to Sherman, who reëmbarked his troops and moved out to Milliken's Bend. Porter dropped down to the mouth of the Yazoo and waited to see what would happen next.

On January 3 Porter sent messengers throughout Sherman's— now McClernand's—army looking for a Catholic priest. Captain Gwin was dying. No priest was found. Late in the afternoon, without the comfort of extreme unction, the gallant captain died.

20.

A TAWDRY VICTORY

Aᴏᴛᴇʀ the Newport Club incident Porter's dislike of West Point generals was sharpened by Mr. Welles's effort to discipline him. In October 1862, Porter had acquiesced in Lincoln's selection of McClernand to command the coöperating army against Vicksburg because McClernand was not encumbered by the military learning of Halleck. He had neither the handsome appearance nor the indecision of McClellan. As a brigadier at Fort Donelson and Shiloh, McClernand had spurned military etiquette and fought hard. In the brief interview Porter had had with him in his hotel room in Washington, Porter had been favorably impressed by McClernand's enthusiasm.

Considerations other than military, however, had induced Lincoln to select McClernand for the important task of opening the Mississippi. After Lincoln had issued his preliminary proclamation of emancipation on September 22, 1862, McClernand had left his post under Major General Grant and come immediately to Washington to inform Lincoln of the dangerous state of public opinion in the West. Lincoln knew McClernand, a fellow townsman, as a versatile lawyer, editor, trader on the Mississippi, and Democratic Member of Congress for ten years.

McClernand poured into Lincoln's ear the best political speech of his life. He began by depicting the widespread suffering of the Western grain and cattle growers. For two seasons this large class of voters had been unable to float their produce down the Mississippi as usual. Railway carriers were inadequate to meet the demands of the military and also to transport the immense supplies of cotton now coming through the Confederate lines. Farmers could not afford to pay the exorbitant freight rates and in consequence were denied a market. They were beginning to listen to defeatists. Down the river they beheld large armies making little progress. The great river, blocked at Vicksburg, had become an inland lake. On every hand they were exhorted by Copperheads, or Southern sympathizers, to end the war. Naturally antagonistic toward the manufacturers of New England, they resented the injection of the abolition issue into the conflict with the South, as this would only serve to prolong the war. The only thing that could prevent the farmers of Indiana, Illinois, and Iowa from seeking a separate peace, said McClernand, was an aggressive campaign to open the river to their products. McClernand wanted authority to wage such a campaign. He would recruit his own armies, influence the election of "war" Democrats in districts where the President's party was certain to lose anyway, and above everything else he would open the Mississippi. Impressed by his recital, Lincoln had given him a limited and semi-secret authority to raise troops in Indiana, Illinois, and Iowa and command them in cooperation with Admiral Porter.

McClernand waged his recruiting campaign during the time of the November elections, and he probably influenced the election of several "war" Democrats. As fast as his troops were raised he sent them to Memphis and Helena, which were already established as points of concentration, and in these towns they were given preliminary drills. For five weeks McClernand devoted himself exclusively to electioneering and recruiting.[1]

Meanwhile Porter was whipping his squadron into shape and waiting impatiently to hear from McClernand. Porter wrote to Welles, who learned from Stanton and Halleck that McClernand would be ready by the first of December. December came. Still no word from McClernand. Porter became acquainted with Grant, who seemed energetic and businesslike. The first week of December passed. Porter made Sherman's acquaintance by mail. On December 14 Porter had given up waiting for McClernand and had pushed on down the river to begin operations with Grant and Sherman.

After the November elections—by which time McClernand's troops were already down at Memphis and Helena—McClernand had wasted an additional five weeks appealing to the War Department to get his semi-secret authority from the President converted into a regular War Department order. Halleck looked upon this as irregular. Stanton hesitated. On December 17 McClernand had become panicky and telegraphed the President and Stanton to learn whether he had been superseded. At last his orders had come. He had hurried to Cairo. Porter had gone down the river without him. McClernand borrowed Navy howitzers and took passage on the ram *Tigress*. At Memphis he learned that Sherman had taken his, McClernand's, hard-earned recruits and gone on without him. McClernand borrowed a bunker of Navy coal and steamed on down the river.

At Milliken's Bend McClernand frowned over the defeat at Chickasaw Bluffs and gave Sherman permission to withdraw the troops from the Yazoo. Newspaper men, already hostile toward Sherman, chattered to McClernand about Sherman's mismanagement of the expedition. An eager light shone in McClernand's eyes. By way of familiarizing himself with conditions in his new command, the political general permitted the reporters to talk on.

On January 4, 1863, with an imperious gesture McClernand assumed command of the army. That his name might in no way be connected with the late disaster, he rechristened his command the "Army of the Mississippi."

General Sherman wrapped himself in a mantle of stoicism. To his family he wrote, "We have been to Vicksburg and it was too much for us, and we have backed out" [2]; to his troops, "A new commander is here to lead you. He is chosen by the President... who ... had the undoubted right to select his own agents"; to his brother John the Senator, "If I can keep down my tamed (?) spirit and live I will claim a virtue higher than Brutus." [3] In his letters he was stoical, but in his heart he was less virtuous and more human. He regarded his supersedure by McClernand as an attempt to humiliate and insult him. McClernand was a politician, not a general. He was conceited and arrogant. McClernand listened to the reporters and apparently accepted their accounts as truth. Worst of all McClernand had no idea what to do with the army now that he had taken it over. He spoke vaguely of opening the Mississippi to navigation and cutting his way to the sea, but his *modus operandi* was not clear. When Sherman asked permission to take Arkansas Post, McClernand immediately appropriated the idea as his own. He had even mentioned this to General Gorman at Helena on his way down the river, he said. Sherman was furious.

Porter shared Sherman's fury at the turn events had taken. He liked this bristling red-haired ex-West Pointer who damned politics, damned the newspapers, and believed in fighting hard. At Chickasaw Bluffs Sherman had fought under the worst conditions possible and had failed through no fault of his own.

This was the situation when a few minutes before midnight on January 4 Sherman and McClernand dropped down the river from Milliken's Bend to the mouth of the Yazoo to see Porter. The two generals boarded the *Black Hawk* and were admitted to the chart room, where they were greeted most informally. Porter had just shifted into his nightgown.

The three men seated themselves at a table, and Sherman explained the proposed expedition to Arkansas Post and his need for two of Porter's ironclads to subdue Fort Hindman—an iron-sheathed, casemate fort on the river side of Arkansas Post upon which the army's light field artillery could have little effect. Sherman suggested that Porter send Captain Shirk or Captain Phelps, since these officers had coöperated in earlier operations on the Tennessee and Cumberland. Sherman wanted to undertake the mission himself to wipe out the defeat at Chickasaw Bluffs.

McClernand interrupted to remind Sherman that in the new organization he commanded only one of the two army corps. Sherman's face flushed. He arose trembling with rage and walked out into an after cabin. Porter's indignation also flared.

"If General Sherman goes in command of the Army," said Porter, "I will go along with my whole force and make a sure thing of it. Otherwise, I will have nothing to do with the affair!"

Just then Sherman beckoned to him, and Porter went out.

"My God, Porter!" whispered Sherman. "You will ruin yourself if you talk that way to McClernand. He is very intimate with the President and has powerful influence."

"I don't care who or what he is, I'll be damned if he shall be rude to you in my cabin!" [4]

Sherman begged Porter for the sake of harmony to waive that. The two returned to the chart room, where they found McClernand poring over a map.

After these outbursts of wrath the atmosphere cleared and the three men worked out the details of the expedition. Since Porter was short of coal and his heavy craft could not stem the current on wood, McClernand agreed to furnish towage for the gunboats. The troops were all ready, as they had not been debarked from the transports. They would set out as soon after daybreak as possible, as Sherman said, to strike the enemy before the reporters could let the cat out of the bag.

"I suppose," said McClernand, "there's no objection to my going along?"

"None in the world," said Porter. If Sherman was willing to waive his rights and go as a subordinate of McClernand, that was Sherman's affair.

The return of the fleet up the river was toilsome and slow. A pair of McClernand's transports was hitched to each of the three heavy turtles, the *Baron DeKalb,* the *Louisville,* and the *Cincinnati.* At Greenwood, Mississippi, where a few days before there had been 10,000 cords of wood along the levee, the returning fleets found only a glowing ash heap.

Rendezvousing at the mouth of the White River the fifty-odd transports and naval vessels on January 9 began ascending this meandering stream.

In its lower reaches the White River looked more like a bayou than a river. There were no houses along its banks, nothing but swamps to echo the hoarse puffs of steam and snatches of soldiers' songs. Having made this feint up White River, the fleets shortly turned through a connecting bayou into the Arkansas River.

In the wider stream their progress was easier. The weather turning suddenly mild, the soldiers abandoned their overcoats and lounged about the decks in shirt sleeves. Habitations along the Arkansas River were few and generally wretched with scanty clearings. At rare intervals were deserted, rambling, plantation houses, with wide verandas rapidly sinking into decay. The negro quarters behind these pretentious structures were invariably in better repair. Here and there on the river's edges were empty corn cribs, the contents of which had been hastily removed and barged up the river. Occasionally a bin was found still burning, the charred ears tumbling into the water.[5]

On the night of January 9 the transports arrived at Notrib's farmhouse three miles below Arkansas Post, and McClernand gave orders to land the troops. Camp fires were lighted; and, pickets having been stationed, the soldiers bivouacked. In the middle of the night a contraband negro on one of the transports had a nightmare and awoke half the fleet with his terrified screams. From the westward through the beautiful clear night came the rhythmical sound of axes felling trees across the road to the fort.

The small village known as the Post of Arkansas, 60 miles above the mouth of the Arkansas River and 117 miles below Little Rock, was situated on a tongue of ground just high enough to be above the reach of floods. French traders in 1685 had established here one of their wilderness outposts. The village, now the county seat of Arkansas County, was used by the Confederates as a base for several regiments of Texas cavalry. On the river front of the village was Fort Hindman, a small square structure with casemates of heavy oak encased in railroad iron. The diminutive fort mounted eleven guns of assorted sizes up to nine inches, and its overabundant store of ammunition had, as the Federals had surmised, been captured with Sherman's ammunition boat, the *Blue Wing*. In addition to the fort the Confederates had entrenched themselves across the approaches by land. To defend the post Confederate Brigadier General Tom Churchill had about five thousand men of all arms.

McClernand's force at Notrib's farm numbered 32,000, and within easy striking distance was General Gorman's army of 12,000 operating along the White River.

Equally overwhelming was Porter's fleet. Any one of his three turtles could have blown Fort Hindman to pieces; and in addition he had the *Black Hawk* with two rifled guns and several tiers of howitzers, the wooden gunboat *Lexington*, the ram *Monarch*, and a whole flotilla of light-drafts under Lieutenant Watson Smith— the *Rattler*, the *Signal*, the *Marmora*, the *Romeo*, the *Juliet*, the *Glide*, the *Springfield*, the *New Era*, and the *Forest Rose*.

The next morning the Federal troops maneuvered to invest Arkansas Post. While George W. Morgan with the XIII Army Corps approached along the river road, a company of artillery and two regiments of infantry obtained a position on the opposite bank above the post, where they could cut off retreat by river; and Sherman attempted to lead his XV Army Corps in a wide detour through the swamps to forestall retreat by land. Sherman's men, however, bogged down in the slough and were compelled to fall back to the high ground along the river over which Morgan's corps had already marched. General McClernand, remaining in the rear aboard the *Tigress*, was troubled by the fact that the Confederates made no attempt to escape. The Confederate general, however, had been ordered to make no retreat and throughout this day was riding along his lines exhorting his men to die in their trenches.

In the afternoon McClernand sent word that the troops were ready to assault. Porter sent the three ironclads to shell the fort at close range, and also moved up the *Lexington* and the *Black Hawk* to send shrapnel into the enemy's trenches. Dust and splinters of wood and iron were kicked up by the explosions. From beyond the fort came the screams of wounded horses. Night fell; but McClernand's troops failed to attack. Their deployment had not been completed as McClernand believed. Porter withdrew his vessels. In the darkness McClernand's troops completed their deployment, massing along the edge of the clearing ahead of the Confederate lines, and bivouacked without camp fires. To repel boarders during the night Porter greased the casemates of his ironclads with tallow.

Sunday January 11 dawned frosty and clear. McClernand transferred his headquarters to a position in the woods not far behind the lines, and sent a man up a tree to witness the fight. During the night the Confederates had added a secondary line of earthworks from behind their fort across to the distant swamps. The old cotton field across which the assault was to be made had its normal quota of gullies and the few trees and logs scattered along the fence rows offered a slight but highly prized protection.

When the troops began firing, Porter moved the turtles once more to an anchorage near the fort and returned the *Black Hawk* to its former position below the ironclads. Watson Smith in the tinclad *Rattler* was ordered to push by the fort and enfilade the new line of earthworks from the rear. Brigadier General Ellet followed Watson Smith up the river in the ram *Monarch*.

In the midst of the action Porter transferred his flag from the *Black Hawk* to the agile little tugboat *Thistle* and circulated among the heavy Pook Turtles, whose heavy guns were now thundering away at the fort. Suddenly the *Louisville* caught fire, but a detail of men from the *Thistle* extinguished it without the ironclad's gunners being called from their battle stations. A reported fire on the *Cincinnati* Porter found to be a false alarm. From the deck of the *Thistle* Porter watched the Confederates' projectiles glance upward from the tallow-greased casemates of his ironclads to fall in the forest on the opposite bank of the river. At length Porter's shells tore through the iron and oak breastworks of Fort Hindman and silenced its guns.

Word now came that McClernand's green troops were retreating across the field, and Porter made all haste to get the *Black Hawk* upstream to board the fort himself. He managed to work his cumbersome flagship past the ironclads and take on board the unemployed regiments from the opposite shore. Quickly Porter warped the *Black Hawk* up to the broken casemates and ran out lines to secure her. The lines parted and he made a second attempt.

He was a few minutes too late. White flags appeared above the broken parapets. All firing ceased. Porter scrambled ashore. A gray clad soldier informed him that Colonel Dunnington, who commanded the fort, wanted to surrender to the naval commander; and Porter received the surrender of Fort Hindman.

McClernand's eyewitness crawled down from his tree. The general mounted his horse and galloped across the clearing. Already the weary defenders were unhooking their ammunition belts and stacking them with their rifles when McClernand arrived. Confederate General Churchill, quivering with chagrin, stated that he had not ordered the white flags to be shown. But he could do nothing about it now. He reluctantly surrendered his sword to General McClernand. In accepting it the political general proved himself not so magnanimous a man as General Grant or General Lee. General Sherman turned away in disgust.

The next morning about three hundred graves were dug. On each side some 150 soldiers had been killed. Over eight hundred of McClernand's men had been wounded in the charge. Porter's losses were negligible. Over the battlefield the little red-flagged hospital wagons were kept busy throughout the day bringing the wounded of both blue and gray to the transports. In all 4,791 prisoners were embarked to be transported to Cairo. All day the Federal troops dragged the ditches for souvenir swords and pistols. They dismantled the army huts and also recovered a part of the ammunition from the *Blue Wing*. In his survey Porter discovered the mail bags of the *Blue Wing*—empty.

The Federals retired down the river through a flurry of snow and anchored off the town of Napoleon. Here McClernand granted his troops leave to go ashore to celebrate the victory and received a message from General Grant disapproving of his "wild-goose chase into Arkansas" so long as Vicksburg, the main objective, remained unsubdued. McClernand complained to Lincoln: "I believe my success here is gall and wormwood to the clique of West Pointers who have been persecuting me . . . Do not let me be clandestinely destroyed, or, what is worse, dishonored, without a hearing." [6] Had he but noticed the date of Grant's message he might have saved himself this anguish, for Grant had written before hearing of the success.

When McClernand presently looked up from his writing, he saw that half the town of Napoleon was in flames. He sent Sherman to bring the troops to their senses and stamp out the blaze.

Meanwhile Porter's dispatches to the Department were carried by gunboat to Cairo, and thence by telegraph to Washington; whereas McClernand sent a messenger on a fast tug to telegraph it from Memphis. Thus the Army report outsped that of the Navy. As a patriot Mr. Welles rejoiced over the good news, if he did first hear of it through the War Department; but he requested Porter to improve his communication service.

"You will," Porter promised the Secretary, "receive the first account of the next battle we have . . ." [7]

The capture of Arkansas Post was widely publicized throughout the North, as was the Chickasaw Bluffs disaster in the South. Thousands who had never before heard of the small Confederate stronghold cheered over its capture. The news came indeed at a propitious moment, for the entire North had just learned of the foundering of the U. S. S. *Monitor* off Cape Hatteras and of the recapture of Galveston by the Confederates—when Porter's old flagship the *Harriet Lane* had been surprised and captured and his mortar steamer *Clifton* burned. The gallant Captains Renshaw and Wainwright had lost their lives, and for the moment the Federal blockade of an important port had been abandoned. From its effect on the political situation the victory at Arkansas Post, however, was not a tawdry affair. For the second time Porter was awarded a vote of thanks by Congress. "If you open the Father of Waters," exulted Gustavus Fox, "you will at once be made an Admiral, besides we will try for a ribboned star." [8]

NAVAL EVOLUTIONS IN THE WOODS

THE Mississippi River had now reached flood stage. Flush with the tops of its levees it rushed through the flat valley, curving, re-curving, doubling back on its course, curving again to the south-ward. It ground out new channels, swept away old bars and islands, enclosed new islands within its restless, drift-littered flood. In spite of its breadth the turbulent river stood from twelve to fifteen feet above the alluvial plain. In hundreds of places between Memphis and Vicksburg it cut through its artificial banks flooding roadways and converting bottom lands on both sides into im-passable swamps.

On January 18 General Grant came down the river from Memphis to Napoleon. Most of the plantations along the river had now been deserted. Many of the mansion houses had been burned, some by Confederate regulars who applied the torch to cotton marked "C. S. A.," which the Confederate Government had purchased from the planters, some by roving bands of draft evaders and guerrillas, some by Federal gunboats in retaliation against bushwhackers and guerrillas. The town of Napoleon was still aflame when Grant arrived.

Grant's commission gave him priority over McClernand. Sher-man begged Grant to take command of the army. Porter backed Sherman. Grant ordered Sherman and McClernand to concentrate their forces above Vicksburg. Then Grant returned to Memphis, took several days to form his plans, and finally, on January 29, brought the remainder of his forces down the river. He absorbed McClernand's forces into the Army of the Tennessee and made Sherman, McClernand, and McPherson commanders of army corps.

By this time Porter had once more assembled his vessels at the mouth of the Yazoo, and was ready for action. Grant and Sher-man came off almost every day to the flagship *Black Hawk* to hold councils of war in Porter's cabin.

Grant's position was exceedingly awkward, for as his biographers agree Grant was still "on trial." Though he sensed the antagonism of his subordinate toward himself, Grant yet hesitated to dismiss McClernand; for he did not know how far the political general had the support of Lincoln. Moreover, the President had expressed a desire that Grant complete the canal opposite Vicksburg which General Williams had started at the time Farragut ran the Vicksburg batteries; and this was tantamount to an executive order.

Sherman, who had been through Chickasaw Bayou to his sorrow and whose troops at Milliken's Bend were camping on the narrow levee by night and shoveling mud in the canal by day, urged Grant to return to Memphis, now that he had demoted McClernand, and approach Vicksburg once more over dry land. But Grant would not listen to this. Such a movement would look like retreat.

In view of the dangerous political situation in the North it was well that Grant did not make what might have appeared to be a backward move. The loss of Galveston had revived the old diplomatic objections to the blockade. Admiral Du Pont, who was soon to lead a squadron of new ironclad monitors against Charleston, had already been discouraged by test performances of these vessels; and the Department nevertheless was coercing him into a purely naval attack which would prove as futile as Farragut's first effort against Vicksburg. The rapid shifting of high commanders in Virginia had given the Federal operations there an air of amateurish bungling. General Rosecrans in the West had paid so dearly for his victory at Murfreesboro that he dared not pursue the retreating Confederate army under Bragg. Copperhead newspapers were clamoring against the Lincoln administration. The enforcement of the draft was provoking dissension that would soon break out in open riots in New York City in which dozens of negroes would be strung up to lamp posts. Bounties for volunteer recruits had risen to $700. On the stock exchange the price of gold had climbed from 132 to 175.

Since Grant would not go back to Memphis, his next best move was to march his army down the Louisiana shore, ferry them across below Vicksburg, and attack the city from the high ground in the rear. He could not send his troops past Vicksburg in the frail transports. And he would have to wait for the Mississippi's backwaters to subside before he could march them down the Louisiana

shore. Yet, simply to wait was at this moment worse than to retreat.

In the conferences aboard the *Black Hawk* Grant and Sherman
and Porter outlined a series of movements which would keep the
naval force and the troops occupied and possibly turn one or another of the enemy's flanks and secure a footing on the dry land
behind Vicksburg.

The plan was that, while Grant's men were digging the canal
opposite the Confederate stronghold and were reconnoitering the
swamps and bayous of Louisiana in search of a western waterway
parallel to the Mississippi down which the troops might descend
in transports to the high ground below Vicksburg, Porter was to
organize a naval expedition to cut eastward across the lowlands of
the Yazoo delta to the headwaters of the Yazoo River and attempt
to find a route around Vicksburg's northern flank.

In the early days before the levee was built the Mississippi
River had been connected with the upper tributaries of the Yazoo
River through a bayou known as the Yazoo Pass, which left the
Mississippi at a point opposite Helena, Arkansas. It was now designed to cut the levee, steam through the old pass, the Coldwater, the Tallahatchie, and thence into the Yazoo River at a
point some 100 miles above Vicksburg, destroy Confederate vessels in the river, and secure a landing for Grant's troops on the
high ground above Haynes's Bluff.[1]

As the Yazoo Pass was more than 200 miles north of Vicksburg,
Porter was compelled to direct the movements of the expedition
from a distance. Most of his gunboats were near Vicksburg; and,
since he was the nerve center for all operations along 3,000 miles
of waterways, he had to stay on the Mississippi where dispatch
vessels could reach him.

Lieutenant Watson Smith was placed in command of the expedition with the newly-completed, turret-ironclad *Chillicothe,*
the old turtle *Baron DeKalb,* the tinclad *Rattler,* and three light-
drafts.

A levee 100 feet wide held the Mississippi from overflowing into
the Yazoo Pass. On February 3 this levee was blasted; and the
river, nine feet higher than the swamps, gushed through, lifting
trees and logs and shoving them through the bushgrown channel
of the old pass. The debris jammed the passage and had to be
cleared away.

The gunboats, held back a week until the overflow approached
the level in the river, at last ran down the chute into the forest

TRANSPORT NAVIGATING A BAYOU. DIFFICULTIES SIMILAR TO THESE CONFRONTED
PORTER'S FLOTILLAS IN THE YAZOO PASS AND STEELE'S BAYOU EXPEDITIONS.

followed by the miscellany of lighter naval vessels and transports bearing Brigadier General Ross's 800 soldiers.

Debris frequently became wedged in the paddle wheels and stopped the vessels. Fortunately, however, among General Ross's men were many experienced foresters, who wrapped chains around the obstructions and dragged them from the channel. The two ironclads being squat, low vessels were able to pass under overhanging trees with comparative ease, but the light-drafts and transports were one or two decks higher and were continually fouling their tophamper. Smokestacks were knocked down, cabins stove in, boats smashed, davits twisted. With axes the soldiers and sailors were compelled to clear an aisle through the trees.

The success of Watson Smith's expedition depended upon surprise and speed of execution; consequently, his men worked like demons for fourteen days before they were able to maneuver their boats through the Pass. Then, having at last entered the more navigable Coldwater River, they encountered a human obstacle —an improvised cavalry force of Confederate "Partisan Rangers" under Brigadier General Featherston. Featherston's men had bivouacked in cotton sheds and were covered with lint. The Federals laughed and called them Featherbed Rangers. But the Rangers crashed through the swamps and felled trees across the channel ahead of the Federal vessels.

Dispatches from the remote wilderness traveled slowly to Porter at the mouth of the Yazoo, and along with the dispatches came rumors that Watson Smith was losing his mind. The strain had in fact brought Smith close to a nervous breakdown. Four weeks had passed before the expedition had covered half the distance to the Yazoo River. Even a less impatient man than Porter might well have been alarmed. This was no moment to risk the capture of so large a force, for Porter had just sent down the river past Vicksburg the ram *Queen of the West* and the new ironclad *Indianola* with her two powerful 11-inch Dahlgren rifles, and both of these vessels had fallen into the hands of the enemy.

Suddenly in the newspapers smuggled over from Vicksburg came news that Watson Smith's expedition had encountered a cotton-bale fort at the mouth of the Tallahatchie and had been beaten back. The exultant Confederates hoped to capture the entire force. The normally imperturbable General Grant became so worried for the safety of General Ross, who commanded the troops in Watson Smith's expedition, that he ordered Quinby with several thousand troops to plunge through the wilderness to relieve Ross.

Porter obtained a pilot who knew the country and pushed a reconnaissance up one of the numerous bayous that branch off from the lower Yazoo. He sounded the channel for thirty miles and was convinced that the Pook Turtles could be gotten up. Along the route he picked up negroes and quizzed them about the chances of finding lateral passageways between the various north-and-south rivers that flow into the Yazoo. Not having time to reconnoiter the entire route, he had to rely on the opinions of his pilot and the escaped contrabands. He returned to the Mississippi, conferred hastily with Grant, and gave orders for five turtles, four mortars, and four tugs to get under way immediately.

On March 14 Porter pushed this force up Steele's Bayou, with Grant accompanying him to complete the plans as the vessels moved along. This second expedition was to ascend Steele's Bayou to Black Bayou, then eastward to Deer Creek, up it to Rolling Fork, then east to the Big Sunflower, and finally down the latter stream to the Yazoo about two miles above Haynes's Bluff. If he could push suddenly into the Yazoo River, Porter might cut off the Confederates who were menacing Watson Smith's expedition farther to the north. If he could not work through, he would at least create a diversion in favor of Smith. If successful, Grant could send troops through the new route to the dry land in the rear of Vicksburg.

Grant left Porter the next day and sent back Sherman with a strong army force to follow in the wake of Porter's flotilla.

The first few days were the easiest, as this part of the bayou was wide and unobstructed. The quartermasters on the bows of the Pook Turtles kept slinging their leads and chanting "quarter less three." There was plenty of water. The seamen were in excellent spirits and blew the whistles to startle the lizards, rats, racoons and possums that sought shelter from high water in the branches of the big trees.

Like his men Porter was in good spirits. Here and there a large cypress tree, smothered with wild eglantine, briar, and grapevines, stood in the middle of the passage; but there was room for the boats to go around it. Porter decided to exercise the turtles at ramming and gave orders for the *Cincinnati* to butt the next big tree. The ironclad rammed its 800 tons against the tree at a speed of three knots and knocked it over about twenty degrees from the perpendicular. The *Cincinnati* backed off and rammed again, and

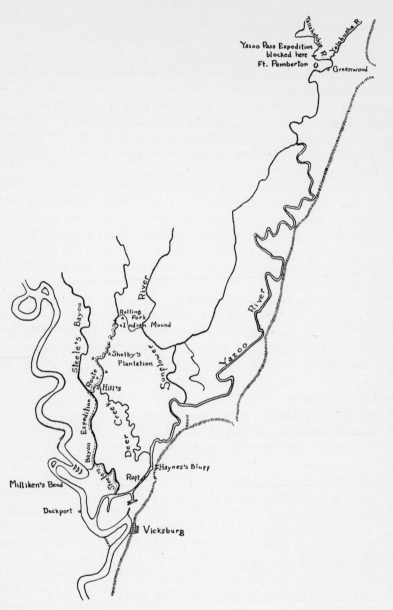

THE LOWER YAZOO DELTA, SHOWING THE ROUTE TAKEN BY PORTER ON THE STEELE'S
BAYOU EXPEDITION.

this time brought it down with a crash. A chain was bent to its branches and the turtle next astern hauled it out of the passage.

The next day when the flotilla turned into Black Bayou, the first of the lateral passageways, ramming became the order of the day. This channel was narrow and full of "devil's elbows." The vessels had to bump into trees and depend on the rebound to turn them around the tortuous bends. On the map Black Bayou wound about like a string faked up and down on a sheet of paper. At times the different vessels were headed in every direction on the compass.

General Sherman came up in a tug late Monday night while Porter was still ramming trees in Black Bayou. Every time a turtle rammed a tree an assortment of lizards, snakes, and weasels would rain on its deck, along with rotten branches and vines. Porter kept a special detail of seamen sweeping the decks. Sherman did not believe a practicable passage could be made for the large transports.

"Before you fellows get through," he prophesied to Porter, "you won't have a smokestack or a boat among you."

"So much the better," said Porter; "it will look like business. All I need is an engine, guns, and a hull to float them." [2]

Sherman stationed his advance troops so as to hold Black Bayou and then steamed back through the watery forest to hurry up his rear transports.

Early on March 17 Porter entered Deer Creek. Deer Creek flowed through a beautiful secluded region that had not yet felt the ravages of war. The ground here was fertile, and plantations were numerous. The people throughout this section had considered themselves safe from Federal invaders; and in contrast to the planters along the Mississippi, who had deserted their homes and withdrawn into the interior with their slaves, livestock, and movables, the planters here had put in their crops as usual. Their gardens were filled with spring vegetables. Their fields had been planted this year to corn, and the young blades were just beginning to tinge the dark alluvium with green. In their barnyards were horses, mules, oxen, cows, pigs, turkeys, geese, and chickens. Their cotton sheds near the boat landings were packed with the crops of the last two years. It was one of these Deer Creek plantations—Shelby's—that had obtained national fame as the setting for *Uncle Tom's Cabin*.

General Pemberton's Confederate troops arrived along Deer Creek about the time Porter did, and Porter's light-drafts had hardly begun loading their decks with "C. S. A." cotton to defray the expenses of the expedition before the Confederates began applying torches to the piles of expensive cotton all along the river. For a Federal about to capture a pile of cotton this was a melancholy sight. Porter fired angrily at the incendiaries and pushed ahead at full speed, his ironclad turtles crashing through wooden bridges, uprooting pilings, and splintering timbers, racing furiously to stop the conflagrations. But the planters on either side collaborated with the Confederate troops in firing cotton, and everywhere made their negroes drive livestock and poultry back from the river banks and into the woods to avoid capture.

Occasionally the flotilla was compelled to run the gauntlet between two pillars of flaming cotton that stood on opposite banks of the narrow stream. Porter then ordered all ports closed, decks wetted, rang two bells to "go ahead fast" and dashed through. He was reminded of the fire rafts at Fort Jackson. On one of these occasions Porter attempted to ride through the flames on the topside of the *Cincinnati*. With him were his nephew Lieutenant George M. Bache, who commanded the vessel, and the helmsman. The hose was pointed up the hatch to the upper deck and everything was drenched with water. But the heat was insufferable. Porter and Bache jumped inside the iron pilot house and the helmsman covered himself with an old, water-soaked flag.

Thirty miles up Deer Creek the channel narrowed and the ironclads squeezed through with difficulty. The overhanging casemates scraped the slimy embankments. However, only a few miles now remained before they would reach the Rolling Fork—last of the lateral bayous which would lead them into the Sunflower, where maneuvering would be easy.

On Thursday night, March 19, Porter was within seven miles of the Rolling Fork. His men were exhausted, and he tied his vessels up for the night. A breathless contraband came alongside and shouted that the Southerners were felling trees across the channel ahead. Porter sent a tug with howitzers to drive the Confederates away, landed a force of 200 men under Lieutenant Murphy to hold the right bank, scribbled a note to Sherman and sent it downstream by his secretary, Charlie Guild, Gustavus Fox's nephew, and finally unleashed the turtles and followed the tug upstream to resume the tedious labor of clearing the channel.

When the tugboat sprayed the woods with grapeshot, the Confederates moved farther upstream, where they managed to fell a giant cypress tree across the channel and halt the tug. Above this they were able to work without hindrance.

The next morning the ironclads dragged the obstructions from the creek. Progress was extremely tedious, but after several miles they came to a stretch where the creek was apparently covered with green scum. The tug rushed into this green part and stuck fast: the bed of the channel was covered with millions of willow switches. Porter crowded steam on the Pook Turtle *Carondelet* and attempted to ram through, but the submerged withes caught in the iron overhang and held the vessel.

Porter ordered out saws, knives, cutlasses, and chisels. The men sitting on planks over the side cut away the withes jammed in the overhang. The *Carondelet* steamed ahead and moved only three feet. Other withes sprang up from under the water and held the *Carondelet* as firmly as before.

Murphy with his 200 men was now entrenched on top of an Indian mound which commanded the right bank of the creek at the entrance into Rolling Fork. But new detachments of Confederates came up the Sunflower River on the other side of the woods, and drove Murphy back to the gunboats.

Next came the news that planters were felling trees behind the fleet. Large gangs of slaves had toiled all night, their determined masters standing over them with shotguns.

Confederate sharpshooters now closed in on the gunboats. Porter clamped down the port shutters and kept his men below decks. Since the river banks were higher than the casemates of his turtles, he could not obtain sufficient elevation to fire his broadside guns. He did manage to get off a few mortar shells, and keep back the attackers during the daytime; but he faced the danger of being boarded during the night before Sherman could arrive.

After dusk Porter wrote a distress message to Sherman on tissue paper, rolled it in a tobacco leaf, and sent it by a faithful negro. He smeared the carapaces of his turtles with slime from the bottom of the stream to make boarding as difficult as possible. Then he unshipped his rudders and drifted the vessels down as far as the new obstructions in the rear. Here Porter stationed his best pickets in the iron-sheathed pilot houses and ordered every other man and officer to keep below. Ports were to be closed, guns loaded with grape and cannister, men to sleep at the guns, everything ready to repel boarders. He put his men on half rations.

In case the Confederates should dam the stream ahead of him, turn the water into Rolling Fork, and thereby strand the fleet,

Porter wrote a detailed general order for blowing up the gunboats.

No mishaps occurred during the night; and on Sunday morning, March 22, Porter crawled out on deck to resume his laborious retreat. He kept up a continual booming of mortars to encourage his men; while enemy sharpshooters filled the air with their twanging bullets. An old quartermaster dragged on deck a section of a smoke stack and offered this ludicrous but effective device to the Admiral as a shield.

At midday rapid skirmishing broke out in the woods below. The Confederates retreated hastily through the bushes. A short time later General Sherman rode up the bank on an old horse with a rope bridle. The men marooned in the flotilla greeted the General with a roar of cheers. Sherman was covered with mud. During the night he had led his men by torches through mud so deep that the soldiers had slung their ammunition belts around their necks and the drummer boys had carried their drums on their heads.

The rescued gunboats now bumped back down the creek, sterns first. A loaded coal barge that sank in their path was broken up and dragged clear, and the coal spread out on the bottom so that the boats could get over it.

The same day Porter received a message from Fleet Captain Breese that Farragut had come up the river during his absence; that Ellet had attempted to run two of the rams past Vicksburg to assist Farragut and that one of these, the *Switzerland,* had been sunk.

Porter boarded a tug and left his now protected fleet to follow him back over the route by which they had come. On the way he passed Sherman's troops strewn all along Deer Creek, celebrating after their skirmish with the Confederates. Some were slaughtering cattle and cooking. Others were wrestling and playing games. Twenty of the merriest, entirely naked, were upon mules' backs forcing their animals to swim the creek and vainly endeavoring to make them climb a steep bank on the opposite side. From the plantation at the mouth of Muddy Bayou soldiers and negroes were bringing down cotton stuffed in pickers' sacks and piling it on board the transports.

Sherman's men cheered the Admiral as he passed.

Porter pulled the tug's whistle rope in answer to the cheers and steamed on to Vicksburg.

RUNNING THE GAUNTLET

WHILE Porter's flotillas were struggling through the Yazoo delta on the crest of the February-March floods in their ingenious but unsuccessful efforts to turn the northern flank of Vicksburg, he was directing the activities of the remainder of the Mississippi Squadron over the 3,000 miles of rivers and preparing to take his ironclads below Vicksburg as soon as the waters should subside and permit the march of Grant's army down the Louisiana shore.

Except during his ten-day absence with the Steele's Bayou Expedition, Porter personally controlled his vast command from the flagship *Black Hawk* at the mouth of the Yazoo. His flotillas on the Tennessee and Cumberland Rivers protected the communications of General Rosecrans. Divisions of his gunboats patrolled continually from Vicksburg to Memphis, from Memphis to Cairo, and after the melting of ice in the Ohio from Cairo up to Pittsburgh. The building of new ironclads was pushed at Cincinnati and St. Louis. Emergency repairs were effected at the navy yards in Memphis and in Mound City.

Shortage of men had compelled Porter to ship 400 contrabands, whose wives and pickaninnies had to be taken aboard with them. A group of these ignorant negroes in their efforts to warm themselves set fire to the station ship at Cairo.

Porter borrowed several companies of General Grant's soldiers to replenish his crews. But as soon as he had cut their hair and trimmed their beards according to Navy Regulations, one of the companies mutinied and had to be sent back in irons.[1]

Smallpox broke out in the Tennessee River flotilla. A case of typhus was reported on the *Conestoga*. Soon the malarial mosquito would be active again.

Porter saw a band of Partisan Rangers fire into his hospital boat, the *Red Rover*; and he became so infuriated that he issued a general order that captured guerrillas were to be strung up to the nearest tree. This drastic order provoked an interchange of sarcastic letters with Confederate General Stevenson at Vicksburg, who threatened like reprisals.

Northern traders swarmed down the river in the wake of the gunboats and transports. Porter and Grant jointly issued an order restricting their activities to territory within the Federal lines. But the traders disregarded regulations and when fired upon by guerrillas complained that they were not protected. Porter's captains caught dozens of traders smuggling contraband articles to the Confederates. Porter arrested such offenders and sent the cotton they had collected to Cairo for condemnation in the admiralty prize court. One of the trader vessels operating beyond the prescribed limits collided with Porter's store ship, the *Sovereign,* and sheared off her side paddle wheel; whereupon Porter ordered Captain Pennock to hold the offending boat at Cairo until her owners had paid a $10,000 fine. "I will make them pay for it if it is a hundred years hence," declared the exasperated Admiral.[2]

Porter's labors were more varied than those of any other naval commander, but his situation enabled him to enjoy more of the amenities of life. He carried a good cow on board the *Black Hawk* for his milk supply, and for supper normally restricted himself to a diet of mush and milk. At other meals he lived generously. A pantry well stocked with delicacies and liquors, and chicken coops well filled with fat hens, ducks, and geese, Porter believed, were the first essentials to health in the river country.

Every morning the mess attendants laid at the Admiral's table as many places as there were gunboats in the neighborhood; and each captain was expected to come on board for breakfast, at which time he would also receive his orders for the day. Porter encouraged his men to be witty in the face of danger. Next to daring in battle came a good humor at the breakfast table, in Porter's estimation. One young man who displayed uncommon energy in confiscating cotton and uncommon ability in selecting bird dogs for the Admiral rose quickly from the rank of seaman to acting lieutenant commander.

On sunny days Porter occasionally found an hour to ride up and down the levee with Sherman or Grant, but his work kept him most of the time at his desk. He began to suffer cramps in his legs from lack of exercise. After hard days he would play his piano or romp around the cabin with his numerous dogs. Another diversion was drawing caricatures and writing burlesque anecdotes, which—recklessly disregarding the fact that they might be seen by the

Secretary—he sent to his brother-in-law, G. H. Heap, correspondence clerk in the Navy Department.[3]

As soon as he had started Watson Smith's expedition into the Yazoo Pass, Porter began his attempts to break up Confederate shipping in the Mississippi below Vicksburg. The river below Vicksburg was included within Admiral Farragut's command, but Farragut's vessels working up the river from New Orleans were blocked at Port Hudson, Louisiana, by an elaborate series of fortifications second only to those of Vicksburg. Every day the Confederates in Vicksburg received shipments of grain and cattle from Louisiana and Texas. Even ammunition from Mexico was brought across Texas and floated down the Red River and up the Mississippi to Vicksburg.

On the last day of January 1863, Porter saw a large steamer unloading stores at Vicksburg. The temptation was too great. He ordered Brigadier General Ellet to run the antiquated *Queen of the West* past the batteries the next morning before daybreak, and ram the Confederate vessel. "It will not be part of your duty," he told Ellet, "to save the lives of those on board; they must look out for themselves, and may think themselves lucky if they do not meet the same fate meted out [by the Confederates] to the *Harriet Lane*. Think of the fate of that vessel while performing your duty, and shout '*Harriet Lane*' into the ears of the Rebels. If you can fire turpentine balls from your bow fieldpieces into the light upper works, it will make a fine finish to the sinking part." [4]

Ellet got his men out early, but the *Queen* was unwieldy, and it was sunrise before he finally got under way. As hundreds of flashes appeared through the smoke, Porter's map makers stationed around the peninsula recorded the locations of enemy guns.

In the swirling current Ellet was unable to butt the Confederate steamer. His own vessel received a pounding from the Confederate shore batteries but got through without serious injury. At steamboat landings below Vicksburg he destroyed quantities of cotton and supplies, and near the mouth of the Red River burned three steamers—in all about $200,000 worth of enemy property.

So profitable was the *Queen's* performance below Vicksburg that Porter decided to gamble an ironclad. He sent down on Friday—February the thirteenth—Lieutenant George Brown in the brand-new *Indianola*, tallest of the ironclads in the squadron because of the upper-deck cabins that Porter had had erected after the first inspection in Cincinnati. With its high decks supported on the outside by massive iron columns, the *Indianola* was indeed an architectural curiosity. Her forward casemate was equipped with two of the most powerful guns yet developed, 14-ton, 11-inch Dahlgren rifles. "Don't be surprised to see the *Indianola*," Porter wrote Ellet. "Don't mistake her for a Rebel." [5] He did not attempt to describe the queer vessel.

The *Indianola* carried sixty days' provisions and two barges of coal. Her guns and those on the *Queen* were sufficient to dispose of all the cottonclads which even the wildest rumors had credited to the Confederates.

On February 21 Colonel Ellet came up from the Red River to Vicksburg on a captured tug. Crossing the peninsula he came aboard the *Black Hawk* to report that his pilot had run the *Queen* aground under an enemy battery near the mouth of the Red River. Ellet had had no time to destroy his vessel and had himself barely escaped capture. A few miles south of Natchez Ellet had met Brown with the *Indianola* and learned that the *Indianola* had suffered no damage in passing Vicksburg. Brown was beating his way slowly upstream against the current with his coal barges lashed alongside.

Porter called a conference of officers.

With the *Queen* added to the enemy, the *Indianola* was now greatly endangered. The *Lafayette,* sister ship to the *Indianola,* had not yet been completed at St. Louis; and Porter had no iron-clads save the old Pook Turtles to send down to Brown's assistance. Whereas the turtles were able to go downstream past Vicksburg, they were unable under their own power to return upstream against the current. A month or so later, when it would be possible to move the army down the river, Porter would need the turtles to shield Grant's fragile transports.

One of his officers suggested that he send down a fake monitor to discourage the Confederates from attacking the *Indianola*. The novel idea pleased Porter and he drew a sketch which the officers pronounced very formidable.

A coal barge supplied the hull for the dummy monitor. Pieces of old lumber and barrel staves were quickly knocked together to make paddle boxes and casemates. Two fourteen-inch logs, painted to simulate guns, were run through the casemate ports. Clay furnaces with tall, pork-barrel funnels were installed, and the whole was smeared with tar. To its foremast was tacked a skull-and-crossbones and across its paddle boxes was the motto: Deluded People Cave In.

On the night of February 24, knots of pitch pine were fired in the clay furnaces, and the wooden monitor was set adrift to run the batteries.

As the dummy rounded the horseshoe at Vicksburg, it drew a heavy fire from the enemy. When it ran aground on the lower side of the peninsula, some of Sherman's canal diggers prodded it out into the current.

Heavy firing was now heard far below Vicksburg, and shortly after daylight Federal pickets on the Louisiana shore reported that the *Queen,* which had appeared off Warrenton, six miles below Vicksburg, during the night had fled down the river on the approach of the dummy monitor.

For two days Porter awaited news of the *Indianola.* On February 26 he wrote Georgy a glowing account of the dummy monitor, "a much better looking vessel than the *Indianola.*" But the *Queen's* appearance and the heavy firing from below Warrenton worried him.

Further news drifted in slowly. On February 27 a negro coal passer from the *Indianola* reported on board the *Black Hawk.* According to the negro the *Indianola* three days earlier had been attacked and captured by six Confederate vessels. Actually, the ironclad, encumbered as she was by coal barges, had fought only two Confederate vessels; but these being lighter and more maneuverable had kept clear of the *Indianola's* guns and by repeated ramming had driven the ironclad ashore and captured it. Four days after the first report another negro member of the *Indianola's* crew emerged from the swamps with an equally exaggerated story of the capture but a true account of the dummy monitor's success. The negroes living on the Louisiana shore, who had fed him while he was hiding in the swamp, had told him that they had seen the *Queen* rush down the river the evening after the capture yelling about a turret-ironclad. Then he had heard an explosion which had sent dead branches crashing in the swamps around him.

The success of the dummy monitor was admitted by the Vicksburg *Whig* on March 5. "We stated a day or two since that we would not then enlighten our readers in regard to a matter which was puzzling them very much. We allude to the loss of the gunboat *Indianola,* recently captured from the enemy. We were loth to acknowledge she had been destroyed, but such is the case. The Yankee barge sent down the river last week was reported to be an ironclad gunboat. The authorities, thinking that this monster would retake the *Indianola,* immediately issued an order to blow her up. The order was sent down by a courier to the officer in charge of the boat. A few hours afterwards another order was sent down countermanding the first. But before it reached the *Indianola* she had been blown to atoms . . ." [6]

Porter quoted the Vicksburg paper in his report to Welles. But the Secretary was already reading the news in the Richmond *Examiner.* "Laugh and hold your sides, lest you die of a surfeit of derision, O Yankeedom!" howled the Southern editor of the *Examiner.* "Blown up because forsooth a flat-boat or mud scow with a small house taken from the back yard of a plantation put on top of it, is floated down the river before the frightened eyes of the Partisan Rangers. A Turreted Monster! . . . The Partisan Rangers are notoriously more cunning than brave." [7]

Not long after this farcical episode Porter heard again that the Yazoo Pass Expedition had been blocked and that Watson Smith was losing his mind. Porter then hurried off on the second futile effort to force a passage into the Yazoo River, the Steele's Bayou Expedition.

When he returned to the Mississippi on March 25 he found that Watson Smith had suffered a nervous breakdown and his command had fallen to Lieutenant Foster of the *Chillicothe.* Quinby's army had relieved Ross so that the northern gunboats, though stalemated, were no longer in danger of capture.

Meanwhile events on the Mississippi had taken a serious turn.

Below Port Hudson Farragut had heard of the capture, but not of the destruction, of the *Indianola;* and had attempted to rush his fleet up above Port Hudson to retake the *Indianola.* Only the *Hartford,* however, with her "little chicken" the tug *Albatross,* had succeeded in getting by Port Hudson. The venerable side-wheeler *Mississippi*—about which so many memories clustered—had grounded under the enemy batteries and had been destroyed by fire.

Arriving below Vicksburg with the *Hartford,* Farragut learned the *Indianola's* fate. Since the sea-going *Hartford* was no more maneuverable in the river than the *Indianola* had been, Farragut now expected at any time to be caught by the agile Confederate vessels. Under these circumstances he had communicated, during Porter's absence up Deer Creek, with Brigadier General Ellet, who had ordered two more of his fast dwindling ram fleet to pass Vicksburg. Contrary to one of Porter's general orders, the ram fleets' insubordinate commander attempted to send the rams past

Vicksburg in *open daylight*. On March 25 the ram *Lancaster* was pounded to pieces under Vicksburg. The ram *Switzerland* got through, with steam pipes shot away, and the loss of several of her men who leaped into the river badly scalded and were drowned.

Porter returned from the vexing Steele's Bayou Expedition about two hours after the *Lancaster* had been sunk. The *Lancaster* was old and rotten, better off Porter thought at the bottom of the river. But her loss meant another black mark for the Navy. When Porter learned that Ellet had sent her past Vicksburg in open daylight he flew into a rage. To make matters worse Ellet now wrote Porter that the Marine Brigade preferred to continue its allegiance to the War Department. Porter immediately relieved Ellet of his command. To Secretary Welles he recommended that the organization be abolished altogether or turned back to the Army. He would have arrested Ellet, but the latter withdrew his impudent letter; whereupon Porter was content to banish Ellet to the guerrilla-infested rivers of Tennessee.

After the moon went down on March 26 Porter drifted a barge of provisions past the Vicksburg batteries to Farragut and entertained Farragut's young son Loyall aboard the *Black Hawk*. "I intended to get over to see you," Porter wrote Farragut the same day, "but General Grant says that it is a very long walk. I have been so much confined to the ship since I have been here that I have almost lost the use of my legs. All my time is spent at my desk, and I get no exercise, which does not agree with me. My trip up the river has been of great service to me, and I feel like a new man . . . Your son got over here safe, and I took him in. I expect he will give you an amusing account of my menage. The first evening he came we had eight dogs in the cabin. I have to resort to all kinds of things for amusement. Loyall was quite at home on mush and cream and fresh butter, all of which we have here in abundance . . . In relation to the *Switzerland,* keep her with you, but please make the commander understand that she is under your command, or he will go off on a cruise somewhere before you know it, and then get the ship into trouble. She is a very formidable ship as a ram, but I would never expect to see her again if she got out of your sight . . . It will be an object for you to remain at Red River as long as possible, and I hope you will do so. It is death to these (Confederate) people; they get all their grub from there." [8] Farragut moved on early the next morning to blockade the Red River and Porter did not get the chance to see him before he left.

During the next few weeks as the level of the river fell, the backwaters began to recede; and Grant started McClernand's division down the Louisiana side toward New Carthage, Louisiana, thirty miles below Vicksburg. As soon as his battered gunboats returned from the Yazoo delta, Porter set all hands to repairing them. The mouth of the Yazoo dinned like a shipyard as hundreds of hammers and saws and sledges and metal shears repaired the smashed cabins and hammered out kinks from smokestacks and stanchions. As a final touch before running the Pook Turtles past Vicksburg Porter gave them a gay coat of paint: hulls black, cabins buff, after the fashion of Nelson's *Victory*. False gun ports were painted on the walls of cabins.

From distant Washington Secretary Welles frowned upon Porter's expeditions in the Yazoo forests and urged him to run the gauntlet with a large force. Fox wrote Porter that the old cry was commencing against Mr. Welles for not giving the people success.

On April 16 Porter had seven ironclads ready to move. Logs were triced up abreast the engines at the waterline to protect them against plunging shot. Three Army transports packed with stores and with forage for horses were also ready to move down. Throughout the day a hush of expectation prevailed in the fleet and among the soldiers who lined the levee.

As if to commemorate the impending event the Mississippi Squadron on this day purchased two of the best private steamers on the river and to one of them gave the auspicious name *Fort Hindman*.

Porter was in excellent spirits. "Our people are too insatiate for success," he wrote Fox on this day. The Rebels at Vicksburg "are like a man inside of a house, windows barricaded, muskets out of a thousand loop holes, a 'cheval de frise' all around, and a wide ditch outside of that—*we* are in the position of boys throwing grass at him and expecting him to cave in—yet we win after all—we don't go backwards, we advance slowly notwithstanding 'Copperheads' and old 'Greeleys,' and by the grace of God, I hope to see us yet with Uncle Abe's foot on Jeff Davis's neck!" [9]

That evening Porter boarded a tug and went up and down the line surveying his fleet of ironclads. His flagship *Benton* was at the head of the line with the tugboat *Ivy* lashed alongside. Captain Walke's newly completed ironclad, the *Lafayette,* second in the line, had the wooden gunboat *General Price* and a coal barge lashed to her starboard side. Then followed the *Louisville,* the *Mound City,* the *Pittsburgh,* the *Carondelet,* each with one or two coal barges. Three Army transports came behind the first six ironclads, and the ironclad *Tuscumbia* as "whipper in" protected the rear.

At 8:45 P.M. the Admiral and his staff went aboard the *Benton.* At nine two white lanterns flashed the signal to get under way.

As they hauled in their anchors, the ships slid out into the current, hugging the Louisiana shore. At first the twin-bottomed *Benton* tried to veer and present her nose to the current, but a few kicks of her wheel counteracted this and sent her drifting down on her proper course. That she might not be prematurely revealed to the enemy, her fireroom hatches were closed, and steam was blown off through special vents inside the paddle box. Her black and yellow hull blended into the darkness along the levee. In the file extending for half a mile astern of the leader, each vessel struggled to maintain the correct distance of fifty yards from the one just ahead. The fuel had been well ignited so that only now and then a puff of smoke escaped into the starlit sky. Past the long line of Army transports they filed, past 50,000 silent soldiers on the Louisiana shore, on past the dredging machines at the north end of Grant's unsuccessful canal, until at length they straightened out along the first shank of the horseshoe curve heading directly toward the Vicksburg hills. Sherman himself with several yawls was at the lower end of the canal below the town ready to rescue any stricken vessels.

At ten-thirty as the lights of the city began to show through the trees Porter started the *Benton's* wheels. Confederate pickets on the spit of the peninsula, sighting the *Benton,* set fire to several houses to spread the alarm. Tar barrels began flaring along the Vicksburg waterfront as Porter's vessels rounded the bend. Muskets began a feeble prelude a few moments before thunder broke from the cannon on the hills.

At the horseshoe curve the current carried the stern of the *Benton* completely around; while from every tier of the Vicksburg fortifications cannon fired down upon the distressed ironclad. The *Benton* righted herself, and steaming within a few feet of the wharf discharged her broadsides as rapidly as her guns could be loaded. Some of her guns were elevated to reach the batteries on the heights, some fired grape and shrapnel at the water batteries, others fired on no particular target save the city itself. So close did the *Benton* pass alongside the town that Porter could hear the clatter of falling bricks as buildings collapsed under the *Benton's* fire. Suddenly a brilliant white glare illuminated the river and the cry arose, "Vicksburg is on fire!" The flare came from a tremendous beacon so arranged as to shed blinding light down both shafts of the horseshoe. Tar barrels blazed red, the burning houses and bonfires were amber, and the calcium flares of the beacon were blinding white.

A single enemy shot tore through the *Benton's* 2½-inch side armor, splintered 40 inches of oak backing through and through, and knocked off inside of the casemate a wall of planking 6 feet square. One seaman's leg was shot away, another's thigh was mangled, a few were slightly wounded by splinters and musket shot.

The *Lafayette*, with her light consort and coal barges, came around the turn, and she too was whirled around by the eddies. A shell exploded in her coal barge, and the lashings had to be cut before the vessel could get back on its course. One of the Pook Turtles was wheeled twice around by the eddies. Only three of the seven escaped this buffeting by the river.

While many of the coal barges had to be cast off before the turtles could right themselves, most of these drifted down to safety; and one was retrieved by its consort while still under fire. Finally the transports, manned chiefly by green volunteers, came under the fire of the batteries. When the eddies whirled them around, they steamed back upstream until Captain Shirk in the *Tuscumbia* turned them back into line. Then a Confederate shell set fire to the transport *Henry Clay,* whose decks for protection had been piled high with cotton and bales of forage. The flames spread instantly throughout the boat, and it had to be abandoned. In the confusion the *Tuscumbia* ran aground, and in backing off was fouled by one of the transports. Thinking the burning transport was an ironclad, the Confederates gave a tremendous yell. In the smoke and flames Porter could not make out for some minutes which of the vessels had been destroyed.

At twelve-thirty Porter drifted below the lower entrance of the canal, and a rowboat pulled out from shore to meet him. It was Sherman.

"*Benton,* ahoy!" he yelled.

"Halloo!" replied Porter.

Sherman climbed on board the *Benton.*

"You are more at home here than you were in the ditches grounding on willow trees," said Sherman. "Stick to this, Porter. It suits you Navy people better." [10] Then Sherman went back to learn how the other vessels had fared.

At two-ten Porter dropped anchor near the head of Diamond Island Bar a few miles below Warrenton. One by one the turtles answered the Coston signal from the flagship and let go their anchors into the silent blackness of the river. Only one of the transports anchored with the fleet. The others had stopped with Sherman's men above Warrenton, badly damaged.

The run past Vicksburg was one of the most colorful pageants of the war, but it was hardy a fight. "The danger to the vessels was more apparent than real," wrote Porter many years later when the events of the war had fallen into their proper perspective.[11] As a pyrotechnical display it was second only to the passage through Forts Jackson and St. Philip. Only a dozen men were wounded, not a single man was killed. "It was a jolly scene throughout," Porter wrote to Fox on the following day, "and I reckon that the city of Vicksburg never got a better pounding. We all drifted by slowly, and opened on them with shell, shrapnel, and canister, as hard as we could fire. I was a little worried when I saw the *Henry Clay* on fire, but I soon saw with a glass that she was [an Army transport and] none of ours ... The scene along the river was beautiful—hundreds of little bunches of cotton all afire, from the *Henry Clay,* were floating down on the water, helping to light up what was already too light for us. These bunches of cotton followed us down the river, and when we anchored below Warrenton, it looked as if a thousand steamers were coming down." [12]

The next morning Porter moved down to New Carthage, Louisiana, where he found that McClernand had mounted a log on cartwheels to bluff the enemy entrenched across the narrow levee ahead of him. After conferring hastily with the General, Porter dropped down and shelled the enemy earthworks. The Confederates retreated, leaving behind their engines of war, which, like McClernand's, were fakes.

On the night of April 22 while Grant was marching the main body of his troops down the western bank to New Carthage, an attempt was made to run six other transports past Vicksburg; although one was sunk the remaining five came through with stores and forage damaged.

Grant planned to ferry his army across at Grand Gulf, Mississippi, forty miles below Vicksburg. He found, however, that the Confederates had now erected many new fortifications at this strategic point and that it would be necessary for these batteries to be reduced before attempting the maneuver.

Accordingly at 8 A.M. on April 29 Porter led his ironclads to the attack. Grant's troops on transports witnessed the fight from the opposite side of the river. On General Grant's tug, anchored about fourteen hundred yards from the scene of battle, was a special commission recently sent out from Washington to observe and report on Grant's fitness for his command.

The fight thus officially witnessed was a ferocious stand-up and knock-down engagement in open daylight. To cope with the southernmost Confederate battery of nine guns on a bluff below and back of the ruined town Porter assigned the *Carondelet*, the *Mound City*, the *Louisville*, and the *Pittsburgh*; while he himself with the *Benton*, the *Tuscumbia*, and the *Lafayette* attacked the group of batteries above the town at the mouth of the Big Black River. The bombardment of Grand Gulf lasted four and a half hours. The enemy's shot hit the ironclads with deadly precision, and several hundred heavy shot pierced the vessels' hulls. The *Tuscumbia's* iron carapace being thinner than the others, shot entering one side came out through the other; and her upper works were demolished. The *Benton's* armor was pierced many times. A shot in her wheelhouse caused her to drift 1,500 yards down the river revolving around and around until her captain nosed her into the bank to bring her under control.

In the midst of the battle, while Porter was standing with several officers on her exposed upper deck to direct the fighting, a 7-inch Brooke shell burst on board killing and wounding several men, including two of the officers who had been talking with Porter. Porter was struck by a flying splinter, but Captain Greer caught him and kept him from falling. This slight injury was the first Porter had received in the thirty-five years since the *Guerrero-Lealtad* battle.

At the end of the bombardment many of the enemy's guns had been dismounted or smothered with dirt, but the losses on the vessels were heavier. Twenty-four men had been killed. On the decks of the ironclads were the cots of fifty-six wounded men.

Deciding to take no chances either in landing his men here or running them past Grand Gulf on the transports, Grant disembarked and marched them farther down the west bank while the transports ran by Grand Gulf after nightfall, under cover of a renewed bombardment from the gunboats.

That night Porter made General Grant and the commissioners comfortable on board his flagship. To elderly General Thomas (Halleck's Adjutant General) he gave up his stateroom. Porter

Courtesy of the Sherman Publishing Company, from D. D. Porter's Naval History of the Civil War

PORTER'S GUNBOATS PASSING THE VICKSBURG BATTERIES, APRIL 16, 1863.

PORTER's BOMBARDMENT OF GRAND GULF, ENGRAVED BY THOMAS NAST FROM SKETCHES SUPPLIED BY WITNESSES

helped General Thomas unpack his carpet bag, and as the General shifted into his long night shirt, Porter mixed a whiskey toddy.

Great complaints about Grant's manner of conducting operations, the Adjutant General told Porter, had come to the President

THE MISSISSIPPI RIVER BELOW VICKSBURG, SHOWING GRAND GULF WHICH PORTER BOMBARDED AND BRUINSBURG WHERE GRANT'S TROOPS WERE LANDED TO BEGIN THE FINAL OPERATIONS OF THE VICKSBURG CAMPAIGN.

from someone in the army before Vicksburg; and Mr. Lincoln had determined to find out for himself the true state of affairs by sending the present commissioners to observe Grant. Here the General stopped and swore Porter to secrecy. Mr. Washburn had been sent as the fast friend of General Grant, Governor Yates as a man on whose judgment the President could depend, and General Thomas as a military expert, who could explain to his colleagues the exact situation of affairs and the defects in Grant's plans if any existed.

"We stopped first," as Porter later quoted the General, "at McClernand's camp to ascertain his style of doing things. He gave us a grand review and a good lunch but had no ice for his champagne."

When Porter handed his guest the toddy General Thomas explained that he carried in his bag the authority to remove General Grant if he found it necessary and give his place to someone else.

"General," said Porter, "don't let your plans get out, for if the army and navy found out what you three gentlemen came for, they would tar and feather you!" [13]

Fortunately the commissioners were pleased with the progress of the campaign and Grant's popularity was not put to this test.

Between April 30 and May 3 Grant ferried his army across to the Mississippi shore of the river at Bruinsburg, under protection of Porter's gunboats, and the great campaign of Vicksburg entered its final stage.

UNVEXED TO THE SEA

W HILE Grant's army was ferrying across at Bruinsburg, Sherman was making a feint up the Yazoo against Haynes's Bluff to distract the Confederates' attention. The gunboats, transports, supply boats, and even the blacksmith boats strung out along the river, whistled and puffed all the smoke they could, while Sherman's 10,000 soldiers debarked, scampered back through the woods, re-embarked, and came up to unload again within view of the enemy. Fleet Captain Breese in Porter's absence made the feint of his gunboats so realistic as to be indistinguishable from an attack. The Confederates scored forty hits on the ironclads *Choctaw* and *DeKalb,* and several light-drafts had to be sent down the river for repairs.[1]

The feint caused the enemy to shift a large body of their reserve troops to Haynes's Bluff and to erect additional batteries. Above all it made them suspect for the moment that the serious maneuver at Bruinsburg was a ruse. By the time they discovered the real state of affairs Grant had landed 30,000 men on hard ground east of the river and was doggedly wedging his way into the heart of Mississippi to isolate Vicksburg from the rest of the Confederacy. With three days' cooked rations in his knapsacks and no provisions for a supply train, Grant pushed into enemy territory determined to feed his army on the produce of the land.

The audacity of Grant's tactics delighted Porter. He would have given his right arm to have been able to march his Pook Turtles overland at the head of Grant's army.

Grant's landing at Bruinsburg caused the Confederates to blow up their magazines and evacuate Grand Gulf. Porter detailed the turtle *Louisville* to complete the demolition of the abandoned stronghold, and since Grant could not arrive behind Vicksburg in less than two weeks Porter decided to make a quick dash up the Red River, relieve Farragut of the blockade at that point, and if possible recapture the *Queen of the West* and the ram *Webb.*

He could do this and get back to Vicksburg, he believed, by the time Grant closed in from the landward side.

At Bruinsburg he transferred his wounded to the battered *Tuscumbia,* and proceeded down the river. About midnight he sighted the *Hartford* at the mouth of the Red River.

The elderly admiral's desk work in connection with the blockade of the western Gulf had been piling up, and he was glad when Porter relieved him of the river duty above Port Hudson. Only a few hours before Porter arrived, Farragut's gunboat *Arizona* had succeeded in pushing up from the Gulf of Mexico through the Atchafalaya Bayou—which Porter had noted the year before as a possible alternative to passing Port Hudson on the Mississippi.

Porter added the *Arizona* to his force of three ironclads and three light-drafts, and pushed on up the Red River into the heart of Louisiana. He wrote General Banks in command of the Federal army at New Orleans requesting that he bring a coöperating force at once to Alexandria.

Sixty miles up the Red River Porter broke through the heavy raft of logs and chains at Fort De Russy—under whose battery the *Queen* had run aground and been captured. Fort De Russy was not yet completed, and its builders had abandoned it on the approach of the Federal gunboats.

Porter hurried on to Alexandria, fifteen miles above Fort De Russy, to find that the Confederates had withdrawn towards Shreveport. Above Alexandria the river was too low for the ironclads to follow.

Twenty-four hours later when General Banks arrived, Porter turned over to him the town, with its noisy crowd of professed Union sympathizers, and detailed Captain Walke to coöperate with the general. He then returned down the river and sent Commander Woodworth to reconnoiter up the Black River and attempt to catch the *Queen* and the *Webb.* At the boat landings Woodworth destroyed stores of salt, sugar, rum, molasses, and bacon to the estimated value of $300,000 but failed to catch either of the Confederate vessels.

Porter set contrabands to work leveling the embankments of Fort De Russy and returned in a tug to the mouth of the Red River, where he boarded the *Benton* and hurried back up the Mississippi toward Vicksburg.

At Grand Gulf Porter learned that Sherman's division had come down from Vicksburg and had been ferried across to the east bank. The *Louisville's* crew had unearthed a number of artillery pieces and stacked them neatly along the bank to be transported up the river. A shelf of clay on one of the knolls had caved in and several rough board coffins of the Confederate dead had tumbled down. Orders were given for the cadavers to be reburied. Grant was reported in the neighborhood of Jackson, Mississippi, winning steadily and thrusting into a position between the Confederate Generals John C. Pemberton at Vicksburg and Joseph E. Johnston at Jackson.

A few miles below Warrenton, on the west bank opposite the plantation of Jefferson Davis' brother Joe, was the sunken *Indianola*. The level of the river had fallen so that the wreck was now almost entirely out of the water. Contrabands from the *Louisville's* crew were at work cleaning the mud out of her. Lieutenant Owen, the *Louisville's* commander, reported the *Indianola's* engines undamaged, and her coal usable.

At Warrenton, six miles below Vicksburg, the turtle *Mound City* had destroyed a water casemate battery constructed of heavy timbers and cotton bales, and had completed the burning of the town itself. Another of Grant's supply boats had been sunk by the Vicksburg batteries.

Porter landed at the lower mouth of the Vicksburg canal and walked across the peninsula. Once more he raised his flag over the *Black Hawk*. Fleet Captain Breese had carried on very well during Porter's absence, though he had exposed his gunboats unnecessarily. Porter set his secretary and clerks to work on the mail that had accumulated.

Porter's mail sometimes piled up at the rate of 300 communications a day, but not all of it was official. Porter received a worried letter from Georgy telling of rumors that he was to be detached from the Mississippi Squadron, that dust was so thick in Washington that she could hardly see across the street, and that the price of sending the children to school in Washington had gone up.

On May 29 G. H. Heap wrote: "Dear Almirante—An extra *Republican* is just out announcing the fall of Vicksburg and that Grant's men put the garrison to the sword...the whole North is on tiptoe of expectation. An extra is published almost every half hour if only to say that no further news has come to hand...fear if they hold out much longer they will be relieved by troops from Tennessee. Brown of the *Indianola* was inmate of eleven prisons before he was exchanged... Well, we can think or talk of nothing just now but Vicksburg—and it is no use concealing the fact that upon our success or failure there, the whole scheme of secession seems to hinge . . ." [2]

George Brown wrote from Washington that he had been imprisoned a long time in Jackson. "General Pemberton was quite anxious for you to hang someone [of the Partisan Rangers] so that he could retaliate on me." [3]

From Cairo Captain Pennock reported that one of his upper teeth had broken off and that he had to go to St. Louis to a dentist, leaving Commander Phelps in charge of the station. "I ordered your coat and pants. The price was high for the material —thirty-four dollars. It was the best we could do. Everything has gone up, at least 50 per cent. I also send ½ dozen shirts and collars—two bottles of bay rum, two jars of pomatum—one bottle benzine, and one box of Bachelor's hair dye (which you say is *intended for Breese*) . . ." [4]

There was a note from Mrs. Duncan, a lady whom Porter and Pennock had entertained at Cairo and whose cotton Porter had protected against seizure not only by the Navy but by the Treasury officials. She was furious because a petty officer had slandered her by calling her a *Rebel,* which she explained was a reprehensible term as it included such sins as lying and false pretenses. "Had it not been for you, Dear Kind Admiral Porter, what should have become of us! I shall feel kindly to every 'blue jacket' for your sake. Ever yours most faithfully, Mary Duncan." [5]

New vessels from the shipyards at Cincinnati and St. Louis were being completed and added to the squadron. New men were sorely needed. With the approach of summer came the malarial mosquitoes, which normally injured the fleet more than the enemy gunnery did. With each new accession to the squadron, Porter was compelled to spread his trained seamen out thinner and thinner. More and more contrabands had to be signed on. Scarcity of trained seamen annoyed him; the heat made him testy. To his old friend Admiral Foote, now in charge of the Bureau of Equipment and Recruiting, Porter wrote on May 16 that if any man could run the squadron better on "niggers and soldiers," Porter wanted him to come out and attempt it. "I often want to sit down and write to you, but there is no leisure time in this squadron, and if I get off a letter to my wife once a month I think myself fortunate. I am here today, and off tomorrow. On the 8th of this month I was in Alexandria, La.; here I am in the Yazoo, a table full of papers of all kinds, and a thousand things to attend to. If I did not cut red tape altogether I should founder.

I have written you about men; do all you can for us. They send us all the rubbish here; we want good men. This squadron will soon number 80 vessels, and we want every one of them. The Rebels are not going to give up this river without a struggle . . ." [6]

If the quality of his crews—scrawny youths, undisciplined Army volunteers, runaway slaves—offended Porter's sense of naval uniformity and discipline, this was a minor difficulty compared to the scarcity of pilots. The Navy Department's regulations limited the pay of pilots to $180 at a time when experienced pilots in private trade along the river were drawing more pay than the Admiral himself, $300 to $400 a month. The Army matched these civilian prices and obtained pilots for their transports, but Porter was compelled to take what pilots he could get for $180, and these were fourth rate. Now that the high waters had subsided, the need for pilots became acute. His squadron could no longer manage with "flat-boat pilots." He wrote the Secretary an urgent letter on this subject while making his last-minute preparations to bombard Vicksburg in coöperation with Grant's army.

He listened anxiously for the sound of Grant's guns in the rear of Vicksburg and paced the *Black Hawk's* deck, glass in hand, nervously scanning the heights of the city.

At last on the morning of the 18th Porter heard skirmishing behind the Chickasaw Hills, where Sherman had made his disastrous assault, and by noon he descried Sherman's blue-coated horsemen dashing along the heights and driving the gray-coats away from their cannon. The men in the fleet sent up a great cheer.

Porter hurried Breese up the Yazoo to establish communications with the army, and by 3 o'clock received messages from Grant and Sherman. Grant had successfully interposed his army between the Confederate Generals Johnston and Pemberton, and was driving the latter into Vicksburg. After two weeks on a diet of foraged "hog and hominy," Grant's men were ravenous for beef and white bread. Porter sent them provisions from the fleet.

The *DeKalb,* dispatched to Haynes's Bluff to shell out the Confederates, found them already evacuating and leaving everything in good order—guns, forts, tents, and equipage of all kinds. The joyous seamen broke out their paint pots and splashed the rock ledges along the Yazoo River with Navy colors.

By May 20 fourteen Confederate forts from Haynes's Bluff down to Vicksburg had fallen into Federal hands. While the army completed its investment of Vicksburg, Porter's men demolished the captured earthworks, spiking guns with nails and priming rods, wrecking gun carriages, blowing up magazines, and burning the encampments, which were permanent and well constructed as if for a long siege. There were miles on miles of entrenchments. Never before had Porter seen such a network of defenses.

To take advantage of the stampede, Porter immediately dispatched a naval force up the Yazoo River. With the land fortifications taken it was an easy matter to force through the river obstructions under Haynes's Bluff. The *DeKalb* and several other gunboats pushed fifty miles up the Yazoo River to Yazoo City, where they destroyed the Confederate navy yard, saw mills, machine shops, planing mills, carpenter shops, and two ironclads on the stocks—the whole estimated at $2,000,000. As soon as this expedition returned Porter sent another which cleared 150 miles of tributary rivers in the Yazoo delta. He was determined that the "granary of Vicksburg," as the Yazoo country was called, should no longer provide sustenance for the enemy.

While these operations were under way Porter hurried his mortar scows into position and ordered them to throw shells into Vicksburg day and night as rapidly as they could fire. The Pook Turtles below the town also contributed their missiles.

The military investment now complete, Grant hoped to take the city by storm, and to this end Porter bombarded day and night. Sherman commanded the right wing of Grant's army beginning at Chickasaw Bluffs, McClernand the left beginning on the Mississippi bluffs below the town, McPherson the center—a very satisfactory disposition of forces in view of the personal enmity of Sherman and McClernand. Grant ordered a general assault for Friday May 22, and requested Porter to annoy the enemy all he could on Thursday night and bombard heavily Friday morning before the attack. This Porter did. From above and below the town he threw in many hundreds of mortar shells, solid shot, and shrapnel. So furious was his attack from the river that he could not hear when the firing on the landward side ceased. McClernand's men captured an outpost, and McClernand reported a lodgment in the enemy's main works, on the strength of which Grant ordered a second assault. The renewed onslaught was repulsed with heavy losses. McClernand's airing of this episode in the newspapers a short while later gave Grant grounds for dismissing him. Ten inches of mud under foot increased the discomforts of this day. At length intrenching tools were brought forward; and, as the soldiers were digging themselves in, Grant wrote Porter that he was now compelled to resort to a regular siege.

From this time on the fighting at Vicksburg lost the glamour of swift movement. The armies settled into a routine of ditch digging and tunneling. Porter's mortars threw into the city a steady rain of shells, more furious at night than in the daytime, for Porter meant to allow the enemy no peace. It was a steady war of attrition. So many head of cattle that had been driven into the town were slaughtered by the mortar shells that the Confederates drove their animals into a secluded valley to the south of the town, but here the cattle were decimated by shrapnel from the lower gunboats and the Confederates once more brought them into the shell-torn city. The sun beat terrifically on besiegers and besieged. On May 25 the stench on the battlefield became so unbearable that Grant and Pemberton agreed upon a two-and-a-half-hour truce and buried their dead.

At Sherman's request on May 27 Porter sent the turtle *Cincinnati* to attack a group of water batteries north of the town. Sherman wanted to outflank these and force an entrance into Vicksburg. He had been informed that certain heavy cannon on top of the hill at this point had been shifted to the rear of the city.

The *Cincinnati,* under Porter's nephew, Lieutenant George Bache, made a bold charge against the water batteries, but too late discovered that the cannon on the hill had not been removed. Shot after shot landed on the *Cincinnati,* penetrated her shield of logs, wet hay, and iron and went out through her hull. Her helmsman was killed. Bache took the wheel and turned the *Cincinnati* into the bank. Here the wounded were put on land, but the vessel drifted into the current and sank while Bache with the remainder of the crew swam ashore. Twenty-five men were killed and wounded and fifteen drowned.

Porter and a party of officers visited Sherman a few days later and Sherman wrote Grant, "I took the party forward to the trenches, the sun glaring hot, and the admiral got tired and over-heated, so that, although we proposed coming to see you, he asked me to make his excuses and say he would come again to make you a special visit. He took the loss of the *Cincinnati* in good part, and expressed himself willing to lose all the boats if he could do any good..." [7]

While Grant was preoccupied with affairs east of Vicksburg,

Porter broke the canons of military etiquette to assist him. On his own initiative he wrote General Hurlbut at Memphis that all available troops ought to be sent down to Grant. Porter even recalled Ellet's insubordinate Marine Brigade and sent its small cavalry force on raids up the Yazoo behind Sherman and then across the river into Louisiana. He mounted heavy Parrott rifles on rafts and platforms along the peninsula, and found these guns to be even more destructive than the mortars. He sent a number of large naval guns and guns' crews to operate with the army on land. As the weeks wore on, and Confederate armies west of the river threatened to break through to assist Vicksburg, Porter stationed his vessels so as to coöperate with the small garrisons of white and black soldiers along the Louisiana shore.

About midnight on June 6 a Confederate force attacked Grant's base at Milliken's Bend. This base was held by 125 white soldiers and about ten times that number of negroes. The Southerners, waving a black flag with skull and crossbones on it, attacked their runaway slaves with ferocity, yelling and war-whooping, and butchering those who were captured. The frightened negroes fell back beyond the levee and fought desperately for their lives. Fortunately two of Porter's gunboats arrived on the scene, obtained a cross fire on the attackers, and drove them back into the woods. The moment Porter heard of it he went up in the *Black Hawk*. He found dead negroes lining the ditch inside the parapet, most of them shot on top of the head. On the other side of the parapet lay an equal number of Confederate dead.

The Marine Brigade which Porter sent to pursue the attackers set fire to the village of Richmond, Louisiana, and returned with gruesome tales of white Federal officers being crucified and burned at the stake for having trained the blacks.

Throughout the month of June conditions in the stricken city became steadily worse. Dozens of deserters floating down the river on logs and planks were picked up by the lower gunboats and sent to Porter for examination. Intelligent contrabands were captured by Grant's pickets. Several of General Pemberton's anxious appeals to General Johnston were intercepted, as well as a letter from the Confederate General M. L. Smith to his wife which revealed the desperateness of Pemberton's position. On more than one occasion Yankee and Rebel pickets laid down their arms and met between the lines for friendly discussions, in the course of which much unofficial information was exchanged.

The steady naval bombardment wounded many but killed remarkably few of the 4,000 inhabitants who remained inside the town, for they sheltered themselves in deep caves under their hills. But cattle, mules, and horses were slaughtered wholesale. During the first week of June bloated carcasses of animals were seen floating down the river. On June 10 Pemberton's supply of beef gave out, and from this time on the Confederate soldiers subsisted on short rations of coarse bread, made of corn, beans, or peas, with one or two slices of bacon per day. The price of wheat flour in the town jumped to $10 a pound and $200 a barrel. The citizens became so infuriated at profiteering merchants that a group of incendiarists set fire to a large warehouse on Washington Street. On June 30 a Confederate diarist recorded: "This day we heard of the first mule meat being eaten. Some of the officers, disgusted with the salt junk, proposed to slaughter some of the fat mules as an experiment ... The soup from it was quite rich in taste and appearance. Some of the ladies ate of it without knowing the difference." "Confederate beef" was the name given to this delicacy.[8]

There was scarcely a house in the town that had not been pierced, and everywhere there were corners missing and walls bulged. From no less than three hundred houses hospital flags were flying. Thousands of Confederate soldiers were debilitated by dietary diseases. Rumors that Johnston or Bragg or Kirby Smith would attempt to break through the line of besiegers nerved the Confederates to further endurance.

Confederate deserters in the last week of June informed Porter that the besieged army would soon attempt to escape across the river on flatboats. Damaged houses were being razed to get lumber, and soldiers were at work whittling paddles. Porter ordered even greater vigilance on the river front, and cautioned his vessels to be ready at all hours to repel boarders. Lookouts were moved up to the tip of the peninsula at night, and a system of rocket signals was devised. When these signals were betrayed to the enemy, new ones were ordered.

On June 25 General McPherson exploded the mine under the enemy's fortifications in his front, and a furious but unsuccessful effort was made to secure a lodgment. On the 27th deserters told Porter that on the Fourth of July the Confederates would fire a salute and surrender. Porter sent this information to Grant, and Grant confirmed it by a similar report obtained through the gossip of pickets.

It occurred to Porter that he might relay this information to the

Vicksburg authorities. Accordingly on June 29, he sent to the gunboat *Price* a bundle of alleged Confederate letters with instructions for Commander Woodworth to put them inside a shell and hurl them into the city. But Woodworth thought of a better way. He made a number of paper kites and flew the letters into the city. Whether or not the letter signed "Many Soldiers," which was later found among General Pemberton's effects, was written by Porter is not known. It may have been. This interesting paper, dated June 28, implores the Confederate General "If you can't feed us, you had better surrender us ... than suffer this noble army to disgrace themselves by desertion. I tell you plainly, men are not going to lie here and perish ... This army is ripe for mutiny, unless it can be fed. Just think of one small biscuit and one or two mouthfuls of bacon per day. General, please direct your inquiries in the proper channels and see if I have not stated stubborn facts which had better be heeded before we are disgraced. From—Many Soldiers." [9]

On July 3 while Porter was directing the bombardment, a semaphore message came from Grant: "The enemy have asked armistice to arrange terms of capitulation. Will you please cease firing until notified, or hear our batteries open? I shall fire a national salute into the city at daylight if they do not surrender." [10]

Porter hushed his fleet. It was the first general silence in more than forty days.

The national salute was not fired into the city at daybreak on the birthday of Independence. As soon as Porter heard that the final articles had been signed, he sent his fastest dispatch boat to Cairo with a telegram for the Secretary: "Sir: I have the honor to inform you that Vicksburg has surrendered to the U. S. forces on this 4th of July. Very respectfully, your obedient servant, D. D. Porter, Acting Rear Admiral." [11] In addition Porter sent his secretary Charlie Guild to Washington as bearer of dispatches.

At 11:30 the Confederate flag was lowered from the courthouse, and the Stars and Stripes run up. From above and below Vicksburg flotillas with flags flying paraded to the city's wharves.

A few minutes after the *Black Hawk* threw out her lines, General Grant and his staff rode down to her gangway and came aboard. Porter and Grant shook hands and congratulated one another. Porter opened his wine lockers and the Army commanders joined the Navy in celebrating the capture of the most important stronghold west of Richmond. Officers and men of the Blue and Gray now fraternized as if they belonged to the same colors.

After dark fireworks were displayed to celebrate the Fourth.

Five days later Port Hudson fell to the combined forces of Admiral Farragut and General Banks, and the Mississippi River at last flowed "unvexed to the sea."

Porter's dispatch boat arrived at Cairo at 11 A.M. on July 7, and Captain Pennock telegraphed Porter's message to Secretary Welles. The news reached the Secretary in the afternoon as he was receiving a delegation from Maine urging naval protection for fishermen. He excused himself and hurried over to the White House. Gettysburg had just been fought, and the President was anxious for General Meade to cut off Lee's retreat into Virginia. Welles found the President "detailing certain points relative to Grant's movements on the map to Chase and two or three others, when I gave the tidings. Putting down the map, he rose at once, said we would drop these topics and 'I myself will telegraph this news to General Meade.' He seized his hat, but suddenly stopped, his countenance beaming with joy; he caught my hand, and, throwing his arm around me, exclaimed: 'What can we do for the Secretary of the Navy for this glorious intelligence? He is always giving us good news. I can not, in words, tell you my joy over this result. It is great, Mr. Welles, it is great!' " [12]

It was no small part of Mr. Welles's pleasure that Porter's message—as Porter had promised after Arkansas Post—had arrived in advance of General Grant's to the Secretary of War and was first heralded throughout the country by the Navy. The price of gold dropped fifteen points, and there were mass meetings, bonfires, and general rejoicings throughout the North.

From the newspapers a few days later Porter learned that Lincoln had signed his permanent commission as rear admiral on the active list. Faithful Captain Pennock at Cairo—who had recently had all his upper teeth extracted—also read the good news in the papers and, noting that the mail from the Department was addressed with the new rank, wrote Porter: "I have ripped all the gold lace off my pants, and will send it down to you with pleasure." [13]

From the permanent rank of commander, Porter was jumped three grades to rear admiral. With something of a flourish he struck off the work "acting" which denoted his former temporary rating. Charlie Guild brought out to him his new commission dated from July 4.

The jubilant letter which Porter in all probability wrote to Georgy upon the receipt of his admiral's commission has not been preserved. The family grocery bills during this period were meticulously preserved. Letters to the Porters, along with transcripts of their own letters to relatives and friends, were saved. Here and there isolated bits from the wartime correspondence between Porter and his wife are quoted in or can be inferred from the letters to relatives and friends. But not one line of their wartime correspondence has survived. From April 6, 1861, when the *Powhatan* sailed for Fort Pickens, to the end of the war Porter's letters to his wife doubtless contained matter not intended for other ears, reckless outpourings of the moment which might have proved embarrassing if published. If they were anything like some of Porter's letters to his brother-in-law Heap, they were full of racy anecdotes which Victorians would not have considered altogether decent.

Porter probably directed Georgy to burn certain of his letters immediately. The chances are that after the war Porter himself collected his letters, used them in writing his reminiscences, and destroyed them when the postwar controversies had made him sensitive to what he termed the "lights of history." At any rate he once advised his friend Admiral Turner to collect his war letters and burn them before some busybody found them and made them public.[14]

Vicksburg was the North's greatest economic victory. With the Mississippi River once more under effective Federal control, men throughout the North lighted bonfires and fireworks, held torchlight parades, and split their throats cheering Lincoln, Grant, Porter, and the preservation of the Union. For the Middle West, as McClernand had pointed out to Lincoln, the capture of King Cotton's citadels along the river meant the remarriage of King Corn to the markets of the world. The capture of Vicksburg effectively silenced doughface and defeatist.

On the diplomatic front Vicksburg along with Gettysburg marked the turning point of the war. Foreign governments, hitherto frankly pro-Confederate in their sympathies, adopted a new tone in their diplomatic objections to the Union blockade, a tone definitely more respectful toward Washington.

With the Confederacy bisected, the Federal military strategy would henceforth be immensely simplified. River traffic would continue to suffer annoyance from roving Confederate guerrillas, but the control of the river, the division of the Confederacy, and the effectiveness of the blockade along the entire line of the Mississippi could not be challenged. Moreover, the main strength of the

Federal armies could now be pitted against the important eastern half of the Confederacy.

For these great advantages the country was indebted to the smooth-running, effective coöperation of Grant and Porter. In the case of Vicksburg the absence of friction between the two branches of the service was truly remarkable. Since on battlefield and in cabinet councils alike the traditional rivalry of Army and Navy normally created sparks of friction which neither of the Departmental headquarters in Washington attempted to conceal, the country was fortunate to have two such men as Grant and Porter fighting together in this the most trying and difficult of all the combined military and naval operations of the war. It is impossible to account for the peculiar success of Grant and Porter except on the basis of the characters of the men themselves. Both were doggedly persistent in pursuing their main objective. Both scorned red tape. Both were fertile in resource, energetic in preparation, and believed with Lord Nelson that "something must be left to chance." Fortunately each man had absolute control over the forces under him. The lack of speedy communication with Washington left each man free to make his own plans according to the exigencies of the moment and to carry them out in the most practical way. Their temperaments were happily congenial, and each respected the professional ability of the other. At the end of the campaign each hastened to accord full credit to the other.

"To the army," wrote Porter, "do we owe immediate thanks for the capture of Vicksburg . . . The conception [of the investment] originated solely with General Grant . . . a single mistake would have involved us in difficulty . . . So confident was I of the ability of General Grant to carry out his plans . . . that I never hesitated . . ." [15]

On the other hand Grant testified, "The Navy under Porter was all it could be during the entire campaign. Without its assistance the campaign could not have been successfully made with twice the number of men engaged . . . The most perfect harmony reigned between the two arms of the service. There never was a request made, that I am aware of, of either the flag-officer or any of his subordinates, that was not promptly complied with." [16] Years after the war Grant had not changed his opinion when he wrote in his *Memoirs,* "Among naval officers I have always placed Porter in the highest rank. I believe Porter to be as great an admiral as Lord Nelson." [17]

24.

WAR, POLITICS, AND COTTON

THE arrival of the river boat *Imperial* at New Orleans on July 16, 1863, with its cargo of produce from St. Louis, was widely heralded. For the moment the Confederacy had been so stunned by the fall of Vicksburg and Port Hudson that even the guerrillas failed to molest the *Imperial* as she steamed down through the long files of abandoned cotton and sugar plantations and blackened, shell-riddled villages and towns. Everywhere the cry went up for resumption of trade along the Mississippi.

Delegations of traders went to Washington, and brought such pressure to bear that Lincoln was compelled against his better judgment to sign permits for traders to operate within the enemy's lines.

Many schemes were devised for getting out cotton from enemy territory. General Banks at New Orleans proposed a plan whereby persons in the Federal armies should negotiate privately with their friends in the Confederate ranks for the release of cotton. Northern cotton speculators, penetrating the South where even military spies had not gone, returned with maps of plantations on both sides of the Mississippi with the locations and descriptions of hidden cotton.[1]

Before the fall of Vicksburg it had been comparatively easy to control the river traders, since traffic was then limited to territory within the Union lines. Boats loading at Memphis and Helena were required to obtain regular clearances from agents of the Treasury Department. Between Memphis and Helena they were licensed to sell small quantities of household articles and provisions only to those families who had appeared in person before the board of trade in Helena or the Treasury agent in Memphis and obtained buyers' permits. Many traders, however, had flouted the Treasury officials, sailed without clearances or with forged papers, and smuggled military supplies to the enemy in exchange for the coveted cotton. Some of these lawbreakers had been caught by the Navy and their vessels seized as prizes.

After the opening of the river, and the resultant increase in traffic, traders' lobbies induced the Treasury Department to relax its stringent laws, issue a lengthy and complicated circular of regulations, and send out an army of Treasury aides to accompany the merchant boats and thereby impart a legal character to their trading operations. To Porter this unhappy procedure was like setting mice to watch the cheese to see that the rats did not get it. "A greater pack of knaves never went unhung," he wrote Sherman.[2] The enormous profits in cotton made it easy for a speculator to bribe a small-salaried Treasury official and land a hundred barrels of salt when he had a permit to land only two. So open was the traffic in contraband goods that guerrillas themselves came down to the banks to make their purchases. Sometimes they held merry drinking bouts on board the trading vessels, and sometimes they simply took whatever they wanted and burned the boat.

Under the benign influence of the President both Army and Navy set about to rebuild with one hand what they had torn down with the other. Abandoned plantations were leased to poor whites of the South who would take the oath of allegiance or to carpetbaggers from the North. The new planters put in crops, but these were often raided by guerrillas. Had the abandoned farms lain idle, the guerrillas would not have been furnished with such an easy source of fresh vegetables, poultry, and forage; and, as Porter moaned, the guerrillas could not have operated so advantageously against the river shipping.

Porter issued orders that the civil population was to be treated with kindness, and some of his men took this too literally. One Sunday morning in September the volunteer captain of the *Rattler* and twenty of his crew donned their best clothes and went to church in the little village of Rodney, Mississippi. Four of the seamen were accompanied by ladies. Suddenly there fell an ominous silence, and the church was surrounded by guerrillas. The leader apologized for interrupting divine services and proceeded to capture the unlucky captain with fifteen of his crew. One of the Federals who by chance had brought his pistol escaped and gave the alarm; and in the commotion four others hid themselves under the wide skirts of their ladies until the church was cleared, when they also got away. The "gallant little dash," as Southern journalists called it, made good copy for their newspapers. The Rodney affair occurred during a season of little naval activity when Porter was tightening the loose discipline of his squadron and "weeding out all cats who can't or won't catch mice." He recommended to Secretary Welles that the captain be at once dismissed from the Navy.

During the fall of 1863 while Sherman was occupying Bragg in northern Alabama and Grant was engaged in the Chattanooga campaign, Porter's light-drafts kept open their lines of communication and supply on the Tennessee and Cumberland Rivers. So numerous were the hidden snags and shallows in these rivers that Porter's anecdote that Captain Phelps lowered spars into the water and jumped his vessels like grasshoppers over the shoals was scarcely nearer fiction than fact. Phelps whose sideburns extended to his epaulettes, was one of the cleverest officers in the squadron and a favorite with Porter.

Throughout the fall and winter of 1863 Porter was in Cairo most of the time to allow Captain Pennock a vacation. Here he renewed his early morning horseback rides. Arriving at his desk by seven in the morning, he seldom left it before ten at night. His mother, who had spent the summer with friends near Hannibal, Missouri, stopped at Cairo to see Porter while on her way back to Chester. Evalina Porter was very feeble now, but her eyes could still flash. She was much concerned over her oldest son William, who was in New York dying of a lingering illness and angrily defending himself in a naval court against charges of insubordination preferred by Admirals Davis and Farragut. William had antagonized both of these officers while he had been on the Mississippi in command of the gunboat *Essex*.

Evalina Porter was much interested in her son's outlook on the war, and she asked his opinion whether she should rent the top floor of Green Bank as an experimental laboratory to a man who claimed to have invented Greek fire.

In November Porter found a job as master's mate for a distant relative, David Y. Porter, a seventeen-year-old youth who had been besieging him with letters for months. Porter liked the boy and gave him a horse to ride at Cairo while not on duty.

Early in December Porter's sister Evelina Cora, wife of Gwynn Harris Heap, died. Porter mourned the loss of his sister. Heap was disconsolate and wrote Porter that he wanted to get a job somewhere away from Washington. Porter arranged with Fox for Heap to come West and assume numerous odd jobs that required diplomacy and tact: negotiation with directors of railroads to speed transportation of Navy supplies, supervision of the pilots whom Porter had been compelled to conscript from the Pilots Association, and like duties.

About the middle of December Porter made a trip to Cincinnati to inspect the ironclads building there for use by the Gulf Squadron in the forthcoming attack on Mobile. The temperature dropped suddenly to below zero, and Porter caught a cold. The Ohio was ice-locked by the time he returned to Cairo. The *Black Hawk,* roomy and comfortable in summer, was now as bleak as an ice box. Her bulkheads were thin, and wind whistled through the cracks. His cold weakened his right lung, and he was compelled to keep to his cabin and hover over his stove while doing his work. Outside the temperature went to twenty below zero. Young David Y. Porter, who insisted on riding horseback, fell ill with double pneumonia. Porter attended him as if he had been his own son but could not save him. With a touch of fatalism Porter wrote to his own mother, "I have seen death in so many shapes within the last year, that I consider the change from life to eternity very philosophically, it is our doom . . ." [3]

In the bitter winter of 1863-1864 the outlook for the Mississippi Squadron was uninteresting, but Porter was in no physical condition to crave action. He did, however, often recall the days before Vicksburg. During that campaign he had developed an enduring friendship for Grant and Sherman. He was glad that the military end of the war had now been turned over to "Grant, Sherman & Company," but he regretted that the two had to operate in different areas. There was something lacking in Grant, Porter would say, that Sherman could always supply, and since the two of them made a very good general, it was a pity that they should be separated.

With the extension of Porter's command to New Orleans, he had been brought into contact with Major General N. P. Banks, the successor to General Butler as commander of the Department of the Gulf. Like Butler, Banks was a civilian general; and, since he had been promoted to his major generalcy from the Speakership of the House, he was one of the highest ranking volunteers in the service. He was a handsome, stately gentleman, who dressed as meticulously as an actor and carried himself like one. Whereas General Butler had antagonized the citizens of New Orleans and treated them as inferiors, General Banks attempted to ingratiate himself with Southern aristocracy by a series of colorful balls at the St. Charles Hotel. Though Banks's policy was less onerous than "Beast Butler's," the people of New Orleans behind his back dubbed him "Dancing Master" Banks. General Banks's position was indeed a difficult one, for in addition to playing host at the St. Charles Hotel he attempted to govern the South's least governable city, to revive the political mechanism of the State of Louisiana, and to conduct military campaigns, at a time when any one of these jobs, properly performed, would have occupied his entire attention.

In the summer of 1863, it was General Banks's misfortune to be confronted with another perplexing problem. The Secretary of State, Mr. Seward, at this time began to fear that Napoleon III's conquest of Mexico might complicate the eventual return of Texas to the Union. Seward explained the situation to Lincoln; Lincoln spoke to Halleck. The latter wrote to Banks that it was desirable to ascend the Red River as far as it was navigable "and thus open an outlet for the sugar and cotton of northern Louisiana," and in a subsequent letter: "It is important that we immediately occupy some point or points, in Texas." [4]

Banks sent one of his adjutants up the river to talk with Grant, Sherman, and Porter. To Grant and Sherman it seemed more desirable for Banks to attack Mobile; but, nevertheless, they promised support the following spring. Porter also agreed to coöperate with Banks in the spring, when the rise of water in the Red River would make possible an advance along that line toward Shreveport.

Meanwhile Banks secured naval coöperation in the Gulf and launched several expeditions into Texas, which were so poorly planned that the Confederates captured two of the naval vessels at the mouth of the Sabine River; and Gulf storms rocked to pieces one of the fresh-water steamers that Banks had employed as a transport. Banks urgently requested Porter to send tinclads into Atchafalaya Bayou as a diversion, but the bar at the mouth of the Red River effectually cut off access from the Mississippi. Porter made a special trip down from Cairo to examine this bar and found it impassable.

With the approach of winter General Banks became increasingly importunate. He urged Porter to send his river gunboats out into the Gulf, and he urged Commodore Bell, who was now acting in Farragut's place as commander of the West Gulf Blockading Squadron, to send his seagoing blockaders into the river to protect New Orleans from guerrillas, although Porter's force in the vicinity of New Orleans was adequate.

At Christmas Sherman came to Cairo to discuss the situation with Porter. Porter wanted Sherman to command the forthcoming expedition against Shreveport, but Sherman was preparing to move against Atlanta and could not jeopardize his main objective. Grant was planning to send General Steele southwestward from Little Rock to coöperate with Banks; and Sherman reluctantly decided to lend General Banks a division of 10,000 men under his trusted general, A. J. Smith, with the understanding that Smith's force should be returned in time to march on Atlanta. Porter was concerned about the navigation in the Red River, but Sherman, who had taught for many years in a military school near Alexandria, assured him that there ought to be plenty of water in the Red River from March until June.

Early in March the Shreveport expedition finally got under way. Porter was still not pleased with the depth of water, but when General Banks suggested that if the expedition failed it would not be the fault of the Army, Porter drew the best Pook Turtles, river monitors, and light-drafts of the Mississippi Squadron across the bar and began ascending the Red River. Porter's flotilla was accompanied by an unwieldy assortment of transports bearing Sherman's 10,000 men under A. J. Smith. The Marine Brigade, now under the auspices of Grant, also swelled the line of transports. From Little Rock General Steele advanced through the wilderness with another 10,000, intending to rendezvous with Banks near Shreveport. Banks at New Orleans, for the moment engrossed in the inauguration of the loyal Governor of Louisiana, placed General Franklin in temporary command of his army of 20,000; and the latter force set out through Opelousas toward Alexandria, where Porter and Banks were to join forces on March 17.

Once again by the time the gunboats forced their way through the channel obstructions, the garrison of Fort De Russy had evacuated without a battle and retired to Alexandria. General A. J. Smith was keenly disappointed that his 10,000 soldiers should have captured but 200 of the enemy.

With chagrin Porter reported to Welles that "Colonel De Russy, from appearances, is a most excellent engineer to build forts, but does not seem to know what to do with them after they are constructed . . . The efforts of these people to keep up this war remind one very much of the antics of Chinamen, who build canvas forts, paint hideous dragons on their shields, turn somersets, and yell in the faces of their enemies to frighten them, and then run away at the first sign of an engagement. It puts the sailors and soldiers out of all patience with them . . . It is not the intention of these rebels to fight; the men are tired of the war, and many of their officers are anxious to go into cotton speculation. A large trade has been carried on between this and New Orleans, the rebels receiving supplies for their cotton . . ." [5]

Captain Phelps with the *Eastport* was sent ahead to Alexandria to cut off the Confederates' retreat and capture shipping; but, though he made all speed, he saw nothing of the enemy and arrived the afternoon of the 15th just half an hour after the last Secessionist steamboat had escaped up the river. Pursuit with the iron-

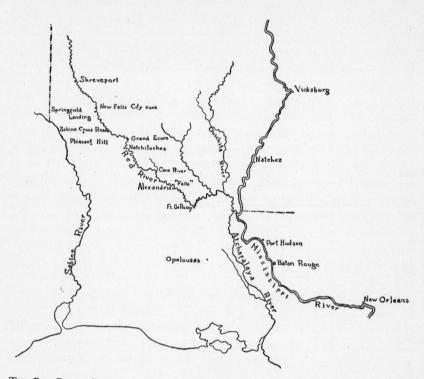

THE RED RIVER, SHOWING POINTS ASSOCIATED WITH THE CAMPAIGN WAGED BY BANKS
AND PORTER.

clad *Eastport* was out of the question because of the rapids just above Alexandria. The channel through these rapids was outlined by rocks that jutted up from the river bed, and the difficulty of navigating it was apparent. One of the escaping steamers, having grounded, had been fired to prevent her capture and was in full blaze when the *Eastport* appeared. On the following afternoon Porter arrived along with A. J. Smith's transports and the Marine Brigade.

While Smith flung pickets around the town, Porter's men

sounded the channel over the falls and reported a scant six feet
of water. A depth of seven and a half feet was necessary to float
the *Eastport*, the heaviest of the ironclads which could possibly be
taken into the upper river. General Banks did not appear until
eight days after the time appointed. His cavalry came in on March
19, his infantry on the 25th and 26th; the trip through Opelousas
with a train of 1,000 wagons had been delayed by rain and boggy
roads.

During this delay Porter detailed the *Benton* and other deep-
draft vessels to collect Confederate cotton from the plantations
between Fort De Russy and Alexandria. An expedition of light-
drafts under Foster was sent up the Ouachita River into northern
Louisiana. Porter landed his horses from the *Black Hawk* and
scoured the country in the vicinity of Alexandria. From the warehouses inside the town the sailors rolled about three hundred bales
of cotton, most of which bore the Confederate Government mark
"X." The sailors painted both ends of every bale "U. S. N. prize"
in tall characters. Quantities of rope and bagging were also secured
from the warehouses, and the sailors scattered over the countryside
to seek their fortunes. At a Mrs. Wilson's plantation they found
a store of unginned fiber, which they ginned and baled. "Jack
makes good bales," remarked the Admiral. Mules and wagons were
also borrowed from Mrs. Wilson to haul cotton from a distance,
but whenever any cotton was discovered within a half mile of the
river the sailors rolled the bales end over end down to their boats.
The coal bunkers of the gunboats were filled to the top in order
to empty the barges for cotton. By the time General Banks
arrived at Alexandria, the Navy had gathered 3,000 bales from the
Ouachita country and a similar number along the Red River and
around Alexandria and had most of it ready for shipment to
Cairo.

When General Banks's headquarters boat, the *Black Hawk*,
arrived and nosed into the wharf alongside Porter's flagship of the
same name, the Navy experienced a mild surprise. From the decks
of the Army's *Black Hawk*, General Banks's soldiers threw off on
the dock quantities of rope and bagging, and down the gangplanks
of the General's "flagship" came a crowd of businesslike civilians
who walked quickly up and down the wharf surveying the Navy's
prize cotton and then ran back to the headquarters boat to talk
with General Banks.

When Porter conferred with Banks, nothing was said concerning
these speculators nor the Navy's seizure of cotton. The military

situation alone engrossed their attention. Upon his arrival Banks received a letter from Sherman admonishing him to return A. J. Smith's division at the end of thirty days, and with the present lowness of the water there was every prospect of the expedition's being held up at the start. Porter's pilots reported that the river was rising slightly, about an inch every twenty-four hours, and the gunboats were ready to ascend as soon as possible.

General Banks now gave orders to his men that private speculations in cotton would not be permitted and that all cotton taken by the Army should be sent to the quartermaster at New Orleans. No assistance was to be rendered to any of the speculators. The firm of Butler & Casey, however, had a permit from President Lincoln, and was to be allowed to follow its own inclinations.

An intense rivalry now sprang up between the sailors and the soldiers. The fact that the soldiers had unlimited wagon transportation irked the seamen, and it infuriated the Army that the sailors had not confined their activities to their own element, or even to short hauls of 50 to 100 yards from the water. Under cover of darkness some of the rowdiest foragers of the flotilla seized Army mules and wagons, branded the mules with Navy initials two feet high, painted the wagons, and scoured the country far beyond the picket lines.

Unsavory rumors began to fly around. Some of the appropriated cotton was the property of alleged Union sympathizers; and occasionally, when one of these succeeded in convincing Porter of his loyalty, Porter would release his cotton. This was done in the case of a Red River pilot named Withenbury, who had immigrated to Alexandria from Cincinnati and whose services as a pilot Porter needed. Usually, however, the owners of seized cotton were set down on the Navy's books as being of doubtful loyalty, suspicious characters, bitter Rebels, etc. When their protests were ignored, they charged Porter with favoritism. Because of Porter's friendship with a Mr. Halliday of Cairo, who appears to have been connected with the firm of Butler & Casey, Porter was accused of sharing in the manipulations of those much favored speculators; but Halliday exhibited the President's signed permit to important persons in Alexandria and silenced these rumors about the Admiral.

Nor was General Banks spared by the gossipmongers. Ex-Governor Yates of Ohio had visited the General just before he left New Orleans, and the story circulated that Yates wanted to run Banks as a dark horse candidate for the Presidential nomination

in the approaching Republican convention. To obtain funds for
this, Yates's crew of cotton speculators was to go through the
country and purchase cotton outright for ridiculously small sums
and thus avoid the delay that accompanied ordinary condemnation
in the courts. Both Breese and Selfridge heard this rumor from
half a dozen sources and so testified a year later before the Congressional Committee on the Conduct of the War, but the rumor
was probably the propaganda of frustrated speculators.

From the testimony compiled by the Congressional Committee,
little truth can be winnowed. By every possible means the traders
attempted to seduce naval officers into lending them aid. Time
after time they importuned Breese and Selfridge to seize their
cotton and take it to Cairo; when, if they could not prove their
ownership in the courts, the Navy would have it. They offered to
pay the officers and seamen one-twentieth of the value of the cotton
if they would do this, and so get the cotton out of the way of
General Banks. For Lieutenant Dominy at the mouth of the Red
River they offered to procure "another stripe" if he would only let
them pass up the river; and, when he refused, they threatened to
have him cashiered.

In the midst of these wranglings General Banks undertook to
hold elections in the various districts of Alexandria. The oath of
allegiance was administered and delegates to a State convention
were elected. Porter regarded Banks's political maneuvering as a
farce. Many people, whose cotton Porter had seized, seemed to take
the oath of allegiance for no other reason than to enable them to
claim the confiscated cotton later on when it was brought before
the prize court.

At last toward the end of March the water over the falls had
risen a sufficient number of inches for the ironclad *Eastport* to
attempt the passage. Phelps crowded on steam and started up, but
his vessel grounded, and three days were lost in dragging her over
by main force. The military criticized Porter for sending his
heaviest vessel first, but Porter was unwilling to risk isolating
his smaller units until he had disposed of the Confederate rams
which were known to be up the river. Thirteen gunboats were at
last got over the rapids, and Porter was ready to set out with
Banks's army for Grand Ecore, about halfway between Alexandria and Shreveport.

For lack of water the deep-draft vessels of the Marine Brigade
could not get over the falls. The Brigade's hospital boat, the
Woodford, was wrecked in the attempt. Smallpox broke out in

the Brigade, and its men were reported on the verge of mutiny. Thus when General McPherson at Vicksburg requested Banks to return this force for the defense of the Mississippi, Banks was glad enough to let them go, although his total force was thus diminished by 3,000 men. The lack of water over the falls also made necessary the establishment of a supply base at Alexandria, and this deprived Banks of the services of an additional 4,000. Add to these mishaps the fact that the Confederates now burned from 200,000 to 300,000 bales of cotton between Alexandria and Shreveport, and the unhappy temper of the expedition can be imagined. On circumstantial evidence the troops laid responsibility for these burnings at Porter's door. The Confederates would not have destroyed their cotton, said the soldiers, if Porter had not begun seizing it. From the extreme anger of Porter's rebuttals, it seems possible that he himself believed this to be the case. But the destruction of cotton at this particular time was merely coincidence; Confederate General Kirby Smith had ordered its destruction on first learning that the Federal expedition had entered the Red River.

While the army marched overland to Natchitoches—an ancient and dingy little Indian and French settlement on a tributary parallel to Red River—the thirteen gunboats of the flotilla worked up to Grand Ecore, a few miles distant from Natchitoches on the main river.

Accompanying Porter and the naval vessels were a number of transports bearing a brigade of A. J. Smith's men under Brigadier General T. Kilby Smith. "Old Kilby" Smith, whom the news reporters were continually confusing with E. Kirby Smith, the Confederate commander of the Southwest Department, was a pious, artistically sensitive man who in appearance resembled Robert Browning but who when occasion demanded was fully capable of "swearing all the hair off his men's heads." [6] He was a cross between the impetuous and philosophical Sherman and his immediate superior, the rough-and-ready, hard-fighting A. J. Smith. Porter greatly enjoyed the friendship of the two Smiths. Indeed, if Porter had not had the full support of these two men he might never have been able (when misfortune overtook him a short while later) to extricate his command from the trap into which it was now falling.

When Porter arrived at Grand Ecore, General Banks shifted his headquarters from Natchitoches to this little unpainted village perched on the ragged, crumbling clay bank of the Red River, and spent several days, amid the usual shootings and flag wavings, holding elections. If General Banks did not realize that he was wasting precious time, the letter he now received from Grant should have been an adequate reminder. Grant wrote: "Should you find that the taking of Shreveport will occupy ten or fifteen days more than General Sherman gave his troops to be absent from their command, you will send them back at the time specified in his note of March ———, even if it leads to the abandonment of the main object of your expedition . . ." [7]

At last on April 7, the Army with its train of wagons and camp followers—the Army having progressed over so many miles of cotton country that every noncommissioned officer now had a servant and every servant a mule—set out by the direct overland route through barren pine forests on the last lap of the march to Shreveport; while the gunboats, leaving seven of the heavier boats at Grand Ecore, pushed over the shallows at this point and worked on up the ever narrowing river.

From Grand Ecore to Shreveport the river is an endless succession of curves. Even Porter's vessels of lighter draft had difficulty making the acute bends without grounding. In his flagship, the tinclad *Cricket,* the Admiral shuttled up and down the line of gunboats keeping a watchful eye on their progress. A hundred miles above Grand Ecore he discovered that despite his advice to the contrary the Army had brought along two of its deeper transports. Kilby Smith shared Porter's wrath, for it developed that the captains of these leased steamboats had gone up against the General's orders in the hope of bringing down cotton. It was too late now to convoy these heavy boats back to Grand Ecore; and, as they grounded continually, they invited guerrilla attacks. About this time Lieutenant Couthouy, one of Porter's most energetic volunteer captains, was shot by a guerrilla and died begging his comrades to assure the Admiral that he had not exposed himself unwarily.

On Sunday, April 10, the flotilla passed Springfield Landing forty miles below Shreveport, where it had been arranged that Banks was to communicate with the gunboats if all was well. Banks's messenger was not here, but Porter, refusing to be alarmed, pushed on. However, he was soon stopped. At Loggy Bayou, a few miles above Springfield Landing, he discovered that the Confederates had gotten a huge steamer, the *New Falls City,* across the river in such a way that her ends extended for fifteen feet on either shore. Filled with mud, she was broken down in the middle, with a sand bar making below her. Across the side of the vessel they had pasted in huge characters an invitation to the "Yankees" to attend a ball in Shreveport.

At 4 o'clock, while Porter and Kilby Smith were reconnoitering the *New Falls City* with a view to blowing her up, the belated courier from Banks appeared with news that the General had been badly defeated and was in full retreat, making it necessary for the squadron and transports to return without delay to Grand Ecore.

As Porter was soon to learn, the defeat of General Banks at Sabine Cross Roads was most fortunate for the flotilla.

25

DAMMING THE RED RIVER

T HROUGHOUT the retreat the Red River failed to produce its usual April rise. The water that had floated the invaders upstream seeped away disastrously from one to two inches a day and threatened to maroon Porter's most valuable ironclads above the rapids at Alexandria. The shoal-draft tinclads might have sprinted downstream, picking up the *Eastport* at the rapids and dragging her along—if they had been alone. But there were the oversize transports whose captains had accompanied the expedition in defiance of Porter's advice and Kilby Smith's orders.

To Porter's chagrin the transports on the return to Grand Ecore snagged continually and had to be towed. Worse yet, Banks's ill-starred retreat ahead of the squadron had left the enemy free to harass Porter. Galloping along the river roads, bands of Confederate cavalry and guerrillas could annoy the boats at one point and by crossing the narrow necks of land attack them again and again as they labored around the bends.[1]

On the afternoon of April 12, when two of the hindmost transports ran aground off Blair's Landing, General Tom Green with 5,000 Confederates elated with rum and their recent victory at Sabine Cross Roads, appeared on the scene with 4 field guns. Kilby Smith's rifles cracked down on the attackers from behind cotton bales and sacks of oats. On the other hand Smith's tall wooden river steamers were riddled by the Confederate field guns. Selfridge in the monitor *Osage* and Bache in the *Lexington* obtained a cross fire on the enemy; but on they came, waving their side arms. The fire of the gunboats scythed them down. Some of the Confederates came so close to the edge that a portion of the bank caved in and one man tumbled into the water within a few feet of the *Lexington's* bow. As General Green galloped across the field, a shot from a naval gun took off his head, and his horse dashed on with its headless rider. The Confederates now withdrew, and the curious seamen who scampered up the bank found hun-

dreds of dead and mangled men. Everywhere the field was littered
with canteens that smelled of Louisiana rum.

Porter arrived at Grand Ecore on April 15 and learned how
General Banks's advance had been checked. On the 8th Banks's
advanced cavalry, isolated from infantry support by its eight-mile
train of wagons, had been attacked by the Confederate General
Dick Taylor and routed. In the confusion the Federal cavalrymen
had dismounted to fight as infantry, and had been thrown back
into the fleeing mob of camp followers. By night the Confederates
had captured over 400 mules, 250 wagons, and 18 pieces of artillery. General Banks had then withdrawn to a village called
Pleasant Hill, where on the following day the Confederates, now
reënforced by General Kirby Smith, again attacked. On this day,
however, the Federals were compactly massed for defense. When
the Confederates bent back one of General Banks's wing divisions,
General A. J. Smith's division had charged through Banks's men
and repulsed the enemy. The Confederates in turn were driven
into the forest while the Federals bivouacked on the field in the
hope of renewing the battle on the morrow. The Federal wounded
lay all night without attention, because in his zeal to secure his
remaining 750 wagons General Banks had unwittingly sent all
the medical equipment out of reach. Before sunrise the next day
General Banks had ordered an immediate retreat to Grand Ecore.
A. J. Smith pleaded for enough delay to collect his wounded, but
General Banks refused. The soldiers complained so loudly against
the commanding general that their officers tightened the discipline
against mutiny. A. J. Smith urged the other division commander,
Franklin, to join him in arresting Banks for incompetence and to
push the expedition on to Shreveport, but Franklin declined so
heavy a responsibility. When Porter arrived on the scene it was
bruited that General Banks was thinking of retreating to Alexandria. If Banks should retreat before Porter's vessels passed below
the rapids at Grand Ecore, Porter would have to destroy his fleet
to prevent capture. A military aide asked a naval officer if the
naval force would not burn its gunboats as soon as the army left,
and the tactless inquiry was reported to the Admiral.

When Porter had left Grand Ecore to ascend the river he had
placed Phelps in charge and had ordered him to watch the rapids
at that point carefully, and to get the *Eastport* into the deeper
water below the town if the river continued to fall. This Phelps
had done, but on the return of the army he had taken the *Eastport*
back above the shallows to protect the troops. The river had now

fallen so low that the *Eastport* could not be got down without being dragged. Moreover, the descent was now blocked by a pontoon bridge the army had built to throw troops upon the east bank against guerrillas. Everyone was thoroughly vexed—even the cotton speculators with the President's permit, for General Banks had seized their boatload of cotton to piece out his pontoon bridge.

Porter urged Banks not to give up the expedition, fearing that if Banks should withdraw he would lose his flotilla. Banks said that strict injunctions from Sherman compelled him to send back A. J. Smith at once. Porter warned that if he did this the Confederates would crush General Steele, now en route from Little Rock to Shreveport, before Steele could be notified of the recent disasters. Banks retorted irrelevantly that the first day's stampede had been wiped out by the second day's victory. Porter choked with rage and apprehension.

He went to A. J. Smith, and Smith promised that whatever Banks might do, he would stay by Porter until he got his gunboats out of the river. Smith had been instructed by Sherman to cooperate heartily with Admiral Porter, "the fast friend of the Army of the Tennessee." To Sherman, Porter wrote explaining the situation: "I assure you that the safety of this army and my whole fleet depends on his staying here. His is the only part of the army not demoralized, and if he was to leave there would be a most disastrous retreat. The army has been shamefully beaten by the Rebels. There is no disguising the fact, notwithstanding the general commanding and his staff try to make a victory. Armies victorious don't often go back as this one has done . . . I cannot express to you my entire disappointment with this department. You know my opinion of political generals. It is a crying sin to put the lives of thousands in the hands of such men, and the time has come when there should be a stop put to it."[2] To Secretary Welles he wrote an official letter in which he tried to contain his wrath, knowing that as an official document it would doubtless get into the newspapers, but along with the official report he sent a lengthy confidential letter: "I do not see why a fleet should not have the protection of an army as well as an army have the protection of a fleet. If we are left here aground, our communications will be cut off and we will have to destroy the vessels. I do not intend to destroy a row boat if it can be helped, and if the proper course is pursued we will lose nothing . . . I wish the Department would give me its views without delay . . . I must confess I feel a little uncertain how to act." [3]

While Porter was writing these letters Phelps transferred the *Eastport's* guns to a raft, to lighten the vessel, and the army withdrew a section of the pontoon bridge. The *Eastport* was dragged over the rapids and started down the river. A mile below these she grounded, but by working all night her tugs got her off the next day. Eight miles below Grand Ecore a small torpedo exploded under her bow. Phelps dispatched his tug posthaste to Alexandria to get a pump boat.

Porter was at Grand Ecore working the light-draft monitors and transports over the rapids, and this work was progressing so favorably that when he heard of the new mishap to the *Eastport* he left Selfridge and Bache in charge of the retreat at Grand Ecore and raced in the *Cricket* to Alexandria to get pump boats for the *Eastport* and to send the heavy turtles out of the lower river into the Mississippi.

Porter met the pump boat *Champion No. 3* coming over the falls at Alexandria and called to her to make all speed. At Alexandria he ordered the Pook Turtles to evacuate the lower river and send back light-drafts from the Mississippi patrols to take their places. A flood of correspondence from Pennock and the divisional commanders on the Mississippi brought bad news. Bedford Forrest's band of backwoods Confederate cavalry had captured Fort Pillow, which had been garrisoned by a few whites and several hundred negroes. Forrest's men were said to have indulged in a sanguinary butchery of all the negroes, savagely ripping open their bellies with bowie knives. Porter sent orders for six of his gunboats to proceed at once to Fort Pillow and recapture it. Then he returned to the *Eastport* with the second pump boat, the *Champion No. 5.*

Phelps had not been able to locate the *Eastport's* leak, but his carpenters had constructed bulkheads to confine the water in the bow. A 20-inch pump was hooked to the engines of the crippled ironclad and she was emptied sufficiently to proceed down the river. After twenty more miles her keel jammed hard on a bed of sunken logs. Her crew labored like madmen. Porter now learned that Banks had begun his retreat from Grand Ecore, leaving the guerrillas in undisputed control of both sides of the river. All but three of his lightest tinclads—the *Cricket,* the *Juliet,* and the *Hindman*—had now been sent down with the transports to Alexandria.

The defenseless pump boats were mere targets. The *Eastport,* with a hole under her bow, her compartments forward filled with water, her bottom wedged in a log jam, and her battery removed, was doomed. Porter gave orders to blow her up.

Early on the 26th the *Eastport's* battle lanterns, cookstove, and other small gear were shifted to the *Cricket.* At 9 A.M. an Army expert attempted to ignite the *Eastport's* magazine by means of an electric battery but was unsuccessful. At 10:30 the guerrillas fired several volleys from the west bank and simultaneously attempted to board the *Cricket,* but the latter's crew cut their hawsers and shoved off. The *Hindman* and the *Juliet* now obtained a cross fire on the Confederates and drove them off while Phelps stowed powder around the *Eastport's* machinery and ran fire trains of cotton and tar to her magazine. Finally at 2:30 P.M. Phelps applied the match. He had barely leaped into his boat when seven explosions occurred in quick succession. Fragments of wreckage rained upon the surrounding boats. The flames worked quickly. Porter rowed up close to the wreck, pronounced it complete, and then pushed on downstream with the tinclads and pump boats. The decks of the latter were crowded with negro families from the neighborhood of Grand Ecore.

For two dozen miles the flotilla of tinclads was unmolested. Porter kept his vessels in close order, prepared at any moment to let go their fire into the woods on either side. Near the mouth of the Cane River 300 guerrillas who had been harassing the rear of Banks's army were sighted. They had a battery of artillery.

Captain Gorringe of the *Cricket* stopped his engines and touched off his bow guns. But the Confederates returned an overwhelming artillery fire.

Porter ordered the little musket-proof tinclad to go ahead fast, but before she could recover headway a shower of 21- and 24-pound shot and shell from 18 guns landed on her, clearing her decks in a moment. The *Cricket* ceased firing, and Porter descended to the gun deck to see what might be done. As he stepped down, the after gun was struck by a shell and disabled. Every man at this gun was killed or wounded. At the same moment the crew of one of the forward guns was swept away by an exploding shell. Porter made up a gun's crew from the contrabands. In the engine room he directed an assistant to take the place of the engineer, who had been killed. A shot had gone through the pilot house and wounded one of the pilots. In less than five minutes the *Cricket* received 38 hits and lost 25 in killed and wounded out of a crew of 50. The pilot steering the vessel was cut in two, and Porter himself took the wheel. As the *Cricket* drifted out of action she caught fire.

Rounding a bend she ran aground, still within the enemy's range but out of sight. Porter's men quickly extinguished the fire and after four hours of working got the vessel off the bar.

Amid the screams of the fugitive negroes in the unprotected pump boats, the captains following Porter withdrew up the river with the intention of passing down after nightfall. In turning around, however, the *Juliet* with one of the *Champions* lashed alongside grounded under the batteries. The *Juliet's* steam pipe was now cut by a shot and the *Champion's* boiler exploded. About eighty negroes were scalded to death. At last Phelps managed to get upstream beyond range, but when night came he wisely decided, because of the uncertainties of the channel, to wait until morning. The next day the *Juliet* and the *Hindman* ran past the batteries as the *Cricket* had done but received less injury because the Confederate gunners devoted most of their fire to sinking the boats loaded with their runaway slaves.

Falling water and other mishaps beyond human control caused the loss of the *Eastport,* but General Banks's inexcusably hurried retirement from Grand Ecore, leaving the fleet unprotected, was responsible for the casualties at Cane River. The destruction of the pump boats, pack-jammed with fugitive slaves, the casualties to the personnel of the fleet, and the placing of the Admiral's life in jeopardy, while they were not overwhelming, were utterly unnecessary losses. By a proper handling of the land forces to cover the naval retreat they could have been avoided. Together with General Banks's lack of frankness at Grand Ecore they completely undermined Porter's confidence in the General and exasperated him.

Thus when Porter arrived above Alexandria rapids with the tag-ends of his squadron, he had no confidence whatever that the General would not repeat the blunder of Grand Ecore and leave Porter's ironclads marooned above the rapids to be further harassed by enemy forces ashore.

Seven feet of water was necessary to float the ironclads over the Alexandria rapids to safety, and Porter's men reported a depth of but 3 feet 4 inches.

Porter went immediately to see General Banks, and once again as at Grand Ecore the General stated that he had no intention of abandoning the squadron. Banks even suggested to Porter that

they might yet continue the campaign if the water should happen
to rise. Porter learned, however, that Banks had received another
letter from Grant ordering him to return A. J. Smith's division.
Since the start of the expedition, Grant had gone to Washington
and had received from the President's hand his commission as
Lieutenant General of the Army, and his words now carried heavy
weight. Among Banks's subordinates Porter could count on only
A. J. Smith for support. General Franklin, another possible source
of assistance, was suffering severely from a wound received at
Pleasant Hill and within a few hours was to be sent home to recuperate. Fortunately, however, General Franklin did not leave
the scene before he had introduced to Porter a midwestern lum-
berman attached to his staff who had a scheme for damming the
river and floating the fleet over the rapids.

When Lieutenant Colonel Joseph Bailey of the Fourth Wis-
consin Cavalry outlined his plan, Porter was at first incredulous.
"If damning would do any good," punned the Admiral, "we would
soon have the ships afloat." To begin with the river was 738 feet
wide at the point where Colonel Bailey proposed to build his
dam. There were two stretches of rapids, lying about a mile apart,
and their combined fall was thirteen feet. The water over the
upper rapids had to be raised at least three feet to enable the gunboats to pass down. The magnitude of the operation was such that
no private company would have considered accomplishing it in
less than six months, but Bailey claimed that with the help of
Banks's large army he could do the work in ten days if Porter
were willing. Porter requested Banks to let Bailey try his experiment. General Franklin requested it, and so did Hunter, who had
brought Grant's latest letter. Banks finally agreed.

On April 30, the huge task of building a dam below the lower
falls was commenced. Banks placed at Bailey's command 3,000
men and between three and four hundred wagons and teams. The
men were picked from pioneer regiments and were experienced
lumberjacks. Along the bank opposite the town where trees were
plentiful, timber was cut and the logs were snaked down to the
river's edge. Companies of men worked in water up to their
waists placing the trees and brush, cross-tying them with heavy
timbers, and weighting them with stones. For miles around, all
the plantation houses and steam mills were pulled down for material. Teams moving in every direction brought brick and stone,
and metal of all kinds from the cotton gins. Stone quarries were
opened along the river above and flatboats were hastily con-

structed to bring down rock. From the Alexandria side, where the forest had long since given way to plantations, a wing dam consisting of cribs filled with stone, brickbats, and scrap iron was run out into the river. A crew of seamen supervised by Captain Langthorne of the turtle *Mound City* set and filled the cribs, also working in water several feet deep. The wing dams were run out about three hundred feet from either bank, and the intervening sluiceway was closed by three Navy barges weighted heavily and sunk in the channel.

While the dam was being built, Porter was busy lightening the ironclads. Whenever possible their iron plating was ripped off, towed upstream in barges and thrown overboard in quicksand to make sure that it could not be salvaged. Guns and ammunition were taken out and carted to the wharf in Alexandria to be reloaded if the gunboats made the passage.

As the work progressed, Porter became very hopeful of success; but his relations with General Banks failed to improve. Banks heard that the Admiral was criticising him, that he had sent a special bearer of dispatches to Washington for that specific purpose. Porter heard that the General had remarked that all the gunboats in the fleet were not worth the price of a day's rations for his large army. One of the bitterest feuds of the war developed between the two men.

To aggravate a bad situation General McClernand now returned to the scene, having been restored to his command by the President. McClernand was stationed below Alexandria to keep guerrillas from erecting batteries and interfering with transports and trading vessels; but the Confederates under the French adventurer, General Polignac, eluded McClernand, set up batteries at Dunn's Bayou, and captured a cotton steamer. The river was so low and the banks so high that two of Porter's tinclads acting as convoy to this cotton boat were unable to obtain a sufficient elevation of their guns and thus were also overwhelmed and had to be destroyed by their crews. The Confederates then captured a quantity of General McClernand's supplies, including clothing; but the latter was retaken a short while later by A. J. Smith's men, who claimed it as a legitimate prize and refused to return the uniforms when McClernand requested them to do so. As a rule Porter quickly forgot petty animosities of the moment, but his feelings against the political generals—Banks, McClernand, and Butler—never left him.

By May 8 the water on the upper falls had risen sufficiently for the *Hindman,* the *Osage,* and the *Neosho* to get through into deep water immediately above the dam. The plan was to get all vessels below the upper falls, and then withdraw the sunken barges from the sluiceway. But early on the 9th the current swept away the barges.

When Porter saw the barges giving way he jumped on his horse and galloped up the bank to the upper falls where he ordered Bache in the *Lexington* to attempt the passage. The *Lexington* was one of the oldest boats of the squadron, and if she were wrecked her loss would not be overwhelming.

The *Lexington* came over the upper rapids just in time, the water visibly falling as she was passing over. She then made for the opening in the dam, through which the water was rushing furiously. Thousands looked on. She entered the gap with a full head of steam, pitched down the torrent, made two or three spasmodic rolls, hung for a moment on the rocks, and was then swept into deep water by the current. Thirty thousand voices cheered.

The *Neosho,* with hatches battened down, followed after the *Lexington* but did not fare as well. Her pilot became frightened as he approached the abyss, and stopped her engine. For a moment her hull disappeared under the water. Everyone thought she was lost. She rose, however, swept along over the rocks with the current, and escaped with only one hole in her bottom, which was stopped in the course of an hour. The *Hindman* and the *Osage* also came through safely.

Colonel Bailey now began constructing wing dams below the upper falls, in a final effort to get the heavier ironclads down the river. Since the beginning of the retreat Porter had worked himself to the limit. Exposure, anxiety for the safety of his flotilla, and uncontrollable anger at General Banks had induced nervous indigestion. Since his horseback ride up the river on the 9th, when the dam had broken through, Porter's legs had swelled with rheumatism. His legs pained him fearfully, but there was no officer at Alexandria to take his place. He had sent Breese down to the mouth of the river and Phelps to Cairo. Selfridge was still marooned above the falls.

Bailey finished the wing dams on the night of the 11th and Porter ordered the Pook Turtles *Mound City, Carondelet,* and *Pittsburgh* to make the attempt. They came through with hatches battened down and carrying a full head of steam. The next morning at 10 o'clock the *Louisville,* and the river monitors, the *Chillicothe* and the *Ozark,* and two tugs came through the chute. A few rudders were unshipped, a few holes gouged out of their bottoms, but all of the boats were safe, requiring only a few hours' patching. Only one man was lost, a seaman swept overboard from one of the tugs. A large fleet of ironclads costing $2,000,000 had been saved to the Union.

Porter collapsed with illness and fatigue. He turned the fleet over to Selfridge and kept to his bed on the *Cricket*, but he remained at Alexandria until his vessels had reshipped their guns and ammunition; then he steamed to the mouth of the Red River. After Breese had helped him aboard the *Black Hawk*, Porter went directly to bed and told Breese to get under way for Cairo.

In April 1864 it was easy for the public to designate the Red River Campaign as one of the war's greatest fiascoes, and such is the verdict of history. A year later the Congressional Committee on the Conduct of the War, after hearing the embittered testimony of participants, could conclude that General Banks had been unwise to conduct elections when he ought to have devoted every energy to the military business in hand, that he ought to have delayed his retreat from Grand Ecore and not endangered the fleet by relinquishing the river banks to the enemy. Admiral Porter also might have refrained from collecting cotton and been more wary in risking the danger of falling water. Seventy years after the event, however, it is apparent that the Congressional investigators did not find fault where it chiefly belonged.

Today it is clear that the fundamental blunder was committed by Washington. If Secretary Seward's desire for a foothold in Texas was of sufficient importance to divert 10,000 of Sherman's troops from the Atlanta Campaign, Washington should have decided that question. Washington ought to have informed Grant and Sherman that the expedition to Shreveport was necessary and thus eliminated the unpardonable interference of Sherman and Grant in the prosecution of the campaign. Furthermore, if Stanton, and his adviser, Halleck, had been convinced that the Red River objective was a valid one, they should have sent another general in command. Banks's earlier blunders in Northern Virginia had proved his ineptitude as a soldier. Either Franklin or A. J. Smith, who were Banks's subordinates, would have fared better. It appears, however, that neither Stanton nor Welles was sufficiently interested in accomplishing Seward's mission; and that President Lincoln—instead of demanding that his cabinet officers come to a clear-cut strategic decision and wage a military campaign divested of side issues—himself contributed an additional handicap when he signed the trader's permit for Butler & Casey. The Red River fiasco, therefore, presents the Civil War's clearest lesson in military and naval strategy. Secretary Welles at least seems to have recognized this fundamental error. He held not the slightest pique against Admiral Porter, and in the succeeding months of the war he was to advance Porter to command on the East Coast to accomplish the last great work of the Navy toward winning the Civil War.

26.
THE SALT-WATER NAVY

Aᴠᴛᴇʀ a week of rest on the *Black Hawk*, the swelling began to go out of Porter's legs; and he was able to prop himself up in bed, screened from insects by the mosquito netting which Pennock had sent down while Porter was up the Red River. Breese brought him the mail and recent newspapers and did his best to turn the Admiral's thoughts away from the Red River Expedition.

In Virginia "Unconditional Surrender" Grant, as he had come to be called, had begun his last campaign against General Lee, and in the Central South Sherman was marching toward Atlanta, wrecking and burning a wide track through the richest "hog and hominy" land in the South. Having the advantage of numbers, Grant planned to outlast General Lee by swapping pawn for pawn while Sherman skirmished through the heart of the Confederacy destroying rails, rolling stock, depots, public buildings, economic resources—in short crippling the South's very sinews of war.

In this final stage of the conflict it was clear to Porter that the Navy's work was to be parallel to that of Sherman. The Confederacy must be cut off absolutely from the rest of the world. The fresh-water navy which Porter commanded must check the widespread smuggling along the rivers. The four salt-water blockading squadrons must make their blockade effective by capturing Mobile Bay and securing an inside station in the Cape Fear River below Wilmington, North Carolina.

It was apparent that there would be no further operations of importance west of the Mississippi. Sitting in judgment as it were on Banks and the Red River affair, Porter wrote Fox, "If the Court knows herself, it is the last one of the kind I will get mixed up in. I shall be sure of my man before I coöperate with any soldier." [1]

The mail which Breese brought him contained letters from Georgy and from his mother. Georgy wrote that Carlisle had now returned from the Naval Academy, and that she was planning to spend the summer with friends at Perth Amboy. His mother wrote that William D. Porter had died on May 1, at St. Luke's Hospital in New York. His mother had heard rumors that the *Black Hawk's* cabin was full of silver taken from the plantations. In the newspapers Porter found himself assailed for having gone on a "cotton raid" with a "piano in his cabin and a pipe in his mouth." The newspaper men were "writing him down" as they had done Sherman after the disaster at Chickasaw Bluffs. The Red River fiasco echoed even in Congress.

J. B. Devoe, a detective assigned to spy duty along the lower river, reported to Porter that the Confederates were using women in an attempt to corrupt naval officers and facilitate smuggling. "In all my investigations here," wrote Devoe, "I have found females of beauty and accomplishment to be employed by the Rebels. ... They manage, by some adroit means, to throw themselves in the way of our officers (always aiming at the commanding officers first) . . . They generally hesitate at no sacrifices to accomplish their designs." [2]

In spite of the abuses, however, the Government could not prohibit all trading along the rivers. Government-paid lecturers had induced settlers to migrate down the river and lease the abandoned plantations. Supplies could not be denied these settlers.

When Porter arrived at Cairo on May 27, he divided his vast territory into ten naval districts and launched a campaign to check smuggling. Acting upon a hint from Fox he sent to the Department an extensive report on the commercial situation in the West, detailing the maze of conflicting regulations promulgated by the Treasury, the War, and the Navy Departments.

Meanwhile Secretary Welles in Washington contemplated shifting Porter to a command in the East. The Secretary's personal feeling toward Porter, which had softened after the fall of Vicksburg, became friendly after Porter's miraculous escape from the Red River. In all the intricate Treasury-Army-Navy disputes regarding the conduct of trade on the Western rivers Mr. Welles gave Porter his whole-hearted support. Through his Assistant Secretary, Mr. Welles began to feel out Porter's views regarding a command in the East.

On May 25 Fox wrote Porter a lengthy letter of congratulation upon his escape from the Red River, in which he remarked, "After you get your feathers smoothed and oiled, I don't see why you should not come East, if you so desire it." [3] And on the 27th Welles wrote that after Porter had made his arrangements to be absent from his squadron for a short period, he would be pleased to have him come to Washington and report in person to the Department.

Porter had become sentimentally attached to the Mississippi Squadron and resisted the thought of change. The huge fresh-water squadron was indeed a complete navy in itself, more diversified than any other naval command and so isolated that most of the Secretary's duties devolved upon its admiral.

Porter managed to find many small matters to delay his trip to Washington. The blacksmiths and carpenters in the Mound City yard went on a strike, and a mysterious fire destroyed the wharf-boat. The Confederates developed a new torpedo resembling coal to be hidden in the Navy's coal barges, thus necessitating the taking of special precautions. Confederate ladies ferrying over from Cairo to the Kentucky shore were strongly suspected of smuggling gunpowder beneath their hoop skirts. Gunboats had to be detailed to keep open the communications of Steele in Arkansas and Sherman on the headwaters of the Tennessee. The newly-completed monitors *Chickasaw* and *Winnebago* had to be sent to Farragut off Mobile Bay. All these matters, however, could have been attended to by Captain Pennock.

On July 3, having completed his arrangements down to the last detail for fireworks on the morrow, Porter set out for Washington, where he arrived on the 6th. Mr. Welles received him cordially. They chatted about Grant and Sherman and discussed the Red River campaign. They talked too about trade and the wholesale smuggling of supplies to the enemy through the connivance of Treasury officials and commanders of the army outposts, as well as through the carpetbagger planters the Treasury had set up along the main river. Mr. Welles was quite pleased with Porter's account of naval affairs in the West. Porter expressed gratitude for the consideration he had shown him personally, and at the end of their conference he gave Porter a leave of absence so that he could join his family at Perth Amboy.

The vacation in Perth Amboy was another turning point in Porter's career, and he was careful not to repeat the blunder of the Newport Club. When Georgy prevailed on him to make a talk before her Women's Club, Porter reported to Fox that he had made a speech "without a mention of politics or the American eagle." [4] He spent several hours each day in the telegraph office receiving dispatches from Captain Pennock and returning directions for his squadron. He romped with his younger children on the beach and went rowing.

More significantly, he turned his attention to happenings on the East Coast. Large salt-water monitors had been built and had been used with good effect to seal the harbor of Charleston against blockade runners. Potentially greater than the monitor class was the *New Ironsides*—more seaworthy because built on the lines of the old sloop-of-war, but equipped with a tremendous belt of iron armor. Vessels of this kind could go anywhere on the high seas and wipe out entire fleets of wooden ships. With the war against the South drawing rapidly to a close, Porter envisioned a vaster conflict with the outside enemies of the country who had furnished ships, munitions, and commissary stores to the Confederacy.

On August 6 Porter learned of Farragut's thrust past Fort Morgan into Mobile Bay. The port of Mobile was now effectively closed to blockade runners. Two days later Porter read that Sherman had taken Atlanta. These successes of Farragut and Sherman made the reëlection of Lincoln a certainty and aroused hope for an early conclusion of the war. The Confederate dollar declined sharply to less than five cents in gold. The Army tried to belittle Farragut's victory at Mobile Bay, as General Butler had belittled Porter's work at New Orleans; but Mr. Welles was comforted by his belief that "the people are not wholly ignorant on the subject." [5]

The realization that the home stretch of the great war had been reached greatly stimulated the Navy Department. Porter was summoned from Perth Amboy to Washington. Consultations were held. Fox's suggestion to place Porter in command of a flying squadron on the Atlantic coast to rid the coast of the last of the Confederate raiders was discussed. Admiral Dahlgren at Charleston was anxious to return home, having (as Fox unkindly observed) found the square flag not so agreeable as his old berth in the Bureau of Ordnance in Washington; and there was talk of shifting Porter into Dahlgren's place to *capture* Charleston—instead of merely maintaining an effective blockade from within the harbor. Porter did not wish to make a change in either of these directions, but he reiterated his gratitude for the favors Mr. Welles had shown him and assured the Secretary of his willingness to go wherever ordered.

More impressive than either the flying squadron or the attack on Charleston was the duty that remained to be accomplished at Wilmington, North Carolina. After Mobile, Wilmington was the only port through which supplies could be run for Lee's army in Virginia. During the last twelve months running the blockade had developed into an art. Scores of long, low, narrow vessels built for the packet lines by the shipyards of Leith and Liverpool were diverted into blockade running. In the past year Acting Rear Admiral S. P. Lee in command of the North Atlantic Blockading Squadron, had captured fifty of these craft, but the profits in running the blockade were so fabulous that new vessels were put into operation faster than they could be captured. A single successful trip frequently earned enough to pay for both vessel and cargo, and some of the runners had made as many as thirty-three trips. The foggray smugglers burning smokeless coal and equipped with telescopic funnels were extremely difficult to see on a dark night. With the shortest of masts and no sails to be silhouetted on the sky these wily blockade runners were frequently able, by suddenly lowering funnels and swinging around upon a course at right angles to a pursuer, to disappear from view in open day. They would put out from Nassau or Bermuda, elude the outer cordon of swift blockaders thrown around the Cape Fear River, twenty miles below Wilmington, North Carolina, and dash through the inner cordon of slower blockaders to the protection of the Confederate forts.

It was particularly difficult to maintain an effective blockade here because there were two channels leading into the river, one through New Inlet, which was guarded by the Confederate Fort Fisher, and another channel some distance to the southwest of New Inlet, which lay under the guns of Fort Caswell. Between these entrances lay Smith's Island and Frying Pan Shoals, jutting far out into the open sea, so that the distance between the channels by sea was nearly fifty miles. Moreover the channels into the river were narrow and tortuous, with bars that shifted as continuously as the bars in the Mississippi, so that it would be impossible for a naval force to dash through into the river as Farragut had dashed through the deep channel opposite Fort Morgan into Mobile Bay. At Wilmington, therefore, a land force would be indispensable to coöperate with the Navy.

After Mobile Mr. Welles had no difficulty in persuading President Lincoln and the War Department to send a coöperating army to attack the forts protecting the channels into Wilmington. Grant detailed General Weitzel to make a reconnaissance at Fort Fisher, which guarded the New Inlet channel; and Welles cast about to find a suitable commander for the naval force. Admiral Lee, who now commanded the North Atlantic Blockading Squadron and in whose province Fort Fisher lay, was a capable man for a routine job. He had served well for two years, but he had, wrote Welles in his diary, "failed to devise and execute any important act . . . The same opportunities in the hands of Porter would have led to more important results." [6] Welles's first choice was Farragut, but Farragut declined because of failing health. "Porter is probably the best man," Welles wrote, "but his selection will cut Lee to the quick. . . . I think Porter must perform this duty. Neither Goldsborough nor Du Pont are men for such service. Nor is Davis. Dahlgren has some good qualities, but lacks great essentials and cannot be thought of for this command . . . I see no alternative but Porter, and, unprejudiced and unembarrassed, I should select him." [7]

Porter was called for a conference, after which Porter and Fox were sent to City Point, Virginia, to see General in Chief Grant. Grant agreed to send General Weitzel with 6,500 men as soon as the naval force was ready. Porter's orders to command the North Atlantic Blockading Squadron were waiting for him on his return from City Point, and the expedition against Fort Fisher was to get under way as soon as possible.

Porter made a flying trip to Cairo and quickly wound up his affairs on the Mississippi. He was genuinely sorry to leave the scene of his immense labors, but in his farewell message to the squadron he struck an optimistic note, "Ere we die, our country will have a debt to pay to those foreign nations who have dared to hamper us . . ." [8]

Fox telegraphed, "When may we expect you? Southern concern is going under. Time flies. . . ." [9] Business men in Pittsburgh, Cincinnati, and St. Louis began cutting prices to prewar levels.

Just as he was about to leave Cairo, Porter received telegrams from the Department requiring him to send two more river monitors to Farragut. He delayed a day and got off the *Milwaukee* and the *Kickapoo*. Like Porter and Welles and everyone else connected with the Navy Department, Farragut was moved by the ancient rivalry with the Army. General Canby of the Gulf Department had been reënforced, and Farragut in spite of a troublesome case of gout was remaining in Mobile Bay to coöperate with the Army in its attack on the city.

On October 3, Porter set out from Cairo for his new command. As he passed through Washington on his way to Hampton Roads, he scarcely stopped long enough to call at the Department or to see his family. The Secretary noted that Porter reluctantly accepted the new command, "but yet he breathes not an objection. ...He will have a difficult task to perform and not the thanks he will deserve, I fear, if successful, but curses if he fails." [10]

Whatever Porter's feelings might have been, when he arrived at Hampton Roads on the 10th he began moving around with great energy. Admiral Lee was down the coast. Porter inspected the ships. He took a trip up the James River to General Butler's canal at Dutch Gap. Porter found naval vessels here doing nothing, although enemy land batteries were within range. By the next morning Admiral Lee still had not arrived. Restless, impatient, scorning red tape, Porter telegraphed the Department: "Shall I assume command before Admiral Lee comes? There is much to be done, and it is necessary." [11] But at 6:40 P.M. Lee arrived on the *Malvern* and the ceremony of shifting the command was postponed until 8 o'clock the next morning.

When Porter's flag reached the masthead of the *Brooklyn*, eighty-seven seagoing vessels of war passed under his command. There were staunch old wooden frigates combining sail and steam, of which the *Colorado,* the *Minnesota,* and the *Wabash* headed the list. There were steam sloops of the *Brooklyn* class; double-enders built to navigate the shallow sounds along the coast; the single-turreted monitors *Saugus, Mahopac, Canonicus;* the powerful and seaworthy double-turreted monitor *Monadnock;* the armor-belted *New Ironsides,* which carried some of the heaviest broadside guns in the world. Added to the list was the important group of captured blockade runners like the *Malvern*—to which Porter shifted his flag immediately after the ceremony on his old friend Alden's sloop the *Brooklyn.* Because of their speed these graceful former blockade runners were useful for running dispatches, capturing other blockade runners, and carrying the admiral.

For the next two weeks picked vessels temporarily detached from other squadrons on the coast arrived at Hampton Roads to participate in the Wilmington expedition. Porter at once began the task of repairing, scrubbing, painting, provisioning, and brightening the discipline of the largest and most powerful naval force that had ever been assembled under one command. The Norfolk Navy Yard was taxed beyond its capacity. Many of the ships lacked full complements. Porter telegraphed for more men, and Fox scoured the Northern yards to obtain them.

One day toward the end of October the Admiral visited City Point to see how the military preparations were coming. To his dismay he found that Grant's enthusiasm for the Wilmington venture had cooled. The pressure of events in Virginia, Grant averred, made it inadvisable to detach Weitzel's force just now. Wilmington, a side issue, would have to wait . . .

If Porter secretly wondered whether the ubiquitous General Butler had opposed sending troops to Wilmington, he did not give his thoughts expression. It was common talk among Butler's enemies that his egregious intellectual prowess overawed and exerted a malign influence over the quiet Grant. After Banks had been relieved of his command, General Butler had become the highest ranking political general in the service; and the fact that he commanded the important Department of the James and North Carolina was sufficient evidence for many that Butler was the most adroit and powerful politician of his day, a menace even to Lincoln. It was from Butler's command that the force to attack Fort Fisher was to be drawn. That fact made Porter regret his unfortunate tilt with the General at New Orleans two years before and induced him to take Mrs. Admiral Porter and pay a call one afternoon in early November upon Mrs. General Butler at Fortress Monroe and later to give dinner parties for the General and his wife on board the *Malvern*.

The delay caused by waiting for the troops gave Porter a chance to become acquainted with his officers. There were now under him five commodores who were from four to ten years senior to him— Thatcher, Lanman, Schenck, Godon, and Radford. He naturally expected to find bitter feeling, but they all met him "in the most cordial manner and ever gave him their heartiest support." Breese had been transferred from the Mississippi to become Porter's fleet captain; and when Charlie Guild, who had been Porter's secretary for two years, resigned, Porter took his second son Carlisle P. Porter aboard the *Malvern* as his secretary.

In many ways the work of the North Atlantic Blockading Squadron was similar to that on the Mississippi. A large smuggling traffic from the eastern shore of Virginia to the Confederates across the bay had to be broken up. Traders with permits from General Butler and his aides pushed up the James and Roanoke Rivers and sold supplies far in excess of the amounts disposed of in these localities before the war. There were the same trade conditions as on the Mississippi, and tradesmen's vessels had to be seized by the Navy for violation of their permits; but merchants here had readier recourse to Washington; therefore, regulating trade was even more complicated than on the Mississippi.

The double coast line along Virginia and North Carolina doubled the routine difficulties. Large flotillas of light-drafts were required to patrol Albemarle and Pamlico Sounds and push up the coastal rivers. Up the Roanoke and the James Rivers just beyond the Federal lines, the Confederates had several ironclad rams built on the model of the famous *Merrimac;* and one of these, the C. S. S. *Albemarle*—now stationed at Plymouth on the Roanoke—had recently threatened to drive out the Federal fleet from Albemarle Sound.

About a week after Porter took command, a thin-faced young lieutenant with wild hair stringing over his shoulders came aboard the *Malvern.* The young man was William B. Cushing, "anchor man" of his class in Annapolis and already more famous than all of his more scholarly classmates. Cushing reported himself ready with his torpedo launch to attempt the destruction of the ram *Albemarle.* At New York he had fitted out three launches. One had been wrecked on the voyage down, and the other had unaccountably vanished. Porter sent the twenty-one-year-old daredevil back to look for the missing boat. Cushing searched and, failing to find it, again presented himself before the Admiral. He was so earnest and confident that Porter gave him permission to go ahead with his one launch and make his attempt.

Porter ordered Commander Macomb, who was blockading the Roanoke River, to assist Cushing and in case the *Albemarle* should come down the river, to fire canister into her ports, board her, pour scalding water on her crew, and capture her if half his vessels were sunk in the process.

The night of October 27 was black with drizzling rain when Cushing sneaked up the Roanoke River to torpedo the ram. Eleven volunteers from the fleet accompanied him in his launch, and he towed along a cutter from the U. S. S. *Shamrock* with a crew to ward off pickets should he be discovered. A few miles below the town lay the wreck of the U. S. S. *Southfield,* sunk by the *Albemarle* a few months before and now used by the Confederates as a station for pickets. Cushing passed by unchallenged, though he steered within twenty yards of the wreck. Nor was he discovered until he was lunging upon the *Albemarle* itself.

The Confederates now sprung their rattle, rang the bell, and commenced firing, at the same time repeating their hail and seeming much confused. The light of a fire ashore revealed the ironclad made fast to the wharf, and surrounded by a pen of logs. Passing her closely, Cushing made a complete circle in order to strike her fairly, and went into her head-on. In a moment his launch was stranded half out of water on top of the logs. The air was alive with musket shot and canister. Quickly Cushing lowered the torpedo boom and by a vigorous pull succeeded in diving the torpedo under the ironclad's overhang and exploding it. At the same moment one of the *Albemarle's* guns was fired. Cushing sprang into the river and swam downstream. Some of his party following after him were captured, some drowned. Completely exhausted, Cushing managed to reach the shore but was too weak to crawl out of the water until just at daylight, when he managed to work his way into the swamp close by the Confederate land batteries. After several hours of traveling in the swamp he came out well below the town, and sending a negro to gain information found that the *Albemarle* was sunk. Floundering through another swamp, he came to a creek and captured a skiff, and with this, by 11 o'clock the next night, made his way out to the Federal ships.

Cushing's daring exploit was one of the bright spots of the war. It accomplished overnight what Porter had been trying to do in his general orders to the squadron. It set a tone. To the fleet Porter wrote, "The spirit evinced by this officer is what I wish to see pervading this squadron. He has shown an absolute disregard of death or danger . . . Opportunities will be offered to all those who have the energy and skill to undertake like enterprises . . . The chances are death, capture, glory, and promotion." [12] In response to this challenge 77 officers, 149 enlisted men, and the entire company of one ship, the U. S. S. *Tuscarora,* volunteered their services. Cushing at once received promotion, the thanks of the Secretary, of Congress, and of the President. Porter showed his own gratitude by elevating Cushing to the command of the flagship *Malvern.*

While waiting for the troops Porter attempted to tighten the Wilmington blockade. He plotted the ocean around Cape Fear and marked the stations for each cordon of blockaders. One line was to be stationed along the coast just beyond gunshot, another line twelve miles out and a third twenty-five. He devised rocket signals to be sent up in the direction of the chase, but the wily runners fired similar rockets in an opposite direction. He placed decoy lights imitating the Confederate signals on shore, and procured calcium lights, to be played on the runners. The blockade was now made more effective than ever. Two million dollars worth of prize vessels were captured in the first few weeks of Porter's command.

Porter made several trips up the James River as far as Trent's Reach, at which place the river had been obstructed by Butler's men to prevent the egress of the Confederate ironclads *Virginia* and *Richmond*. The right wing of General Butler's army rested on the James River at this point, and the Federal ships, by good spotting, could hit the Confederate batteries beyond the obstructions. Porter sent up several of the idle monitors from Hampton Roads to Trent's Reach for target practice.

The Navy was ready to begin its attack on Wilmington, but the military forces were still delaying. Mr. Welles complained to the President about the dilatoriness of the Army. "Every other squadron has been depleted and vessels detached are concentrated at Hampton Roads and Beaufort, where they remain, an immense force lying idle, awaiting the movements of the army... if the expedition cannot go forward for want of troops, I desire to be notified, so that the ships may be relieved and dispersed for other service ... The season for naval coast operations will soon be gone ...and the autumn weather so favorable for such an expedition is fast passing away." [13]

Upon the receipt of Mr. Welles's message Mr. Lincoln did not go to the War Department to hurry up Mr. Stanton; neither did he order the Navy to disperse the magnificent naval force now gathered at Hampton Roads and Beaufort. He simply waited for matters to straighten themselves out.

Near the end of October it occurred to General Butler that Fort Fisher might be attacked by a gigantic torpedo, after which the troops might march in with comparative ease and take possession of the works. The explosion of a group of English powder magazines at Erith on the Thames had suggested this idea to General Butler. According to newspaper accounts the British disaster had blown down and damaged certain poorly constructed houses within a wide radius. Windowpanes had been shattered as far as fifty miles away in the suburbs of London. On November 2, when General Butler passed through Washington on his way to New York to supervise the elections in that city, he explained his idea to various Washington officials including Gustavus Fox. A boat loaded with 300 tons of powder with proper mechanisms for firing was to be taken as close under the walls of the fort as possible and the entire mass ignited instantaneously.

Fox took up the suggestion at once. Whether he believed that the concussion from such an explosion would be sufficient to blow down the fort or not, he saw in Butler's scheme an opportunity for getting the necessary troops for the expedition. Fox won the support of Welles and Porter for the idea.

Two days later the Chief Engineer of the Army submitted an unfavorable report on General Butler's project, and five days later the Chief Engineer assembled a council of Army and Navy officers at the home of Captain Wise of the Naval Ordnance Bureau for a round table discussion of the matter. General Grant had no faith in the experiment. General Delafield's historical summary of previous magazine disasters presented an overwhelming weight of unfavorable evidence. Yet, in spite of research and competent military opinion, it was decided to put Butler's project into execution.

Porter was given orders to prepare for the expedition a useless steamer that could carry 300 tons of powder.

27.
FORT FISHER FALLS

Washington's decision to launch a ship-torpedo against Fort Fisher was not remarkable simply because a board of ordnance experts had frowned on the project. Various experts had opposed Ericsson's *Monitor* and Porter's idea of a smothering bombardment of mortar shells, and a number of decidedly "crackpot" innovations had proved to be worth the risking—Cushing's torpedo launch, the Confederate semi-submersible submarines popularly known as Davids, and Porter's dummy battleships.

The decision was remarkable, however, for the light it casts upon the Washington high command. The Navy accepted General Butler's novel idea in order to get the coöperation of a detachment of Butler's troops for the forthcoming attack. Porter and the Navy, as well as Grant and the War Department officials, believed that General Weitzel would command these troops; and General Butler gave no forewarning whatsoever that he himself planned to accompany the expedition. A situation wherein a subordinate political general could thus keep his plans to himself boded ill for the success of the campaign. Certain of the political generals like Banks and Butler were so notoriously inept as soldiers that Washington ought to have kept them under rigid control, out of humanitarian regard for the armies entrusted to their care as well as to insure the success of important campaigns. Though such a control was recognized in certain quarters as desirable it was thought necessary, doubtless for political reasons, not to exercise it. In November 1864, General Grant was general in chief of all the Federal armies, and yet he exercised no more actual control over Butler than formerly he had over the political general Mc-Clernand. And Washington, so anxious to forget the unpleasantness of Red River that they neglected to heed its obvious lessons, was again confiding too much discretion to a military subordinate, merely because of his power in politics.

With General Butler's plans as yet unrevealed Porter speeded the preparation of the powder boat.

It did not take long to pick the old and shaky *Louisiana* to become the shell of the mammoth torpedo. But to send her to Beaufort, North Carolina, the nearest naval base above Fort Fisher, and to disembowel her of everything but her boilers and machinery to make space for her powder charge required six weeks. General Butler offered to send the Army's contribution of 150 tons of powder to be loaded at Beaufort, but to save time and avoid double handling Porter ordered the *Louisiana* up to Hampton Roads, where the Army's powder was stored. When General Delafield's unfavorable report threatened to make difficulties for General Butler, Fox wrote Butler to go ahead with his plans, and promised that the Navy would furnish the entire 300 tons of powder if necessary. The General, however, obtained his half of the powder load, and detailed men at Fortress Monroe to carry it on board. As if to cement their new *entente cordiale* the General and the Admiral undertook a second joint expedition up the Roanoke River, and Butler's orders to his subordinate on this occasion were sent unsealed for Porter's approval before being dispatched.

Admiral and Mrs. Porter dined with the General and Mrs. Butler at Fortress Monroe, and the compliment was repaid with a dinner and dance aboard the flagship *Malvern*. On the latter occasion Porter's favorite, woman-shy Tom Selfridge, fell in love with Ellen Shepley, the daughter of one of Butler's aides who had lobbied against Porter during the New Orleans controversy.[1]

On November 26, when an inventor of Greek fire planned to demonstrate his pyrotechnics against the Southern forts near Dutch Gap, Butler telegraphed to Porter an invitation to "come up this pleasant day and I will go down with you in the morning..."[2] Porter wired that he would start up immediately. The Greek fire display made no lasting impression on Porter's mind, but the return down the river on General Butler's *Greyhound* did.

The vicinity of Dutch Gap was a kind of neutral ground between the two armies where prisoners were exchanged and stragglers congregated. Several of the latter hid themselves on board the *Greyhound* and rode down the river as far as Bermuda Hundreds, where they were put ashore.

The *Greyhound* had made but five or six miles below Bermuda Hundreds when a mysterious explosion blew open her furnace door and scattered coals through the fire room. Pumps were applied and the fire was partially subdued, but in a few minutes it burst out on deck through the sheathing of the steam pipe, and got beyond control. Porter put his own shoulder under the captain's gig and helped the steward get it over the side. Everyone on board was saved. But unfortunately several of the general's horses were trapped, and their screams rose above the flames and steam.

About the first of December General Grant's interest in Fort Fisher was revived by rumors that Confederate forces had been withdrawn from Wilmington to reënforce Savannah against Sherman. Now was the time to strike at Fort Fisher and at Wilmington. On the second of December Grant came down to Hampton Roads from his headquarters at City Point for a conference aboard the *Malvern*. The *Louisiana's* masts and fittings had now been removed. Her decks forward of the boiler bulkheads had been converted into a vast magazine, and she was all ready to receive the powder. Porter explained how the powder would be stowed above the water line to give the explosion its greatest lateral force. The upper heads were to be removed from the barrels, and running along over the open barrels and in and out among the hundreds of bags of powder would be a network of Gomez fuse. This fuse ignited at the rate of a mile in four seconds. To explode as much of the powder as possible at the same instant, neat clockwork devices had been placed in different parts of the ship. At first Porter like Grant had been skeptical about the powder boat, but now that he had entered into the project he went at it with energy. Porter's enthusiasm and his assurance that everything would be ready in four days inspired Grant with a glimmer of hope.

However, Grant's hope deserted him on his return to City Point, and he wrote Butler to notify the Admiral and get General Weitzel's force off at once, with or without the powder boat. Butler did not deliver this message. Instead he telegraphed to inquire when Porter could be ready. And a few days later the *Louisiana*, very wobbly and top-heavy, sailed for Beaufort to take on the remainder of her load from the Navy's powder magazines.

By December 8 the entire expedition was prepared to sail. Though the weather now turned foggy, General Weitzel's troops with five days' rations and three days' cooked meats were embarked on the transports; and a number of cavalry horses were also loaded. At the last minute an order from Grant called for the carrying of a larger number of intrenching tools and these too were shipped.

At this point two mishaps befell the expedition. The first was unavoidable. A strong southwest wind brought five days of storm and delay. While at this season of the year rough weather was to be expected, the delay was irksome. But the second misfortune could and should have been avoided. Contrary to all previous plans it now appeared that General Butler intended to accompany Weitzel on the expedition. All the gestures of coöperation between the Admiral and the General were nullified, for naval men interpreted Butler's action as an effort to gain publicity. The memories of New Orleans incensed Porter anew. Porter even suspected Grant of deceiving him, not knowing that Butler's intentions were quite as great a surprise to Grant as to everyone else. As a matter of official courtesy Grant had communicated with Weitzel through Butler, since Butler was Weitzel's immediate superior. Porter wrote Fox bitterly that he feared the movement would now prove a failure. The politic Fox showed this letter around in Washington to clear the Navy should anything adverse happen. Indiscreetly he showed it to a Mr. Whitely who told Mrs. Butler, who wrote the General—but too late to affect the expedition.[3]

The revival of animosity between Butler and Porter resulted immediately in the departure of the Army and Navy forces from Hampton Roads in an order apparently the reverse of what had been planned, each in ignorance of the movements of the other. It had been planned that Porter, with the slow monitors, was to get off a day ahead of the transports. On the windy and rainy morning of the 12th Porter saw the transports which had been loaded for four days leave their anchorage at Bermuda Hundreds and set out. Porter assumed that they were sailing for Beaufort. General Butler, however, in order to deceive the enemy, had ordered the transports to sail first to the northward up the Chesapeake and into the Potomac; but since he did not inform Porter, he deceived the Navy more than he deceived the enemy. On the 13th Porter set out for Beaufort, where to his astonishment he failed to find the transports.

Porter set his men to loading the remainder of the 300 tons of powder on the *Louisiana* and on the 16th steamed out to the blockading fleet, which was now assembled out of sight of land about twenty-five miles off Fort Fisher.

General Butler arrived at Beaufort a few hours later on the 16th and in the afternoon steamed down the coast in his huge transport, ostensibly looking for Porter, but actually playing his telescope over the notched horizon of Fort Fisher. Steaming inshore he did not see Porter's fleet, which was below the horizon twenty miles to the east, and he virtually disclosed the Federal plans to the Confederates.

On the 18th, the powder boat joined the fleet, and Porter sent Breese back to Beaufort to find the General and inform him that the powder boat would be exploded that night. General Butler dispatched Weitzel to request a few days' delay. The troops had now eaten their five days' rations; and, since many of the transports were not equipped with condensers, Butler's vessels were compelled to put in to Beaufort for water as well as food. Porter consented to this delay, with the understanding that the *Louisiana* was to be blown up on the first favorable opportunity thereafter.

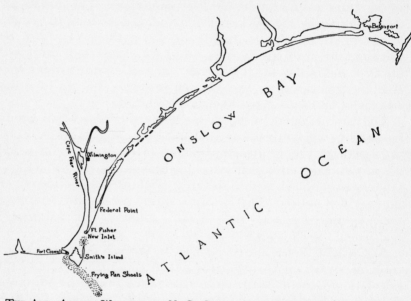

THE AREA AROUND WILMINGTON, N. C., SHOWING THE FEDERAL BASE AT BEAUFORT, THE ENTRANCES TO CAPE FEAR RIVER, AND FORT FISHER.

From the 15th to the 18th, there had been a smooth sea, but from the 19th to the 23rd, it blew a gale. The transports remained in Beaufort Harbor; but the fleet, including even the monitors, rode out the storm at anchor in the raging sea. It was the first time such a fleet had ridden out a storm at anchor.

On the afternoon of the 23rd, when the sun appeared and the breakers along the coast began to subside, Porter dispatched a fast vessel to inform General Butler that he would explode the powder boat before 2 o'clock the next morning. He allowed sixteen hours for the message to reach the General and for the transports to make the landing place a few miles above the fort. The vessels of the fleet were held back twelve miles from the explosion with steam down and fires drawn, for no one knew what the effects of so large an explosion might be.

Captain Rhind was ordered to build a good fire of pine knots on the after deck of the powder boat as a supplement to the clockworks. Though the clearness of the night augmented the chance of discovery, Captain Rhind carried the powder vessel under her own steam to a point within 300 yards of the northeast salient of Fort Fisher, set the clockworks, fired the pine knots, and ran out his anchors. A fast tug then carried him twelve miles out to sea where steam was blown off and fires were drawn. The minute for the explosion by the clockworks arrived, but nothing happened. Five, ten, fifteen minutes passed, and still nothing happened. By this time the fire from the pine knots had completely enveloped the after end of the ship. Finally at 1:40 A.M., twenty-two minutes after the time set, a monster column of flames shot up from the *Louisiana,* and four sharp reports were heard.

The cargo of the ship-torpedo had not exploded but had simply burned like a gigantic firework. A few panes of glass on the naval ships were cracked. Confederate soldiers bivouacking on the beach where General Butler planned to land his troops felt the sand vibrate beneath them. Within the great sand fortress nothing out of the way was noticed. The lookouts, mistaking the detonation of the 300 tons of powder for a boiler explosion, reported merely that one of the Union gunboats had come to grief.

At daylight Porter moved his fleet in through a slowly settling cloud of powder dust to attack the fort. According to the Admiral's calculations General Butler should have been able to get his troops down from Beaufort to the landing beach by 8 o'clock. But at 8 o'clock the transports failed to appear. Porter delayed until shortly after midday, when he despaired of the troops and began his bombardment. According to the lithographed instructions issued by Porter the ironclads and monitors under Commodore Radford moved in within a thousand yards and shelled the land face of the fort, which commanded the approach down the finger-like peninsula. Divisions of wooden frigates and double-enders, taking position on great arcs of circles outside the monitors and extending below the end of Federal Point, directed their attack chiefly against the sea face and the high mound battery near the tip of the finger. Particular targets for each individual ship had been indicated on the chart.

While the fight was progressing Porter kept his little dispatch boat continually on the move to different portions of the lines. In the *Malvern* he steamed in and out among the thundering ships. One of the ships fell out of line and passed the *Malvern* within hailing distance.

"What's the trouble?" Porter shouted.

"My 100-pounder has exploded."

"Then why in hell don't you go back and use your other guns?"[4]

Porter saw that another vessel had edged off too far from the regular line. He sent the commanding officer a card dispatch informing him that, if he desired, the Admiral would show him the way into action.

"Where are you going now?" shouted Porter as one of the double-enders came steaming out of danger.

"To repair a damage in my side," was the reply.

"Go back to your place, or I will send you and your boat to the bottom," was the order given in return.

"Those who are acquainted with the prompt, energetic manner in which Admiral Porter dispatches business," wrote the New York *Times* correspondent on board the *Malvern*, "will readily perceive that orders given in the midst of a hot engagement were not studied, but suited to the emergency."

The bombardment continued furiously for an hour and a half with excellent effect. Most of the guns of the fort had been silenced. Porter then ordered slow bombardment until nightfall. Every wooden structure in the fort went up in flames.

Throughout the remainder of the day Porter saw nothing of General Butler. General Weitzel brought a note from him and made arrangements for the fleet to assist in landing troops the next morning, December 25, at 8 o'clock.

On Christmas Day Porter directed a renewal of the bombardment and detailed Captains Alden and Glisson to the duty of getting the troops on shore. Alden had less temper and more tact than any officer in the fleet, and Glisson had befriended General Butler two years ago by hauling the latter's grounded transport off Frying Pan Shoals and enabling him to continue his voyage to New Orleans. The guns from Fort Fisher were now firing only intermittently. The two diminutive Confederate batteries behind sand banks near the chosen landing place of the troops were shelled by two of Porter's gunboats as the soldiers landed.

The garrisons of these batteries—old men and boys of the junior and senior reserves of North Carolina—surrendered immediately, one group to the army and another to six or seven sailors who could not resist the holiday impulse to wade ashore and capture them.

Impatient at the slowness of the landing, Porter ran the *Malvern* close to Butler's vessel and shouted through his speaking trumpet, "How do you do, General?"

"Very well, thank you," replied the General.

"How many troops are you going to land?" asked the Admiral.

"All I can," replied the General.

Not satisfied with this cryptic answer, Porter hastened additional gunboats to expedite the landing, but only 2,500, or about a third of the army, were put ashore.

The rapprochement through speaking trumpets was far from sufficient to restore the *entente cordiale* between the commanders. They saw the situation from vastly different points of view and were too angry to come together for an interchange of views.

General Butler, as he later told the Congressional Committee, believed that Porter had deliberately exploded the powder vessel prematurely in the hope that it might destroy the fort and the Navy hog the victory.

Butler himself did not land. While his 2,500 troops engaged the pickets of the enemy, General Weitzel reconnoitered the land face of Fort Fisher from close range. A company of Federals made a dash to the parapets and captured a Confederate flag which had been shot down by the Navy. Another company killed a messenger and captured his horse. General Weitzel reported that out of nineteen Confederate guns bearing on the land approach only two had been dismounted. He could not report how many of the seventeen remaining guns had their muzzles packed with the sand kicked up by shells hitting on the parapet. The prisoners told Butler that a division from Richmond had just arrived in Wilmington to reënforce Fort Fisher, and on the basis of these reports General Butler disregarded Grant's specific instruction that after landing the troops should consider themselves victorious, and should then entrench themselves and lay siege to the fort. Instead of assaulting as Porter hoped he would do or entrenching as Grant had ordered, Butler gave the command to reëmbark and return to Hampton Roads.

General Butler sailed, leaving about seven hundred of his men on the beach to be gotten off through the surf by Porter the next day. Porter at once sent his aide, Lieutenant Preston, to Washington with dispatches and a plea that the Secretary obtain an army under a different commander. He sent Breese to Savannah to beg

Sherman to participate. Sherman wrote him a sympathetic letter which Porter sent Welles. The more Porter thought and wrote about the fiasco, the more it seemed to him the fort could have been carried.

Several potent newspapers upheld Butler and denounced the Admiral. But Lincoln, Welles, and Grant backed Porter. Lincoln's Executive Order No. 1 for 1865 relieved Butler of his command and banished him to his home in Lowell.

Welles wrote Porter that his course was heartily approved by the Department and that everything would be done to send another army properly commanded. Grant wrote Porter to please hold on and he would send back the *same troops and without the former commander!*

To assuage their disappointment the seamen on the *Malvern* created a medal for General Butler in tooled leather. One side displayed a pair of legs in the act of running, surmounted by a major general's straps, and the reverse carried an inscription of presentation to the General "in commemoration of his heroic conduct before Fort Fisher, Dec. 1864." [5]

One of Porter's friends in New York sent him a clipping from the New York *Evening Telegram* of December 30, 1864, commenting on his published report of the fiasco. "Admiral Porter writes as though even in his official capacity he remained a man. ... Most official reports have only an official character about them. They smack of the dust and rust of office. They deal with grammatical truisms and stilted phrasing. They are very correct in the mention of dates and figures, and they are singularly exact in the lists of casualties. But they give information without ideas. The words have no soul in them; the sound has only a fact-and-figure sense ... Admiral Porter's report has soul and life in it."

The failure of the first expedition was a stimulus to Porter for the second. The reënforcement of Fort Fisher would make the job more difficult. January storms would make fleet maneuvers increasingly hazardous. But a second failure would bring applause for General Butler, which was unthinkable.

To inspire the Confederates with overconfidence Porter caused his vessels to limp away from the scene of action a few at a time, most of them under tow. The Richmond *Whig* exulted over the apparent crippling of the Federal armada: "Where is it now? Beaten, scattered, sunk, dispersed all over the ocean." The Richmond *Whig* moralized that if Porter had but pitched "that Jonah

Copyrighted by the Review of Reviews, from the Photographic History of the Civil War

ADMIRAL PORTER (*center*) AND HIS STAFF ON BOARD THE U.S.S. *Malvern*. LIEUTENANT W. B. CUSHING, WHO SANK THE C.S.S. *Albemarle*, IS AT THE EXTREME LEFT. THIS PHOTOGRAPH WAS TAKEN SHORTLY AFTER THE FORT FISHER POWDER BOAT FIASCO OF DECEMBER 24, 1864.

Courtesy of U. S. Naval Academy

The Bombardment of Fort Fisher, January 15, 1865, as Seen from the Mound Battery, Drawn by J. M. Alden and Lithographed by Endicott & Co.

Butler" into the sea, the elements might have dealt with Porter more kindly.

Upon the withdrawal of the Union fleet to Beaufort the Confederate ladies of Wilmington came down to Fort Fisher, and spread a picnic for the defenders under the scrub pines from whose shelter Weitzel had made his reconnaissance.

At Beaufort Porter again stored his ships with ammunition and sent them back out into the open sea to ride out the storms and inure the crews to hardships.

To make doubly certain that the fort would be properly assaulted Porter organized a landing party of sailors and marines to storm the fort from the beach at the same time the army attacked. "The sailors will be armed with cutlasses, well sharpened, and with revolvers," read his general order No. 81. "When the signal is made to assault ... board the fort on the run in a seaman-like way."[6]

Four hundred marines were to entrench themselves as near the fort as possible and cover the 1,600 sailors as they scaled the walls. Should the mound battery fire into them after they had taken possession of the main works, the sailors were to fling the captured Confederates over the parapets and take shelter in the bombproof traverses.

Delayed for several days by storms, the new expedition finally set out from Hampton Roads on January 6, its destination unknown even to General Terry, now in command of Butler's troops, until it reached the open sea. On the 8th it arrived at Beaufort, where storms again delayed the attack. The many conferences between the new General and the Admiral were frank and friendly.

On the morning of the 13th, the fleet renewed its bombardment. Between 8:30 A.M. and 2 P.M. 8,000 troops were tumbled ashore through a rolling surf. The troops entrenched themselves for defense on ground covered with litter from the recent Confederate picnic.

A strong wind hampered the fleet the next day, but the ironclads anchored near the shoals scorned the danger of shipwreck and poured a steady rain of shells into the fort, knocking down the line of palisades and cutting wires leading to the subterranean torpedoes over which the troops would have to advance.

On Sunday January 15 the fleet opened with terrific energy. At 10:30 the signal was given for the landing parties of sailors and marines to get under way. Small boats were lowered from each vessel on the side away from the fort. The seamen rowed to the beach, took their ducking in the surf, landed, formed in companies. Fleet Captain Breese commanded these "boarders." Lieutenants Preston and B. H. Porter—two of the Admiral's aides —led the *Malvern's* contingent and carried the Admiral's flag. The Admiral's son Carlisle P. Porter with pistol and cutlass ran up the beach beside Breese at the head of the seamen.

The bombardment of the land face of Fort Fisher continued until 3 o'clock, when General Terry gave the signal for the fleet to shift the direction of its fire. Immediately every whistle in the squadron blew off a deafening shriek, and the naval guns were pointed away from the troops. Over the beach the sailors and marines raced toward the eastern salient. So great was the excitement that the marines failed to hear their officers ordering them into the intrenchments and ploughed on through the deep sand along with the sailors. The sharpened cutlasses of the sailors glistened in the sunshine. The marines had no time to pick off the Confederates who flocked to defend the eastern salient.

Few of the party reached the battlements. Enemy sharpshooters let loose a fire which mowed them down. Those who could, broke and fled back down the beach. Lieutenants Preston and B. H. Porter were killed at the head of the line. The attack of the sailors was a failure, but it diverted the attention of the Confederates from the main attack by the army on the other side of the peninsula.

Terry's men entered the fortress and fought desperately from one traverse to another. Confederates and Federals grappled and gored each other over the tops of bombproofs. The dead were trampled twelve men deep between these mounds. From 3 o'clock in the afternoon until 10 the fight continued. The fire of the *New Ironsides* and the monitors was so accurately directed that when Porter signaled to learn whether it menaced the Federals, General Terry signaled "No."

At 10 P.M. Terry sent up rockets announcing victory. The flagship answered with rockets, Coston signals, and a blast from her whistle. The entire fleet gave three cheers, and crisscrossed the sky with rockets. Officers and seamen took turns venting their emotions by hauling on whistle ropes. Many blue Costons were lighted, and the sky scintillated with rockets.

Fort Fisher had fallen.

28.

THE END OF THE REBELLION

ALL night troops, sailors, and marines swarmed over the giant fortress. From bombproof to bombproof they waved their flickering torches and removed the wounded from under the mounds of mangled corpses, sand, and charred timbers. They rifled the Confederate commissary of its supply of spirits and celebrated the victory. They picked up souvenirs for the folks back home.

Their officers noticed a group of them peering into ammunition cellars with their uncovered torches and called them away, stationing armed guards before the doors. The main magazine, however, many yards back from the traverses, the Federal officers did not see. About daylight several prowlers entered this powder chamber, and at 7 A.M. it exploded, killing and burying 200 Federal soldiers. A rumor circulated that the Confederates in the forts across the river had exploded the huge magazine by means of a galvanic battery.[1]

Porter was buoying the New Inlet Channel and pushing his light-drafts over the bar into the river when the explosion occurred. He left the *Malvern*, went up the river in a cutter, and entered the fortification over the route taken by General Terry's troops less than twelve hours before. He found that gun after gun had been dismounted, carriages splintered, platforms torn up, muzzles packed with sand. He was so elated by the victory that he forgave General Weitzel—the expert engineer—for having pronounced the place impossible of assault. Fort Fisher, Porter said, was more powerful than the famous Malakoff, which he had seen a few days after its capture in 1855 when engaged on the first camel expedition. Below the eastern salient of Fort Fisher Porter examined the magnificent 150-pounder Armstrong gun which its English inventor had presented to Jefferson Davis. This piece of ordnance was mounted on a polished mahogany carriage with brass trimming.

The reporter for the Baltimore *American*, who at the time of

Porter's visit was also walking through the fort, "breakfasting on horrors, that I might know of what I speak," found many large guns "dismounted and tumbled down. Among these are entangled Rebel dead in almost every shape and position, some standing on their feet and others on their heads, all glaring and grinning ghastly alike upon the passerby." [2]

Soon after Porter returned to the cutter, the *Malvern* outside the rips in the roadstead fired a fifteen-gun salute. Porter hurried out to his ship and found that the Secretary of War had arrived. Mr. Stanton had been to Savannah to see Sherman and had stopped at Fort Fisher not knowing that it had fallen. Stanton was jubilant over the victory. General Terry presented him with the captured Confederate colors.

At 1:30 the next morning, while Porter was writing commendatory letters for the five commodores who were now being detached from his squadron, the magazine of Fort Caswell was blown up by its Confederate garrison and the fort evacuated. Wilmington, the last port of the Confederacy, was now effectively sealed.

During the short time that Porter had commanded this squadron and in spite of the increased vigor of his blockade, the Confederates had run in through the port of Wilmington 8,632,000 lbs. of meat, 1,507,000 lbs. of lead, 1,933,000 lbs. of saltpetre, 546,000 pairs of shoes, 316,000 pairs of blankets, 500,000 lbs. of coffee, 69,000 rifles, and 43 cannon, while enough cotton to pay for these purchases was exported.

An intercepted telegram from General Lee to one of the officers in the fort stated that if Forts Fisher and Caswell were not held he would have to evacuate Richmond.

On January 19 Porter caused the Confederate signal lights on the mound to be relighted, and two blockade runners, the *Stag* and the *Charlotte,* came dashing into the river where they were seized by Porter's sailors. The blockade runners were loaded with arms, blankets, and shoes, as well as an assortment of liquors, silks, laces, and Empress Eugénie bonnets.

Porter's official dispatch to Welles of January 20, announced that General Terry had enough troops to hold Fort Fisher against the entire Confederacy. Immediately afterward Porter explained in a private letter to Fox that his official dispatch "was written to mislead the Rebels, for they read our morning papers almost as soon as we do. The fact is we cannot hold this place unless heavily reënforced at once." [3] "The reaction after the last month's excitement," Porter wrote Fox on January 21, "has quite broken me down, my mind was on a stretch for a long time, and when the work was over I collapsed. I am all right again today and have not smoked more than twelve cigars." [4]

In spite of the victory Porter continued to chafe over the fiasco at Christmas. He held Grant responsible for having sent Butler on the first expedition. In a personal and confidential letter to Welles on the 24th Porter expressed freely his bitterness against Grant and attributed the honor of the ultimate victory to the persistence of Secretary Welles.

During the lull before the final operations against Richmond, General Grant came down on January 28 to see Porter and to inspect the captured forts. Grant spent four hours as Porter's guest on the *Malvern* and explained that he had never intended that Butler should have accompanied Weitzel on the first expedition. The old friendship between Porter and Grant, begun at the siege of Vicksburg, was revived. When Grant returned north, he immediately sent back General Schofield with an adequate force to coöperate with Porter in capturing Wilmington.

The channel of the Cape Fear River was strewn with torpedoes and pilings, and the shores were lined with forts that mounted almost as many guns as Fort Fisher. The sludgy rice fields on either side made going difficult for the armies of Schofield and Terry, but the campaign against Wilmington was pushed with vigor.

Porter now had only one monitor left, for he had released all but the *Montauk* before the push to Wilmington had been decided on. He wrote Admiral Dahlgren begging him to return two of the monitors for this duty, and failing to obtain them— since Dahlgren was employing them to reduce Charleston—Porter constructed a dummy monitor out of an old scow and some canvas and barrel staves. Lieutenant Cushing piloted this dummy battleship up the river on a flood tide and drew the fire of the forts. On February 21 one of Porter's officers wrote that "Johnny Reb let off his torpedoes without effect on it, and the old thing sailed across the river and grounded in flank and rear of the enemy's lines on the eastern bank, whereupon they fell back in the night. She now occupies the most advanced position of the line, and Battery Lee has been banging away at her, and probably wondering why she does not answer. Last night after half a day's fighting, the rebs sent down about 50 torpedoes; but although 'Old Bogey'

took no notice of them, they kept the rest of us pretty lively so
long as the ebb tide ran ..." [5]

On February 22 the Confederates abandoned Wilmington. General Schofield's troops occupied the town and Porter's vessels
came up to the wharves. The fleet was welcomed by a crowd of
negroes who sang, shouted, and danced. The joy of the negroes
was genuine, for the Confederate Congress had just decided to
conscript blacks into the army. When Porter fired a Washington's
Birthday salute in honor of the victory, the negroes scattered in
all directions. The capture of Wilmington gave to Sherman another important base for his final operations against Confederate
General Joseph E. Johnston, who commanded the remnants of
the Confederate armies south of Richmond.

In the closing weeks of the war there was little for Porter's fleet
to do. Up the Roanoke and James Rivers the Confederates had a
few rams, which, it was rumored, would try to break through. On
January 24, the three Confederate rams on the James River had
attempted to come down on a flood tide but had grounded in the
neighborhood of the obstructions at Trent's Reach, and Porter's
division commander in the James River had allowed them to
retreat unmolested. Had the Confederate rams succeeded in attacking City Point at this time, they might have destroyed the vast
warehouses of military stores and upset Grant's plans for the
spring campaign. Since Porter was occupied at Fort Fisher at
the time, Welles had sent Farragut to the James River; and upon
Farragut's recommendation and Grant's, Commander Parker had
been relieved.

Porter was so furious when he heard of Parker's delinquency
that he prescribed drastic measures to cope with any similar
situation in the future. The naval commander in the Roanoke
was ordered to fit spar torpedoes on the bows of every gunboat,
and to run all together at any ram that should show itself, "No
matter how many of your vessels get sunk ... Have all your large
rowboats fitted with torpedoes also ... sling a good sized anchor
to an outrigger spar, and let it go on her deck, and by letting go
your own anchor keep her from getting away until other vessels
pile in on her ... If you can get on board of her, knock a hole
in her smokestack with axes, or fire a howitzer through it, and
drop shrapnel down into the furnaces ... Get a net or two across
the river ... [to] clog her propeller ... Don't place timid men in
your torpedo boats, but choose those who won't flinch from anything ... A full blow from all your vessels (don't be afraid of dam-

aging them) would, I think, sink her in a short time; the torpedoes would, certainly ..." 6 For the James River Squadron, which now contained four monitors, Porter's orders provided that row after row of vessels, linked with heavy chains, should surround any enemy rams attempting to get through. "Boats will also be ready with poles with nets on them to clog the rams' propellers. ... All other vessels not mentioned will be thrown across the channel, and the cocks turned to let them go on the bottom and obstruct the passage before and behind the rams ... Everyone must set his wits to work, and have no such word as fail." 7 Porter earnestly desired an opportunity to try these measures, but his wish was not granted. Henceforth his naval force was doomed to wait for the Army to end the war.

On March 3 Porter left Beaufort for Washington, where he arrived the day after Lincoln's second inauguration. Washington was packed with the usual inaugural crowds. Scintillating chatter ran through the salons. Lincoln's famous words "with malice toward none and charity for all" awakened lively speculations regarding the President's attitude toward the Confederate leaders after the fall of the Rebellion. What would happen to Jefferson Davis, the greatest of all the Confederates? How soon would the war be over? The President had avoided any definite statement of policy. His address had been very solemn and dignified; but the ceremonies as a whole had been woefully without plan, as Porter learned. Secretary Welles, who saw everything from the perspective of a small-town newspaperman, recorded in his diary that "All was confusion and without order,—a jumble. The Vice-President made a rambling and strange harangue, which was listened to with pain and mortification by all of his friends. My impressions were that he was under the influence of stimulants ... Speed, who sat at my left, whispered to me that 'all this is in wretched bad taste.' ... I said to Stanton, who was on my right, 'Johnson is either drunk or crazy.' ... Seward says it was emotion on returning and revisiting the Senate ... I hope Seward is right, but don't entirely concur with him." 8

On March 7 Porter appeared before the Joint Committee on the Conduct of the War and gave his version of the Red River campaign and the Powder Boat expedition to Fort Fisher. In both cases he said exactly what he thought; and his language, as was that of Banks and Butler, was beyond the limits of parliamentary privilege. Years later Porter wrote, "Congress did not get at the truth, nor did it desire to do so. Wherever it stuck down a spade it struck a politician." [9] After completing his testimony before the Committee, Porter proceeded to City Point, where he took over the direction of the local squadron.

City Point, Virginia, the headquarters of the largest army ever assembled in America, afforded an unusual panorama. A stroll along its docks and warehouses gave Mr. Stillson, a reporter for the New York *World,* a "somewhat blasphemous impression" that with the quartermaster's department all things were possible. From the lower level of its waterfront and freight yards he ascended one of the numerous stairways built along the cliff to the upper plain where the troops were quartered. This part of the village Mr. Stillson described as "A maze of flapping canvas, and muddy streets, with here and there a patched up ruin of a house lifting its roof and chimneys above the general level. Log and pine cabins, roofed with tarpaulin, abound. Grant's headquarters in a royal old Virginia mansion with broad verandas, commanded an extensive view of the river." [10] Everywhere there were offices, storehouses and bakeries. The "grand" bakery turned out 120,000 loaves per day. There was a "bull pen" for Confederate captives. On the outskirts beyond the tents were wagon parks and stables for horses.

On March 24 President Lincoln, with Mrs. Lincoln and his son Tad, came down on the *River Queen* to City Point. Lincoln wanted to be near the front when the Army set out on its last campaign. He was nervous. Now that the end was in sight, he wanted it to come quickly.

Lincoln told Porter that he wanted the war over and the men sent home to get their crops in. Since the Navy's job was now virtually completed, Porter was able to spend most of the next ten days escorting the President. They took long horseback rides over the country behind the Union lines, puzzled over the maps of Richmond and Petersburg, and enjoyed the hospitality of the Army officers at City Point. Lincoln enjoyed "knocking around" in the Admiral's barge. He enjoyed Porter's bonhomie and his endless store of burlesque anecdotes about the war. Lincoln had a droll way of referring to General Butler which delighted Porter.

"Well," said Mr. Lincoln on one occasion, "I don't think, Admiral, your friend the General was very much of an engineer."

Porter cordially agreed with him.

"I don't think," continued Lincoln, "that your friend the General was much of a general either."

In this Porter also agreed. [11]

On March 27 General Sherman arrived at City Point for a final conference with Lincoln and Grant before beginning his offensive in North Carolina. Porter was at Trent's Reach when Sherman's boat came in, but he hurried down at once to greet his old companion.

Early on the 28th Grant, Sherman, and Porter boarded a tug and went out to the *River Queen* to confer with the President and discuss the prospects of an early and final victory.

"Let them surrender and go home," said Lincoln. "They will not take up arms again. Let them all go, officers and all, let them have their horses to plow with, and if you like, their guns to shoot crows with." [12]

When the President was at rest or listening, his legs and arms seemed to hang almost lifeless; and his face was careworn and haggard. But, when he himself began to talk, his face lighted up, and he was the perfection of good humor and fellowship.

About noon the conference ended. Sherman returned to North Carolina in the fast ex-blockade runner *Bat,* which Porter loaned him; and at 6 A.M. on the 29th Grant's armies set out to attack Lee at Petersburg and Richmond. Porter's oldest son David Essex Porter, a second lieutenant of volunteers, marched with the army toward Petersburg.

At 9 o'clock on March 29 General Grant bade the President good-by and set off aboard his headquarters train for the front. Not to be outdone by the generals, the President and the Admiral took an excursion up the Appomattox River, where Porter ordered several gunboats to push up to protect Grant's pontoon bridge. Heavy firing from the direction of Petersburg was heard at 3:40 P.M.

That night Porter reported to Fox, "Uncle Abe is having a good time down here, and would have had a better one had he come alone. Mrs. Lincoln got jealous of a lady down here, and rather pulled his wig for him. We put him through the Navy and did all we could to make him forget the cares of office, for which he seems grateful . . . The old gentleman seems to like the quiet here and will stay some days longer." [13] A short time earlier he had written, "I don't wear a long feather, big boots, and spurs, and have a long sword jingling after me, which I know is very impressive, but I keep a good larder, and some good champagne which is always a passport to a sensible man's heart." [14]

During the next few days Lincoln and Porter spent most of their time in the telegraph hut at City Point, piecing together the fragments of information as they came in and tracing the army's movements on the maps. Thursday and Friday it rained and the army's covered wagons, crawling over the muddy roads, sank to their hubs, but mushed steadily on. From time to time the direction of heavy firing shifted from the south side of the Appomattox to Petersburg and to the upper James.

On April 1 Mrs. Lincoln went back to the Capital on the *River Queen,* and Lincoln accepted a cabin on the *Malvern.* The President's bunk was too short for his length, and he was compelled to fold his legs the first night, but Porter's carpenters remodeled the cabin on the sly, and the second morning Lincoln appeared at breakfast with the story that he had shrunk "six inches in length and about a foot sideways."

The vigils in the telegraph hut were so agitating that on Saturday night Porter arranged for the monitors at Trent's Reach to make a demonstration for the President's amusement. That night, Mrs. Admiral Porter being on the *Malvern,* the regimental band of the One Hundred and Fourteenth Pennsylvania Volunteers came on board and serenaded. As soon as the moon went down, the monitors up the river set off rockets, burnt blue lights, and kept up a brisk cannonade for half an hour. Lest any of the commanders should mistake the purpose of the affair and risk encountering torpedoes, Porter ordered them specifically not to change their position and explained: "The only object is to make a noise." [15]

The next day at General Ord's request Porter sent a detachment of 500 seamen up the Appomattox River to bring down 3,000 captured soldiers to the bull pen at City Point. All day the firing at Petersburg was very heavy, and from midnight until 4 A.M. on the 3rd the sky in that direction was lighted by fire. Grant telegraphed that Petersburg had just been taken and invited Lincoln to come up.

Accordingly at 9 o'clock Lincoln, Tad, and Porter set out by rail. The railroad was a temporary affair winding in an eccentric path around and over the hills. As the Presidential train was laboriously climbing one of the wooded ridges, a locomotive suddenly appeared upon its crest and plunged down out of sight, followed by freight cars. It rose again immediately in front and rattling by with a whistle and a roar, ascended another camel's back of ground, and disappeared within a wood.

The rails ended at Patrick Station, and from here Lincoln and Porter rode horseback the remaining three miles to Petersburg.

Petersburg had been the strongest Confederate position immediately to the south of Richmond.

When Lincoln and Porter returned to City Point that afternoon at 5 o'clock, they learned that Richmond, too, had been evacuated that same day and occupied by General Weitzel's troops. They also learned that the Confederate ironclads above Trent's Reach had been blown up. Porter ordered his squadron to clear away the obstructions and fish the torpedoes out of the James River.

Lincoln's joy was without bounds. At last the four long years of nightmare were over. In spite of Secretary Stanton's telegram begging him not to expose himself, Lincoln declared that he must see Richmond. "I have not a particle of the bump of veneration on my head," wrote Porter years later in his reminiscences, "but I saw more to admire in this man, more to reverence, than I had believed possible...he was not the man to assume a character for feelings he did not possess. He was in some respects as guileless as a child. How could one avoid liking such a man?" [16]

By 9 o'clock the channel of the James had been cleared, and Lincoln and Porter set out to visit Richmond. The party consisted of the *River Queen*, the *Malvern*, the *Bat*, the transport *Columbus*, and a tug. They passed Trent's Reach and steamed cautiously up the river past the wreckage of the Confederate ironclads. Thirty miles above City Point, where the channel narrowed through a forest of obstructions, they found their passage blocked by the Confederate flag-of-truce boat *Allison*.

Admiral Farragut, who had entered Richmond the day before with General Weitzel and was now returning down the river, was aboard the stranded *Allison*. Impatient at the delay, Lincoln and Porter entered the latter's barge and towed by a light tug made their way through shallow water around the obstructions. In this way they might have made the trip to Richmond very quickly, but Lincoln sent the tug back to help Farragut, and the tug grounded. Lincoln and Porter proceeded up the river in the barge, escorted only by three aides and the twelve husky seamen who manned the oars. A more modest equipage than had been planned, but one that would get them to Richmond.

It was a mild spring day. Birds were singing in the orchards on either side of the river, and the trees were in bloom. As the party pulled up the river they saw a wide curtain of smoke rise on the horizon ahead. Richmond was on fire. On evacuating the city the Confederates had fired their magazines and warehouses of cotton and tobacco; and bursting projectiles had dropped over the town, setting fire to a wide swath of dwellings and buildings in the business district.

The party landed about one block above Libby Prison. Porter formed ten of the sailors into a guard. They were armed with carbines. Six marched in front and four in rear, and in the middle with the President and the Admiral walked Captain Penrose, Lincoln's military aide, Captain Adams of the Navy, and Lieutenant Clemens of the Signal Corps.

Lincoln with his tall hat towered more than a foot above the thick-set Admiral, whose flat seaman's cap emphasized his five feet seven inches.

Crowds of negroes and poor whites surged around the party, shouting and chanting. Porter felt anxious for the President's safety, but Lincoln, good politican and friendly, unaffected man, was flattered and amused by the curious masses.

When a little girl ran out of a house with a bouquet of flowers, Lincoln stopped and thanked her. Negroes wailing halleluiahs greeted him as their Messiah, and Lincoln stopped to admonish and talk to them about good citizenship.

Everywhere there were men and women carrying bedclothes and other household effects saved from the fire. Here and there on the sidewalks were stragglers from the Southern Army. The Confederate Government warehouses had been broken open after the troops had withdrawn. The gutters were running with liquor. Many barrels of bacon, ham, cornmeal, and quantities of tobacco and blankets and gray cloth, so carefully reserved by the Confederate quartermaster, had been seized by the populace. The streets were littered, but the crowds were orderly, though semi-hysterical from want of sleep and from excitement. About noon the Presidential party reached General Weitzel's headquarters, Jefferson Davis's residence, from which the Confederate President had fled less than thirty-six hours before.

In the afternoon General Weitzel detailed a cavalry escort to accompany the President as he rode around the city. Porter and Weitzel rode with him in the low, open carriage. They drove through the burned district, where white and colored Federal troops were yet laboring to extinguish the fires; and visited the Capitol, Castle Thunder, and the infamous Libby Prison, not far from the starting point of the morning's march through the city. The old sign board "Libby & Sons, Ship Chandlers and Grocers" had never been taken down. The prison's doors were now open and both inmates and wardens had vanished.

In the afternoon the *Malvern* worked her way up to the suburb known as the Rocketts and fired a salute of thirty-five guns. Lincoln spent the night on the *Malvern* and the following morning directed Porter to return to City Point.[17] Mrs. Lincoln came down from Washington on the 6th with Senator Sumner. These visitors were sent to Richmond; while Lincoln remained with Porter; for, as Lincoln confided, he wanted to see no one from Washington. On the 8th the President said good-by to the Admiral. He was in a merry mood. In the opinion of his private secretary the President had enjoyed his most carefree holiday in four years.

On the 10th, when word came of the surrender at Appomattox Court House, the fleet fired a national salute. The winding river echoed and reëchoed as each of the vessels fired its thirty-five guns.

On April 14 Porter hoisted his flag aboard the *Tristram Shandy* and steamed north for a brief vacation. When he docked the next morning in Baltimore, he learned that Lincoln had been shot. He immediately went by train to Washington. Everywhere people moved about in little groups talking excitedly in undertones. So lately joyous over their great victory, they were now overwhelmed by the new disaster. Porter entered the city. Learning that Lincoln had died, the hard little man whose trade had taught him to jest in the heat of battle bowed his head and wept.

As we arrive at the final, black-trimmed page of the Civil War it is interesting to bring into focus the changes that the war had wrought in Porter's character and career. His early service on the *Powhatan* at Fort Pickens, on the blockade, and chasing the *Sumter* ideally suited him at this time; for, though he had the makings of a great squadron commander, he was as yet far too much of an individualist to have made a good one. He was too quickly exasperated by what he considered the professional delinquencies of his superior officers. His character was not set in the mold, and this was well, but despite his forty-eight years his attitude was still that of a young man and required the seasoning of experience before he could successfully cope with the personnel difficulties of a large squadron. His service on the *Powhatan,* moreover, led him to the realistic conclusion that single-ship glories—such as had been the vogue in his father's day—were not so desirable now as were the coördinated activities of many ships.

Porter's tendency to ignore tradition and his inveterate love of experimentation were valuable assets in a war where innovation played so large a rôle. His plan for the attack on New Orleans showed Porter at his best as an innovator in tactical method. Of deeper significance, however, it revealed a sensitiveness to the strategic need of the hour, ability to see the problem of the war as a whole—which is after all the very first requisite of a great commander.

The Mortar Flotilla afforded him his first experience in command of a large number of ships and men, and he executed the work of his particular division to perfection. But whenever it became necessary for him to coöperate with certain older officers in Farragut's fleet, it must be admitted that his attitude lacked charitableness and sympathetic understanding. Only his affection for Farragut and the latter's genius in composing minor difficulties between the men under him saved the junior commander from the dangers of his own intense individualism.

The Newport incident—which came near to wrecking Porter's career, as Fajardo had wrecked his father's, and from the selfsame fault of plain speaking—taught Porter a much needed lesson in circumspection, another highly desirable trait in a commander. It by no means, however, undermined his boyishness of spirit. Throughout his service as commander of the Mississippi Squadron Porter's table talk within his official family continued to be as gaily bantering and buoyant as ever; but in his dealings with outsiders, though always frank and aboveboard, he exercised restraint, unconsciously perhaps emulating the sympathetic and understanding manner of Farragut.

The maturing of Porter's attitude into a happy combination of frankness and restraint was the fundamental reason for his successful coöperation with Grant in the Vicksburg campaign. No other extensive joint military and naval mission of the war was so remarkably free from friction. His ability to adjust his personality so as to lead effectively this large, heterogeneous squadron with its multitude and diversity of objectives won for Porter the right to rank with the greatest American commanders.

To the last, however, Porter was not able to reconcile himself to the employment of political leaders as generals. Under the circumstances the services of these officers were entirely necessary; and many men like Dix and Logan distinguished themselves, although the ineptitude of others stigmatized their class as a whole. In simple justice to the several scores of political generals who were hard working, conscientious, and patriotic, as well as in justice to Porter's fame, it must be remembered that the men who bungled the Red River campaign and the first attack on Fort Fisher were the worst generals in the service.

The alternation of spectacular victories with spectacular defeats did not mar Porter's prestige. The Government rewarded Porter as it did no other Civil War leader. Four times he was given the Congressional vote of thanks, a greater number than any other naval officer received. In three years he was jumped from lieutenant to rear admiral, overleaping three grades, a distinction unique in American annals, and perhaps in any navy of modern times. In official and popular estimation at the end of the war Porter stood with Farragut, who was many years his senior; and in 1866, when Congress created the new grade of Admiral of the Navy for Farragut, it advanced Porter to the distinctive grade of Vice Admiral.

PART THREE
THE FOUR-STARRED FLAG

And a gala, four-starred flag
awaving at the mainmast head ...

RIVALING WEST POINT

A T the close of the Civil War the United States had the largest force of ironclad steamships in the world. European attachés in Washington had been impressed by the mid-winter operations of the ironclads along the stormy coast off Fort Fisher, and within the next twelve months England and France were alarmed by the successful voyage across the Atlantic of the ironclad warships which the United States sold to the Kingdom of Sardinia and by the good will journey to St. Petersburg of the unwieldy, double-turreted U. S. monitor *Miantonomah*. Downing Street admitted the error of Her Majesty's Government in allowing Confederate raiders to be fitted out from British shipyards. Napoleon III hurriedly withdrew his army from Mexico and abandoned the unfortunate Emperor Maximilian.

In the spring of 1865, however, the United States ignored her vast naval prestige. Her leaders, weary of war, plunged with military abruptness into the complicated problems of reconstruction. Vast volunteer armies were mustered out of the service. Work was suspended on naval vessels under construction. Thousands of seamen and hundreds of volunteer officers were mustered out of the Navy. Hundreds of ships of all categories were decommissioned.

Gideon Welles read correctly the signs of the times. One of his first acts after the establishment of peace was to place Porter on waiting orders, for he well knew that service afloat was now for men who had not specifically placed themselves on record as anxious for a foreign war.

In May the Secretary appointed Porter to the Board of Visitors to witness the examinations at the Naval Academy and report on the "state of police, discipline, and general management of the institution."

On the outbreak of hostilities, when the secession of Maryland was hanging in doubt, the U. S. S. *Constitution* had carried the loyal remnants of the Naval Academy away from Annapolis to the safe study ground of Newport, Rhode Island.[1] Here in an old hotel with a pretentious Parthenon façade the Academy had existed for four years under the guidance of elderly Commodore Blake and a set of scholastic teachers who flunked many midshipmen who might have been passed to fill emergency needs in the fleet. Both Porter and Welles had been irked by the Naval Academy during the war. The Secretary's son had been tossed overboard from the schoolship with a rope around his waist and towed back and forth; and the Admiral's second son had had to resign, although later at Fort Fisher he had demonstrated his fitness for the service.

During the most colorful period of American history the Academy had pursued an uninteresting course. Most of the naval officers who had been attached to it before the war had entered active service, and their places had been filled by civilian teachers. The few officers who remained were considered by such men as Porter to be "Miss Nancys" without sufficient professional energy to break away from the scholastic routine.

As a professional school the Academy had retrogressed during the war. During the greatest period of naval invention the world had ever seen the Academy had followed the course mapped out in the days of wooden ships, sail propulsion, and smoothbore cannon. Enterprising midshipmen might read in the newspapers about ironclads, turret monitors, steam engines, propellers, electric batteries, mortars, rifled guns, torpedoes. But they had no classroom facilities for studying about these interesting naval innovations. Even the out-of-date course of study was handicapped. The Academy's library of a few thousand volumes, which had been boxed and brought from Annapolis, had never been uncrated.

The atmosphere of the institution was conservative and puritanical. According to Midshipman Benjamin, whenever boisterous youngsters requested permission to play cricket in Tuoro Park, they were rebuked. The Commandant of the Academy, the Superintendent reported, "is a communicant of the Presbyterian Church, never uttered a profane word, never smoked a cigar, and never knew the taste of even a glass of wine."

In the summer of 1865 after many conversations with Porter the Secretary appointed him superintendent of the Naval Academy.

There was much to be done before the Academy could be restored to its old home at Fort Severn in Annapolis. During the war the Academy grounds had been used by the Army as a hospital base. Buildings would have to be cleared and disinfected. New buildings would have to be constructed to make room for the newer branches of naval studies developed during the war. The grounds, for four years cluttered with Army tents, sutlers' shacks, and grog shops, would have to be cleared, lawns restored, gardens planned and planted. Changes in the faculty of the old Naval Academy would also have to be made. New life would have to be infused into the institution.

In Annapolis Porter would surround himself with his favorites and develop cliquism, Secretary Welles believed; but along with his bad qualities he had certain positive characteristics which made him the logical man for the job. "The high rank of the new Superintendent," proclaimed the *Army and Navy Journal*, "his wide fame, and his fine capacity for discipline, will be a great source of strength to the Academy."

Porter entered upon his new duties with enthusiasm, for his dream of a war with Europe was to him a stimulating reality. The thought never left him that one day he would lead these youngsters into battles on the high seas. Porter wanted his young officers to be resourceful, practical, alert for scientific developments. He wanted them to be as well drilled in the manual of arms as the cadets at West Point, but beyond that he wanted them to be well grounded in their own profession. He wanted them to be gentlemen, tactful, diplomatic, at ease in any drawing-room. Porter had learned from experience that naval officers need social finesse as well as skill and courage in battle.

To develop this character in his midshipmen Porter's aims were simple, and compared with the policy of the institution in the past, drastic. He was determined to make the course of instruction more practical and more professional. He would secure voluntary obedience to the regulations by trusting to the personal honor of the midshipmen. He would inaugurate an elaborate system of physical exercises and athletic sports which would divert the midshipmen and at the same time cultivate self-reliance. Porter saw no reason why the Academy should not be built up into a flourishing national institution rivaling West Point.

Making the Academy more professional was a pleasing task to Porter. As instructors for the midshipmen, he brought to the Academy a group of interesting young officers who had made names for themselves in the war. K. R. Breese, who had been Porter's fleet captain both on the Mississippi and at Fort Fisher, was detailed as Assistant to the Superintendent. R. L. Phythian, one of the heroes of Fort Fisher, became the head of the Department of Astronomy,

Navigation, and Surveying. John S. Barnes, who had served in both Atlantic squadrons, was to teach in the Department of Mathematics along with J. G. Walker, one of Porter's most energetic officers on the Mississippi and also a nephew of Senator J. W. Grimes of the Naval Committee. Porter foresaw that he should have to have political support if he were to accomplish his aims during the present period of peace-time retrenchment in the Navy.

Not all the officer instructors were from Porter's squadrons. George Dewey, who had been with Farragut at Mobile, William T. Sampson, and Winfield Scott Schley—three officers who would win fame later in the War with Spain—were also members of Porter's faculty.

Tom Selfridge, one of Porter's favorite younger officers, however, Mr. Welles had ordered to China. The lad presently came to see Porter. His earnest, youthful face, fringed with luxuriant sideburns, was unusually serious. He wanted to marry Ellen Shepley, but this he could not do if he were ordered to China for three years. Porter had a chat with the Secretary and secured for Selfridge a new assignment as assistant to the Commandant and instructor in Seamanship and Naval Tactics; whereupon the marriage was performed, and the newly-weds were added to Porter's entourage at the Academy.

When the school ships *Constitution* and *Santee* arrived at Annapolis in September, the courses as well as the faculty had been rearranged. Integral calculus had been abolished, and only the simpler forms of mathematics remained. The theoretical science of ethics had been extracted from the Department of English Studies and assigned to the chaplain, to be taught, not by the old method of "boning," but by "familiar lectures."

Professional courses had been elaborated and made more practical. To make the studies of seamanship and gunnery more attractive, the developments of the past few years were illustrated by a large number of models of ships, guns, torpedoes, fuses, etc. Fully-rigged ship models were used to expound the principles of sailing, and midshipmen were themselves required to name the parts and reef and furl according to command. Every Saturday drills in making and furling sails were held on the school ships; and midshipmen were exercised in sending down spars and topmasts, as many of their fathers had done in the old Navy. These drills were repeated and repeated until the midshipmen could strip a ship to a girtline in the short space of seventeen minutes. Whenever distinguished guests visited the institution during the next four years, they were entertained with exhibitions of seamanship that awed the most skeptical sailor.

The stress on practical gunnery was symbolized by the removal of the gunnery museum to the old chapel building on the completion of the new. Midshipmen were taught to cut fuses, test torpedoes, and operate electric batteries. Infantry and artillery drills were frequent. Thirteen-inch mortars—reminiscent of the Admiral's own struggle against the New Orleans forts—were mounted on the sea wall, and only upper classmen were allowed to exercise these weapons. Midshipmen mounted scurrilous flags on the mortars and chalked them with uncomplimentary inscriptions, but drills went steadily on. Gunnery lectures were designed to keep pace with the times; and Porter strictly enjoined the professors to leave the minds of the midshipmen unprejudiced "so that when they shall have arrived at maturer years, and had more experience, they be better able to judge for themselves, without following in the ruts of their instructors." [2]

The old platform at the water's edge which had been rigged up in times past to resemble a ship's deck was abandoned, and the *Santee* was converted into a gunnery ship from which whole broadsides were fired, despite the fact that window glass and retorts in the adjoining laboratory of Experimental Philosophy were shattered. The ironclad monitor *Tonawanda* was also secured as a practice ship for the midshipmen.

The greatest innovation in the curriculum was the establishment of a Department of Steam Enginery. Chief Engineer W. W. W. Wood ("William Wonderful" as the boys called him) became the head of this new branch. A steam engineering building was constructed and fitted out with working models of every type of engine. The famous torpedo launch which Cushing had used to sink the *Albemarle* was fitted with engines and miniature sails, its object being to combine study with amusement.

In October 1867, the Admiral was to have gone out in her for her trial spin, but a temporary illness prevented him. The toy exploded, killing engineer Eben Hoyt and wounding two seamen. The disaster dampened the ardor of this department for a time; but the new brick steam building remained, with its grounds ornamented with captured guns and a fountain presented by the engineers of the Navy.

When the Academy was founded in 1845, the midshipmen by act of Congress had been created "gentlemen"; but earlier Superintendents had accepted this legislative fiat with a grain of salt, and to maintain discipline had established a system of espionage. With a stroke of his pen Porter abolished spying and placed midshipmen on their honor to uphold the regulations. Before the week was out, the upper classmen began their hazing of newcomers; whereupon Porter ordered an investigation which in effect hazed the upper classmen. On October 9 a rowdy youngster having conducted himself improperly during seamanship drill in the maintop of the *Santee*, committed the more serious fault of "violating the truth"; whereupon he was "prohibited from all associations with his classmates for the space of thirty days." A clever midshipman who had made an examination of his professor's notes expressed his sense of the impropriety of his own conduct, and after a sharp lecture by the Superintendent was reinstated. Another was reported for smoking and card playing and sentenced to four hours per day of guard duty until further notice, and one was similarly punished for putting a dummy in bed with his roommate for the purpose of deceiving the inspector of rooms.

A midshipman marched many hours of guard duty carrying one of the muskets he had allowed to be spat full of tobacco juice. Guard duty finally usurped the function of demerits; and, whenever it was performed in what Porter considered to be "an unseamanlike manner," the number of hours was increased. Sometimes more drastic punishments had to be inflicted and offenders were placed in solitary confinement and fed on bread and water. For yet more serious offenses they were confined in dark rooms and armed guards stood watch before their doors. When a midshipman so confined escaped by a Jacob's ladder from the third floor of the recitation building, the marines were sent out across Annapolis to bring him back.

The pranks of the midshipmen reminded the Admiral of the peccadilloes of his own youth, and in secret he chuckled as he dispensed justice. "Midshipman Jenkins," he ordered, "who does not know how to behave himself at the mess table will mess by himself on board the *Constitution* until further orders." The midshipmen who kicked their football into the basket of the cake man had their spending money cut off until the damage was paid for. Several midshipmen who stamped their feet during a mechanics lecture were required to stand ten hours of guard duty. "Midshipman Thompson (First Class) who plays so abominably on a fish horn," wrote the Admiral, "will oblige me by going outside the limits when he wants to practice or he will find himself coming out of the 'little end of the horn.'"[3]

"I loosen or tighten the reins according as they conduct themselves," declared Porter in a report to the Department. "My rule is to bear with offending midshipmen as long as I think there is anything in them to justify keeping them here—their insubordination can be checked with punishments, their mischiefs with guard duty... As long as a boy is only mischievous or full of life and spirit, I stand up for him."[4]

The health of the future officers of the Navy was carefully guarded. Each boy was required to take one bath a week, though excessive cleanliness was discouraged by a small fee exacted by the barbers for each additional bath. In fair weather during the fall and spring outdoor infantry and seamanship drills were the regular order of the day. To make the manual of arms agreeable as well as instructive the naval and marine bands turned out every day and marched ahead of the ranks of midshipmen. The bandsmen who hitherto had worn uniforms of ecclesiastical cut now wore uniforms of blue trimmed with red and gold, and performed under the direction of a "flaming drum major."

No longer was music discouraged at the Academy. If the Admiral objected to fish horns, he fostered the development of musical clubs and allowed the leaders of these organizations many liberties in cutting classes. A dramatic club was also formed under the versatile direction of Midshipmen Park Benjamin and Sam Very. A gay company of young officers and their wives—who contrary to all previous custom now had quarters in the yard—came to the midshipmen's musicales and blackface comedies. The young Navy wives followed the lead of Mrs. Admiral Porter in entertaining the midshipmen at tea; and, if the atmosphere in general was more worldly than heretofore, it was tempered with the refining influences of feminine society. On the dark cold mornings of winter midshipmen were no longer required to trek across the yard to chapel. Short prayers were said at breakfast.

In converting the Academy into a "smart ship" a great deal of attention was given to athletic exercises and sports. Gymnastic requirements were rigid, but the variety of athletic sports was ample to interest the most inert midshipman. The best French fencing masters presided over the *Salle d'Armes*. Drills included broad sword and ancient seaman's cutlass as well as the foil. First classmen were coached in the art of boxing. Interclass meets in other sports were featured. Sometimes the Admiral himself would enter the boxing ring against first classmen amidst the loud cheers of the midshipmen. Baseball was introduced and games were played with outsiders, but on such occasions the Admiral required his midshipmen to take their sport seriously and drill for the match. "I don't want anyone to come down here and beat us at anything," [5] he declared. Both clubs were organized in each of the classes and races were held.

When the guns were removed from the antiquated Fort Severn in the southeast corner of the sea wall to the *Santee,* the fort was converted into a well appointed gymnasium and armory. The galleries surrounding the main floor communicated with fencing and boxing rooms. On the ground floor bowling alleys and shooting galleries were fitted out, and midshipmen were enjoined to use plenty of powder. The Government had a considerable store of powder left over from the war, which Porter felt might thus be put to good use.

In the architectural center of the brick-walled, ten-acre reservation—midway between the gymnasium and "Rascality Row" where the professors lived—was the Superintendent's house. During the war this plain, two-story colonial house, sixty-five by twenty-one feet, had been used by the Army as a recreation hall. In September 1865, after Porter's workmen had hauled away the billiard tables, beer bottles, and checker boards, Mrs. Porter supervised its redecoration and moved her furniture up from Washington.

All six of the Porter children were here at some time during the first year, and the house was filled to capacity. David Essex, twenty, who had been breveted captain for meritorious service during the final operations before Richmond, was mustered out of the service with his company of volunteers and was at home for a month before he obtained a commission in the Regular Army. The oldest son had a restless, roving temperament. After enduring two years in the peace-time Regular Army he resigned against his father's wishes, went west, found work in a flour mill, nearly died of double pneumonia. The Admiral was much exasperated by his "riding buffaloes and scalping Indians"; but Essex returned home finally, married Lily Abert, daughter of one of General Banks's aides on the Red River expedition and settled in Washington. [6]

The second son, Carlisle, was quieter than Essex, though not less dashing and brave. His participation with the seamen in the attack on Fort Fisher had endeared him to the Admiral, but the depression that overtook the Navy after the war kept him at home for several years. He worked as one of his father's secretaries until he obtained a commission in the Marine Corps.

Sixteen-year-old Theodoric came with his father to the Academy as a midshipman. He was the athlete of the family—standing number one in fencing during his plebe year. Because he chatted French with Sword Master Bonnafous he stood number nine in languages—though not so well in mathematics. Tod was well liked by his classmates. His demerits in conduct increased in number from year to year, and like the other boys he did his turns at guard duty.

Eleven-year-old Richard lived with his parents at the Academy until, after he had had the mumps, measles, and scarlet fever, his father sent him to the Pennsylvania Military School at Chester. He was an honest, high-spirited lad, who criticized his teachers and freely admitted it. When the headmaster confined him in the coal bin for his frankness, he ran away and went into business for himself.

The two girls of the family—Elizabeth, 13, and Elena, 9—assisted their mother in entertaining the midshipmen. Both went horseback riding with their father over Strawberry Hill. In a manner quite disconcerting to Annapolis in 1865 they rode astride their horses. Elizabeth danced with the midshipmen and by 1869 had fallen in love with Midshipman Leavitt C. Logan, one of the most promising youths at the Academy.

Mrs. Porter made her house the social center of the Academy. She set an extravagant table at all times and dressed well. Her house guests included General Grant, General Sherman, members of Congress, foreign naval officers and naval attachés, and a wide circle of the Admiral's friends in the Navy. At the dinner table opposite her immaculately groomed husband she kept up an animated conversation in competition with the boisterous gaiety of her spouse. Her bright brown hair was parted in the center and coiled in soft braids at the back. For evening she wore a string of pearls with a pendant across her smoothly brushed hair to lessen the severity of her coiffure. In her dress she tempered the mode to her outstanding beauty and dignity and chose to appear most often in a rich blue or deep old rose.

Mrs. Porter's social accomplishments added much to the new regime at the Academy. During the war eighty new grog shops had been licensed in Annapolis, and Porter was determined to provide recreation for the midshipmen within the walls.

Once a month the Admiral and Mrs. Porter led the quadrille

which opened the dances at the gymnasium. These dances were colorful affairs, attended by the officers on the station and the élite of Annapolis as well as the midshipmen. The floor of the armory was highly polished, ceilings were decorated with Japanese lanterns and streamers, the walls lined with rifles and bayonets. Awkward midshipmen were turned over to dancing masters to have their faults corrected, for social grace was regarded as an important corollary to military precision.

The hops in the armory created a stir among advocates of the old order, and Commodore Goldsborough, who had been Superintendent of the Academy before the war, exclaimed, "Yes, sir, there is a distinctive difference between then and now. In my time we educated the head. Now, by Neptune, they educate the heels!" [7] Nor were such remarks confined to the older officers. Young officers and their wives, who enjoyed the social events but who were coerced into attendance by the example of the Admiral and Mrs. Porter, chattered slyly about "Porter's Dancing Academy."

The fame of the institution at last began to rival that of West Point. In February 1867, when an Austrian admiral visited the Academy, the regiment turned out on dress parade to welcome him. The midshipmen scurried aloft on the school ship and furled and unfurled sails and unshipped and shipped the spars and masts so dextrously as to win large applause. Throughout the fleet it came to be recognized that Vice Admiral Porter had given a tone to the once modest institution. Whenever older officers visited Annapolis they were met by specially appointed reception committees.

In June 1867 President Johnson visited the Academy. When the Presidential steamer turned the buoy in the roadstead twenty-one guns blazed from the *Santee*. The guns were immediately reloaded. As the Presidential party entered the Academy grounds another salute of twenty-one guns was fired. When the President was received at the door of the Maryland Governor's mansion, he was presented to the officers on the station, who wore formal dress. The Regiment of Midshipmen was drawn up in parade formation. Every seaman on the station had been ordered to wash his face for the occasion, and the proper officers had taken steps to insure compliance with this order. The file of marines gave five ruffles. The band clad in new uniforms played the "Star-Spangled Banner." And at the close of the ceremonies the *Santee* fired a third volley of twenty-one guns.[8]

Incidentally Porter's bid for the President's favor was not without motive as far as the Academy was concerned. The few acres of low ground surrounding the ancient fort were not sufficient room for a flourishing national institution. Porter was determined that the Academy should expand. Already he had begun sending young J. G. Walker down to Washington to state the Academy's needs to his uncle, Senator J. W. Grimes, who was a member of the Naval Committee. In view of the general cutting down of the Navy at this time, the task of securing an appropriation of $200,000 to purchase the mansion and grounds of the Governor of Maryland was not easy. The number of Congressional appointments to the Academy had also been cut from two to one per member. But Porter adroitly achieved his end, and in addition to the Governor's mansion with its four acres of lawns and gardens he managed to purchase three other tracts, thus increasing the Academy's size from ten acres to about one hundred and fifty acres.

Porter's health was poor during the whole of his stay in Annapolis. "This vile climate is getting me by inches," he wrote his aging mother at Chester; "I scarcely know what it is to sleep at night . . . I am half dead with neuralgia . . . It is seldom that I can write without feeling such pain in the back of my head and over the eyes that I have to lay down my pen—indeed I never write to anyone but yourself. All my work being done by dictating . . . Neither can I read without feeling as if I were going to faint. All my letters have to be read to me when they are of any length, and a newspaper seems to drive a wedge right into my eyes. I am in fact in a dreadful nervous condition (I suppose it is) and out of 5 doctors I have had none of them seem able to relieve me . . . The strain of the war is telling on me, and I want relaxation . . . Nothing that I eat agrees with me . . . I don't look sick, have a fair appetite at times and a longing for sweet things which don't agree with me . . ." [9]

His illnesses, however, were known to few people outside of his family. Whenever possible he eliminated desk work. The preceding Superintendent had been praised by the Board of Visitors for writing an average of a thousand letters per year to the parents of midshipmen. This work Porter discontinued. To Fox Porter confided that he supposed Secretary Welles would be glad to have Captain Blake back as Superintendent, "Blake did all his writing to the mama's which I never do." [10] Only one parent elicited a response in Porter's handwriting by addressing him as "Rev. D. D. Porter." To this Porter could not resist the urge to write a tactful reply.

Mr. Welles was not troubled by Porter's neglect of parents, but he was disturbed by the Vice Admiral's growing interest in Washington politics. The Secretary jotted down many premonitions in the pages of his diary. And as events were to prove the Secretary's secret fears were prophetic.

PORTER IN THE NAVY DEPARTMENT

O N January 13, 1864 Porter had written Fox that "Grant could not be kicked into the Presidency, he would not have it at $40,000 per year; he doesn't like anything but fighting and smoking and hates politics as the de'il does holy water." [1] General Banks, whose Presidential ambitions were notorious, had ruined his own chances in the disastrous Red River campaign, just as the first attack on Fort Fisher had eliminated General Butler.

If Porter had had the slightest idea that the hard-fighting, hard-smoking, hard-drinking General Grant would ever become a candidate for the Presidency, he would never have been so indiscreet as to write Gideon Welles that Grant had been culpable for sending Butler to Fort Fisher. On January 24, however, in the heat of the victory over Fort Fisher, Porter had confided to the Secretary exactly what he thought. He could not, of course, foresee Grant's emergence into politics or his own future embarrassment when his enemies in the Navy Department should steal his confidential letter from the files for publication in the New York papers.

After Grant's visit to Fort Fisher, Porter had at once forgotten the difficulty—and the letter to Welles.

Throughout Porter's career at the Naval Academy Grant had been a frequent visitor at the institution, and the relations between the General and the Admiral had progressed from mutual admiration to friendship. Finally when the Republican party nominated Grant for the Presidency, Porter volunteered his testimony that the General was a teetotaler! The absurd testimony probably won few votes outside of naval circles, for temperance was not an issue of the campaign.

Prior to General Grant's campaign for the Presidency, Secretary Welles wrote in his diary that the Vice Admiral was angling for the office of Secretary of the Navy. But Gideon Welles's manage-

ment of the Navy during the four years following the war had
infuriated many naval officers—including Porter—and Mr. Welles
was shrewd enough to foresee the rejoicings on the day that he left
the Department. Porter's political influence thus became a source
of annoyance to Welles throughout his last years in office. During
the attempt to impeach President Johnson it was rumored in
Washington that if Senator Benjamin Wade succeeded in sup-
planting Johnson, he would make Porter Secretary of the Navy.
With the failure of the impeachment Welles's fears were not for
long allayed. After Grant was nominated—and before his election
—Porter accorded him Presidential salutes whenever the nominee-
general visited the Academy. This irked Welles greatly, but he
spoke of it only in private, and exulted when Congressman
Edmund on the eve of Grant's inauguration created an agitation
to exclude Army and Navy men from civil positions in Washington.

If Porter desired the title of Secretary of the Navy he left
no documentary evidence of his ambition. On December 13,
1868 General Sherman wrote Porter that there was a possibility
that he might be given this post. The President-elect, however,
kept his own council. Two days after the inauguration the appointment was still not made, and the *Army and Navy Journal*
speculated that neither Porter nor Farragut would care to enter
the cabinet. Grant placed his former aide, General Rawlins, in
the War Department. Rawlins was a volunteer, not a West
Pointer, and his appointment could arouse no controversy. Apparently Grant wanted Porter as Navy Secretary but feared to brook
the opposition of the anti-military block in Congress by appointing
him outright. At last he appointed Adolph E. Borie—a wealthy
Philadelphia merchant who knew nothing about the Navy—and
assigned Porter to special duty in the Department as Mr. Borie's
mentor.

On the morning of March 9 when the appointment was announced, Grant summoned Porter from Annapolis. The Admiral
hurried to Washington on a special train. Mr. Borie was a modest,
simply dressed gentleman, fifty-nine years of age—two years older
than Porter and about the same height. He wore short white
whiskers and a moustache slightly darker. His hair was iron-
gray, eyes dark hazel, very bright and keen. He was courteous, gen-
tlemanly, easily approached. Porter liked him at once, and their
friendship was destined to be lifelong in spite of the many up-
heavals that occurred in the Navy Department during Mr. Borie's

brief tenure of office and in spite of the fact that Mr. Borie later loaned the Admiral considerable sums of money which the latter was slow in repaying.

In his first two days as Secretary, Mr. Borie issued more general orders than Mr. Welles had in the last two years. On March 13 the *Army and Navy Journal* approved the "healthful influence of the new administration ... How much *need* there is of some 'rattling among dry bones' the readers of the *Journal* will have learned from the severe comments we have been making for more than five years on some branches of its management." On the 27th the New York *Times* hailed Mr. Borie as "the Van Tromp of the Navy Department—he sweeps the sea, so to speak, with a broom (new) at his masthead, and with the reality as well as the fear of change, perplexes a great many of our ancient mariners, as well as those who with a slight change may be called *marines.* Order is Heaven's first law; and he means to enforce it ... Liberty and equality are good things in their way, but there might be too much of them on board a man-of-war."

The Washington correspondent of the New York *Herald* wrote that "Like a giant refreshed after eight years of slumber, the Navy Department buckles on its business boots and starts in for the race of reform under General Grant. Borie is hardly a week at his post when he has run half through the gamut of Naval reform; but not all, nor a half nor a third of the credit of this to Borie. Behind him, with every rope, boom, and spar at his fingers' ends, with a mind that takes in at a glance, as another's might the alphabet, the whole American Navy and its organization, from the cooking galley to the etiquette of an admiral's reception—its wants, its wastes, its capacity for improvement, its *morale,* in short, its everything, stands Admiral David D. Porter, who comes at the request of General Grant, and of Secretary Borie, to give his valuable advice and assistance in remodeling and renovating the entire Navy ... On the first floor, in a wide, mellow lighted room of the Department, Secretary Borie receives his visitors and attends to the duties of his position. He is rapid in his movements, spends no time with loafers who simply come in to sit down and have a talk, but shows them out and bids them a pleasant good-morning. He is up to his eyes in business, contemplating other reforms ... Borie, with Admiral Porter as his assistant, will give us the model Navy of the world."

The news concerning the Navy Department was reported daily to the retired Secretary. Faxon, late Assistant Secretary, who had

acted as Head of Department during the "interregnum" from
March 4 to 9, was the first to unburden his feelings to Mr. Welles.
With the best of intentions Faxon had commenced to explain to
Secretary Borie the mechanism of the organization. The Admiral
had peremptorily interposed, saying that Faxon could tell him
and that he would inform Mr. Borie. Commodore Melancthon
Smith told Welles that Porter was "trying to flourish and make a
noise in order to be noticed in the newspapers," that he had
appointed a large number of boards to examine ships, engines,
etc., and overlooked the Bureaus, which could furnish all the information. It was alleged that Porter had told Commodore Smith
and other Chiefs of Bureaus that if they wanted anything, to apply
to *him,* not to the Secretary.[2]

John Lenthall, chief naval constructor, confided to ex-Secretary
Welles that he thought Mr. Borie well disposed, but feeble, timid,
inefficient, dwarfed and overborne by the arrogant and meddle-
some Vice Admiral. Paymaster Bridge hated Porter but was afraid
to say so, and Mr. Welles was amused and disgusted with his
timidity. Commodore Jenkins moaned that Porter devoted his
time to picking flaws with the previous administration. "In all
this," concluded Welles, "poor Borie was a passive tool. He is now
a mere clerk to Vice Admiral Porter, not the Secretary of the
Navy." [3] Nevertheless, when the "Lord of the Admiralty" placed
the dispatch boat *Tallapoosa* at Mr. Welles's service to convey his
personal effects to his home in Hartford, the ex-Secretary was
"glad to accept." How far the Vice Admiral's liberality might be
justified, mused Mr. Welles, "is a question which I shall not
scan." [4] Had the ex-Secretary but known that the *Tallapoosa* drew
too much water to get over the bar into the Connecticut River,
and that he would have to unload his furniture at New London
and express it 100 miles by rail from that point—at an expense
just double what it would have been if he had shipped it
originally in a regular trading vessel—Mr. Welles would probably
have denounced the Porter-Borie regime long before he arrived
at his home in Hartford.

After his return to Hartford the ex-Secretary attacked the Admiral with caustic eloquence. He believed that Porter's mind had
been turned by too rapid promotion during the war, that he was
selfish and overly ambitious. Mr. Welles's onslaughts in the *Galaxy*
magazine gave voice to the resentment of hundreds of others
whose fortunes had suffered from Porter's vigorous renovation of
the Navy Department. Welles's printed eloquence carried far. His

ill-tempered contrasts of Porter with Farragut did much to create popular legends about the two greatest naval officers of the Civil War; and the difference between their accomplishments has been exaggerated. Concerning Farragut *nil nisi bonum* was Welles's postwar motto; for Porter *nil nisi malum.*

Back of Porter's renovation of the Navy Department in the spring of 1869, however, there was a very real threat of war with Great Britain . . .

The settlement of the *Alabama* claims had been bungled by Radicals in Congress. Charles Sumner, chairman of the Senate's Committee on Foreign Affairs, had not only demanded that Britain pay for Federal vessels actually sunk during the war by Confederate raiders built in British yards, but that she repay America for the loss of her great merchant marine, including ships that had been shifted to foreign registry. The sum was grotesque—two and a quarter billion dollars, or half the total cost of the war. The British press denounced the indirect claims, and American newspapers deplored "British hypocrisy." Hindered by unwise laws designed to compel them to patronize American shipyards, American shippers had refused to rebuild the lost merchant marine. In the summer of 1868 Porter had written a magazine article advocating the abolition of these laws. It was a sensible article; and as a corollary to the merchant marine he called for a reformation of the Navy. "The millions we have spent," he declared, "have produced nothing in the shape of a navy with which we could assert the rights that have been violated by England—the nation which helped to drive our commerce from the ocean. . . . Let us husband our resources, build up an army and a navy, and then our motto may be *nemo me impune lacessit.*" [5]

The coming of General Grant to the Presidency after the pacific regime of Andrew Johnson was interpreted by many in the spring of 1869 to be a resurgence of America's military spirit; and Porter's work in the Navy Department did, in all probability, exert an influence on the diplomats who were soon to negotiate a peaceful settlement of the *Alabama* claims.

The Welles regime had not only decommissioned many blockaders but had allowed the ironclad fleet to deteriorate. In 1865 America had had the largest ironclad fleet in the world, and the practicability even of the double-turreted monitor in the open sea had been demonstrated in 1866 when Gustavus Fox had taken the *Miantonomah* to Russia. In the last four years America had allowed her ironclads to rust; while both England and France, profiting by America's costly experiments, had pushed ahead. To get the navy yards in shape for a building program was the first task Porter attempted. He ordered a board of admirals to survey the yards. He ordered existing vessels to be refitted for immediate duty overseas. There were not enough suitable ships in readiness to relieve the flagships at that time on foreign stations.

During the last four years Mr. Welles had given over so much of his authority to the various bureaus that the unity of the Department had been to a large extent destroyed. His office had become a honeycomb of bureaus, each acting as a separate organization rather than as a part of the centralized naval authority. The bureaus had extended their authority down through all gradations and branches of the service, not only at Washington but everywhere in the yards and on the vessels themselves. It had come to be the practice for bureau officials on ships and yards to send their reports not through their immediate superiors, the captains and commandants, but direct to the bureau concerned. Porter ordered the signs that had been posted in navy yards indicating the bureau to which different subdivisions belonged to be replaced with simple signs—"Medical Office," "Navigation Office," "Office of Docks and Yards," etc., and he ordered the officials of these subdivisions *to report to the Department via their commanding officers.*[6]

The process of abolishing the cellular formation of the Department and restoring its former unity was by no means easy. Mr. Isherwood, the talented and distinguished head of the Steam Bureau, lost his job. One after another the other heads of bureaus were shifted to other duties. Politicians interceded, but Porter hung a sign outside the Secretary's door warning office seekers and their political friends not to enter. He issued general orders forbidding anyone connected with the Navy to discuss politics or bring political pressure to bear on the Secretary. "All such applications must be made direct to the Secretary of the Navy, who is supposed to be the best judge . . ."[7]

With iron determination Porter set out to brighten the discipline of the service. He tackled the question of the relative rank of line and staff officers, which had troubled Mr. Welles and was destined to harass Mr. Borie until he resigned at the end of four months and would continue to harass every succeeding Secretary of the Navy after Borie down to the year 1926. In the pre-Civil War Navy, surgeons, paymasters and engineers—the noncombatant staff group—were simply called Surgeon, Paymaster, or Engineer of the Navy. Promotions for officers of the line were provided for by law in the second year of the war, but promotions for staff officers lagged until 1863, when Secretary Welles arbitrarily decreed that staff officers might rank with line officers after fewer years of service. The constitutionality of Welles's departmental executive order had been upheld by Attorney General Bates, but line officers were dissatisfied.

On March 9, when Porter and Borie entered the Department, an instance existed on board the U. S. S. *Franklin* which illustrated the complaint of the line officers. The *Franklin's* surgeon, paymaster, and engineer all had the rank of captain, the two former taking precedence over the line-officer captain commanding the ship. The commanding officer had 20 years of sea service to his credit, the surgeon 12, the paymaster 12, and the engineer 8. On March 10 this condition so vexing to the maintenance of discipline was changed by Secretary Borie. General Order No. 89 specified that "Commanding and executive officers, ashore and afloat, will take precedence over all staff officers." On the eleventh an order provided that hereafter staff officers of the various corps should remove part of the gold lace from their sleeves and substitute stripes of colored velvet which would serve to identify them. The new distinguishing stripe for medical officers was of cobalt blue; for paymasters, white; for engineers, red. In order to make this change as inconspicuous as possible, a change in the uniforms of both line and staff was ordered. Uniforms had been changed several times since 1860, with the creation of new grades, and Porter's war letters testify that he had been personally irked by the lavish outlay of gold braid. Rear Admiral Ammen had satirized Secretary Welles's taste in matters of uniform in an anonymous letter to the *Army and Navy Journal* in 1866, by saying that the stripes around an admiral's arm were so numerous as to "remind one of a barber's pole."

The attempt to cover the demotion of the staff, however, was unsuccessful. The staff took their grievances to politicians and newspaper editors. Horace Greeley of the *Tribune* became a powerful mouthpiece for the malcontents.

When Senator Grimes introduced the Porter-Borie bill for the reorganization of the Navy, which provided for a Board of Survey composed of admirals who would give technical advice to the Secretary, as well as providing for the rank of staff officers within their own corps, and assimilating rank as in the British Navy "with but after" the line, Greeley led the attack for the staff corps. "Old Salts" of the line, Porter in particular, were denounced as withholding from the staff their honest due. Line officers were "un-American and aristocratic," affecting to regard the staff as "an inferior race of beings, holding a nondescript position between the able-bodied seamen and landlubbers." The provisions of the Grimes bill, the *Tribune* alleged, would make assistant surgeons, assistant paymasters, and assistant engineers— all capable men who, "unlike the line paid for their own education"—"take rank below the chubby little ensign who just came out of school yesterday." Admiral Porter rated the staff as "rather less than gentlemen and a little better than boatswains." Good men, it was declared, would be driven out of the service and shiftless mediocrites would take their places.

The Navy Department replied to Greeley through the *Army and Navy Journal:* "In a recent editorial article, the public was informed that (according to the provision of the Grimes bill) the surgeon was not permitted to come on the quarter-deck unless a line officer was sick; and we are also treated to a long rigmarole of such stuff, which made every intelligent staff officer blush for the advocate of his side of the question . . . The *Tribune* constantly holds up the line officers as an aristocracy, and prates of their 'shining' presence and 'awful' dignity, in which no staff officer can appear without feeling an uncomfortable sense of inferiority . . . Under our form of government, honorary rank and titles are ignored, as opposed to Republicanism. Military and naval rank are conferred not as personal distinctions, but simply to signify command, and the nature of such command . . ." In the arguments of both sides the question of discipline and the question of reward for distinguished service became much confused.

Porter had hoped to rush the Grimes bill through Congress to secure immediate action on what he considered the larger issue—the creation of a Board of Survey, which in effect would have operated like the Board of Navy Commissioners in his father's day. Grimes put it through the Senate without reference to the Naval Committee, but in the House it was blocked on the floor. Porter and Borie, appearing before the House Naval Committee, presented a letter from Grant urging speedy action; but the entire measure was defeated by the inclusion of the relative rank clause. Congress laid the bill on the table and adjourned until December, and Senator Grimes took a boat to Europe.

Thus far the reformation of the Navy Department had infuriated ex-Secretary Welles, the dismissed heads of bureaus, the surgeons, paymasters, and engineers of the Navy, a few politicians, and Mr. Greeley of the *Tribune*. Porter's next move affected all the workers of the navy yards and scores of Congressmen whose rights of patronage were violated.

Porter wanted to push repair work in the yards, and he was handicapped for money. During the previous administration the workers in the navy yards had been brought under the eight-hour law and their pay had remained the same as they had formerly received for ten hours of work. From the new Attorney General, Mr. Hoar, Porter obtained the opinion that the Navy under the law could not compel workers to labor more than eight hours, but that the law did not require the Department to pay more than eight-tenths of what had formerly been paid for ten hours. Mr. Borie issued an order based on the new Attorney General's decision, and was immediately waited upon by General Banks, the author of the eight-hour law. Mr. Borie replied that, if Congress wanted the Secretary to pay full wages for eight hours, Congress would have to specify this. Congress had now adjourned. Delegations of navy yard workers applied for relief to their Congressmen, and Congressmen brought pressure to bear on President Grant. It was an embarrassing moment for Grant, since politicians were already disgruntled over the administration's system of nepotism. The *Army and Navy Journal* suggested "they thought they would be able to grind their axes, but they are distressed because the noise of grinding is so low."

Finally on May 22 Grant yielded to the pressure and reversed the Navy Department's decision. It was a blow to Vice Admiral Porter, but one that could not well have been avoided. To show that his sympathies were still with the Admiral, however, the President three days later became Porter's guest at Annapolis for a merry round of entertainment and a ball that lasted until 3 o'clock in the morning.

Opposition to the Porter-Borie regime had now become nation-wide. Many minor acts of the administration were singled out for censure. Porter had reversed the decision of a court-martial on his nephew, Lieutenant-Commander George M. Bache, who had been navigating officer on the U. S. S. *Sacramento* when that vessel went aground on a reef in the Indian Ocean. The captain of the vessel had been playing chess at the time of the disaster, Bache peacefully smoking his pipe forward of the chicken coops. Secretary Welles had administered a public reprimand to Bache. In spite of the fact that the Judge Advocate in the case upheld

Porter for reversing the decision again Bache, the press raised a cry against Porter; but Grant endorsed his action.

Another troublesome matter for Porter was the changing of ships' names. Ships named for moderately well-known Indian tribes, and ships that had become famous during the war were not affected. To find Indian names for a large number of ships Mr. Welles had thumbed through the whole of the post-route directory and had chosen such names as *Tunxis, Umpqua, Suncook, Wassuc, Naubuc, Squando, Wissahickon.* Unable to pronounce many of these names of the "root-digger" Indians, sailors had applied to them a sort of Billy Bowlegs nomenclature that was not flattering to the service. "Imagine a sailor joining a ship called Sassy-cuss, Shacky-macks-on, Am-I-a-noo-sucker, Countycook, Sun-of-a-cook, My-aunt-dont-know-me, Mush-I-loose, or Pompey's-noo-suck," derided the *Army and Navy Journal.* Of the unusual names in this list—*Sassacus, Shakamaxon, Ammonoosuc, Contoo-cook, Suncook, Miantonomah, Mosholu,* and *Pompanoosuc*—several were too famous to admit of change. Porter changed the names of the bomb vessels *Etlah, Klamath,* and *Koka* to *Aetna, Vesuvius,* and *Stromboli,* believing the latter more appropriate "from the fact that they will pour out metaphorical lava on the heads of any indiscreet Britishers that may approach too near them." The legislature of New Hampshire arose to denounce these innovations as "heathen." The *Journal* supported Porter, "but there's something appropriate in the idea of the U. S. S. *Niobe* shedding a fifteen-inch tear into H. M. S. *Latona.* Hardly appropriate to name a monitor for one of the prophets, better the heathen gods." The controversy over nomenclature persisted until the next Secretary effected a compromise.

By the middle of April, affable, peace-loving Secretary Borie had had enough of his job. He told a delegation of Pennsylvanians who came to congratulate him on his appointment that his health might soon require him to retire. When Porter offered to resign to save Mr. Borie's political career, the Secretary not only refused to permit this but issued an order authorizing Porter to sign orders for the Secretary, a novel procedure which provoked further opposition to Porter.

Throughout the reformation in the Navy Department Porter had continued living in Annapolis and commuting to Washington. On June 4, the graduation day, the officers and midshipmen of the Academy gave an elaborate farewell ball in honor of Mrs. Admiral Porter.[8]

This was one of the most colorful social events in the history of Annapolis since colonial times. Nearly 4,000 persons came from New York, Philadelphia, Baltimore, and Washington. At 9 A.M. the steamer *Tallapoosa* arrived from Washington having on board President Grant; the Honorable J. A. Creswell, Postmaster General; the Honorable J. D. Cox, Secretary of the Interior; the Honorable E. R. Hoar, Attorney General; the Honorable J. C. B. Davis, Assistant Secretary of State; Mr. Thornton, the British Minister; together with many ladies of their households. Salutes of twenty-one guns were fired from all the men-of-war in Annapolis Roads. After President Grant had delivered diplomas to the graduating class, there were dress parades, crew races, mock aquatic tournaments. At 10 o'clock the grand ball began. In front of Fort Severn were brilliantly lighted pavilions. Avenues of light led to the two entrances. The façade of the new, three-story, brick dormitory for midshipmen was bedecked with Chinese lanterns, while a calcium light, such as the Confederates had used to light the scene at the passage of Vicksburg, flared from its tower. The Marine Band from Washington provided music in the yard. The Naval Academy Band furnished "inimitable" dance music. Around the highly polished dance floor the walls were ornamented with muskets, swords, flags. There were "spooney corners" with mottoes "Beware, Beware, She's Fooling Thee," "Who Enters Here Leaves Hope Behind."

At 10 o'clock the quadrille was led off by President Grant and Mrs. Porter; then came Secretary Borie and Miss Sherman, the Postmaster General and Miss Minnie Sherman, General Sherman and Miss Borie, Vice Admiral Porter and Mrs. Grant. The event was covered by many reporters, and what they saw depended largely upon the editorial policies of their respective papers. There was glamour and hero worship. There was cynicism. For Mr. Borie the event was as tragic as it was colorful; in one of the dances the Secretary slipped and fell. The incident was suppressed in all but one of the newspapers.[9] The dancing went on through the "German," and ended at 2 A.M. But Secretary Borie was deeply mortified, and a few days later he resigned his Secretaryship and returned home to Philadelphia.

The new Secretary, Mr. George Robeson, gradually eased Vice Admiral Porter from his exceptional position in the Department; and in the following year, after Farragut's death had left vacant the office of Admiral of the Navy, the new Secretary assumed a neutral position on the question of Porter's elevation to Admiral. The host of enemies that Porter had made during his four months as actual head of the Navy would seriously affect his chances of becoming Admiral Farragut's successor in the highest position the Navy had to offer.

THE GRANT-PORTER IMBROGLIO

ON Sunday August 14, 1870, Admiral Farragut died of paralysis at the home of his relative Commodore A. M. Pennock at the Portsmouth, New Hampshire, Navy Yard. Admiral Farragut had found the controversies of the Porter-Borie regime vexing. Deploring the changes made in his uniform and flag, he had objected to the new insignia of rank and the Department had authorized him to continue wearing the old one which he had himself designed in 1866 when the office of Admiral was created, although his illness had prevented his calling the attention of the Department to his flag.

The appointment of Porter to succeed Farragut was, in the opinion of the *Army and Navy Journal,* "a foregone conclusion." A month after Farragut's death President Grant issued to Porter his commission as Admiral, subject to confirmation by the Senate. But the forces whom Porter had antagonized now endeavored to defeat his confirmation.

The attack on Porter was led by ex-Secretary Welles. In the November issue of the *Galaxy* magazine Mr. Welles exposed the machinations of Seward, Meigs, and Porter which in April 1861 had diverted the *Powhatan* from the Fort Sumter expedition to the relief of Fort Pickens. The ex-Secretary presented a cogent array of evidence which would have damaged Porter before any jury had not the attendant circumstances been explained. General Meigs offered a rebuttal through the pages of the *Journal,* and Porter too refuted certain of Mr. Welles's interpretations.

The *Journal* claimed a victory for Porter. "His name is now presented to the Senate for confirmation to the highest grade, with an assent so general that his enemies can only hope to defeat his appointment by abolishing the grade of Admiral altogether." It was rumored that certain Congressmen would attempt to do just this. It was whispered that one of Porter's enemies was in possession of a letter which he had written to Secretary Welles con-

demning General Grant, and planned to publish it. A Congressman friendly to the Admiral offered to take up the cudgels for him
against his old enemy General Butler, who was leading the opposition to his appointment in the House. Porter declined the offer
and refused to believe that such a letter as the one hinted about
was in existence. But the rumor and the whisper both proved to
be well founded.

On December 2 the New York *Sun* and the *World* published
the attack on General Grant which Porter had written Welles
during the let-down after Fort Fisher, when the heat of battle had
given way to bitter rumination over the failure of Butler to cooperate. Grant's alleged culpability for having allowed Butler
to accompany the first expedition was depicted in Porter's most
trenchant style. Porter had jumped to his conclusions on the evidence in hand without stopping to consider that there might be
evidence which he did not have. The best that can be said for
this letter is that it was marked "private." Inasmuch as the temporary misunderstanding had been cleared up by the time it
arrived, Mr. Welles might well have destroyed this letter; but instead he had made a copy of it in his personal letter book, and
placed the original on file in the Department, where Porter's
enemies might—and did—find it.

When President Grant read the damaging epistle written by a
man he had considered his friend he became terribly depressed.

The publication of the unfortunate letter was condemned generally by most of the newspapers. The New York *Times* denounced it as "a morbid desire for making mischief and creating
bad blood, by opening anew for gossip and comment a condition
of circumstances that were long since modified, explained and
buried." The *Times* laid responsibility for the act at the door of
Mr. Welles. It was true that Mr. Welles had a "penchant for scandal which seemed to increase with age," and that he had shown his
copy of this letter to Governor Hawley, a friend of the Admiral's.
But a later investigation fixed the guilt upon a subordinate in the
Department who had had access to the files.

Naturally Porter was even more distressed than President
Grant. He admitted the genuineness of the letter and publicly
condemned himself for having written it. For years the Fort
Fisher episode had been explained and his relation with General
Grant had been one of friendship. There was little Porter could
do to recover Grant's friendship, and what he could do he did.
He turned over his war journal to the correspondent of the

Herald, who published excerpts to reveal the Admiral's real feelings toward the General both before and after the letter to Welles was written. Porter called immediately at the White House to explain, but Grant had not yet recovered from the shock and the interview was painful. On December 3 Porter wrote Grant a long and dignified letter accepting all blame and urging him to consider their relationship in recent years as the best refutation of the letter he had written while under a wrong impression. This was published and hailed by the papers as an appropriate and manly *amende honorable.*

Porter's friends came to his assistance. From Philadelphia his friend ex-Secretary Borie wrote consolingly that "I heard the President himself say just after reading your letter to Welles, 'the greatest naval officer in this country and perhaps in any other.'" [1] Grant told Porter's friend, General Beale, that he harbored no ill will toward the Admiral. Beale wanted him to extend Porter an invitation to come and see him again. Grant said, "No, I will stop in there myself some of these days."

Beale asked, "Can I tell the Admiral that?"

"Certainly," said Grant.

Within a week after the unfortunate publication, the New York *Herald* announced that "The Grant-Porter Imbroglio...soon lost the fictitious importance that was attached to it at first."

During the imbroglio Porter suffered an attack of pleurisy. He had recovered by December 23, and apparently regarded the incident as closed. On December 23 he wrote Admiral Turner at Philadelphia, apropos of a similar gossip started about the relations of Turner and the late Admiral Farragut: "As the atmosphere seems to be full of an epidemic of bringing to light people's letters, I might as well tell you all I know of this matter now, and then let it be forever forgotten. A few months after Farragut's return from California, and after his first great sickness, he became very much exercised in mind about a forgery of his name that he asserted had been committed by Paymaster Looker of the Navy, and he wrote several communications to the Department showing in his weak condition evidently a great deal of distress of mind. He also demanded to see a letter which you wrote about him from California. The Secretary...sent an officer to see him and show him your [Turner's] letter, so he wouldn't have a copy of it. Of course the Admiral was rather indignant when he read the letter and gave utterance to some little expletives not used in saintly places. He then produced a letter which he said he had received from you after a visit you had made to the Naval Academy and read it to the officer, offering to give him a copy to bring to me. The letter was not very complimentary to myself and was somewhat in the style of the unfortunate one I wrote about General Grant. The officer declined bringing me a copy until he could consult with me. When the officer returned to Washington and asked me if he should write Farragut for a copy I laughed and said 'No, I don't want to see it. Turner likely had the dyspepsia when he wrote it and a man is not responsible for what he says when his stomach is out of order. Besides,' I said, 'Turner and I are good friends now and I care nothing about it. Navy officers will talk of each other and don't mean half they say. I never want to hear any more about it'...It never made a particle of difference in my feelings toward you ... Old Gardner I am told, who was always officious, had got hold of the letters and was about to publish them when God Almighty 'shuffled off his mortal coil.' I am sorry for Gardner's death but at the same time I am better pleased than if he had lived to publish the letters. Why some people take a devilish pleasure in sowing dissension among friends I cannot imagine ... You refer in your letter to a little misunderstanding that occurred between us some years ago ... As the whole affair grew out of a foolish sensitiveness on my part you were not to blame in the matter. I had forgotten the thing entirely until you referred to it, and I never had an unkind feeling toward you in my life. I suppose some of those letters will be raked up by some fool and I think you had better get hold of them and burn them. There are some navy officers who are delighted with these little exposés. They call them the 'lights of history.' There now. I have said all that can be said about this and when you come to Washington come to see me and we will laugh at it over a glass of good sherry old Lanman sent me after blowing him up in a dispatch, showing that he did not harbor animosity." [2]

The Grant-Porter imbroglio was but trifling compared with the attack on the floor of the House; where, since Grant declined to withdraw Porter's nomination, a motion was made to abolish the grade of Admiral, and thereby defeat Porter's confirmation. This motion was championed by General Benjamin F. Butler himself, and on this familiar battleground the General's tactics were brilliant, cunning, unscrupulous.

Butler's strategy was to lower Porter's prestige by raising that of the late Admiral Farragut. The circumstances surrounding Farragut's last days, death, and funeral ceremonies did, indeed, lend a certain air of plausibility to General Butler's interpretations. The private funeral in Portsmouth in August was out of proportion to the honors the country ought to have bestowed on Farragut. The newspapers of the country had commented so severely upon its inadequacy that elaborate obsequies in New York had been carried through on September 29. Torrential rains had drenched and saddened the final procession. The President and many of his cabinet had moved in the procession. Admiral Porter, ill at the time, was absent. It was well known in the navy that Farragut had been disappointed with his position as Admiral, and had rightly felt that his promotion had placed him "on the shelf." Newspapers after his death had sentimentalized this neglect of Farragut by the Department.

While the Grant-Porter affair was at its height General Butler arose on the floor of the House and proclaimed that "the brave, frank, open-hearted sailor who had just died (Admiral Farragut) had with his dying lips said to his attendants, 'Never raise that flag over me, nor carry it before my coffin—that flag which has been imposed upon me by the man who expects to become my successor!'" [3]

The effect of this speech was immediate. Within the next ten days Porter's nomination—favorably reported upon by the Senate committee—was twice discussed on the floor of the Senate without result. On December 17 the *Army and Navy Journal* reported that the matter remained *in statu quo*.

Porter worried. In his letter book was a copy of a letter he had written to Commodore Pennock on August 12, when he learned of Farragut's probably fatal illness, in which Porter had expressed sympathy for Mrs. Farragut and hope that the Admiral might yet recover. "He has conferred great fame upon the Navy and we cannot do him too much honor ... I am still in hopes his attack may pass off, though he would still have a continuation of his sufferings ..." It would have been fatuous to have published this letter. Porter scanned the papers anxiously, hoping that someone would refute General Butler's charge. Day after day the coveted statement failed to appear. On December 19 Porter's impatience overcame him and he wrote Pennock, "If Admiral Farragut ever uttered such words, they dim the reputation he so fairly earned, for as you well know I was his best friend and warmest supporter from the time he first assumed command at the outbreak of the Rebellion until his death. I would have preferred that the denial of the speech imputed to Admiral Farragut

should have come from you without any suggestion of mine . . .
The silence of those who were about the Admiral's bedside concerning the truth of General Butler's remarks gives some founda-
tion for the report that Farragut had used those words, although
perhaps the best proof that he made use of no such expressions
is to be found in Butler's statement that he did . . ." [4]

Meanwhile an explanation of Farragut's difficulties over his
flag, written by "an ex-officer of the Navy," appeared in the *Herald*
and was quoted (on December 17) by the *Journal*. "The commanding officer of a squadron carries what is called a broad pennant, or flag especially denoting his rank. The pennant is carried
at the masthead; and when Admiral Farragut was engaged at
Mobile and below New Orleans the flag he carried as commander of the fleet was one with a blue field and four white stars.
While at the island of Minorca, on board the *Franklin*, he was
shown a book describing the ensign carried by his ancestor, Sir
Pedro Farragut, in the eleventh century, at that time being governor of Aragon. Strange to say the flags were similar, with the
addition in the Spanish flag of a horseshoe with one nail in it.
When Commodore James Alden was placed at the head of the
Bureau of Navigation, he changed the pennant of the Admiral
to one of similar dimensions, having alternate red and white
stripes. This was done entirely without the wish of Admiral
Porter, who is in no way responsible for the change. Commodore Alden has at different times stated that it was made
in accordance with his [Farragut's] own wish. Further than this,
Admiral Farragut's friends here assert that, while he regretted the
change, and probably would have taken steps in regard to it
had he lived, he did not attribute that change to Admiral Porter, nor did he ever use the last nine words of the sentence quoted
by General Butler. The question of whether Admiral Porter is
or is not fitted for the position of Admiral it is not my intention
to discuss; but his gallantry and devotion to our country at all
events demand that we do not, without the most incontrovertible
evidence, allow a man well known to have been his [Porter's]
enemy to place in the mouth of the honored dead words which
are calculated to throw discredit on his services."

On December 21 Commodore Pennock replied to Porter's inquiry. He had not written earlier because he was waiting for the
return of Farragut's son in order to get his testimony also. Neither
Pennock, nor the deceased Admiral's son, nor any of the officers on
the station had ever heard Farragut utter anything like the re-

marks attributed to him by General Butler. They had all of them been "constantly at his bedside."

Pennock's evidence probably would not now have erased the legend propagated by General Butler even if Porter had published it. Porter was content merely to have the proof in his possession as a piece of tangible evidence to show friends.

During the Christmas and New Year recess General Butler circulated a rumor that he had in his possession a letter of Porter's about Farragut similar to the scurrilous one Porter had written about Grant. This was an old trick, and one that had been recently used; but it would serve as a reminder of the Grant-Porter imbroglio, and might, Butler evidently hoped, serve to bring to light another rash Porter letter.

New letters, however, failed to appear, and Ben Butler was forced to resort to another subterfuge. On January 12—the day before the confirmation was to be brought up in a secret executive session in the Senate—Butler caused to be published in the Washington *Daily National Republican* an anonymous letter which, it was announced, "came into the hands of General Butler, who gave it to the public lest some one might suppose that he would be swerved in his execution of public duty by threats of slanders, which, if true, can be investigated." The anonymous epistle began, "The Admiral has heard that a letter is said to be in hands hostile to him, purporting to have been written by him to Admiral Farragut, assailing General Grant..."

There followed a remarkable list of accusations which "P." threatened to prove against "B." if the letter were made public; though "P." stoutly asserted that the letter was false, he cringingly implored "B." not to make it public, and threatened, if he did to prove the enclosed charges against "B." The style of the letter was a neat imitation of Porter's, even to errors in punctuation and grammar.

On the afternoon of January 13 at 1 o'clock the Senate locked its doors, and the question of the confirmation was fought out in secret session. The opposition, reported the *Journal,* "was active and vigorous, but the fact that other nominations were dependent on this, and the position in which the Acting Admiral would be thrown by a rejection of his appointment, helped to carry the day in his favor. The wiser judgment of the Senate prevailed over the prejudices of the moment." The vote was 31 to 10 in favor of Porter.

That evening the new Admiral of the Navy received the congratulations of his friends at his residence, 1710 H Street. Among his well-wishers were Governor Geary of Pennsylvania, Governor Newell of New Jersey, and a number of Senators and Representatives, as well as naval officers. The next day he suffered another attack of pleurisy and was bedfast for two days.

On the 19th he received his final commission as "Admiral of the Navy," to become second of the three American naval officers to receive the rank. King William of Prussia, who on this same day in the great *Salle des Glaces* in Versailles was crowned Emperor William I of Germany, was, indeed, no happier than David Dixon Porter.

32.

THE SECOND ADMIRAL

For twenty years the "Lord High Admiral of the U. S. Navy," as General Sherman affectionately nicknamed Porter, enjoyed his rank and the dignified comfort of his mansion at 1710 H Street, N. W. The austere, three-story brick and stone house represented the architectural fashion of the 1820's. Ivy vines ran up its granite corners, spread over its plain brick walls around gothic windows and up to the tessellated cornices. On the inside it was comfortable and roomy. The kitchen, always an important room in the Porter household, was located in the basement as in other Washington homes of the day, but was light and airy for the lot sloped to the rear. On the ground floor on one side of the winding central staircase was a ballroom forty-two by twenty-six feet, on the other a dining room behind which was a small drawing-room with a southern exposure. On the second and third floors were the bedrooms. On the third floor was the Admiral's study. The study was paneled in walnut. Low bookshelves ran completely around the walls. Above the shelves the walls were arrayed with swords and cutlasses, reminiscent of Commodore Porter's study at Meridian Hill. There were models of torpedoes and torpedo boats. Above the small fireplace was an autograph of Lord Nelson framed in wood from the *Victory*. In a near-by frame was the last letter written by Admiral Farragut. Three large tables in the center of the room held one of the new typewriting machines and a comfortable litter of reference books and papers to remind the Admiral of his gala days on the *Black Hawk*. Under one of the windows was a tall desk at which the Admiral usually stood to do his writing.[1]

In the early days Number 1710 H Street had been occupied by Secretary of State Joel R. Poinsett, whom Porter remembered as American Minister to Mexico in the days before the *Guerrero-Lealtad* battle. During the Civil War it had housed Lord Lyons and the British Embassy. In 1869 Porter purchased it with $95,000 of his Civil War prize money, and after his promotion to Admiral of the Navy found it the most convenient location in Washington. It stood next door to the convivial Metropolitan Club, of which Porter was a member, within a stone's throw of the White House, and but five minutes' walk from the Navy Department.

Like Meridian Hill, 1710 H Street became a mecca for politicians and naval officers. Porter kept his pantry stocked with fine wines. Hard liquor came into the house a bottle at a time, but frequently, the merchant carefully itemizing "March 31— 1 bottle whiskey; April 1—1 gal. syrup, 1 bottle whiskey; April 8— 1 bottle whiskey; April 18—1 bottle whiskey . . ." [2]

Porter often declared that a good dinner and a glass of champagne was a passport to the heart of any sensible gentleman. His own stomach he had punished with rich foods during the war— when he had considered generous living the only means of keeping fit for his enormous labors—so that he was now compelled to eat sparingly. In spite of her own increasing invalidism Mrs. Porter set a more extravagant table than ever. Prairie hens, eggs, robins, canvasback ducks, steaks, chops, cutlets, mackerel, rockfish, lobsters, sausage, tongue, all manner of fruits and vegetables, cakes, and gallons of ice cream were included in Mrs. Porter's menus for a single week.

In the fall of 1871 the Admiral's aged mother died in Chester, and Porter carried her remains to Woodlawn Cemetery in Philadelphia for burial beside the Commodore. During the seventies Lieutenant Theodoric Porter married Bettie Mason of Annapolis; Elizabeth married Lieutenant Leavitt C. Logan of the Navy; Lieutenant Carlisle Porter of the Marine Corps married Carrie Catron; David Essex Porter married Lily Abert, daughter of General Abert. Soon there were grandchildren with curly brown hair and dancing eyes visiting at 1710 H Street. The Admiral fondled them; and, when they pattered upstairs on all fours, the Admiral admitted them to his study, where he carried them on his shoulder and danced them on his knee.

Civil War prize money continued to flow into Admiral Porter's coffers during the seventies, supplementing his $13,000 salary. He was able to afford summer homes at Narragansett Pier and Perth Amboy, and to spend a considerable time away from Washington in search of health at resorts in Virginia, Maryland, and Pennsylvania.

His duties as Admiral required him to make frequent trips to inspect the navy yards on the Atlantic Coast, to supervise the trials of new vessels constructed for the Navy, to aid the Secretary with professional advice and make annual reports on the state of the Navy. Since the war, naval expenditures had steadily declined, and after 1870 the annual appropriation dropped to less than $20,000,000. To keep ships in operation on low cost Porter advocated the continuance of masts and sails on steam vessels of all types. To enable these clumsy craft to function as rams Porter invented a bowsprit which could be removed in half an hour. He advocated elaborate drills in shipping and unshipping masts and spars. He advocated the use of steam capstans on all ships. He invented lifeboats and life rafts. He invented torpedo vessels equipped with spar torpedoes similar to the one Cushing had used to sink the *Albemarle,* but so rigged as to be operated mechanically. His masterpiece was the torpedo boat *Alarm,* which was equipped throughout with devices operated by electricity.

In 1874 when Spanish officials summarily shot a number of American adventurers filibustering in the interests of Cuban independence, Porter was offered command of the squadron in the event of war. But the war was postponed, and the second Admiral like the first was doomed to end his days in inactive life ashore. After much effort he collected funds and erected at the foot of Capitol Hill on Pennsylvania Avenue the monument to seamen killed during the war. He helped to erect the Farragut statue in Washington.

In the scandals of Grant's administration the Navy Department did not escape investigation. When Secretary Robeson's dealings in the matter of the Delaware-Chesapeake Canal were investigated in 1876 the Admiral was for some weeks too ill to testify. He did not want to testify, for he felt that the Secretary's dealings had not been above question. However, when Robeson's friends rumored that Porter might be culpably involved, he had no other alternative than to appear before the committee. He tried, he said, to let Robeson off as lightly as possible. But the newspapers hailed his testimony as a frank and honest exposé of the Secretary, and this brought down on Porter the antagonism of the Secretary.

On August 10, 1876, when Secretary Robeson placed Porter on "waiting orders"—which would have reduced the Admiral's pay from $13,000 to $8,000—Porter considered it an act of reprisal and immediately took his case to the President. His old friend General Sherman interceded with Grant. Grant told Sherman that he would "stretch his authority to the limit," and Porter was given active duty. From Sherman, Porter also heard that Secretary Robeson was resisting the distribution of Civil War prize money in a certain case because Porter "gets the lion's share." Whether or not this charge—which was told Sherman by Judge Taft—was justified is not known. The whole question of naval prize money was very involved.

Because of Robeson's opposition Porter went less often to the Department, and turned to writing. His first work, a *Memoir of Commodore David Porter,* is his best. The *Memoir,* which he published in 1875, was the first full-length portrait of his father. It is full of anecdote and controversy. Like all of Porter's historical works it is chiefly a feat of memory, and subject to the usual deficiencies of such writing. The *Memoir* is, however, a spirited narrative—the only published work which gives a comprehensive account of the Commodore's (and Porter's own) experiences in the Mexican Navy. The *Memoir* achieved considerable success and is largely responsible for the legendary fame which surrounds the elder Porter. Its chief defect is its propaganda. The *Memoir* abounds with expressions of the anti-British feelings of the Post-Civil War Era and with arguments favoring a larger Navy. Porter seems to have had certain qualms of conscience over the amount of propaganda injected into this work. His friend and literary adviser, John S. Barnes, wrote him, "Where you don't want to say anything, make the Commodore say it . . . He had cause and reason for saying a great many things and so far as I can judge, he said them, as you do, very emphatically." Porter, however, did not disguise the propaganda with quotation marks but wrote it out boldly as the sentiments of the author. Far too much of the Commodore's portrait is a likeness of the son. A true romanticist, the author beheld in the tribulations of his subject too many parallels in his own career.

After the *Memoir* came a torrent of fiction—*Arthur Merton, The Adventures of Harry Marline,* the two-volume *Allan Dare and Robert Le Diable.* Imitations of Marryat, filled with reminiscences of the sea, hodgepodges of sentiment and ludicrousness, utterly chaotic in form and substance, they had no other recommendation than the author's famous name. Porter paid a fifth-rate San Francisco playwright $500 to cut-and-paste a drama out of *Allan Dare.* The première of the play in New York was a gala event. Admiral Porter, Mrs. Porter, and General Sherman occupied one of the boxes; and in an intermission between acts the audience cheered the venerable author.

"The Admiral handles fate like an old Aeschylus," proclaimed one critic. The play ran for two weeks in New York and then toured the country, but did not boost the sales of the novel. *Allan Dare* took its publishers far down in the red, and did not even pay the type-setting bill.

Civil War reminiscences both Union and Confederate, were popular during the seventies and eighties. The autobiography of the "ex-pirate," Raphael Semmes, provoked one of the loudest discussions in the North. William Tecumseh Sherman's *Memoirs*, angrily read throughout the South, brought its author a fortune.

In 1885 Porter published his *Incidents and Anecdotes of the Civil War* which was not the conventional postwar autobiography but a delightful joke book in which he was an important figure. It was not filled with self-justification nor the prejudices of wartime. The old animosities cropped out, of course; but Porter treated them lightly or impartially. *Incidents and Anecdotes* mentioned many dignified personages of history, but the incidents were allowed to appear only in anecdotal dress. Serious-minded participants in the struggle saw themselves wearing comic masks, furiously and energetically enacting scenes of an *opéra bouffe* war not unlike the Civil War. Banks, McClernand, and Butler were portrayed, but no more harshly than the Admiral.

The Admiral himself was permitted to carry on flirtations with pretty Southern ladies who posed as Unionists to save their cotton—incidents which were not wholly denied the Admiral in real life, but which in the joke book were much exaggerated and more pleasant.

In the *Incidents and Anecdotes* the author made many honest confessions. Porter's attitude toward the South had become one of sympathetic understanding. The South had suffered many just grievances—at the hands of its own politicians as well as of the abolitionists of the North. They had fought a brave and gallant fight against heavy odds and had nobly lost. He felt that it would be better to deal with such things by way of jest because the animosities engendered on both sides had been already too much exaggerated.

There were, naturally, many military morals to be drawn from the struggle. Civilian generals with Presidential ambitions ought never to have been allowed to command armies.

But even this was lightly managed in a burst of doggerel:

Now all you old fellows who have studied the laws,
Who make a good living by quibbles and flaws,
Who ne'er had a gun or a sword in your paws,
 Deceiving whose trade is,
 Old men and old ladies,
Don't mount heavy boots and a long 'yaller sash,'
Or expose your rich coat, or bright *sabretasche*
In battle or skirmish, or where there's a chance
Of a shot from a pistol or a poke from a lance.
Be wise, stay at home, read Blackstone and Wheaton,
And study Coke's tactics, where you can not be beaten.[3]

In 1886 Porter took leave of fiction and autobiographical fiction and published his most ambitious volume, *The Naval History of the Civil War*. He made an honest effort to deal fairly with his subject; but the task was beyond the scope even of professional historians of his day. Porter had the files of the Navy Department at his disposal, but the impetuous Admiral, who "wrote more in three months than any ordinary writer would do in a year," preferred to resort to memory rather than labor through the mountains of documents in the Navy Department. His desire to deal fairly is evident from the many things he wrote derogatory to himself in the chapters on the Red River campaign.

More serious than the faults of memory were the fallacies the aging Admiral fell into. "No naval officer during the war would have dared to write anything in his official reports that was not strictly correct, for there were too many witnesses (and interested ones) who would not have hesitated to impeach the veracity of any officer who made anything but a proper report." [4]

The Admiral had forgotten, or ignored, the fact that he had himself many times written but a part of the truth in his official dispatches; that such was a common practice in view of the fact that the Secretary was expected to make official dispatches public; that he had himself in the Red River fiasco followed up his incomplete official dispatches by confidential ones to the Secretary and private, personal letters to the Assistant Secretary—three distinct categories of reports to tell the *complete* story of the episode. War conditions had rightly sanctioned this method as the most effective means of censoring an unlicensed press.

The Admiral's *Naval History* was unquestionably partisan. But it was certainly not more so than that of Mr. Boynton, written shortly after the war. Even the best history of the naval war, Maclay's, published in 1893, contained glaring inaccuracies.

In the latter eighties the Admiral's health failed rapidly. On March 10, 1889 the golden wedding anniversary of Admiral and Mrs. Porter marked the end of the gala social events at 1710 H Street. Many dignitaries attended this reception and listened to the Admiral declare that he was still a young man and good for another war. President Harrison, upon hearing that the Admiral and his lady while newly-weds nearly fifty years ago had attended the inauguration ball of his grandfather, President William Henry Harrison, broke a precedent and came to the golden wedding. The newspapers reported the golden wedding as the outstanding social occasion of the year. Many anecdotes of the second Admiral's career were recalled, and he was widely praised.

About a month after the golden wedding came the centennial of George Washington's inauguration as President,—a celebration which proved to have a curious aftermath for Admiral Porter. Assigned by the Department to the temporary command of the naval vessels in New York Harbor, he experienced from April 30 to May 2 his last command afloat. Newspapers were full of the Admiral's doings in the Civil War. A new generation had grown up since the war, and the achievements of the Hero of Fort Fisher once more became a topic of conversation. Unfortunately it was impossible to eulogize Porter without mentioning General Butler. And Butler's name provoked wrathy reminiscences both North and South. New Orleans again denounced "Beast Butler," and recalled the famous story that Butler had run off with the spoons of the St. Charles Hotel. Northerners, remembering the fiasco of the first attack on Fort Fisher, circulated anew the Butler ballads, wherein the "best hated general who ever lived" was made the scapegoat for many of the Federal defeats.

Vexed by this notoriety General Butler sought to divert the public's attention from Fort Fisher to New Orleans, where, he alleged, Admiral Porter had shown the white feather by running away from the forts!

Had the Admiral been a younger man, he might have ignored this preposterous charge. But Porter was now an old man, worn out by his immense labors; and a new generation unfamiliar with the war had arisen. At first Porter tried to laugh, but eventually the charge of cowardice got under his skin.

To prove his thesis Butler searched the Navy Department for the log of the *Harriet Lane,* and, failing to locate it, suggested that the Admiral might have removed it. News reporters questioned the Admiral, and Porter reminded them that the *Harriet Lane* had been captured by the Confederates at Galveston on January 1, 1863. The laugh was turned on Butler by the reporters. A cartoonist for the magazine *Judge* drew a cover design depicting the Admiral in full feather escorting the "widow" Butler through New Orleans. The widow's market basket was filled with spoons, and the dog tagging at her heels wore the face of Charles Dana of the New York *Sun*. There were many laughs.

The redoubtable Butler now published a pamphlet purporting to prove Admiral Porter's "cowardice and falsehood...from... Porter's own self-contradictions." [5] The substance of this leaflet was extracted from the Admiral's own joke book—the *Incidents and Anecdotes!*

When Porter became angry enough to declare that "Butler is a fool," the fight began in earnest, for Butler was as proud of his intellect as Porter was of his courage.

Sensational newspapers persisted in fanning the flames, and neither the General nor the Admiral tried to check them. The Boston *Globe* for May 8, 1889, reported: "The general looked well and was apparently not worried by the fight. He had a sprig of mignonette and a big rose in his buttonhole, and he chewed on his gum with great zest. Age had not blunted his combative qualities." Another interviewer recorded: "Admiral Porter himself looks vigorous and combative. Years do not appear to have robbed him of his love of fight. His full beard has in it more of brown than gray and his aquiline nose stands out between sharp black eyes that sparkle with animation as he talks. His manner is extremely pleasant and gracious. So full of gentleness is it that it is a surprise to those who know him well to read the violent language that has fallen from his lips concerning his present antagonist. It happened that while I was in his office, a little girl toddled up the steps from the domestic part of the house. 'Ah!' said the Admiral, leaning forward in his chair and holding out his arms, 'Here comes the little anti-Butler angel,' as he lifted the little curly-headed grandchild to his knees and caressed her tenderly. Then he sent her trotting away, and in another moment was striding up and down the floor of his library as if it were a quarter-deck, while a stream of violent language fell from his lips as he denounced Butler."

At length the maudlin aspect of the controversy began to pall. A cartoonist depicted "The Last Battle of the Late War," with

VOL. 16 NO. 396   MAY 18 1889   PRICE 10 CENTS

ENTERED AT THE POST OFFICE BY NEW YORK AS SECOND-CLASS MATTER,   COPYRIGHT 1889 BY THE JUDGE PUBLISHING CO.

THAT IRREPRESSIBLE WIDOW.

WIDOW BUTLER (*an envious old party*) — "You can't scare me with your bluster, Mister Admiral. Who ran away at New Orleans ?"
ADMIRAL PORTER — "Spoons!"

COVER DESIGN OF *Judge* AT THE HEIGHT OF THE PORTER-BUTLER FEUD.

Butler standing in a sewer bombarding the Admiral with filth. Another jested, "This row betwixt the porter and the butler is a real kitchen shindy." "Let us have peace," cried the more sedate papers; and the quarrel came to a close.

For the reputation of the second Admiral the quarrel with Butler was well-nigh fatal. It inspired the new generation with something akin to disgust. For the man who had done more than any other naval officer—Farragut not excepted—to win the war for the Union, to permit himself to slip so far beneath the limits of decorum was little short of tragic. Porter's flair for plain speech affected him in his old age as that fault had affected his father. The fact that Admiral Porter was in his dotage when the crisis arrived mattered nothing. The public, perhaps rightly, does not weigh evidence in a fine scale.

In 1890 while the Admiral was summering in Newport, against the advice of his physician he took a long and strenuous walk, after which he suffered a heart attack. Dr. Wales, lately Surgeon General of the Navy, pulled him through and got him back to Washington.[6] He lingered through the fall and early winter. At times his mental faculties became obscured, and he failed to recognize the friends who came to see him. In his conscious moments he would joke with the doctors and chide them for telling him that he was to die. They were trying to frighten him into taking care of himself, he said.

At 6:30 A.M. on February 13, 1891, he awoke as usual and ate breakfast. At 8 o'clock his youngest son Richard, who attended him constantly, noticed a change and ran for the nurse and Dr. Wales. At 8:30 the Admiral gave a slight gasp and died, sitting bolt upright in his chair. Richard held one of his hands, and his daughter, Mrs. Logan, the other. George Ann, for long an invalid, was unable to be at her husband's side when he died.

When President Harrison announced the death, Congress adjourned. Flags were half-masted on the White House, on the Navy Department, and throughout the fleet.

At high noon two days later the ships of the Navy fired fifteen minute guns. A marine stood watch at the door of 1710 H Street. President Harrison, Vice President Morton, Cabinet members, Governors, Congressmen, ranking rear admirals of the Navy, generals of the Union and of the Confederacy passed through the doorway of the house. Lining the sidewalk opposite were commodores, captains, lieutenants of the Navy in full dress with swords. At Seventeenth Street the Marine Band was formed. Behind them were sailors and marines—as many as had stormed the salient of Fort Fisher.

Silence fell along the street. The ivy vines that covered the old mansion to its cornices rattled in the breeze. The file of officers snapped to attention as briskly as though the scene were the deck of a flagship when an admiral was leaving the ship. The purple coffin was carried out through the doorway. General Joseph E. Johnston, late of the Confederate Army, was among the officers who lifted the body on its way to Arlington. The gala, four-starred flag of the second Admiral was lowered from the mainmast head ...

APPENDIX

NOTES

BIBLIOGRAPHICAL REFERENCES

Manuscript collections and published works frequently referred to in these notes are designated by the following symbols and abbreviations:

L. of C.—Manuscript Division of the Library of Congress. Letters and other papers mounted in folios are listed under "David Porter Papers" and "David D. Porter Papers"; when loose papers are in folders, the number of the folder is given; unsorted papers are referred to as "D. D. Porter Collection."

N.H.S.—Naval History Section of the New York Historical Society, 170 Central Park West, New York City.

N.R.L.—Naval Records and Library, Navy Department, Washington, D. C.

Van Ness.—Private collection of Mrs. Carroll Van Ness, Owings Mills P.O., Md.

O.R...Navies. I—*Official Records of the Union and Confederate Navies in the War of the Rebellion.* Series I. 27 vols. Washington, D. C. 1894-1917.

O.R...Armies.—*Official Records of the Union and Confederate Armies in the War of the Rebellion.* 127 vols. Washington, D. C. 1880-1900.

Fox Corr.—*Confidential Correspondence of Gustavus Vasa Fox,* Assistant Secretary of the Navy, 1861-1865. Edited by Robert Means Thompson and Richard Wainwright. 2 vols. Printed for the Naval History Society by the De Vinne Press. New York. 1918, 1919.

Welles Diary—*The Diary of Gideon Welles,* Secretary of the Navy under Lincoln and Johnson. With an Introduction by John T. Morse, Jr. 3 vols. Houghton Mifflin Company. 1911.

Incidents.—Porter, D. D. *Incidents and Anecdotes of the Civil War.* D. Appleton-Century Company. 1885.

CHAPTER ONE

1. Porter, David. *Journal of a Cruise Made to the Pacific Ocean in the U. S. Frigate Essex, 1812-1814.* 2 vols. N. Y. (2nd Edition) 1822.

2. Porter, D. D. *Memoir of Commodore David Porter.* Albany. 1875.
3. Bryan, W. B. *A History of the National Capital.* 2 vols. Macmillan. N. Y. 1914. Vol. 2, p. 5.
4. Paullin, C. O. *Commodore John Rodgers.* Arthur H. Clark Company. Cleveland, 1910. p. 316. By permission of the publishers.
5. Paulding, J. K. *John Bull in America.* London. 1825. p. 309 ff.
6. In all of the early chapters reminiscences found in scrapbooks and unpublished letters in the various manuscript collections have been used.

CHAPTER TWO

1. Porter, David, *An Exposition of the Facts ... Which Justified the Expedition to Foxardo.* Washington, D. C. 1825.
2. Log of the *John Adams* for 1823 and 1824. N.R.L.
3. Paullin, C. O. *Commodore John Rodgers.* Arthur H. Clark Company. Cleveland. 1910. p. 318. Reprinted by permission of the publishers.
4. Reference 1 above and *Minutes of the Proceedings of the Courts of Inquiry and Court Martial in Relation to D. Porter.* Washington, D. C. 1825.
5. For some details of Fajardo and the West Indian pirates the *Daily National Intelligencer,* April 7, 1823 to April 19, 1825, has been used.

CHAPTER THREE

1. Porter, D. D. *Memoir of Commodore David Porter.* Albany. 1875.
2. Poinsett, J. R. *Notes on Mexico.* Philadelphia, 1824.
3. The best account of the *Esmeralda's* cruise and her fight with the *Lealtad* is in "Letter Book U.S.N.A." pp. 879-895, D. D. Porter Collection. L. of C.
4. Newspaper reports of David Porter's adventures as commander of the Mexican Navy given in *Niles Register,* Vols. xxxiii, xxxiv, and xxxvii; and in *Daily National Intelligence,* May 22, 1827 to April 23, 1828.

CHAPTER FOUR

1. Porter, D. D. *The Adventures of Harry Marline.* D. Appleton-Century Company. 1885. pp. 9 and 17.
2. Log of the *United States.* May, 1832, ff. N.R.L.
3. Willis, N. P. *Summer Cruise in the Mediterranean on Board an American Frigate.* London. 1835; and the same author's *Pencillings By the Way.* 3 vols. London. 1835.
4. The Philadelphia *Press* on March 12, 1889, when the golden wedding celebration of Admiral and Mrs. Porter was in the news, printed this reminiscence of their courtship.

5. Captains' Letters. October, 1834. N.R.L.
6. Cajori, F. *The Chequered Career of Ferdinand Rudolph Hassler*. The Christopher Publishing House. Boston. 1929.
   Further information on the Coast Survey and Hassler may be found in *Second Volume of the Principal Documents Relating to the Survey of the Coast of the United States, from October, 1834, to November, 1835*. Published by F. R. Hassler, Superintendent of the Survey. N. Y. 1835. See also West, Richard S., Jr. "The Beginnings of the Coast Survey" U. S. Naval Institute *Proceedings*. May, 1935.
7. This information about the family is derived from letters in the D. D. Porter Collection, L. of C.
8. Sands, B. F. *From Reefer to Rear Admiral*. Frederick A. Stokes Company. N. Y. 1899. pp. 121-123.
9. The two letters quoted in this paragraph are dated October 28, year not given, and October 18, 1845. N.H.S.
10. Letter dated November 19, year not given. N.H.S.
11. Letter dated October 16, year not given. N.H.S.
12. Letter not dated. N.H.S.

CHAPTER FIVE

1. D. D. Porter Collection, L. of C., folder No. 5, contains Porter's report dated June 5, 1846, to Secretary of the Navy George Bancroft; and his "Journal," a lengthy and detailed account of his trip across the island. See also Porter D. D. "Secret Missions to Santo Domingo," *North American Review*. Vol. 128, pp. 616-630.
2. News clipping, dated May 1, 1846. D. D. Porter Collection. L. of C.
3. Porter's letter of September 19, 1846. Officers' Letters, Ships of War. N.R.L. This item is quoted in Soley J. R. *Admiral Porter*. D. Appleton-Century Company. 1903. pp. 59-60.
4. Semmes, R. *Service Afloat and Ashore, During the Mexican War*. Cincinnati. 1851.
5. Officers' reports in N.R.L. are the primary sources for this narrative of the War with Mexico.
6. Porter's letter dated August 28, 1847. N.H.S.

CHAPTER SIX

1. For Porter's surveys in New York Harbor see Bache, A. D. *Report of the U. S. Coast Survey*. 1848.
2. Porter's cruises in mail steamers are referred to in Officers' Letters, Ships of War. Vols. 42 to 52. N.R.L.
3. Adams, F. C. *High Old Salts*. Washington, D. C. 1876. p. 73.
4. Letter from Porter to his mother, dated August 8, 1850. N.H.S.

5. The "Crescent City Affair" is fully reported in the New Orleans *Daily Picayune,* from September 7 to October 27, 1852.
6. The speeches quoted in this paragraph are from the New Orleans *Daily Picayune,* October 12, 1852.
7. Letter from Porter to his wife, dated February 21, 1854. Folder No. 6. D. D. Porter Collection. L. of C.
8. D. D. Porter Collection. L. of C.

CHAPTER SEVEN

1. Letters and reports concerning Porter's camel voyages are published in full in *Senate Executive Document No. 62.* 34th Congress, 3rd Session.
2. Simpson, E. (Compiler) *A Treatise on Ordnance and Naval Gunnery.* N. Y. 1862.
3. The letter from Porter to G. H. Heap, dated April 15, 1858, is included in the volume labeled "Memorials of Rear Admiral David D. Porter, U.S.N." D. D. Porter Collection. L. of C.
4. Porter to his mother, dated "March 28th 18—" from Portsmouth, N. H., D. D. Porter Collection. L. of C.
5. "Private Journal of Lieutenant S. C. Rowan, on the U.S.S. *Delaware,* 1841-43." N.R.L.
6. "Reports of Officers on Corporal Punishment and the Spirit Ration." 1850. N.R.L.
7. Adapted from an account in the D. D. Porter Collection. L. of C. Two similar versions of Porter's call at the Davis home are in *Incidents,* pp. 8-11; and Welles *Diary,* Vol. 2, pp. 255-256.
8. Divorce proceedings, William D. Porter against Elizabeth Ann Porter. September 10, 1861. Hall of Records. New York City.

CHAPTER EIGHT

1. Porter's interviews with Seward and Lincoln are adapted from *Incidents,* pp. 13 and 15; and from one of Porter's papers labeled "Copied from Journal in tin box. February 13, 1873, for General Crawford." D. D. Porter Collection. L. of C.
2. These four letters are from *O.R. . . Navies.* I. Vol. 4, pp. 108-109.
3. Idem. p. 108.
4. Porter's interview with Foote is adapted from papers in the D. D. Porter Collection. L. of C.
5. *O.R. . . Navies.* I. Vol. 4, p. 234.
6. Idem. p. 236.
7. Idem. p. 112.
8. Idem. p. 112.

CHAPTER NINE

1. Principal sources for this chapter are *O.R. . . . Navies.* I. Vol. 4; *O.R. . . . Armies.* Series I. Vol. 1, pp. 393-418; and Log of the *Powhatan.* N.R.L.
2. *O.R. . . . Navies.* I. Vol. 4, p. 123.
3. Idem. p. 124.
4. *O.R. . . . Armies.* Series I. Vol. 1, p. 403.
5. *Fox Corr.* Vol. 2, pp. 74 and 79. Porter to Fox, July 5, 1861.
6. *O.R. . . . Navies.* I. Vol. 4, pp. 125-128.
7. *Incidents.* pp. 35 and 36.

CHAPTER TEN

1. Principal sources for this chapter are *O.R. . . . Navies.* I. Vols. 4 and 16; and the Log of the *Powhatan,* N.R.L.
2. *O.R. . . . Navies.* I. Vol. 16, p. 534.
3. Idem. p. 534.
4. Idem. p. 572.
5. Idem. p. 572.
6. Idem. pp. 571-572.
7. *Fox Corr.* Vol. 2, pp. 73-79.
8. *O.R. . . . Navies.* I. Vol. 16, p. 602.
9. *O.R. . . . Navies.* I. Vol. 1, pp. 65, 622 ff.

CHAPTER ELEVEN

1. Principal sources for this chapter are *O.R. . . . Navies.* I. Vols. 1 and 16; Log of the *Powhatan,* N.R.L.; Semmes, R. *Memoirs of Service Afloat,* During the War Between the States. Baltimore. 1869.
2. *O.R. . . . Navies.* I. Vol. 1, p. 68 ff.
3. Idem. pp. 92-95.
4. *O.R. . . . Navies.* I. Vol. 16, pp. 750-751.
5. Idem. pp. 726-727. Extracts are quoted from the New Orleans *Daily True Delta* of October 13 and 15, 1861.

CHAPTER TWELVE

1. Principal sources for this chapter are *O.R. . . . Navies.* I. Vol. 18; and Officers' Letters, Ships of War, N.R.L.
2. *Incidents.* p. 64.
3. Sources for the inception of the New Orleans campaign are Blair, M. "Opening the Mississippi," *United Service Magazine,* January, 1881; Welles, G., article in the *Galaxy* magazine for November, 1870; *Incidents;* and Gideon Welles Papers, L. of C.
4. *Fox Corr.* Vol. 2, p. 89. See also West, Richard S., Jr. "The Relations Between Farragut and Porter." U. S. Naval Institute *Proceedings,* July, 1935.

5. *O.R...Navies.* I. Vol. 18, p. 3; and Gideon Welles Papers, L. of C.
6. Blair, M. "Opening the Mississippi," *United Service Magazine,* January, 1881.
7. *Incidents.* p. 109.
8. *O.R...Navies.* I. Vol. 18, p. 42 ff.

CHAPTER THIRTEEN

1. *O.R...Navies.* I. Vol. 18, pp. 15-24.
2. Farragut, L. *The Life of David Glasgow Farragut.* N. Y. 1879. p. 215.
3. Fox to Porter, February 24, 1862. D. D. Porter Collection, folder No. 4. L. of C.
4. *Fox Corr.* Vol. 2, p. 87.
5. New York *Times* for April 2, 1862.
6. Principal source for this chapter is *O.R...Navies.* I. Vol. 18.
7. Osbon, B. S. *The Cruise of the U. S. Flag-Ship Hartford, 1862-1863:* being the narrative of all her operations since going into commission, in 1862, until her return to New York in 1863. From the private journal of William C. Holton. New York. 1863. p. 19.
8. *O.R...Navies.* I. Vol. 18, p. 267.
9. Idem. p. 136.
10. From *Surgeon of the Seas,* By C. S. Foltz, Copyright 1931. Used by special permission of the Publishers, The Bobbs-Merrill Company. p. 213.
11. From a printed letter by John Guest, Captain, U.S.N., dated January 10, 1872, and apparently written in reply to an article in the *Galaxy* magazine by Gideon Welles. Van Ness.
12. *O.R...Navies.* I. Vol. 18, p. 134.

CHAPTER FOURTEEN

1. Principal source for this chapter is *O.R...Navies.* I. Vol. 18; but *O.R...Armies* and various newspapers have supplied some details.
2. The account of the surrender of the forts is adapted from Porter's "detailed report" of April 30, 1862, *O.R...Navies.* I. Vol. 18, pp. 361-374; and from material in the D. D. Porter Collection, L. of C.
3. *O.R...Navies.* I. Vol. 18, p. 314.
4. *Fox Corr.* Vol. 2, p. 107.

CHAPTER FIFTEEN

1. *O.R...Armies.*
2. *O.R...Navies.* I. Vol. 18, p. 393.
3. Idem. p. 427.
4. *Fox Corr.* Vol. 2, p. 103.
5. *O.R...Armies.*

6. Moore, F. *The Rebellion Record*. Vol. 5, "Poetry and Incidents" section, p. 6. N. Y. 1863.
7. *Fox Corr*. Vol. 2, p. 100. In this letter of May 10, 1862, Porter requests Fox to delete the remark from his report.
8. "Memorials of Rear Admiral David D. Porter, U.S.N." D. D. Porter Collection, L. of C.
9. *Fox Corr*. Vol. 2, p. 95.
10. Idem. pp. 97-100. Two letters dated April 8 and May 10, 1862.
11. *O.R...Navies*. I. Vol. 18, p. 577.
12. *Fox Corr*. Vol. 2, p. 115.
13. Idem. p. 113.
14. Idem. p. 114.
15. Idem. pp. 101-102.

Chapter Sixteen

1. *O.R...Navies*. I. Vol. 18, p. 559.
2. Folder No. 4, D. D. Porter Collection. L. of C.
3. *O.R...Navies*. I. Vol. 18, p. 586.
4. Idem. p. 597.
5. *Fox Corr*. Vol. 2, p. 124.
6. *O.R...Navies*. I. Vol. 18, p. 638.
7. Idem. pp. 641-642.

Chapter Seventeen

1. *Fox Corr*. Vol. 2, p. 126.
2. Idem. p. 127.
3. Adapted from Porter's letter of "explanation" to Fox, dated September 10, 1862. *Fox Corr*. Vol. 2, pp. 135-137.
4. Adapted from material in D. D. Porter Collection. L. of C.
5. *Incidents*. pp. 120-121.
6. *O.R...Navies*. I. Vol. 23, p. 373.
7. Welles *Diary*. Vol. 1, pp. 157-158.
8. Idem. p. 167.
9. Porter to his mother, October 7, 1862. David D. Porter Papers. Vol. 6. L. of C.
10. *Incidents*. p. 122.

Chapter Eighteen

1. For descriptions of vessels in the Western Flotilla see articles in *Battles and Leaders of the Civil War*. 4 vols. D. Appleton-Century Company, 1884; biographic accounts of A. H. Foote, C. H. Davis, John Rodgers; Crandall, W. D. *History of the Ram Fleet and the Mississippi Marine Brigade*. St. Louis. 1907; officers' reports in *O.R...Armies* and *O.R...Navies*. I; and statistical information in *O.R...Navies*, Series II. Vol. 1.

2. Principal source for this chapter is *O.R...Navies*. I. Vol. 23; newspapers and *O.R...Armies* have also been consulted.
3. *O.R...Navies*. I. Vol. 23, pp. 424-425.
4. Adams, F. C. *High Old Salts*. Washington, D. C. 1876.
5. New York *Herald*, December 5, 1870, quotes this passage from Porter's "Journal."
6. *Memoirs of Thomas O. Selfridge, Jr.*, Rear Admiral, U.S.N. With an Introduction by Captain Dudley W. Knox, U.S.N. G. P. Putnam's Sons. 1924. pp. 116-117.

Chapter Nineteen

1. *Incidents*. pp. 126-127.
2. From newspapers, some of which are quoted in Moore, F. *The Rebellion Record*. Vol. 6. 1863.
3. Quoted in *The Growth of the American Republic*. By Samuel E. Morison and Henry Steele Commager. Oxford University Press. 1930. p. 591.
4. Principal source for this chapter is *O.R...Navies*. I. Vols. 23 and 24.

Chapter Twenty

1. Principal sources for this chapter are *O.R...Armies*. Series I, Vol. 15, Part 2, pp. 420-894; and *O.R...Navies*. I. Vol. 24.
2. *The Home Letters of General Sherman*. (Edited by M. A. De W. Howe.) Charles Scribner's Sons. 1909. p. 235.
3. *The Sherman Letters*. Charles Scribner's Sons. 1894. p. 182.
4. Adapted from *Incidents*, p. 131.
5. Newspaper accounts, some of which are in Moore, F. *The Rebellion Record*. Vol. 6. Doc. 101. 1863.
6. *O.R...Armies*. Series I. Vol. 17. Part 2, pp. 566-567.
7. *O.R...Navies*. I. Vol. 24, p. 127.
8. *Fox Corr*. Vol. 2, p. 156.

Chapter Twenty-One

1. Principal sources for this chapter are *O.R...Navies*. I. Vol. 24; Moore, F. *The Rebellion Record*, Vol. 6. 1863; Sherman, W. T. *Memoirs of General William T. Sherman*, By Himself. 2 vols. N. Y. 1875; D. D. Porter Collection, L. of C.; and various newspapers.
2. *Incidents*. p. 147.

Chapter Twenty-Two

1. Principal sources for this chapter are those listed under note 1 for Chapter Twenty-One.
2. *O.R...Navies*. I. Vol. 24, p. 200.

3. "Memorials of Rear Admiral David D. Porter, U.S.N." D. D. Porter Collection. L. of C.

4. *O.R. . . Navies.* I. Vol. 24. p. 218.

5. Idem. p. 370.

6. Idem. p. 396.

7. Richmond *Examiner,* March 7, 1863, quoted in Moore, F. *The Rebellion Record.* Vol. 6, Documents, p. 427.

8. Farragut, L. *The Life of David Glasgow Farragut.* N. Y. 1879. pp. 348-351. (Quotations from two letters of the same date, March 26, 1863.)

9. *Fox Corr.* Vol. 2, p. 168.

10. Adapted from *Incidents.* p. 177.

11. Porter, D. D. *The Naval History of the Civil War.* The Sherman Publishing Company, N. Y. 1886. p. 311.

12. *Fox Corr.* Vol. 2, p. 170.

13. *Incidents.* p. 182.

Chapter Twenty-Three

1. Principal sources for this chapter are *O.R. . . Navies.* I. Vols. 24 and 25; *O.R. . . Armies;* Moore, F. *The Rebellion Record.* Vols. 6 and 7; and Officers' Letters, Mississippi Squadron, N.R.L.

2. Officers' Letters, Mississippi Squadron. Letter dated May 29, 1863. N.R.L.

3. Idem. Letter dated May 31, 1863.

4. Idem. Letter dated May 2, 1863.

5. Idem. Letter not dated.

6. *O.R. . . Navies.* I. Vol. 24, p. 678.

7. *O.R. . . Navies.* I. Vol. 25, p. 56.

8. *Rebellion Record.* Vol. 7, Documents. p. 170.

9. *O.R. . . Navies.* I. Vol. 25, pp. 118-119.

10. Idem. p. 102.

11. Idem. p. 103.

12. Welles *Diary.* Vol. 1. p. 364.

13. Officers' Letters, Mississippi Squadron. March–August, 1863. N.R.L.

14. Letter dated December 23, 1870. "U.S.N.A." letter book. D. D. Porter Collection. L. of C.

15. *O.R. . . Navies.* I. Vol. 25, pp. 279-280.

16. *Battles and Leaders of the Civil War.* 4 vols. D. Appleton-Century Company. 1884. Vol. 3, p. 538.

17. Soley, J. R. *Admiral Porter.* (Great Commanders Series.) D. Appleton-Century Company. 1903. p. 486.

Chapter Twenty-Four

1. Principal sources for this chapter are *O.R. . . Navies.* I. Vols. 25 and 26; *O.R. . . Armies; Report of the Joint Committee on the*

Conduct of the War. Vol. 2; Moore, F. *The Rebellion Record.* Vol. 8, 1865.

2. *O.R. . . Navies.* I. Vol. 25, p. 521.

3. Porter to his mother, December 29, 1863. David D. Porter Papers. Vol. 6. L. of C.

4. See *O.R. . . Armies* and *Report of the Joint Committee on the Conduct of the War.* Vol. 2.

5. *O.R. . . Navies.* I. Vol. 26, p. 29.

6. Interesting sidelights on the Red River campaign are afforded by Smith, W. G. *Life and Letters of Thomas Kilby Smith.* N. Y. 1898.

7. *Report of the Joint Committee on the Conduct of the War.* Vol. 2, p. xliv.

Chapter Twenty-Five

1. Principal sources for this chapter: see note 1, Chapter Twenty-Four; and Log of the *Cricket.* N.R.L.

2. *O.R. . . Navies.* I. Vol. 26, p. 56.

3. Idem. p. 47.

Chapter Twenty-Six

1. Porter to Fox, May 27, 1864. D. D. Porter Collection. L. of C. Principal sources for this chapter are *O.R. . . Navies.* I. Vols. 26, 10, and 11; Moore, F. *The Rebellion Record;* Welles *Diary;* the *Army and Navy Journal;* and various newspapers.

2. *O.R. . . Navies.* I. Vol. 26, p. 752.

3. Idem. p. 325.

4. D. D. Porter Collection. L. of C.

5. Welles *Diary.* Vol. 2, p. 115.

6. Idem. p. 161.

7. Idem. pp. 146-147.

8. *O.R. . . Navies.* I. Vol. 26, p. 572.

9. Idem. p. 574.

10. Welles *Diary.* Vol. 2, p. 172.

11. *O.R. . . Navies.* I. Vol. 10, p. 552.

12. Idem. p. 618.

13. *O.R. . . Navies.* I. Vol. 11, p. 3.

Chapter Twenty-Seven

1. See Marshall, J. A. (Copyrighter) *Private and Official Correspondence of General Benjamin F. Butler,* During the Period of the Civil War. 5 Vols. Norwood, Mass. 1917. Vol. 2, p. 148. Principal sources for this chapter are *O.R. . . Navies.* I. Vol. 11, and other items listed under note 1, Chapter Twenty-Six; *Report of the Joint Committee on the Conduct of the War.* Vol. 2; Fox Papers, N.H.S.; Porter Papers, Van Ness; Log of the *Malvern,* N.R.L.

2. *O.R...Navies.* I. Vol. 11, p. 96.
3. *Report of the Joint Committee on the Conduct of the War.* Vol. 2, pp. 95 ff. and 216.
4. New York *Times* for December 31, 1864.
5. Van Ness.
6. *O.R...Navies.* I. Vol. 11, p. 427.

CHAPTER TWENTY-EIGHT

1. Principal sources for this chapter are *O.R...Navies.* I. Vols. 11 and 12; Moore, F. *The Rebellion Record; Army and Navy Journal;* Log of the *Malvern,* N.R.L.
2. Baltimore *American* for January 24, 1865.
3. Porter to Fox, January 20, 1865. N.H.S.
4. Fox Papers. N.H.S.
5. *O.R...Navies.* I. Vol. 12, pp. 34-35.
6. Idem. p. 9.
7. Idem. p. 52.
8. Welles *Diary.* Vol. 2, pp. 251-252.
9. D. D. Porter Collection. L. of C.
10. New York *World* for December 26, 1864.
11. D. D. Porter Collection. L. of C.
12. See *Memoirs of General William T. Sherman,* By Himself, 2 vols. N. Y. 1875. p. 324 ff. A copy of Porter's letter to Sherman, confirming Sherman's account of the conference with Lincoln on board the *River Queen,* is in the Chicago Historical Society.
13. Porter to Fox, March 28, 1865. N.H.S.
14. Porter to Fox, February 10, 1865. N.H.S.
15. *O.R...Navies.* I. Vol. 12, p. 95.
16. *Incidents.* pp. 283-284.
17. Log of the *Malvern.* N.R.L.

CHAPTER TWENTY-NINE

1. Principal sources for this chapter are Benjamin, P. *The United States Naval Academy.* G. P. Putnam's Sons. 1900; "David D. Porter's Naval Academy Order Books, Nos. 1 and 2," Superintendent's Office, U. S. Naval Academy; Thomas G. Ford's unpublished manuscript "History of the Naval Academy," U. S. Naval Academy Library; Porter Papers, N.H.S.; U. S. Naval Academy Registers; Lull, E. P. *Description and History of the U. S. Naval Academy,* from its origin to the present time. Annapolis, 1869; Soley, J. R. *Historical Sketch of the United States Naval Academy.* Washington. 1876; *Army and Navy Journal.*
2. Lull. op. cit. p. 25.
3. Order Book No. 2. October 25, 1867.

4. Porter to the Secretary of the Navy, December 27, 1867. Quoted in Ford Ms., Chapter 20.
5. Order Book No. 1. April 11, 1867.
6. D. D. Porter Collection. L. of C.
7. Quoted in Ford Ms., Chapter 20.
8. Newspaper clipping included with Ford Ms.
9. Excerpts from various letters from Porter to his mother. N.H.S.
10. Porter to Fox, March 11, 1866. N.H.S.

CHAPTER THIRTY

1. General Letters, Mississippi Squadron. N.R.L.
2. Welles *Diary*. Vol. 3, p. 553.
3. Idem. p. 560.
4. Idem. pp. 580-581.
5. D. D. Porter Collection. L. of C.
6. *Army and Navy Journal.*
7. Idem.
8. Idem. June, 1869.
9. Newspaper clipping in Ford Ms.

CHAPTER THIRTY-ONE

1. David D. Porter Collection, Folder No. 4. L. of C.
2. Idem. "U.S.N.A." Letter Book.
3. See West, Richard S., Jr. "The Relations Between Farragut and Porter." U. S. Naval Institute *Proceedings*. July, 1935.
4. David D. Porter Collection. "U.S.N.A." Letter Book. L. of C.

CHAPTER THIRTY-TWO

1. Newspaper clipping, Van Ness.
2. D. D. Porter Collection. L. of C.
3. *Incidents.* p. 124.
4. Porter, D. D. *The Naval History of the Civil War*. The Sherman Publishing Company. N. Y. 1886. Preface p. iii.
5. Butler, B. F. "Statement of Facts in relation to Admiral D. D. Porter's claim not to have run away from forts St. Philip and Jackson, in April, 1862, by which his cowardice and falsehood are fully shown from official documents and Porter's own self contradictions." Boston. 1889.
6. Obituary notices in the Washington *Post* for February 14 and 15, 1891.

BIBLIOGRAPHY

I. Manuscript Collections

A. The material belonging to Mrs. Carroll Van Ness contains transcripts of some of Porter's wartime official dispatches and letters to Government officials; copies of the Admiral's annual reports; scattered manuscript chapters of Porter's published works; a 40,000-word essay entitled "My Career in the Navy Department"; original postwar letters from U. S. Grant and W. T. Sherman showing that Grant harbored no animosity after the "imbroglio" and that Sherman was a close personal friend of Porter; letters from minor participants in the war, dated 1889, deploring the Porter-Butler quarrel and calling to mind reminiscences of the war; a printed letter dated January 10, 1872, from Captain John Guest, U. S. Navy, exonerating Porter from charges made by ex-Secretary Welles in the *Galaxy* magazine; newspaper scrapbooks covering (1) contemporary narratives of the passage of the New Orleans forts and (2) the Porter-Butler controversy of 1889.

B. The Manuscript Division of the Library of Congress contains many personal papers relating to Admiral David D. Porter and to his father, Commodore David Porter of the War of 1812. In addition to the several volumes of letters entitled "David Porter Papers" and "David D. Porter Papers," there are a number of folders (about twelve) which contain unassorted original letters to Admiral Porter, some of his household accounts, cancelled checks, chapters from his published books; Lieutenant David D. Porter's "Journal" on San Domingo and his Dominican report to the State Department, dated June 5, 1846; his letter "to Georgy," dated July 21, 1854, from Melbourne, Australia; a letter book marked "U.S.N.A."; an extract concerning the *Powhatan* episode with the notation "copied from Journal in tin box, February 13, 1873, for General Crawford"; a volume entitled "Memorials of Rear Admiral David D. Porter, U.S.N.," containing Porter's correspondence with his brother-in-law G. H. Heap between 1858 and 1863; and duplicates of many orders and dispatches that are on file in the Navy Department. The bulk of the David D. Porter Collection remained in storage until 1930, when it was acquired by the Library of Congress.

C. The material in the Naval History Society, New York City, includes Porter's commission as "Admiral of the Navy," and family letters saved over a period of years by Porter's mother, Evalina Anderson Porter.

D. The Eldridge Collection in the Henry E. Huntington Library and Art Gallery contains some 11,000 Porter documents, chiefly telegrams and reports, duplicates of material in the Navy Department.

E. The Chicago Historical Society has Porter's account of the conference on board the *River Queen* in which Lincoln was quoted as approving General W. T. Sherman's lenient policy toward Confederates who should surrender.

F. The U. S. Naval Academy Library has an unpublished manuscript entitled "History of the U. S. Naval Academy," by the late Professor Thomas G. Ford, to which the writer is indebted for details of Naval Academy life from 1866 to 1869. Also useful for this period are "David D. Porter's Letter Books, Nos. 1 and 2" which are in the Superintendent's Office at the U. S. Naval Academy.

G. By far the most significant and voluminous body of manuscript material is in the Naval Records and Library of the Navy Department. Much of it is published in the *Official Records ... Navies,* but by no means all. Constant reference to the original documents has been made. In general the naval correspondence is organized under the categories: "Officers' Letters, Ships of War," "Captains' Letters," "Letters to Port Admirals," "Admirals' and Commodores' Letters," "Squadron Letters." Such miscellaneous manuscripts as the "Private Journal of Lieutenant S. C. Rowan, on the U.S.S. *Delaware* 1841-43" and the reports of officers on "Corporal Punishment and the Spirit Ration, 1850," have been found useful for details. Logs of the vessels on which Porter served have been examined for important periods.

II. Government Documents and Publications

1. *Official Records of the Union and Confederate Navies in the War of the Rebellion.* Series I, 27 vols., 1894-1917; Series II, 3 vols., 1921-22.
2. *Official Records ... Armies.* Series I-IV, 128 vols., 1880-1900.
3. Annual reports of the Secretaries of the Navy.
4. "Minutes of the Proceedings of the Court of Inquiry and Court Martial in relation to D. Porter, etc." 1825.
5. Coast Survey. House Document No. 57, 27th Congress, 2nd Session; "U. S. Coast Survey Reports" for the following years: 1816-1843, 1845, 1847-48; House Report No. 43, 27th Congress, 3rd Session, 1842.
6. San Domingo. Senate Executive Document No. 17, 41st Congress, 3rd Session, 1870-71.

7. Flogging in the Navy. Statutes at Large. Vol. 9, 31st Congress, 1st Session.
8. Red River and Fort Fisher Expeditions. *Report of the Joint Committee on the Conduct of the War.* Vol. II. 1865.
9. U. S. Naval Academy Registers, 1859-1870.
10. The *Congressional Globe,* 1870-71.

III. NEWSPAPERS

The following newspapers, in the files of the Library of Congress and in scrap-books listed above under "Manuscript Collections," have been examined for various dates between 1824 and 1891, inclusive:
1. Baltimore. *American.*
2. New Orleans. *Daily Picayune.*
3. New York. *Herald, Sun, Times, Tribune, World.*
4. Richmond. *Daily Dispatch, Examiner, Sentinel, Whig.*
5. Philadelphia. *Press.*
6. Washington, D. C. *Daily Morning Chronicle, Daily National Republican, Evening Express, Evening Star, National Intelligencer, Post, Star.*

IV. MAGAZINE ARTICLES AND PAMPHLETS

Army and Navy Chronicle, March-April, 1839, 1863-71.
Army and Navy Journal, 1863-91.
Barnes, J. S. "With Lincoln from Washington to Richmond in 1865." *Magazine of History.* Extra Number 161. Reprinted by William Abbott, Tarrytown, N. Y., 1930.
Blair, M. "Opening the Mississippi." *United Service Magazine,* Jan., 1881.
Butler, B. F. "Statement of Facts in relation to Admiral D. D. Porter's claim not to have run away from forts St. Philip and Jackson, in April, 1862, by which his cowardice and falsehood are fully shown from official documents and Porter's own self contradictions." Boston, 1889.
Colvocoresses, G. P., "Admiral Porter." U. S. Naval Institute *Proceedings,* 1908.
Edinburgh Review, vol 124, p. 185 ff., "The American Navy in the Late War" (Farragut and Porter).
Neeser, R. W. "Historic Ships of the Navy: *Cricket.*" U. S. Naval Institute *Proceedings,* 1934.
Niles Register, vols. xxxiii, xxxiv, xxxvii. (David Porter in the Mexican Navy.)
"Memorial of David Dixon Porter from the City of Boston." Boston, 1891.
Old South Leaflets. vol. iii, No. 56. Article on "The Monroe Doctrine." Boston (No date given.)

Porter, D. D. "Secret Missions to San Domingo." *North American Review.* vol. 128, 1889.

Rowan, S. C. "Recollections of the Mexican War," U. S. Naval Institute *Proceedings,* 1888; "The War With Mexico." Same, 1882.

Southern Historical Society Papers. vol. 23, p. 187 ff.

Weed, T. "Early Incidents of the Rebellion." *Galaxy.* 1870.

Welles, G. Article in *Galaxy,* November, 1870.

West, R. S., Jr. "The Relations of Farragut and Porter," U. S. Naval Institute *Proceedings,* 1935; "The Beginning of the Coast Survey," same, 1935; "Watchful Gideon," same, 1936.

V. BOOKS

In the following selected list of books the author has made extensive use of the *Diary of Gideon Welles,* the *Confidential Correspondence of Gustavus Vasa Fox,* and the *Battles and Leaders of the Civil War,* for which he is indebted to Houghton Mifflin Co., the Naval History Society, and the D. Appleton-Century Company, respectively. Books from which brief direct quotations have been used are indicated by asterisks.

* Adams, F. C. *High Old Salts.* Washington, D. C., 1876.

Alden, C. S. *George Hamilton Perkins, U.S.N., His Life and Letters.* Boston, 1914.

Allen, G. W. *Our Navy and the Barbary Corsairs.* N. Y., 1905.

——. *Our Navy and the West Indian Pirates.* Salem, Mass., 1929.

Ammen, D. *The Atlantic Coast.* N. Y., 1883.

——. *The Old Navy and the New.* Phila., 1893.

Bancroft, H. H. *History of Mexico.* vol. V. San Francisco, 1885.

Barnes, J. S. *Submarine Warfare.* N. Y., 1869.

Benjamin, P. *The United States Naval Academy.* N. Y., 1900.

Bennett, F. M. *The Steam Navy of the United States.* Pittsburgh, 1896.

Blaine, J. G. *Twenty Years in Congress.* 2 vols., Norwich, Conn., 1886.

Boynton, C. B. *The History of the Navy During the Rebellion.* N. Y., 1868.

Bradford, G. *Confederate Portraits.* N. Y., 1914.

——. *Damaged Souls.* N. Y., 1922.

Bradlee, F. B. C. *Blockade Running During the Civil War.* Salem, Mass., 1925.

Buel, C. C. (see Johnson, R. J.).

Butler, B. F. *Butler's Book.* Boston, 1892.

Cajori, F. *The Chequered Career of Ferdinand Rudolph Hassler.* The Christopher Publishing House, Boston, 1929.

Cole, A. C. *The Irrepressible Conflict. 1850-1865.* (History of American Life Series, Schlesinger and Fox, Eds.). N. Y., 1934.

Crandall, W. D. *History of the Ram Fleet and the Mississippi Marine Brigade*. St. Louis, 1907.

Cutting, E. *Jefferson Davis: Political Soldier*. N. Y., 1930.

Davenport, C. B. (assisted by Scudder, M. T.): *Heredity of Naval Officers*. Washington, 1919.

Dewey, Admiral George. *Autobiography*. N. Y., 1913.

Du Pont, H. A. *Rear Admiral Francis Du Pont*. N. Y., 1926.

* Farragut, L. *The Life of David Glasgow Farragut*. N. Y., 1879.

* Foltz C. S. *Surgeon of the Seas*. Indianapolis, 1931.

Garland, H. *Ulysses S. Grant, His Life and Character*. N. Y., 1898.

Gibbs, G. F. (compiler and illustrator). *A Collection of Songs and Poems by Cadets at the United States Naval Academy*. Washington, D. C., 1889.

Gleaves, Rear Admiral A. (Ed.): *The Life of An American Sailor: Rear-Admiral William Hemsley Emory*. N. Y., 1923.

Greeley, H. *The American Conflict*, A History of the Great Rebellion in the United States of America. 2 vols., Hartford, 1866.

* Grant, U. S. *Personal Memoirs*. 2 vols., N. Y., 1885-1886.

Hay, J. (see Nicolay, J. G. and Hay, J.).

Headley, J. T. *Farragut and our Naval Commanders*. N. Y., 1866.

Hoppin, J. M. *Life of Andrew Hull Foote*. N. Y., 1874.

* Howe, M. A. DeW. *Home Letters of General Sherman*. N. Y., 1909.

* Johnson, R. J. and Buel, C. C. (Eds.). *Battles and Leaders of the Civil War*. 4 vols., N. Y., 1884-1887.

Johnston, J. E. *Narrative of Military Operations Directed During the Late War Between the States*. N. Y., 1874.

Jones, J. B. *A Rebel War Clerk's Diary at the Confederate States Capital*. 2 vols., Phila., 1866.

Knox, Dudley W., Captain, U.S.N. *A History of the United States Navy*. (With an introduction by William L. Rodgers, Vice Admiral U.S.N.). N. Y., 1936.

Latané, J. H. *A History of American Foreign Policy*. (Revised and enlarged by Wainhouse, D. W.). N. Y, 1934.

Leslie, F. *Illustrated History of the Civil War*. N. Y., 1895.

Lewis, C. L. *Admiral Franklin Buchanan, fearless man of action*. Baltimore, 1929.

———. *Matthew Fontaine Maury, the pathfinder of the seas*. Annapolis, 1927.

Lewis, L. *Sherman, Fighting Prophet*. N. Y., 1932.

Liddell Hart, B. H. *Sherman: Soldier, Realist, American*. N. Y., 1929.

Lossing, B. J. *Pictorial History of the Civil War*. 3 vols., Phila., 1866-1868.

Lull, E. P. *Description and History of the U. S. Naval Academy from its origin to the present time*. Annapolis, 1869.

Maclay, E. S. *A History of the United States Navy from 1775 to 1898*. 2 vols., N. Y., 1898.

Mahan, A. T. *Admiral Farragut*. (Great Commanders Series.) N. Y., 1892.

——. *The Gulf and Inland Waters*. N. Y., 1883.

Marshall, J. A. (copyrighter). *Private and Official Correspondence of General Benjamin F. Butler, During the Period of the Civil War*. 5 vols., Norwood, Mass., 1917.

Martin, J. H. *Chester*. Phila., 1877.

Mason, A. L. (Ed.). *Memoir and Correspondence of Charles Steedman*. Cambridge, 1912.

Mechlin and Winder (compilers). *Naval and Marine Laws*. Washington, D. C., 1848.

* Moore, F. *The Rebellion Record, A Diary of American Events*. 12 vols., N. Y., 1861-1867.

Morris, C. *Heroes of the Navy*. Phila., 1907.

Myers, W. S. *The Republican Party*. N. Y., 1928.

Neeser, R. W. *Statistical and Chronological History of the United States Navy, 1775-1907*. 2 vols., N. Y., 1909.

Nevins, A. (Ed.). *The Diary of John Quincy Adams*. N. Y., 1928.

Nevins, A. *The Emergence of Modern America, 1865-1878*. (History of American Life Series, Schlesinger and Fox, Eds.). N. Y., 1927.

Nicolay, J. G. and Hay, J. *Abraham Lincoln, A History*. 10 vols., N. Y., 1890.

Norris, W. B. *Annapolis: Its Colonial and Naval History*. N. Y., 1925.

* Osbon, B. S. (Ed.). *The Cruise of the U. S. Flag-Ship Hartford, 1862-1863 ... From the private journal of William C. Holton*. N. Y., 1863.

Owsley, F. *King Cotton Diplomacy*. Chicago, 1931.

Paine, A. B. *A Sailor of Fortune: Personal Memoirs of B. S. Osbon*. N. Y., 1906.

Paulding, J. K. *John Bull in America*. London, 1825.

Poinsett, J. R. *Notes on Mexico*. Phila., 1824.

* Porter, David. *An Exposition of the Facts ... which justified the expedition to Foxardo*. Washington, D. C., 1825.

——. *Journal of a Cruise Made to the Pacific Ocean in the U. S. Frigate Essex, 1812-1814*. 2 vols., N. Y. (2nd Edition), 1822.

Porter, David Dixon. *The Adventures of Harry Marline*. N. Y., 1885.

——. *Allan Dare and Robert Le Diable*. 2 vols. N. Y., 1885.

* ——. *Incidents and Anecdotes of the Civil War*. N. Y., 1885.

* ——. *Memoir of Commodore David Porter*. Albany, 1875.

* ——. *The Naval History of the Civil War*. N. Y., 1886.

Preble, G. H. *History of the Navy Yard at Portsmouth, N. H.* Washington, D. C., 1892.

Rhodes, J. F. *History of the United States, 1850-1896.* 8 vols., N. Y., 1920.

Rives, G. R. *The United States and Mexico, 1821-1848.* 2 vols., N. Y., 1913.

Roosevelt, T. *The Naval War of 1812.* N. Y., 1882.

* Sands, B. F. *From Reefer to Rear Admiral.* N. Y., 1899.

Scharf, J. T. *History of the Confederate States Navy.* Atlanta, 1887.

Schwab, J. C. *The Confederate States of America, 1861-1865, a financial and industrial history of the South during the Civil War.* N. Y., 1901.

Seitz, D. C. *The Dreadful Decade.* Indianapolis, 1926.

——. *Horace Greeley.* Indianapolis, 1926.

* Selfridge, T. O., Jr. *Memoirs of Thomas O. Selfridge, Jr. Rear Admiral, U.S.N.* (With an Introduction by Captain Dudley W. Knox, U.S.N.). N. Y., 1924.

Semmes, R. *Memoirs of Service Afloat, During the War Between the States.* Baltimore, 1869.

* ——. *Service Afloat and Ashore During the Mexican War.* Cincinnati, 1851.

* Sherman, W. T. *Memoirs of General William T. Sherman, By Himself.* 2 vols., N. Y., 1875.

Simpson, E. (Compiler). *A Treatise on Ordnance and Naval Gunnery.* N. Y., 1862.

Smith, W. G. *Life and Letters of Thomas Kilby Smith.* N. Y., 1898.

* Soley, J. R. *Admiral Porter.* (Great Commanders Series. Edited by James Grant Wilson.) N. Y., 1903.

——. *The Blockade and the Cruisers.* N. Y., 1883.

Spears, J. R. *The History of Our Navy.* 4 vols., N. Y., 1897-1899.

Stryker, L. P. *Andrew Johnson, a Study in Courage.* N. Y., 1929.

Tate A. *Jefferson Davis, His Rise and Fall.* N. Y., 1929.

* Thompson, R. M. and Wainwright R. (Eds.). *Confidential Correspondence of Gustavus Vasa Fox, Assistant Secretary of the Navy, 1861-1865.* 2 vols., N. Y., 1918-1919.

Turnbull, A. D. *Commodore David Porter, 1780-1843.* N. Y., 1929.

Wainwright, R. (See Thompson, R. M.)

Walke, H. *Naval Scenes and Reminiscences.* N. Y., 1877.

* Welles, G. *The Diary of Gideon Welles* (With a preface by Edgar T. Welles and an introduction by John T. Morse, Jr.). 3 vols., Boston, 1911.

Welles, G. *Seward and Lincoln.* N. Y., 1874.

Westcott, A. F. (Ed.). *Mahan on Naval Warfare.* Boston, 1918.

Wilkinson, J. *The Narrative of a Blockade Runner.* N. Y., 1877.

* Willis, N. P. *Summer Cruise in the Mediterranean on board an American Frigate.* London, 1835.

Woodward, W. E. *Meet General Grant.* N. Y., 1928.

INDEX